SAMURAI, WARFARE AND THE STATE IN EARLY MEDIEVAL JAPAN

Warfare in early medieval Japan was intimately linked to social structure. Examining the causes and conduct of military operations informs and enhances our understanding of the tenth to fourteenth centuries – the formative age of the samurai.

Karl Friday, an internationally recognized authority on Japanese warriors, provides the first comprehensive study of the topic in English. This work incorporates nearly twenty years of ongoing research, drawing on both new readings of primary sources and the most recent secondary scholarship. It overturns many of the stereotypes that have dominated views of the period.

Friday analyzes Heian-, Kamakura- and Nambokuchō-period warfare from five thematic angles. He examines the principles that justified armed conflict, the mechanisms used to raise and deploy armed forces, the weapons available to early medieval warriors, the means by which they obtained them, and the techniques and customs of battle.

A thorough, accessible and informative review, this study highlights the complex causal relationships among the structures and sources of early medieval political power, technology and the conduct of war.

Karl F. Friday is a professor of Japanese History at the University of Georgia. A specialist in classical and early medieval Japanese history, he has also written widely on samurai culture and Japanese warrior traditions.

Warfare and History
General Editor
Jeremy Black
Professor of History, University of Exeter

Air Power in the Age of Total War
John Buckley

*The Armies of the Caliphs:
Military and Society in the
Early Islamic State*
Hugh Kennedy

*The Balkan Wars, 1912–1913: Prelude
to the First World War*
Richard C. Hall

English Warfare, 1511–1642
Mark Charles Fissel

*European and Native American Warfare,
1675–1815*
Armstrong Starkey

European Warfare, 1660–1815
Jeremy Black

European Warfare, 1494–1660
Jeremy Black

The First Punic War
J.F. Lazenby

*Frontiersmen: Warfare in Africa Since
1950*
Anthony Clayton

*German Armies: War and German
Politics, 1648–1806*
Peter H. Wilson

The Great War 1914–1918
Spencer C. Tucker

*The Irish and British Wars,
1637–1654. Triumph, Tragedy,
and Failure*
James Scott Wheeler

Israel's Wars, 1947–1993
Ahron Bregman

*The Korean War: No Victors,
No Vanquished*
Stanley Sandler

Medieval Chinese Warfare, 300–900
David A. Graff

Medieval Naval Warfare, 1000–1500
Susan Rose

Modern Chinese Warfare, 1795–1989
Bruce A. Elleman

*Modern Insurgencies and
Counter-insurgencies: Guerrillas
and their Opponents since 1750*
Ian F.W. Beckett

*Mughal Warfare: Imperial Frontiers and
Highroads to Empire 1500–1700*
Jos Gommans

Naval Warfare, 1815–1914
Lawrence Sondhaus

Ottoman Warfare, 1500–1700
Rhoads Murphey

The Peloponnesian War: A Military Study
J.F. Lazenby

Samurai, Warfare and the State in Early Medieval Japan
Karl F. Friday

Seapower and Naval Warfare, 1650–1830
Richard Harding

The Soviet Military Experience
Roger R. Reese

Vietnam
Spencer C. Tucker

The War for Independence and the Transformation of American Society
Harry M. Ward

War and the State in Early Modern Europe: Spain, the Dutch Republic and Sweden as Fiscal–military States, 1500–1660
Jan Glete

Warfare and Society in Europe, 1792–1914
Geoffrey Wawro

Warfare and Society in Europe, 1898 to the Present
Michael S. Neiberg

Warfare at Sea, 1500–1650
Jan Glete

Warfare in Atlantic Africa, 1500–1800: Maritime Conflicts and the Transformation of Europe
John K. Thornton

Warfare, State and Society in the Byzantine World, 565–1204
John Haldon

War in the Early Modern World, 1450–1815
edited by Jeremy Black

Wars of Imperial Conquest in Africa, 1830–1914
Bruce Vandervort

Western Warfare in the Age of the Crusades, 1000–1300
John France

War and Society in Imperial Rome, 31 BC–AD 284
Brian Campbell

Warfare and Society in the Barbarian West
Guy Halsall

War in the Modern World since 1815
edited by Jeremy Black

World War Two: A Military History
Jeremy Black

SAMURAI, WARFARE AND THE STATE IN EARLY MEDIEVAL JAPAN

Karl F. Friday

LONDON AND NEW YORK

First published 2004
by Routledge
2 Park Square, Milton Park, Abingdon, Oxon, OX14 4RN

Simultaneously published in the USA
by Routledge
270 Madison Ave, New York NY 10016

Routledge is an imprint of the Taylor & Francis Group

Transferred to Digital Printing 2010

© 2004 Karl F. Friday
Typeset in Bembo by
BOOK NOW Ltd

All rights reserved. No part of this book may be reprinted or reproduced or utilised in any form or by any electronic, mechanical, or other means, now known or hereafter invented, including photocopying and recording, or in any information storage or retrieval system, without permission in writing from the publishers.

Library of Congress Cataloging-in-Publication Data
Friday, Karl F.
Samurai, warfare & the state in early medieval Japan / Karl F. Friday.– 1st ed.
p. cm. – (Warfare and history)
Includes bibliographical references and index.
1. Japan–History, Military–To 1868. 2. Samurai–History. I. Title: Samurai, warfare and the state in early medieval Japan. II. Title. III Series

DS838.5.F756 2003
952'.02–dc21   2003011681

British Library Cataloguing in Publication Data
A catalogue record for this book is available from the British Library

ISBN 0–415–32962–0 (hbk)
ISBN 0–415–32963–9 (pbk)

FOR MY PARENTS, WHO STILL THINK
I'M CRAZY TO DO THIS FOR A LIVING

CONTENTS

	List of figures	xi
	Acknowledgments	xiii
	Introduction	1
1	The meaning of war	19
	The concept of Just War	20
	Private war	23
	Feuding and self-help	29
	Ritual war	32
2	The organization of war	34
	Hired swords and franchise armies	36
	Equilibrium and revolution	43
	The Kamakura vassal corps	44
	Officers and the chain of command	49
	Warbands and warbonds	53
3	The tools of war	63
	Manufacture and procurement of weapons	64
	Projectile weapons	68
	Shock weapons	77
	Protective weapons	89
	Horses and tack	96
4	The science of war	102
	The way of the horse and bow	103
	Shaping battle	112
	Ambushes and raids	115
	Fortifications and strongholds	119
	New wine in old bottles	128

CONTENTS

5	The culture of war	135
	Reputation, honor and warrior personality	137
	Deception, guile and surprise	140
	Battle cries and self-introduction	145
	Prisoners of war	149
	Head-hunting	152
	Non-combatants	155
	Epilog	164
	Notes	169
	References and bibliography	199
	Index	231

FIGURES

2.1	Chains of command in the provincial military and police system of the eleventh and twelfth centuries	43
2.2	Yoritomo's chain of command	50
2.3	Chains of command in the late Kamakura military/police system	53
3.1	Japanese bow designs in cross-section	70
3.2	Bow oscillation	71
3.3	Early medieval arrows	72
3.4	*Ebira* and *utsubo*	73
3.5	*Warabite katana, kenuki-gata warabite katana, kenuki-gata katana, kenuki-gata tachi* and *tachi*	81
3.6	Sword shapes in cross-section	82
3.7	Methods of forging Japanese swords	85
3.8	*Naginata* and *kumade*	86
3.9	*Hoko, yari* and *naginata* blades	88
3.10	Japanese shields	89
3.11	The components of Japanese armors	91
3.12	Construction of *ōyoroi*	92
3.13	Mounted warrior in *ōyoroi*	95
3.14	Medieval Japanese saddle and tack	98
4.1	Possible angles of attack for mounted archery encounters	110
4.2	Maneuver options for subsequent passes	111
4.3	A mid-twelfth-century warrior residence	121
4.4	*Sakamogi*	123
4.5	A *yagura* and *kaidate*	125
5.1	Heads collected and displayed on the battlefield	153
5.2	Presentation of heads	154

ACKNOWLEDGMENTS

Some historians are born to certain projects, others have projects thrust upon them. This book falls into the latter category. It began in 1996, with the proverbial offer I could not refuse, in this case an invitation from Jeremy Black to write a volume on early medieval Japan for his "Warfare and History" series. As I took up the task, I was surprised and delighted to discover that I was in pursuit of that rarest of medievalist's game: a hot topic. In the mid-1990s, an eager pack of young scholars (if, indeed, those of us on the dark side of forty still qualify for that description), as well as a handful of senior historians in Japan, descended with considerable fury on the subject of warfare among the early samurai—an issue that had not attracted attention from serious scholars in decades. Since that time, several dozen excellent books and articles on this topic have appeared, immeasurably enriching my own perspectives on the matter.

This on-going explosion of new scholarship, and the demands of some rather heavy-duty administrative assignments for the history department whose paychecks feed me and my family, has stretched this project out considerably beyond its originally anticipated completion date. I must, therefore, begin my acknowledgements by thanking Prof. Black and the folks at Routledge for their patience and forbearance. Thanks, in particular to Alex Ballantine, Jane Blackwell, Ruth Jeavons, James Cooke and to my copy editor, Caroline Richmond.

Much of the research for this study was funded by a grant from the Japan Foundation, whose support I most gratefully acknowledge. I am also deeply indebted to Profs. Seki Humitake and Ōhama Tetsuya, and the University of Tsukuba; and to Profs. Kondō Shigekazu, Ishigami Eiichi, and the rest of the faculty and staff of the University of Tokyo Shiryōhensanjō for giving me places to work, and for the time they took away from their own labors to assist me with mine.

A special round of thanks goes to Kondō Yoshikazu, Kawai Yasushi, Suzuki Masaya and Tom Conlan, who shared invaluable advice, information, and copies of their numerous publications; to Wayne Farris, for his generous help with some questions concerning economic issues, and for a stimulating e-mail debate about Japanese crossbows that helped me clarify my thoughts on the

ACKNOWLEDGMENTS

issue; to Yamamoto Isao for pointing me toward contacts and materials I would not have found otherwise; and to Torkel Brekke for nudging me into deeper investigation of questions concerning the rules of war.

I am also deeply grateful to Cappy Hurst, Andrew Goble, Hitomi Tonomura, Mickey Adolphson, Bruce Batten, Roy Ron, Paul Varley, Ethan Segal, Gordon Berger, Will Bodiford, Thom Whigham and Peter Hoffer, for their support, encouragement – and above all – their friendship throughout this project.

To my deep regret, I did not finish this book in time to include one more name on this list: that of my mentor and friend Jeffrey Mass, whose untimely passing has left an enormous hole, not only in all of our hearts, but in our field as well. I can only hope that Jeff has spent these last two years contentedly arguing *bakufu* politics with Yoritomo.

As always, my most profound debt is to Chie, my wife and my best friend. She not only put up with me before and during this long project, listened patiently to my thoughts and rantings, and offered cogent responses and suggestions, she also drew the artwork for many of the illustrations that adorn this book. I could not have done this without her, and I could not have wanted to.

INTRODUCTION

> War is the father of all things.
>
> Heraclitus, sixth century BCE
>
> War is the greatest plague that afflicts mankind; it destroys religion, it destroys nations, it destroys families.
>
> Martin Luther, *Table Talk*, 1569

On the second day of the fifth month of 1213, the weather was cloudy. So, too, was the political future of the thirty-year-old Kamakura shogunate. That afternoon, as the hour of the monkey (3:00–5:00 pm) opened, three or four hundred horsemen and foot soldiers led by Wada Yoshimori and his kinsmen stormed eastward from Yoshimori's home, and through the streets of Kamakura toward the residence of the shogunal regent (*shikken*), Hōjō Yoshitoki.[1]

Yoshimori, a warrior from Sagami province, had been one of the first to rally to the cause of Minamoto Yoritomo, when the future Lord of Kamakura raised his war banners in 1180. Appointed head of Yoritomo's Board of Retainers (*samurai-dokoro*) that same year, Yoshimori many times distinguished himself in both battlefield and administrative service to the regime.[2] By 1213, however, Yoshitoki and his sister, Masako (the widow of Yoritomo, who died in 1199), appear to have identified him as an obstacle to their domination of the shogunate. In the spring of that year, Yoshitoki found the pretext he needed to pick a fight, arresting two of Yoshimori's sons and his nephew Tanenaga on charges of conspiracy against the shogun. Although he subsequently released the sons in deference to Yoshimori, Yoshitoki rejected Yoshimori's pleas on behalf of his nephew. Instead, he paraded Tanenaga, trussed up like a common thief, before Yoshimori and his assembled men. A month later, he compounded this insult by seizing Wada house lands that should, by right and custom, have been entrusted to Yoshimori. Yoshimori spent the next month assembling troops and allies.[3]

By early afternoon on the second, it must have been obvious to anyone out and about in Kamakura that something unusual was afoot, for horses and men had been assembling in and around Yoshimori's home all morning. The Wada compound stood opposite the Tsurugaoka Hachiman shrine, at the north end of the city, and faced Yoshitoki's home, across the Wakamiya-ōji, the main avenue

INTRODUCTION

running through Kamakura, between the shrine and Yūhigahama beach. A force the size of the one Yoshimori had gathered could scarcely have been contained within the walls of his residential compound, nor could the sounds – or smells – of dozens of horses have been hidden from even the least attentive passers-by. Yoshimori probably attempted to conceal the bulk of his army in the woods, to the northwest of his residence, but he was rapidly losing any possible advantage of surprise. Indeed, Yoshitoki, occupied in a game of *go*, was receiving multiple reports of the goings-on across the street. At length, he quietly slipped out the back gate of his compound, and moved to the shogun's residence, a block and a half to the northeast. In the meantime, the shogun, Sanetomo, and his mother, Hōjō Masako, left their home, to hide in the chambers of the chief administrator (*bettō*) of the shrine.

Yoshimori's plan appears to have centered on capturing or killing Yoshitoki. Toward this end, he split his forces into three groups, sending one to invest the south gate of the shogun's home, and the second to surround Yoshitoki's residence. In the meantime, Yoshimori himself led the third group to attack the home of Yoshitoki's confederate, Ōe Hiromoto. Hiromoto's men were engaged in a drinking party, and were easily taken by the Wada troops pouring through their front gate; but Hiromoto himself had already slipped away, to join Yoshitoki at the shogun's residence. Yoshitoki's home was also quickly overrun, although the men left behind to guard it put up a valiant struggle, claiming numerous casualties from the Wada forces.

Yoshimori and his men then moved on to the Yoko-ōji avenue on the south side of the shogun's residence, where they ran into a group of horsemen hastily deployed by shogunal retainer Hitano Tadatsuna, and reinforced by Miura Yoshimura. Yoshimura, a close kinsman of Yoshimori, had in fact been a confederate to the plotting for the day's attempted coup, but had gotten cold feet at the last minute, and warned Yoshitoki instead. His sudden appearance in the Yoko-ōji must have been Yoshimori's first indication that he had been betrayed. The ensuing mêlée filled the streets for several blocks, as mounted warriors dodged around and past one another, shooting, pausing to identify new targets, and charging again. For the next two hours the combat raged on without clear lines or advantage to either side until, at the hour of the cock (5:00–7:00 pm), Wada troops under Asaina Yoshihide broke through the gate and stormed into the south garden of the shogunal compound, shooting down the defenders there and setting fire to the buildings. Yoshitoki and Hiromoto continued the fight "while screaming arrows [*narikabura*] flew and sharp blades flashed."[4]

Yoshimori's warriors, we are told, "were each man worth a thousand, each fighting like the heavens and the earth and the angry thunder." None more so, however, than Asaina Yoshihide, who "manifested strength as though he were a god; and none who opposed him escaped death."[5] The shogunate's official history of the battle offers four stirring testimonials to his valor and skills.

Among Yoshihide's victims was Yoshimori's nephew Takai Shigemochi, who "had not taken part in his family's plotting, but had come to the shogunal residence alone to throw down his life." Which, as it happens, is exactly what he did, almost literally. Yoshihide and Shigemochi rode at one another and, having already emptied their quivers of arrows, "cast away their bows and aligned their bridles, seeking to determine cock from hen." Drawing their daggers, the pair took hold of one another and grappled. Shigemochi momentarily gained the upper hand, throwing Yoshihide from his mount, only to lose his own balance and topple to the ground with him. The tussle continued for several minutes, until "at length Shigemochi was struck down." Before Yoshihide could get back onto his horse, however, another warrior, Sagami Tomotoki, came running at him, his long sword in hand. Once again Yoshihide prevailed.[6]

After regaining his mount, Yoshihide rode back through the gate and southwest into the Yoko-ōji, where he spotted Ashikaga Yoshiuji beside a bridge that spanned the ditch surrounding the shogunate's administrative head-quarters (*mandokoro*). Yoshiuji wheeled and whipped his horse to flee, while Yoshihide galloped forward, catching Yoshiuji by the shoulder plate (*ōsode*) of his armor. In almost the same instant, however, Yoshiuji leaped across the ditch, leaving Yoshihide clutching the shoulder plate, astonished that Yoshiuji's horse had managed the jump without breaking its legs or throwing its rider. Unable to follow on a mount already fatigued from a battle now entering its third or fourth hour, Yoshihide pulled up, and glared across the ditch at Yoshiuji, while onlookers around them clapped and cheered. A moment later, he turned and galloped around to the bridge, intent on renewing his pursuit. But just as he reached the crossway, a warrior named Taka no Shikan broke from the crowd and rode to support Yoshiuji. Yoshihide quickly killed him but, while the two were thus engaged, Yoshiuji escaped.

By this time it was growing dark, and the Wada men and horses were becoming exhausted. They were also running out of arrows. At length, Yoshimori ordered a withdrawal southward, down the Wakamiya-ōji, to the beach. Hōjō Yasutoki (Yoshitoki's son) and his men pursued them, clashing at Nakashimōma bridge, and at the Komemachi and Ōmachi intersections along the way. In the meantime, Ōe Hiromoto and his troops pulled back to guard the administrative headquarters and the documents stored there.

The fighting continued sporadically throughout the night. By dawn, Yoshimori and his men were nearly out of provisions, and worn out from more than twelve hours of combat; they were also cold and wet, from the light rain that had been falling since midnight. To make matters worse, they were pinned down on the beach by Hōjō troops, who controlled all the major arteries running northwest into the city. As Yoshimori contemplated his increasingly bleak options, however, his fortunes abruptly changed. At the hour of the tiger (3:00–5:00 am), Yokoyama Tokikane, a warrior from southern Musashi, rode onto the beach from the west, along the old Tōkaidō road, at the head of an enormous contingent of troops under several dozen of his sons, nephews, retainers and allies. Tokikane had, in fact, been part of Yoshimori's plotting from the start. The two had agreed to open hostilities together on the morning of the third. Tokikane, arriving according to plan, must have been startled to find himself in the middle of a battle already long underway. As Tokikane's troops shed their straw rain coats, making a pile "said to form a mountain," the allied forces now numbered some 3,000 mounted troops.[7]

Curiously, however, Yoshimori did not move quickly to exploit his now overwhelming advantage in numbers, a miscalculation that proved to be his undoing. While he delayed – perhaps in order to allow his warriors time to rest – troops belonging to the Sōga, Nakamura, Futamiyama and Kawamura houses, "as tumultuous as the clouds and as stirred up as bees," took up positions and erected shields and barricades across the Wakamiya-ōji and other streets leading from the beach. Nevertheless, thoroughly cowed by the size of the enemy forces, the Hōjō allies held in place, in spite of orders to attack. Meanwhile, Yoshitoki and Hiromoto were about to turn things around yet again.

At the hour of the snake (9:00–11:00 am), the pair drafted and countersigned a letter of instruction (*migyōsho*) under the shogun's personal seal, declaring the Wada and Yokoyama to be rebels and enemies of the state – turning what had, to this point, been a private conflict between Yoshimori, Yoshitoki, and their respective allies into a government-sanctioned pursuit of outlaws. They then put the letter to dramatic use, dispatching it by courier to shogunal vassals in neighboring provinces, and simultaneously arranging to have it read before the troops forming ranks on the beach. The effect was spectacular. Yoshimori's and Tokikane's allies deserted them *en masse* for Yoshitoki, and what was now the government army.

Stunned by this sudden reversal of fortune, Yoshimori led his remaining forces in a desperate attempt to cut their way up the Wakamiya-ōji to Yoshitoki, in the shogun's residence. Amazingly, although once again outnumbered, the rebels were still able to advance, scattering many of the shogunate's presumably less than highly motivated allies in their wake. When Hōjō Yasutoki, the government commander on the front, sent a messenger for instructions, a surprised and frightened Sanetomo could only respond with an exhortation to firm up defensive efforts.

At this juncture, fate and superstition intervened on behalf of the Hōjō. As the Wada and Yokoyama warriors galloped through the streets, Ōe Hiromoto composed an appeal for help and dispatched it, along with two poems in his own hand, to the Tsurugaoka Hachiman shrine. At about the same time, one of Yoshimori's key allies, Tsuchiya Yoshikiyo, closing in on the shogunal compound, was suddenly struck and killed by an unidentified arrow. Seeing this, and noting that the arrow had come from the north, the direction of the shrine, the Kamakura men began to shout that the arrow had been a divine one (*kami kabura*), sparking a rally that slowly built to a rout. By the hour of the cock (5:00–7:00 pm), the rebels were in flight. Yoshimori's eldest son, Yoshinao, was shot down by shogunal houseman Iguma Shideshige. A short time later Yoshimori himself, and three of his other sons, fell to Edo Yoshinori. Yoshihide and 500 of his horsemen managed to reach the beach, where they had prepared escape boats, and put to oars for Awa, while six other Wada commanders and the remaining rebel forces scattered and fled by land. Yoshitoki collected the heads of Yoshimori and the other principals, and put them on display in a temporary hut erected on the beach. Afterward, the victors held a party at Yoshitoki's home that lasted for two days.

According to a report presented three days later, casualties on the Wada side included 142 ranking warriors of the Wada, Yokoyama, Tsuchiya, Yamanouchi, Shibuya, Mōri, Kamakura and Hemmi houses, in addition to a presumably much larger number of "retainers and lesser figures not listed." Another twenty-eight warrior leaders were captured alive. Yoshitoki and his allies had lost only fifty named warriors, while "over a thousand servants of the Minamoto [shogunate] suffered wounds." The shogunate confiscated just over two dozen properties and titles from Yoshimori's allies, redistributing them among Yoshitoki and his men as rewards.[8]

While the skirmishing attendant to the Wada rebellion can hardly be ranked among the celebrated battles of the Kamakura period, it nevertheless exemplified the warfare of the era – in its origins and goals, in the organization of the forces involved, and in the weapons and tactics by which it was fought. Indeed, the flames and smoke and noise and rain and mud and stench and heroics and cruelties and allegiances and betrayals of the second and third days of the fifth month of 1213 reflect the broader face of battle in tenth- to fourteenth-century Japan. So, too, does the warfare of this early medieval epoch reflect the broader face of the age itself. A careful study of early medieval warfare informs and deepens our understanding of the Japanese world, such as it was during the Heian, Kamakura and Nambokuchō periods.

For Heraclitus was wrong. War is not the father of all things, it is the offspring – a quintessential human institution intimately intertwined with two other quintessentially human institutions, society and polity. War can create, define and defend both states and peoples, but it is also created, defined and delimited by them. The purposes for wars and the means by which they are conducted are set forth by the polities and the societies that fight them.

From the mid-tenth century until the late nineteenth, warfare in Japan was the province of professional men-at-arms, known variously as *bushi*, *tsuwamono*, *musha*, *mononofu* or – more popularly among Western audiences – *samurai*. This warrior order came into being, during the early Heian period to serve the imperial court and the noble houses that comprised it – as hired swords and contract bows. Its members ended the Nambokuchō era as the *de facto* masters of the country. Intriguingly, however, the "rise of the *bushi*" was less a matter of dramatic revolution than one incremental evolution, occurring in fits and starts.

Around the turn of the eighth century, the newly restyled imperial house and its supporters secured their position at the apex of Japan's socio-political hierarchy with the promulgation of an elaborate battery of governing institutions modeled in large measure on those of T'ang China. These included numerous provisions for domestic law-enforcement and foreign defense. Contrary to popular belief, these institutions were not simply adopted wholesale, they were carefully adapted to meet Japanese needs. But the various goals and requirements of the state were often in conflict with one another, with the result that the *ritsuryō* (the statutory, or imperial state) military apparatus incorporated a number of unhappy compromises. Problems inherent in the system at its inception were, moreover, made worse by changing conditions as the principal threats the state armies were designed to meet – invasion from the continent and regional challenges to the new, centralized polity – dwindled rapidly. By the mid-700s, the court had begun to reevaluate its martial needs and to restructure its armed forces, tinkering and experimenting with mechanisms for using and directing a new and different kind of soldiery, until a workable system was achieved around the late tenth century.[9]

The warrior order that would monopolize the application of arms throughout the medieval and early modern eras emerged rapidly during the ninth and tenth centuries, as incentives toward private arms-bearing received new impetus from a variety of directions. First and foremost among these was the dismantling of the *ritsuryō* military apparatus, and the concomitant amplification of the role of elites – members of the upper tiers of provincial society and the lower echelons of the court nobility – in the new military establishment. Bit by bit, the government ceased trying to draft and drill the population at large and concentrated instead on co-opting the privately acquired skills of martially talented elites through a series of new military posts and titles that legitimized the use of the personal martial resources of this group on behalf of the state. In essence, the court moved from a conscripted, publicly trained military force to one composed of privately trained, privately equipped professional mercenaries.

The expansive socio-political changes taking shape in Japan during the Heian period broadened other avenues for parlaying skill at arms into personal success as well. As it happened, government interest in the martial talents of provincial elites and the scions of lower-ranked central noble families dovetailed with growing demands for these same resources spawned by competition for wealth and influence among the premier noble houses of the court. State and personal needs served to create continually expanding opportunities for advancement for those with military talent. Increasingly, from the late eighth century onward, skill at arms offered a means for an ambitious young man to get his foot in the door for a career in government service and/or in the service of some powerful aristocrat in the capital. The greater such opportunities became, the more enthusiastically and the more seriously such young men committed themselves to the profession of arms. The result was the gradual emergence of an order of professional fighting men in the countryside and the capital that came to be known as the *bushi*.

At the heart of these developments lay a phenomenon that is often summarized as the privatization of the workings of government, or, more accurately, as the blurring of lines separating the public and private persona of those who carried out the affairs of governance. While it has become somewhat unfashionable today to employ the concepts of "public" and "private" in discussions of the early medieval era, these terms do, in fact, appear regularly in sources for the period and are not only useful, but critical to understanding political developments. "Public," in this context, indicates the notion of a corporate entity – the state – having an existence above and beyond the sum of its parts, as well as to activities overtly sanctioned by the laws and procedural regulations of that entity. "Private" refers, then, to the personal affairs and relationships of the units – the families and individuals – who made up the collective.

During the Heian period, the identity between hereditary status and office-holding, a cardinal feature of the *ritsuryō* polity from its outset, grew increasingly deeper and more rigid. Eligibility for any given post in the bureaucratic hierarchy became progressively more circumscribed, limited to smaller and smaller numbers of houses. Gradually, as the prospect that descendants of particular families would hold the same posts generation after generation turned more and more predictable, many offices – and the tasks assigned them – came to be closely associated with certain houses; and key government functions came to be performed through personal, rather than formal public, channels, rendering "public" and "private" rights and responsibilities harder and harder to distinguish.[10]

From the late ninth century onward, court society and the operations of government were increasingly dominated by powerful familial interest groups headed by senior courtiers (*kugyō*), who established complex networks of vertical alliances with low- and middle-ranked nobles.[11] Intense political competition at court made control of military resources of one sort or another an invaluable tool for guarding the status, as well as the persons, of the top courtiers and their heirs. Efforts on the part of the great court families to assemble private military forces and to press for control of state military assets were, therefore, ongoing from the inception of the *ritsuryō* state. As the system evolved, *kugyō* vied with one another to recruit men with warrior skills into the ranks of their household service, and to staff the officerships of the military units operating in the capital with their own kinsmen or clients.[12]

Waxing opportunities to parlay skill at arms into advancement through official and semiofficial channels were paralleled and reinforced by profound changes occurring in the fundamental relationship between the court the countryside. While the provinces were by no means simply left to fend for themselves in matters of law and order, the mechanisms by which they were kept bound to the center evolved considerably between the eighth and eleventh centuries.[13] In the public sphere, the signal changes revolved around the tax system, which was amended to make tax collection a problem between the central and provincial governments, rather than one between the court and individual subjects. Henceforth, revenue quotas were set province by province, and provincial officials were made accountable for seeing that they were met, as well as for making up shortfalls – out of their own pockets, if necessary. The means by which the taxes were actually collected were left largely to the discretion of the provincial governors and their staffs, who, in turn, delegated most of the burden to local elites charged with assembling whatever revenues were deemed appropriate from the specific locales in which they had influence. For their part, the local elites welcomed and encouraged such policy measures as opportunities for increasing their personal wealth and power. In the event, the new tax structure proved lucrative to all involved, turning provincial officials and local managers alike into tax farmers, who collected revenues beyond their assigned quotas and pocketed the surplus.[14]

Local elites and provincial officials were not, however, the only ones coming to view the agriculturalist residents of the provinces as simple resources for enhancing personal wealth. "Agents of temples, shrines, princes and officials" of the court were also "disobeying provincial governors, ignoring district officials, invading provinces and districts and using their prestige and influence" to pressure residents there, as well as "forcibly impressing men and horses," "robbing tax shipments," and "confiscating by force boats, carts, horses and men."[15]

Thus, by the mid-Heian period, the provinces had become a forum for competition for wealth and influence between three groups: provincial resident elites; provincial government officers; and the "temples, shrines, princes and officials" of the court. At the axis of this competition were the middle-ranked court nobles whose careers centered on appointments to provincial government offices. Such career provincial officials (*zuryō*) forged alliances with the lofty aristocrats above them to ensure a continued succession of posts. At the same time, many found that they could use the power and perquisites of their offices, and the strength of their court connections, to establish landed bases in their provinces of appointment and to continue to exploit the resources of these provinces even after their terms of office expired.[16]

Against this backdrop, some residents of the provinces were discovering that service to the court was not the only use to which martial skills could be applied. By the ninth century, a significant element was turning to banditry, as either an alternative or an addition to public service. In response, provincial governors, compelled by a need to defend themselves and their prerogatives against outlawry and armed resistance, as well as by the desire to maximize the profits that could be squeezed from taxpayers, began to include "warriors of ability" among the personal entourages that accompanied them to their provinces of appointment. A substantial number of *zuryō* also took up the profession of arms for themselves.[17]

Military skills and resources were undoubtedly useful to provincial officials in winning the respect of, or intimidating, armed residents of their provinces. But, far more importantly, they could also enhance an up-and-coming *zuryō*'s prospects at court, by opening doors to the patronage of important aristocrats and to posts in court military units.

By the tenth century, military service at court and service as a provincial official had become parallel and mutually supportive careers for the members of several middle-ranked courtier houses collectively known as the *miyako no musha*, or "warriors of the capital." The most illustrious of these belonged to

INTRODUCTION

a handful of competing branches of the Seiwa Minamoto – or Genji – and the Kammu Taira – or Heishi.*

Miyako no musha were, to borrow a pet phrase of the late Jeffrey Mass, "bridging figures," who maintained close economic and personal ties in both the capital and the provinces. Many developed marriage and other alliances with local figures, and held packages of lands scattered about the countryside, which provided them with income. But they resided primarily in the capital, and looked chiefly to the central court for their livelihoods. To provincial governors and their families, Kyoto was the source of the human and physical resources that made their provincial business activities possible, as well as the marketplace for the goods they brought from the country.† It was, nevertheless, mainly the central direction of their career emphasis, rather than pedigree or residence as such, that distinguished "warriors of the capital" from "provincial warriors."[18]

The latter were, broadly speaking, men of two main types of ancestry: descendants of cadet branches of central court houses – the Minamoto, the Fujiwara, the Tachibana and the Taira – that had established bases in the provinces; and the scions of families that traced their descent back to pre-*ritsuryō* provincial chieftains. The genealogies of medieval warrior houses suggest a preponderance of the former group. But the reliability of such records is open to some question, and in practice both groups intermarried and interacted so thoroughly as to become functionally indistinguishable.

Heian court marriages were uxorilocal or neolocal, and polygamous or serially monogamous. Children reckoned descent primarily from their father, and took his surname, but they were usually raised in their mother's home, and inherited much of their material property from her. Often, moreover, when the bride's family was of significantly higher station than the groom's, the children – and sometimes the new husband – adopted the surname of the bride's father. *Zuryō* sent to work in the provinces took their marriage customs with them. Numerous edicts forbidding the practice make it clear that provincial officials took wives

---

* The term Genji derives from the Sino-Japanese reading of the surname Minamoto. The Seiwa Genji, then, were the Minamoto lines that claimed descent from Emperor Seiwa (r. 858–76). Seiwa had nine sons who bore the surname Minamoto. Of these, the most important military families descended from his sixth son, Sadazumi, through his son Tsunemoto. Similarly, "Heishi" comes from the Sino-Japanese reading of the surname Taira, and the Kammu Heishi were the branches of the Taira descended from Emperor Kammu (r. 781–806). The warrior lines began with Kammu's eldest son, Katsurahara, through his son and grandson Takami and Takamochi. Takamochi fathered eight sons; the descendents of four established formidable reputations for themselves as military servants of the court for several generations.

† Japan's capital city was known as Heian-kyō during the Heian period; the name "Kyōto" did not come into popular use until the medieval era. In order to minimize confusion, however, I have adopted "Kyoto" as a convenient label for the city throughout its history.

9

and sons-in-law from provincial elite houses with considerable frequency. As a result, surnames such as Taira, Minamoto and Fujiwara gradually supplanted those of the older provincial noble families among the leading houses of provincial society.[19]

Superficial similarities between the samurai and the knights of northern Europe make it tempting to equate the birth of the samurai with the onset of "feudalism" in the Japanese countryside; but such was not the case. Heian Japan remained firmly under civil authority; the socio-economic hierarchy still culminated in a civil, not a military, nobility; and the idea of a warrior order was still more nascent than real. Warrior leaders still looked to the center and to the civil ladder for success, and still saw the profession of arms largely as a means to an end – a foot in the door toward civil rank and office. During the Heian period, warriors thought of themselves as warriors in much the same way that modern corporate CEOs view themselves as shoe makers, automobile manufacturers or magazine distributors: just as the latter tend to identify more closely with CEOs in other industries than with the workers, engineers or middle managers in their factories, design workshops and offices, so too did *bushi* at all levels in the socio-political hierarchy identify more strongly with their non-military social peers than with warriors above or below them in the hierarchy.[20]

Bushi class-consciousness – a sense of warriors as a separate estate – did not begin to emerge until the thirteenth century, after the Kamakura shogunate was in place. The new institution created the category of shogunal retainer (*gokenin*) as a self-conscious class of individuals with special privileges and responsibilities. It also narrowed the range of social classes from which *bushi* came, by eliminating or supplanting the *miyako no musha* houses in all military affairs outside the capital. Its founder, Minamoto Yoritomo, consciously helped foster this new sense of warrior identity by holding hunts and archery competitions, which were staged in an atmosphere not entirely unlike those of medieval European tournaments.[21]

The sequence of events that led to the birth of Japan's first warrior government began in 1156, when Yoritomo's father, Yoshitomo, and his long-time rival Taira Kiyomori found themselves fighting on the same side of a dispute between a reigning and a retired emperor. In the ensuing Hōgen Incident (named for the calendar era in which it occurred), Kiyomori reaped what Yoshitomo considered to have been far more than his fair share of the rewards distributed to the victors. The enmity this precipitated led to the Heiji Incident (again named for the calendar era) of 1159, a poorly conceived and clumsily executed attempt by Yoshitomo to eliminate his rival. This time, several days of bloody fighting left Yoshitomo and most of his supporters dead, and Kiyomori as the premier warrior leader in Japan. For the next two decades, Kiyomori's prestige and influence at court grew steadily, capped by the marriage of his daughter, Tokuko, to the reigning emperor, Takakura, in 1171, his seizure and confinement of the retired emperor Go-Shirakawa in 1179, and the accession of his grandson to the throne as Emperor Antoku in 1180.

INTRODUCTION

That same year, however, Yoritomo issued a call to arms, parlaying his own pedigree, the localized ambitions of provincial warriors, and the upheavals within the court into a new and innovative base of power. Exiled at thirteen years of age, in the wake of the Heiji Incident — and therefore dispossessed of the career path that would otherwise have been his by right of patrimony — Yoritomo had been effectively locked out of the system, unable to advance his interests through traditional means. His response was to initiate what amounted to an end run around the *status quo* hitherto existing between the central nobility and warriors in the provinces.[22]

Seizing on a pretext of rescuing the court from Kiyomori — in answer to a plea broadcast by Prince Mochihito, a frustrated claimant to the throne — Yoritomo announced that he was assuming jurisdiction over all lands and offices in the east, further declaring that, in return for an oath of allegiance to himself, henceforth he (Yoritomo) would assume the role of the court in guaranteeing whatever lands and administrative rights an enlisting vassal considered to be rightfully his own. In essence, Yoritomo was proclaiming the existence of an independent state in the east, a polity run by warriors for warriors. The ensuing groundswell of support touched off a countrywide series of feuds and civil wars subsumed under the rubric of Yoritomo's crusade against Kiyomori and his heirs.

In the course of this so-called Gempei War (the name of which derives from the Sino-Japanese readings for the characters used to write "Minamoto" and "Taira"), however, Yoritomo revealed himself to be a surprisingly conservative revolutionary. Rather than maintain his independent warrior state in the east, Yoritomo instead negotiated a series of accords with the retired emperor Go-Shirakawa that gave permanent status to the Kamakura regime, trading formal court recognition of many of the powers Yoritomo had seized for reincorporation of the east into the court-centered national polity.

Yoritomo's successes at first breaking the east free from court control and then reintegrating it to the imperial fold both raise scholarly eyebrows — for he was hardly the first eastern warrior leader to attempt either feat. The most famous warrior rebellions of the Heian period began in 939, when Taira Masakado seized control of the provincial government offices in Hitachi, and in 1028, when his grandson Taira Tadatsune ravaged the government compound in Awa. Masakado's insurrection climaxed with his claiming for himself the title "New Emperor." Tadatsune's reach did not extend so far, but his grasp held the provinces of the Bōsō peninsula — Kazusa, Shimōsa and Awa — for the better part of three years, and left much of the region in ruin.

And yet, a careful look at these and similar events during the Heian period demonstrates how strong the underlying ties between the periphery and the center remained, in spite of the loosening of bonds and the expansion of local freedom of action that developed during the epoch. Freedom of local action was not the same as independence, or even autonomy, for the simple reason that the warriors themselves did not yet think in those terms. Even Masakado and Tadatsune, whose insurrections are among the most momentous events of the period, were not willfully in defiance of central government authority – at least not initially. Their quarrels were local, not national; their insurgency was aimed at specific provincial officials and their subordinates and policies, not the national polity. And when they found themselves branded outlaws and rebels, their first – and most enduring – instincts were to seek reconciliation with the state, through the offices of their patrons at court.[23]

Neither Masakado nor Tadatsune – nor any of their epigones – were, however, successful in their efforts. Before Yoritomo, whenever powerful warriors stepped too far out of line and posed a challenge to central authority, the court was always able to find peers and rivals more conservative in their ambitions and assessments of the odds against successful rebellion to subdue them. There was little need, therefore, for the court to bargain with felonious warrior leaders. Yoritomo's theretofore unprecedented achievements were possible because of the sheer scale of the autonomous zone he was able to seize, and because his timing was fortuitous.

When he raised his standard in 1180, he was tapping into a wellspring of intra-familial and inter-class frustration with the structure of land-holding and administrative rights in the provinces. This discontent brought him a vast following. Nevertheless, it by no means earned him a *universal* following – a point that is perhaps more significant to understanding the socio-political dynamics of the period than was Yoritomo's revolution itself. The battle lines in the Gempei War were not really drawn between the "Gen" and the "Hei" (that is, between the Minamoto and the Taira); there were men of Taira kinship on Yoritomo's side and of Minamoto on Kiyomori's. The real conflict was between those, on the one side, who were sufficiently dissatisfied with their lot under the *status quo* to chance an enormous gamble and those, on the other, who were content with their current situation – or simply more conservative in their thinking or more skeptical of Yoritomo's chances for success. The former group signed on with Yoritomo, while the latter fought for the Taira.

The same dynamic that had brought Yoritomo to power, however, necessitated his moves toward reconciliation with the court. As his following mushroomed, he was quick to recognize two key precepts relating to his circumstances and to the nature of authority: first, that the forces he had unleashed were inherently unstable, and could all too easily expand beyond his control; and second, that his only cogent claims to preeminence over other eastern warrior leaders were rooted in his pedigree and his exploitation of Mochihito's warrant against Kiyomori – that is, that his incipient feudal lordship was in fact inextricably bound to the court-centered socio-political structure.

As it happened, the powers-that-were in the court were just as unhappy with Yoritomo's enemies – the Taira, and Minamoto Yoshinaka – as they were with him. In contrast to the circumstances prevailing during previous warrior uprisings, the events of the 1180s left the court with no more palatable choice available to send as champion against Yoritomo, making rapprochement with him the least of several evils.

INTRODUCTION

The resulting Kamakura shogunate was in effect a government within a government, at once a part of and distinct from the imperial court in Kyoto. Dominated after Yoritomo's death by the Hōjō family, who established a permanent regency over a succession of figurehead shoguns, the regime exercised broad administrative powers over the eastern provinces, and held special authority over the warriors, scattered nationwide, whom it recognized as its formal vassals (*gokenin*). After the Jōkyū War of 1221, an ill-fated attempt by a retired emperor, Go-Toba, to eliminate the shogunate, the balance of real power shifted steadily toward Kamakura and away from Kyoto. By the end of that century, the shogunate had assumed control of most of the state's judicial, military and foreign affairs.

In the meantime, *gokenin* across the country discovered that they could manipulate the insulation from direct court supervision Kamakura offered them in order to lay ever stronger and more personal claims to lands – and the people on them – which they ostensibly administered on behalf of the powers-that-were in the capital. Through a ratcheting process of gradual advance by *fait accompli*, a new warrior-dominated system of authority absorbed the older, courtier-dominated one, and real power over the countryside spun off steadily from the center to the hands of local figures.[24]

By the second quarter of the fourteenth century, this evolution had progressed to the point where the most successful of the shogunate's provincial vassals had begun to question the value of continued submission to Kamakura at all. The regime fell in 1333, as the result of events spawned by an imperial succession dispute.

Both the imperial house and the loyalties of the court had, since the 1260s, been divided between competing lineages descended from Emperor Go-Saga (r. 1242–6): the Senior, or Jimmyōin, line deriving from Go-Saga's eldest son, Go-Fukakasa (r. 1246–59); and the Junior, or Daikakuji, line, descended from his younger brother Kameyama (r. 1259–74). The shogunate, which had taken an active hand in matters of imperial succession since the Jōkyū War, was able to keep this rift under control by arranging a compromise whereby the two lineages would alternate in succession. In 1218, however, Emperor Go-Daigo, of the Junior line, came to the throne, and immediately set about reorganizing the power structure around himself.[25]

In 1331 Kamakura discovered that Go-Daigo had been plotting its elimination, and responded by forcing his abdication, and later his exile to the remote province of Oki. At this, Emperor Kōgon, of the Senior branch, ascended the throne. In the second month of 1333, however, Go-Daigo escaped from Oki and took refuge with supporters, who had continued to be active in working against the shogunate, under Go-Daigo's son, Prince Moriyoshi. Kamakura responded by dispatching armies under Ashikaga Takauji and Niita Yoshisada to subdue the "loyalist" forces and recapture Go-Daigo. But, in mid-course, both commanders turned on the shogunate, Takauji attacking and destroying its offices in Kyoto, and Yoshisada marching on Kamakura itself. In the sixth month of 1333, Go-Daigo returned to Kyoto, insisting that he had never formally abdicated, and proclaiming the start of a Kemmu (named for the calendar era) Restoration of imperial rule. Within three years, however, he found himself once again driven from power by the very men who put him there.

In 1335 Takauji changed sides yet again, and by the middle of the following year he had destroyed Go-Daigo's coalition, forced the once-and-future monarch to abdicate for a second time, and established a new shogunate, headquartered in the Muromachi district of Kyoto. Go-Daigo fled to the mountains of Yoshino, south of Kyoto, where he and his remaining supporters set up a rival court, insisting that the Takauji-sponsored succession of Emperor Kōmyō in Kyoto had been illegitimate, and therefore illegal. Thus began the six-decade long Nambokuchō (literally, "Southern and Northern Court") era, the longest and most significant dynastic schism in Japanese history.

Warfare between the two courts broke out immediately, and rapidly spread across the country.[26] Leading warriors – including Takauji and his brother Tadayoshi! – shifted sides again and again in response to advantages and opportunities of the moment, playing each court off the other in much the same way that the court had once kept warriors weak by pitting them against one another. As this happened, it took a predictably heavy toll on imperial authority. By the time the third Ashikaga shogun, Yoshimitsu, tricked the southern pretender, Go-Kameyama, and his followers into returning to Kyoto – subsequently reneging on his promise to reinstitute the old system of alternating succession – whatever remained of centralized power in Japan was in the hands of the shogunate.

The end of the Nambokuchō era thus marks a convenient point for dividing the early medieval epoch from what followed. In subsequent decades, warriors, not emperors or courtier houses, dominated not only the countryside, but the entire socio-economic and political structure of Japan. Fifteen Ashikaga shoguns reigned between 1336 and 1573, when the last, Yoshiaki, was deposed; but only the first six could lay claim to having actually ruled the country. The dynamic *modus vivendi* that had characterized the early medieval era – in which private or provincial military power had been balanced by public authority emanating from the top down or the center out – were gone. Meaningful power now depended on pyramids of control and relationships built from the ground up, as scores of feudal barons, called *daimyo*, contested with one another for control.

The study presented in the five chapters of this volume is not about wars, but about what wars and warfare meant, and why they took the form they did, within the socio-political structure of early medieval Japan (defined, for our purposes here, as the tenth through the fourteenth centuries). It examines early medieval Japanese warfare from five thematic angles, focusing primarily on the Heian and Kamakura periods. The following chapters, then, explore the purposes of the military and military activities, the principles according to which armed conflict was justified or condemned, the mechanisms through which armed forces were raised and deployed, the form of weapons available to early medieval warriors, the means by which they obtained them, and the techniques and customs of battle.

INTRODUCTION

My aim throughout is to highlight the delicate balance, the interpenetrated, interdependent, causal relationship that held between the structures and sources of political power, the objectives and purposes of warfare, the composition and organization of military forces, and the tactics and equipment of war.

The conclusions presented in this study are built from a wide variety of sources, ranging from legal documents to picture scrolls to works of literature. Reconstruction of battlefield ethics and behavior presents a particularly thorny historiographical challenge, which merits a bit of elaboration here, before I move on to the first chapter.

Until very recently, historians' images of early medieval warfare were predominantly shaped by facile analyses of literary wartales (*gunkimono*), particularly the *Heike monogatari*, the classic saga of the Gempei War. This masterpiece bristles with vivid descriptions of battles and other encounters between warriors so detailed they even record the colors of horses ridden and clothing worn. Long assumed to have been built closely around accounts compiled shortly after the occurrence of the events they portray, and preserved more or less verbatim henceforth, *Heike monogatari* and other *gunkimono* beckon historians as compelling, and readily accessible, sources of information on early medieval warfare. Modern literary scholars have, however, raised considerable doubt about the historical reliability of these chronicles, observing that much of the most compelling detail contained in the narratives was in fact manufactured largely of whole cloth.

Kenneth Butler's careful reconstruction of the textual development of *Heike monogatari*, for example, demonstrates that, while the outline forms of the great medieval wartales were first committed to paper shortly after the occurrence of the events they portray, these antetype accounts lacked the meticulous descriptions of battlefield behavior that have shaped our images of early *bushi* warfare. The *Heike monogatari* as we know it today is the result of a merger of enrichments and embellishments developed by traveling entertainers (*biwa-hōshi*) into the original stories and written texts (said merger having occurred in stages over the course of the thirteenth and fourteenth centuries). The *biwa-hōshi*, Butler argues, produced these embellishments by manipulating stereotyped themes and formulae common to oral tale composition all over the world. The best-known (and most analyzed) version of *Heike monogatari*, the Kakuichi-bon, was recorded in its present form in 1371, after nearly 200 years of elaboration and enhancement on the lutes of jongleurs.[27]

Heike monogatari is, moreover, a heavily thematic narrative. Its central purpose is to explain how and why the once-mighty Taira fell from power and grace. It casts the Taira defeat as inevitable and shapes everything to this fatalistic theme of certain, predictable fall: Kiyomori and his heirs, it tells us, lost because they could not have won. Among the most important devices applied toward this end is the consistent exaggeration of a dichotomy alleged to have existed between the fierce, rough-and-ready Minamoto warriors of the east and the genteel, courtified Taira partisans of the west – a stereotype that has no evidential basis outside the *Heike monogatari* and its sister texts, but which has colored and dominated historical perceptions of early warriors for centuries.[28]

Similar problems of distortions introduced by the entertainment or didactic purposes for which they were written plague other literary texts as well, even those no *biwa-hōshi* ever sang. So too, do Hollywood-esque problems of anachronism and physical, biological or mechanical implausibility introduced by the authors' lack of familiarity with real battlefields. The sharpest-eyed of historians have, in fact, been commenting on the latter problem for generations. In his famous 1891 essay on why "*Taiheiki* Has No Value for Historians," Kume Kunitake, for example, offered several illustrations of this sort of scientific error in *Taiheiki*, a chronicle of the Nambokuchō wars. Among the most interesting of these is one concerning the battle at Akasaka Castle in 1331. *Taiheiki* alleges that,

> Those within the castle took up ladles with handles ten or twenty feet long, dipped up boiling water, and poured it onto [attackers attempting to pull down the castle walls]. The hot water passed through the holes in their helmet tops, ran down from the edges of their shoulder-guards, and burned their bodies so grievously that they fled panic-stricken.[29]

The problem with this assertion, notes Kume, is twofold: first, a ladle with a 10- or 20-foot handle would become far too heavy to lift if it held more than a very small amount of water; and second, water dropped from a height quickly spreads out and is cooled by the air as it falls. Boiling water poured onto attackers from atop even fairly low castle walls would, therefore, be warm, not scalding, when it reached its targets.[30]

It would seem, then, that a truly scrupulous reaccounting of tenth- to fourteenth-century battlefield customs and behavior must ignore literary texts entirely. But, however desirable, this sort of approach is simply not feasible.

Diaries, letters, public documents and court histories – the sort of sources scholars deem most reliable – are maddeningly laconic in their discussions of battles. Most, particularly those dealing with the period before the 1180s, tell us little more than the time, place and results of encounters between warriors. By the late twelfth century, it had become customary for warrior leaders to compile petitions for reward, called *gunchūjō*, which were in turn based on battle reports (*kassen teioi chūmon* or *kassen teioi jikken-jō*) submitted by their subordinates. The earliest surviving example of this sort of document dates from 1265, but it is plain that the practice of compiling them began much earlier. *Gunchūjō*, therefore, offer an additional window on the late thirteenth and fourteenth centuries. The Kamakura shogunate's official chronicle of its own history, *Azuma kagami*, moreover, quotes and cites such reports frequently, and uses them as the base for detailed descriptions of battles in its entries.[31]

Azuma kagami is, in fact, the most dependable – and therefore the most useful – single source for information on early medieval Japanese warfare, for it is, at a minimum, a roughly contemporaneous chronicle written by warriors about warriors. Nevertheless, it covers only the years between 1180 and 1266 – that is, only the middle third of the period under scrutiny in the present study – and is far from comprehensive even for that span of time.

For a fuller understanding of early medieval warfare, historians have little recourse but to depend, at least in part, on sources that are fictionalized to an uncertain degree, and therefore less than completely trustworthy. These include pictorial as well as literary records.

One of the most promising avenues of research is analysis of the numerous illustrated scrolls (*emaki*) that depict the wars and other military adventures of the early medieval era. A dozen or so *emaki* produced during the late thirteenth and fourteenth centuries survive, although with the singular exception of Takezaki Suenaga's illustrated petition for rewards, the *Mōko shūrai ekotoba*, all of these scrolls postdate the events they portray by a half-century or more. They are, therefore, most reliably interpreted as reflecting conditions during the late Kamakura and Nambokuchō eras, when they were drawn. Sadly, no comparable resources exist for the Heian and early Kamakura periods.[32]

Historians can also make use of some of the early variant texts of the *Heike monogatari*. The most helpful of these are the Engyōbon version and the *Gempei jōsuiki*, both written down during the early thirteenth century. These accounts differ considerably – sometimes dramatically – from the more familiar Kakuichi-bon, and, if approached with appropriate caution and skepticism, are indispensable sources of information.

For the Heian and Nambokuchō periods, we also have numerous literary accounts of warriors and warfare, ranging from anecdotes in didactic tale collections such as the *Konjaku monogatarishū* to longer chronicles of specific wars, such as *Shōmonki* and *Mutsuwaki* (which relate Taira Masakado's rebellion and the so-called Former 9 Years' War of 1055–62), to epic sagas such as *Taiheiki*, which spans some forty volumes. To be sure, these are tales and stories, not historical records, and must be used carefully. But if they have been embellished and sometimes deviate from fact, they nevertheless reflect the perceptions – the images of warriors and battles – of men who lived roughly contemporaneously to the events depicted. As such, they can at least be trusted to be far closer to portraying "how things actually were" (to use von Ranke's famous phrase) on early medieval battlefields than the Kakuichi-bon *Heike monogatari* and other *gunkimono* written centuries after the fact. The general credibility of the Heian literary works is, moreover, underscored by the fact that their portrayals of warriors and warfare are consistent with one another and with those in other sources for the period, even as they are at odds with much of the imagery of the later *gunkimono*.

The portrait of early medieval warfare that emerges from close analysis and cross-comparison of this diverse mixture of evidence is different but no less colorful than that found in the traditional literature. The early *bushi* were a fascinating enigma: men of fierce, self-sacrificing courage, whose lives centered on the concept of honor but who seemingly held no notion of fair play; men seen by some of their contemporaries as "of imposing visage, great martial skills, courage, discretion and discrimination," and by others as, "no different from barbarians . . . like wild wolves, butchering human flesh and using it as ornaments for their bodies."[33]

I begin my reproduction of this portrait with an examination of what early medieval warriors were fighting about.

1

THE MEANING OF WAR

> A just war is hospitable to every self-deception on the part of those waging it, none more than the certainty of virtue, under whose shelter every abomination can be committed with a clear conscience.
> Alexander Cockburn, *New Statesman and Society*, 1991

> You cannot have good laws without good arms, and where there are good arms, good laws inevitably follow.
> Niccolo Machiavelli, *The Prince*, 1514

Warfare – armed conflict between organized bands or bodies – may well be a ubiquitous phenomenon, occurring in all times and all places that humans have grouped themselves into exclusively defined troupes; but *war* is anything but a universal construct. While men everywhere and every when have taken up arms, the purposes and objectives toward which they strive are as varied as the clothing they wear and the languages they speak. The meaning of war is highly particularized to specific times and places, and always susceptible to change brought on by social or technological evolution.

Carl von Clausewitz's famous definition of war as "an act of force to compel our enemy to do our will," and "a continuation of political intercourse with the intermixing of other means," rings true for modern Western audiences.[1] But while his views may have been typical of the age and place in which he penned them, they were expressed in defiance of historical reality. Warfare and martial power have forms and purposes beyond resolving interstate disputes – beyond even killing enemies or protecting oneself. And some of these are more important or more common in premodern societies than the shapes and objectives we associate with "war" today. Warfare can also be a form of communication. It can be a means of divination or other intercourse with deities. It can be a competition, a means of entertainment or self-expression. It can serve a judicial function, or be a symbol of the power of the observers of its exercise over those who perform it.

And if the identity of war is contingent on time, place and circumstance, still more so are the rules of war, the bases for distinguishing between acceptable and unacceptable grounds for resorting to arms. Societies differentiate just from unjust wars, warriors from brigands, and even guerrillas from terrorists. Yet one people's or one age's holy cause is another's malefaction. In practice, moreover, a culture's ideas about why wars are – or should be – fought are interwoven with its customs and routines for fighting them.

This chapter explores the ways that the socio-political climate in which the early *bushi* functioned shaped early medieval Japanese customs and beliefs regarding the purposes of armed conflict, and the principles that separated righteous from criminal hostilities.

The concept of Just War

Modern Western ideas concerning the purpose of armies and war trace back to antiquity and the political philosophers of Greece and Rome. Aristotle, who coined the term and the concept of Just War for the Hellenic world, saw it not as an end in and of itself, but as a means to higher goals. He cast war in the light of conflict to further peace and justice, which in turn rested on the concept of natural law, a universal and self-vindicating morality rooted in religious or cosmic sanction. Under this view, war became acceptable only as a last resort and only when conducted so as not to preclude the restoration of a lasting peace.

To this the Romans appended the role of the polity. As defined by Cicero, a war could be just only when conducted by the state, which excluded revolution and rebellion, and only when accompanied by a formal declaration of hostilities. The Romans further saw war as analogous to the process of recovering damages for breach of contract in a civil suit, with the injured city-state enjoying rights to seek compensation and redress, and acting as advocate, judge and sheriff. Against an enemy from whom Rome sought to recover lost goods, whether real property or incorporeal rights, warfare was not a willful exercise of violence but a just and pious endeavor occasioned by injustices propagated by the enemy. Conversely, combat waged without a proper *causa belli* or without state sanction was not war but piracy (*lactrocinium*).[2]

Early Christians rejected war *in toto*. This position was not, however, due to any explicit prohibition of war in the New Testament. It derived instead from an effort to apply what was taken to be the mind of Christ. And it offered a new vision of peace that centered on well-being and security, but without physical characteristics. Christian peace was the absence not only of war but of contention. The earliest forms of Christian pacifism had as much to do with rejection of politics and worldliness as with abhorrence of violence itself.

After Constantine, however, the clear separation of the Church and the world ceased to exist, and Christianity could no longer be pacifist in the same way it had been. As a result, it began to focus on the evil of violence itself, and to attempt some reconciliation of Christian ideals with the necessity of using armed force in governance. Against this background Augustine formulated a doctrine centered on the twin themes of permission and limitation. Christians, whether acting as individuals or collectively in war, could engage in violence only under circumstances that met key criteria: right authority, just cause, right intention, proportionality, last resort, and the end of peace.[3]

Japan generated no significant dialog of its own on what circumstances rendered it right and proper for the state to direct its military power at its own subjects or at outsiders, and instead drew the philosophical base it needed for such decisions from Chinese – predominantly Confucian – principles. China produced a staggeringly prodigious volume of theoretical work on war. One estimate puts the total number of treatises at 1,340 books in 6,831 volumes, of which some 288 books, containing 2,160 volumes, survive today. Most of the original thinking on military theory was developed during the Chou period, with later texts focusing on interpretation of older ones. The Warring States era (475–221 BCE) in particular saw the emergence of a rich commentary on warfare, both in specialized works on military theory and strategy, such as Sun Tzu, and in more general works by Legalist, Taoist, Confucian and other thinkers.[4]

Post-Ch'in dynasty political theory cast the governing institutions of the state as nothing more – and nothing less – than a conduit for the expression of the will of the sovereign. Government officials were held to be advisors and sometimes surrogates acting *in loco parentis* for the emperor, who was himself the earthly agent and custodian of the cosmic order, with authority over and responsibility for his subjects analogous to those of a father for his children. The emperor's role in the social order applied equally to domestic and foreign affairs, which formed a single continuum with the emperor at the center of a series of radial zones of influence. Any disruptions of the social order, from petty crimes and familial disputes in the capital to armed conflicts abroad, were thus transgressions against the proper cosmic order and deserving of imperial attention.

When all was as it should be, the virtuous and proper conduct of the ruler exerted a powerful edifying effect on his subjects, driving them toward righteous behavior without further need for coercion, just as ideal children acquire moral rectitude from their parents' example. But where, owing to shortcomings on the part of the ruler or the subjects, this was not enough (as was usually the case in the real world), the next best alternative was the law and the state, which encouraged virtuous conduct by reward and discouraged misbehavior by punishment. Recourse to war – to the violent coercion of large numbers of people – was justifiable only when all else had failed.

Thus war, in the Chinese scheme of things, could be pursued only by the rightful sovereign, and only if conducted as a matter of last resort. At the same time, the righteousness and the justice of *any* military action the emperor and his ministers deemed it necessary to pursue could not be questioned, save in retrospect. The success of any military venture was in itself proof that the campaign had been in accord with the cosmic order, and therefore by definition right and just.

Chinese ideas about war made their way into Japan along with other bits of Chinese culture over the course of the fifth, sixth and seventh centuries, and provided the framework for the military institutions of the imperial (*ritsuryō*) state, which in turn served as the core principles of the state's military system from the eighth through the end of the fourteenth century. Following the Chinese model, the Japanese court viewed both warfare with foreign powers and peoples and domestic law-enforcement as essentially the same activity. Outside the capital, military defense and police functions were carried out by the same units and officers, following the same procedures (see Chapter 2). And military adventures outside the parameters of the state were justified with the same rhetoric as police actions within it. The court's efforts to establish control over northeastern Honshu, ongoing from the late seventh to the early ninth century, for example, cast these campaigns as "pacification" efforts (*seii*), and the *emishi* people against whom they were directed as criminals and rebels:[5]

> Because [military action] brings hardship to the people, We have long embraced broader virtue [and have eschewed war]. [But] a report from Our generals makes it clear that the barbarians have not amended their wild hearts. They invade Our frontiers and ignore the instructions of the Sovereign. What must be done cannot be avoided. . . . Immediately dispatch the army to strike down and destroy in a timely fashion.[6]

> These bandits are like wild-hearted wolf cubs. They do not reflect on the favors We have bestowed upon them but trust in the steepness of [the terrain around their bases] and time and again wreak havoc upon Our frontiers. Our soldiers are a dangerous weapon, but they cannot stop [these depredations]. Be it thus: mobilize 3000 troops and with these cut off the rebel progeny; with these put out the smoldering embers.[7]

Thus the Japanese court, like its Chinese paragon, laid claim to an authority whose boundaries often exceeded its real power, and whose implications left scarce room for debate concerning the parameters of Just War. The *ritsuryō* polity equated its existence, and the socio-political structure over which it reigned, with morality and the cosmic order. Military actions undertaken in order to preserve – or enhance – the imperial order were – must be – Just War, while any and all other recourses to force of arms were by definition selfish, particularistic and unjust.[8]

The *ritsuryō* codes enshrined these notions in their provisions reserving control and direction of all but the most minor military and police affairs for the emperor and his court. Overall administration of the state's armed forces was conducted by the Ministry of Military Affairs (*hyōbushō*) and the five offices under it. Its responsibilities included the supervision of military officers; the administration of troop registers, armories, pastures, war-horses, public and private pack animals, boats, fortifications, signal fires, and postal roads; the oversight of the manufacture of weapons; the collation of military communications from the provinces; and the calculation of overall troop strength and the balance of forces in the various provinces. All these functions were handled at the provincial level by the governor and his staff (all of whom were central appointees), who also conducted annual inspections of weapons, boats, livestock and the like, and forwarded the information collected to the Ministry of Military Affairs for collation.[9]

Any mobilization of more than twenty troops could be undertaken only by imperial edict. The procedures for promulgating such writs were complex, and required the concurrence of the Council of State (*daijōkan*). This meant that a decision to employ armed force could be effected only with the broad consensus of the ruling class. The issue would first be discussed by various deliberative bodies and decided on by the Council of State, whereupon an imperial edict was petitioned for and an order to fight issued in the emperor's name. The Ministry of Military Affairs would then be directed to calculate and report on the number of troops available for mobilization, the number appropriate for the current campaign, and the specific units most suitable for mobilization. This report would thereupon become the base upon which the Council of State would issue preparation and mobilization instructions "pursuant to an order from his imperial majesty."[10]

Private war

By the mid-tenth century, the court had discarded most of the elaborate, Chinese-inspired military apparatus established under the *ritsuryō* codes, an excision that in part facilitated and was in part facilitated by the birth and rapid growth of a new order of professional fighting men in the capital and the countryside. From this time forward, the state maintained no armies of its own, depending instead on the members of the emerging *bushi* order deputized to act as its "claws and teeth." The military institutions of the early medieval period centered on privately armed, privately trained warriors commissioned with new titles that legitimized their use of personal martial resources on behalf of the court.[11]

Bushi acquisition of a monopoly over the *means* of armed force did not, however, lead quickly or directly to warrior autonomy in the *application* of force. For in contrast to Europe, where knights and feudal lordship arose together from the confusion of the waning Carolingian empire and the onslaughts of Norse marauders, the wellspring of samurai warfare lay within a secure and still-vital imperial state structure.

In northwestern Europe, the anarchic situation brought on by the breakup of the Roman empire and the collapse of universal government rendered Augustine's theories of war, premised on sovereign states under responsible governments, moot and inapplicable. Augustine's injunction against self-defense by private individuals was cast aside after state protection became impossible. The Church met the new reality with continued efforts to keep war within the framework of the law, which was itself modified and adapted. Stress shifted from the protection of life and honor to the protection of property, and the sanction for this was increasingly found in the doctrine of natural law, rather than in the injunctions of the New Testament. To this Thomas Aquinas added the proposition of proportion: recourse to arms was permissible only if the foreseeable damage would not exceed that of the injury sustained or of submission.[12]

In the meantime, outside the Church, warfaring had become a profession, not a public service. Knights fought because their honor obligated them to do so, because their contractual obligations to their lords required them to, and because war brought profits. And they fought as individuals, as private contractors, not as salaried soldiers. Irrespective of the causes for which they took up arms, knights supplied themselves and their men, paid their own expenses, and saw rights acquired by and against them personally, not for or against the sides for which they fought.

Even so, it remained critical that wars receive public sanction. Without this, a conflict could not be a public action, and the knights involved could claim no legally enforceable title to the ransoms and booty they captured. This principle was an outgrowth of earlier dictates that only "competent authorities" could declare war. But the political structure of the era introduced a thorny problem: for who among the hodgepodge of princes, popes, emperors, kings, barons, dukes and other feudal lords of the Middle Ages constituted a "competent authority" with the right to make war? By the late Middle Ages a growing, *de facto* consensus placed sovereignty – and with it the power to declare war – in the hands of kings and a few other great lords. Nevertheless, the complex realities of power in medieval Europe meant that there could never be a clear and absolute polarity between public and private warfare.[13]

In classical and early medieval Japan, many of the same considerations applied, but the situation was, at least initially, considerably more clear-cut. From the perspective of the law – of the state as a corporate entity – recourse to arms was acceptable when and only when it was sanctioned by the state *in advance*. The principle that final authority and formal control rested with the central government remained a key feature of Japan's military and police system from the late seventh century until well into the fourteenth: the state jealously guarded its exclusive right to sanction the use of force throughout the Heian and Kamakura periods, and it attempted to do so, albeit with lessening success, under the Muromachi regime as well.

Under the *ritsuryō* system, all violations of the law outside the capital were first to be reported to the local district government office. District officials were empowered to dispose of most misdemeanors (that is, crimes punishable by light or heavy beating) themselves. More serious crimes were reported to the provincial governor, who was authorized to handle minor felonies (crimes punishable by a period of labor service). For major felonies – armed robbery, murder or rebellion – governors were required to advise the Council of State of the situation and await its instructions. Only the central government could authorize the mobilization of troops to apprehend the felon or pass judgment on him following his capture.[14]

Substantially the same procedures remained in place throughout the Heian period. Court orders to capture criminals or suppress rebellions continued to be issued by the Council of State in the form of *tsuibu kampu*, or "Warrants of Pursuit and Capture."[15] Any form of military action undertaken without such a warrant was subject to punishment. "To muster more than twenty warriors without a special order has been forbidden by law again and again," noted one source, while a petition to the Council of State reminded that body that "the mustering of private warriors has been repeatedly forbidden."[16]

Warrants carried with them six basic powers. They:

- authorized the mobilizing of troops;
- gave the commander full authority over his troops, including the right to punish those who violated orders or failed to report for duty;
- authorized the commander to take whatever action he deemed necessary to accomplish his mission, including the use of deadly force;
- canceled any immunity from arrest or prosecution enjoyed by monks, high-ranking courtiers, and other people of privileged position;
- authorized the government forces to commandeer food and supplies as needed;
- authorized rewards for warriors who fought on behalf of the government.[17]

After the 1180s, many of the court's military/police functions shifted to first the Kamakura and then the Muromachi shogunates, but the essential premise of central control over the right to violence remained intact. The Kamakura regime's first and most important piece of legislation, the *Goseibai shikimoku*, was unequivocal on this issue:

> No person, even one whose family have been hereditary vassals of the shogun for generations, shall be able to mobilize troops for military service without a current writ.[18]

The Muromachi regime had similar policies. A 1346 supplement to the shogunate's primary legal code, the *Kemmu shikimoku*, insists that:

> Even those who have cogent, long-standing complaints must first petition the Shogun and follow his judgment. To willfully initiate hostilities with attendant loss of life constitutes a crime that cannot easily be tolerated. In the case of offensive warfare, even when the original petition is justified, usurpation of [the Shogun's authority in this area] constitutes a crime that will not be tolerated. Still more so when there is no justification. Henceforth, this will be strictly forbidden. Violators shall, in accordance with the original law [of the *Goseibai shikimoku*], have their property confiscated and be subject to exile. Accomplices shall also have their property confiscated. If they have no property,

they shall be exiled, in accord with the details just outlined. Cases of defensive warfare by persons other than the lawful holder of the lands shall constitute the same crime as offensive warfare. If a person acts out of justifiable reason, judgment shall be made according to the particulars of the case.[19]

Thus, until the mid-fourteenth century at least, Japanese law made an unambiguous distinction between lawful military action, in which one (or more) of the parties involved possessed a legal warrant, and unlawful, private fights. But there are important complications to what might otherwise have been a very simple picture here. For, legalities notwithstanding, it is clear that warriors did engage in fighting for reasons other than being called to service on behalf of the state, that they were doing this from the very beginning of their history, and that they felt morally justified in doing so.

One of the most important forms of private warfare during the late classical and early medieval periods was *bushi* involvement in the political intrigues of the upper court aristocracy. While political authority during this era still derived from the emperor through the *ritsuryō* bureaucracy, real power took an oligarchic form in which various powers-that-were, or *kemmon* (literally, "gates of power"), as Kuroda Toshio dubbed them, ruled through a combination of public and private assets and channels. These *kemmon* included powerful courtier houses, major shrines and temples, and – after the twelfth century – the shogunate. Each sat at the apex of a substantial chain of vertical alliances, with individuals, families and institutions below it in the socio-political hierarchy. The *kemmon* served as a patron for these clients, retainers and followers, vouchsafing their careers, political interests, land rights, and other economic resources. In exchange, the clients performed personal services for their patrons, and followed their instructions in the execution of any official duties.[20]

The competition between the *kemmon* for wealth and influence was often intense. And in this struggle, control of martial resources of one sort or another could be a crucial asset. Dramatic or large-scale examples of recourse to arms in pursuit of political aims were rare, but attempts at assassination and intimidation were common enough that military retainers were needed to protect the persons, as well as the status, of the top courtiers and their heirs.[21] The great houses and religious institutions, accordingly, assembled private military forces and pressed for control of state military resources, a development that is reflected from early on in the recurring references in amnesty edicts to the crime of stockpiling weapons.[22]

The attitude of warriors toward participation in this sort of private martial service is neatly showcased in an anecdote involving Minamoto Yorinobu, said to have taken place around 990:

> Yorinobu was a retainer of [Fujiwara Michikane]. Now and then he would say, "If I were to be ordered by my lord to kill [his rival,

Michitaka], I would take up my sword and run to his home; who could defend him against me?" When [Yorinobu's father,] Yorimitsu heard this, he was greatly surprised, and restrained Yorinobu, saying, "In the first place, the likelihood of successfully killing him would be exceedingly small. In the second place, even if you were to succeed, this evil deed would prevent your lord from becoming Chancellor. In the third place, even if he were to become Chancellor, you would have to protect him unerringly for the rest of his life, which would be all-but impossible."[23]

Clearly neither Yorinobu nor his father was bothered by the fact that the action he was contemplating was illegal. Their concerns about the advisability of the action center exclusively on its practicality. The fact that Yorinobu's patron would order the hypothetical assassination, and that it would stand a reasonable chance of success (or, as their discussion determined, that it would not), was justification enough for them.

From the perspective of the warriors involved, military actions undertaken on behalf of aristocratic employers were not, of course, very far removed from actions conducted in possession of warrants. In either case the warrior acted on orders from above. From the mid-ninth century, public and private rights and responsibilities with respect to many key government functions were becoming increasingly hard to separate. Under such circumstances, warriors probably made little practical distinction between orders from state officials and (private) orders from courtier patrons.

But not all private warfare was initiated by or for the aristocracy. Warriors were also taking to the saddle in their own interests.

Early *bushi* had a highly developed sense of personal honor, and were rarely averse to bloodshed in order to protect or advance it. Breaches of etiquette and failure to show proper respect often led to violent consequences. Anecdotes in the *Konjaku monogatarishū*, for example, tell of a warrior who was shot for failing to dismount from his horse in the presence of a higher-ranked *bushi*, and of Minamoto Yorinobu ordering the death of a warrior for being rude. *Nihon kiryaku*, a court-sponsored history, relates that, in 989, two *bushi* in the capital got into a quarrel over drinks and "went to war," in the process shooting down several officers sent to quiet them. *Azuma kagami* describes even more colorful incidents, such as one in 1241, that began when Miura Yasumura and some of his relatives were having a drinking and dancing party in a "lascivious house" near Shimoge Bridge in Kamakura, while warriors of the Yūki, Oyama and Naganuma households were having a similar party near the other end of the bridge. At some point during the festivities, Yūki Tomomura took it into his head to practice some long-distance archery, and began chasing and shooting at a dog outside the house. Unfortunately, one of his arrows went wild, and ended its flight in a screen in the house where the Miura were gathered. Tomomura sent a servant to ask for the arrow back, but the Miura refused, instead scolding

Tomomura for his rudeness. An argument quickly ensued and before long both sides had assembled mounted troops and began a full-scale battle.[24]

Malicious gossip carried between warriors by third parties could also prompt *bushi* to gather troops and take to the field.[25] The seriousness of gossip and personal insults is reflected in the language of shogunal laws:

> Battle and killing often arise from a base of insults and bad-mouthing of others. In momentous cases the perpetrator shall be punished by exile; in lighter cases, he shall be punished by confinement. If, in the course of judicial proceedings, one party should bad-mouth the other, the dispute shall be settled in favor of his enemy. Further, if his argument is otherwise without merit, he shall have another of his holdings confiscated. If he has no holdings, he shall be punished by exile.[26]

Filial piety and familial honor were a third cause of private warfare.[27] Large-scale vendettas were surprisingly rare, but attempts to avenge slights or crimes against family members were common enough and troublesome enough to merit specific mention in twelfth-century shogunal law:

> Furthermore, in the case of a son or grandson who kills the enemy of his father or grandfather, said father or grandfather shall also be punished for the crime, even if he protests that he had no knowledge of it, because the father or grandfather's enmity was the motive that gave rise to the act. Furthermore, if a son should kill in order to seize a man's post or steal his valuables, the father shall not be judged guilty, provided he maintains he had no knowledge of the act and has documentary proof of this.[28]

Overt attempts at self-aggrandizement by armed force provided yet another source of unsanctioned military encounters. Such skirmishes were a minor, albeit ongoing, phenomenon from the tenth century, and became increasingly commonplace during the Kamakura and Muromachi periods, a point I shall return to shortly.[29]

Warriors were also sometimes drawn into the quarrels of their vassals and retainers. Taira Masakado's rebellion (935–40), which first became a matter of mutiny against the central government when Masakado led troops into Hitachi province to plead the case of one of his men with the acting governor of Hitachi, is probably the best-known example of this phenomenon.

A less famous case occurred in 1091, when Minamoto Yoshiie and his younger brother Yoshitsuna were pulled into a dispute between their retainers, Fujiwara Sanekiyo and Kiyowara Norikiyo, over land rights. The confrontation set the entire court in a uproar, and resulted in the sealing of the gates to the capital and the mobilization of troops from several provinces.[30]

Feuding and self-help

In principle, the state's exclusive right to sanction violence ought to have robbed private war of any rectitude; but clearly it did not. Instead, the notion of Just War seems to have broadened over the course of the tenth to thirteenth centuries, making increasing room for the existence of legitimate battle, even in the absence of formal legality. Significantly, but not surprisingly, this expansion of the parameters of what constituted just cause for employing organized violence paralleled the rise of the *bushi*. In particular, the state's willingness to tolerate at least small-scale military activities conducted for enhancing or preserving personal profit grew at a pace just a few steps behind the court's dependence on private warriors for law-enforcement. The government's increasingly liberal attitude toward private conflicts between *bushi* can be seen in the punishments meted out to violators of the peace, which varied considerably with time and political circumstance.

Tenth- and eleventh-century warriors engaged in private fighting at their peril: in 1049, for example, Minamoto Yorifusa, a former governor of Kaga, clashed with troops belonging to Minamoto Yorichika, the governor of Yamato, near a temple in Nara, causing the deaths of several monks by stray arrow shots. The court responded by arresting both warriors and exiling them. Similarly, in 988, Taira Korehira and Taira Muneyori found themselves banished as the result of a private feud. A century later Fujiwara Motohira was called swiftly to task for his armed attempt to defend long-held perquisites over his lands in Mutsu province, and escaped punishment only by pleading ignorance of the incident and by offering the troop commander during the incident, his nephew and retainer Inunoshōji Sueharu, as a scapegoat; Sueharu was executed, along with five of his men.[31]

The court was only slightly more lenient when unauthorized military actions served the public interest. The most celebrated case in point began in 1083, when Minamoto Yoshiie, serving as governor of Mutsu, found himself drawn into a conflict between two powerful warriors resident in the province, Kiyowara Sanehira and Kiyowara Iehira. As Yoshiie prepared to move against Iehira, he informed the court that the Kiyowara were in rebellion against the state, and asked for authorization to proceed. But the court, suspecting that Yoshiie's motives were more personal than public, refused to endorse the campaign. Undaunted, Yoshiie went ahead anyway, launching what became known as the "Latter Three Years' War" of 1083–7. Once he had secured his victory, Yoshiie petitioned the court for rewards for himself and his men. Kyoto, however, stood firm in its refusal to sanction the action, forcing a frustrated Yoshiie to reward his troops from his own pocket. Yoshiie had violated the court's rules of war, and thus no reward could be forthcoming. Perhaps, however, because his campaign was helpful to the state, or perhaps because of his tremendous popularity in both the provinces and the capital, he was able to avoid serious punishment. A scant four years before the campaign in the north, Yoshiie himself had been sent by the court to "pursue and capture" Minamoto Shigemune for engaging in a private fight with Minamoto Kunifusa in Mino.³²

The Kamakura shogunate, forced to maintain a delicate balancing act between satisfying its mandate from the court to maintain law and order and not alienating its vassals, on whose support it depended for continued existence, was much more tolerant than the imperial court of small-scale private warfare in the provinces. In Kamakura times, armed incursion into neighboring lands and use of force to extort estate residents and proprietors alike became commonplace. While shogunal edicts described attempts at self-aggrandizement through force of arms as "outrages" (*ranbō*), "evil acts" (*akugyō*) or "depradations" (*rōzeki*), severe punishments were almost never imposed.

The experience of Terao Yoichi Shigekazu, in the late 1270s, is a revealing case in point. Having been disinherited, on grounds of disloyalty, in favor of his brother, Shigemichi, Shigekazu attempted to reclaim his patrimony by force, invading his father's home, seizing crops, robbing shipments of rent and tax goods, and terrorizing residents on his brother's lands. In response to a lawsuit filed by Shigemichi and his mother and sister, the shogunate confronted Shigekazu with the charges, and gave both sides opportunity for explanation and rebuttal. At length, the shogunate determined that Shigekazu's defense was "utterly without reason" and that his actions had been "matchless savagery," and confirmed the claims of the plaintiffs to the disputed lands, without prescribing any punative actions to be taken against Shigekazu.³³

Most often, those judged guilty of activities of this sort were, like Shigekazu, simply ordered to cease and desist. Occasionally recalcitrant warriors were threatened with fines, imprisonment, or the confiscation of their lands and titles, but such threats were seldom carried out. Warrants for arrests were issued and punitive campaigns conducted only when a warrior's military activities were judged to threaten the security of court or the shogunate itself.³⁴

During the fourteenth century, the existence of rival imperial courts made it impossible to distinguish public from private war, inasmuch as both courts claimed to be issuing public calls to arms. *Bushi* could therefore justify almost any recourse to violence as public, which lent an unprecedented legitimacy to feuding, with the predictable result that violence became endemic. At the same time, the inability of any central authority to provide meaningful protection for property rights, or to secure public safety, made warriors more and more reliant on self-help in resolving disputes. Sixty years of this sort of ambiguity reified the custom of warrior self-help, and the shogunate found itself unable to recover control of the situation, even after the era of two courts ended, in 1392. The warrior-dominated, centripetal polity that was taking shape rejected the hoary premise that *bushi* were only administrators and custodians of lands that actually belonged to some *kemmon* in the capital, and affirmed instead a new concept of comprehensive and inalienable possession (*honryō*) determined by physical occupation rather than the overlapping perquisites of titles (*shiki*) distributed by the court.³⁵

It is clear, then, that warriors engaged in private warfare with growing frequency and impunity over the course of the early medieval period. But it is also clear that this represented not a broadening of central government acceptance of private warfare, but a shrinking ability to stop it. In this respect Japan differed markedly from Europe, where feuds and duels were legal and legitimate activities, serving clearly defined purposes and with clearly defined rules and boundaries.

In early medieval Europe, engaging in or even starting a feud did not, in and of itself, mark lords as lawless violators of the peace. Censorship along these lines applied only to those who engaged in conflicts that were seen to be unjustified. Far from being simply the expression of an atavistic drive for revenge and destruction, the medieval European feud was a legal instrument, akin to a lawsuit. The legitimacy of a feud depended on the existence of a just claim: feuds were a struggle for Right aimed at retribution and reparation for violations of rights. A feud waged without legal grounds was held to be unlawful and "willful." It was described in surviving documentation as "plunder," "unjust war" or "tyranny." In the legal terminology of the age, "willfulness" (*Mutwille*), which originally referred to any conscious and deliberate act, came to indicate an action that was not only premeditated but also legally unjustified.[36]

From the thirteenth century, however, as the feudal structure began to take on its classic, pyramidal shape – emerging from the more chaotic lines of authority and responsibility that characterized the early medieval era – church authorities and canon lawyers began to argue for a distinction between *duellum*, the innumerable petty feuds pursued by knights owing service to a common liege, and *bellum*, major enterprises involving large-scale military action and waged by sovereign authorities. The distinction between these constructs provided the rationale for restricting the right to violence to a small number of princes at the top of the feudal social order, thereby refining the notion of *jus ad bellum*. The ambiguity of what did and did not constitute sovereign authority during the high Middle Ages made the suppression of private war difficult, even in the face of increasing acceptance of the principle that only public wars were legal and legitimate. The solution came only in the fifteenth and sixteenth centuries, as the system of distributing and recognizing plunder formalized – so that only soldiers enrolled on the official muster lists of armies could share in the booty – and as the increasing costs of war limited the raising of such forces to kings and a handful of other great lords.[37]

Private warfare in early medieval Japan, on the othe hand, corresponded closely to what European legal scholars termed *guerre couverte*, or covert war: private war between two lords who held their lands from the same sovereign. In such conflicts no legal rights attached to any captured property. This, of course, made the affixing of one's private disputes to some public cause attractive to the point of being imperative, for it was the public sanction – irrespective of whether or not the "sanctioning" authority was even aware of one's participation – that rendered ransom, arson, rape and plunder legitimate.[38] Similarly, the legal structure of early medieval Japan made no allowance for the pursuit of private ends through violence. While central authorities were forced, with increasing frequency, to look the other way during private squabbles between warriors, they never dropped their pretense that such activities were criminal. And *bushi* took great pains to cloak their warfaring under the mantle of state authority – a habit that persisted even in the late sixteenth century, long after central government had all but ceased to exist.

Ritual war

Foreign powers, domestic lawbreakers, and personal enemies were not the only antagonists against whom early *bushi* and their institutional forebears directed their martial power. For not all adversaries of the state or the throne were human.[39]

Under the *ritsuryō* polity and its antecedents, the Japanese emperor emerged as a sacerdotal monarch reigning over a liturgical community of noble houses. The operations of this liturgical community were conducted as much through the rituals and ceremonies that filled the court calendar as through the sorts of activities modern audiences conventionally associate with governance. To the Japanese of the Nara, Heian and Kamakura eras, ritual and ceremony were not quaint or meaningless customs designed to occupy the time of bored courtiers, they were a visible symbol of the social order and served an important function in vitalizing and renewing the polity. Thus it is an error to think of court politics as having become ceremonial during the Heian period (as textbooks and survey histories often contend), for, from the very beginning, court ritual and ceremony *were* politics.[40]

As such, defense of the emperor and of the state involved more than just guarding the security of his corporeal body, and military service extended into the realm of magic and exorcism. Participation in rites of this sort was, in effect, an alternative type of military service, one equally valued at the time as police work and battlefield activity. In premodern societies, technology and magic were not separable phenomena. It should not be surprising, then, that the military arts, being just one more kind of technology, also had a magical function in premodern Japan.[41]

In fact, magical and exorcistic military functions were considered important enough to warrant the creation of a guard unit specializing in them. The *Takiguchi*, formed in the late ninth century as a detail of bodyguards attached to Emperor Uda's private secretariat, the *Kurodō dokoro*, was composed of men recruited for their martial skills, and yet there are virtually no sources that portray Takiguchi guardsmen engaged in ordinary personal defense or law-enforcement activities. Their main function seems, rather, to have been exorcism and divination.[42]

Among their duties was a rite called *meigen* ("sighing bowstring") or *tsuru-uchi* ("striking the bowstring"), which involved the drawing and releasing of bows without shooting arrows. This was performed at regular hours throughout the night, and on such occasions as births, illnesses, thunderclaps or other inauspicious omens, and – intriguingly – prior to an emperor's entry to his bath.

It was also performed by Takiguchi whenever they came on duty. This is the background to the scene in the *Genji monogatari* in which Genji, frightened by an apparition in a dream and by the Yūgao lady's sudden illness, summons a servant and orders him to

> "Tell the escort to twang his bowstring and keep shouting." . . . The servant, a member of the Takiguchi, could be heard twanging his bow with expert skill . . .. The sound reminded Genji of the imperial palace. The roll call would be over by now; the guardsmen were probably twanging their bows and proclaiming their names.[43]

Rites such as *meigen* reflect a belief that the bow was more than just a prosaic weapon, that it was a magical instrument with the power to drive away evil spirits and disperse ghosts. The notion that weapons could be used to ward off evil and invite good fortune probably derives from Taoist practices, but it was thoroughly ingrained with native Japanese (Shintō) ideals by the start of the *ritsuryō* era. It was expressed at court not only in meigen exercises, but also in the numerous wrestling (*sumai*) and archery (*jarai*) ceremonies held throughout the year.[44]

★ ★ ★ ★ ★

The proliferation of private warfaring that occurred over the course of the early medieval period was symptomatic of a fundamental change in Japanese definitions of Just War, one that centered on the replacement of courtier values with those of the *bushi* themselves. While the former focused narrowly on central government sanction, the latter broadly embraced the right of warriors to fight on the personal authority of courtier or *bushi* patrons, as well as in pursuit or defense of private profit or matters of honor.

The new ethic was nascent during the Heian period, but *bushi* remained politically constrained enough that they were obliged to bow to courtier rules and definitions governing their *droit de guerre*. The Gempei War (1180–85) unleashed widespread local violence conducted under the banner of public war, and the Kamakura shogunate that emerged from this fighting found itself unable fully to constrain small-scale private conflicts, because it depended for its existence as much on the backing of its own warrior vassals as on the credibility of its promises to the court to maintain law and order. The fourteenth century witnessed six decades of more or less constant civil war, fueled by two competing centers of political legitimation, which made it both possible to wrap almost any private fight in the banner of the larger public war and impossible for either government to restrain its warriors, lest they simply change allegiance to the other side.

The result was the end of any meaningful distinctions between public and private warfare, and of the ability of governments to assert the primacy of centrally dictated law over warrior self-help. Henceforth, *bushi* notions of Just War would prevail.

2

THE ORGANIZATION OF WAR

> An army is composed for the most part of idle and inactive men, and unless the General has a constant eye upon them, and obliges them to do their duty, this artificial machine, which with greatest care cannot be made perfect, will very soon fall to pieces, and nothing but the bare idea of a disciplined army will remain.
>
> Frederick the Great, military instruction from the King of Prussia to his generals, c.1745

> Organization doesn't really accomplish anything. Plans don't accomplish anything either. . . . Endeavors succeed or fail because of the people involved.
>
> Colin Powell, "A Leadership Primer," 2000

Warfare in early medieval Japan was the province of warriors, but only belatedly of warlords. From the tenth century onward, battles were fought by a warrior order that armed, trained and organized itself; but armies were raised and retained with the backing of state authority – sometimes allocated, sometimes borrowed, and sometimes fabricated – through most of the 1300s. The history of Japanese military organization is, in fact, a story dominated by dialectics between personal and institutional authority, and between localized and centralized sanctions, jurisdictions and structures of command.

While "national armies" of the Yamato confederation era had been knit together from forces independently raised by the various noble houses, and led into battle under the banner of the Yamato sovereign, by the close of the seventh century, the king cum emperor and his court had successfully subsumed the whole of Japan's military resources under their control. Henceforth, centrally appointed officers and officials oversaw all military units and activities, and direct conscription – supervised by the imperial court – replaced enlistment of troops through provincial chieftains.[1]

Under the new system, all free male subjects between the ages of twenty and fifty-nine, other than rank-holding nobles and individuals who "suffered from long-term illness or were otherwise unfit for military duty," were liable for induction as soldiers, or *heishi*.² Conscripts were enrolled in provincial regiments (*gundan*), which were militia organizations, akin to modern national guards. Once assigned and registered as soldiers, most men returned to their homes and fields. Provincial governments maintained copies of regimental rosters, which they used as master lists from which to select troops for training; for peacetime police, guard and frontier garrison functions; and for service in wartime armies.

Although peasant draftees thus provided the vast majority of the manpower for the *ritsuryō* military units, descendants of the old provincial nobility and lower-ranked central court nobles were by no means excluded from military functions. They served as officers in the new provincial regiments, manned the military guard (*hyōefu*) units that protected the innermost gates to the imperial palace, and acted in several other capacities as well. Recruitment for such posts was competitive; the principal criterion was martial aptitude and skill. Accordingly, the military talents and resources of provincial elites – a cornerstone of the Yamato confederation armies – remained a vital and integral element of the *ritsuryō* military system too. And as the latter began to warp and buckle under the pressure of changing socio-political conditions, the role of privately trained and equipped elites expanded.[3]

In the seventh century, when the specters of Chinese invasion and regional insurrection loomed large, the *ritsuryō* framers had seized upon across-the-board mobilization of the peasantry as a key part of the answer to both dangers. The militia-based system they designed ensured central control of military resources, enabled the court to corner the market on military manpower, and made it possible for a tiny country like Japan at the turn of the eighth century to muster large-scale fighting forces when necessary, without utterly destroying its economic and agricultural base.

By the middle of the eighth century, however, the political climate at home and abroad had changed sufficiently to render the provincial regiments anachronistic and superfluous in most of the country. As visions of Chinese ships appearing over the horizon faded, and former provincial chieftains came to accept the *ritsuryō* state structure, military affairs in most of the country quickly pared down to the capture of criminals and other police functions. For this, the unwieldy infantry units based on the provincial regiments were neither necessary nor well-suited.[4] Small, highly mobile squads that could be assembled with a minimum of delay and sent out to pursue raiding bandits were far more appropriate to the tasks at hand. In the meantime, diminishing military need for the regiments encouraged officers and provincial officials to misuse the conscripts who manned them.[5]

The state responded to these challenges with a series of adjustments, amendments, and general reforms, centering on the privately acquired martial skills of elites and the diminishing use of troops conscripted from the ordinary peasantry. The provincial regiments were first supplemented with new types of forces, and then, in 792, eliminated entirely in all but a handful of provinces.[6]

This measure was in many respects but one more step in an ongoing series of reforms and modifications directed toward a rationalization of the state's armed forces: the regiments were eliminated in favor of a more select fighting force. Nevertheless, the 792 edict has a special significance, for it created an institutional vacuum in the military establishment. The court had recognized the weaknesses of the earlier system and moved to correct them. It had identified its best source of manpower – the rural gentry and lower central aristocracy. But it had not yet worked out an alternative organizational framework that would put these forces to the best use.[7]

As the court struggled with those issues, it slowly groped and experimented its way toward a system that centered on commissioning professional mercenaries with new military titles legitimating their use of private martial resources on behalf of the state – a principle that would characterize military affairs in Japan until the modern era. The evolution of military posts during the Heian period and beyond reflects the emergence of the *bushi* across the same span of time. The two processes were, in fact, reciprocal: deputizing provincial elites and members of the middle and lower central aristocracy with military titles inevitably had a catalytic effect on the development of private martial resources under these leaders, which in turn led to the introduction of new assignments and the modification of existing ones.

Nevertheless, the cardinal features of the system that came together in the mid-Heian period persisted well into the Nambokuchō era. Outstanding among these was the bifurcation of organizational principles, and therefore the degree of cohesion, that characterized warrior associations and confederations. At the tactical level, military units formed around personal relationships and personal connections. Early samurai "armies" were hodgepodge conglomerations of small warbands led by individual *bushi*. At the strategic level, however, the organization of warfare in early medieval Japan remained closely integrated with the framework of the *ritsuryō* state and surprisingly obedient to visions of centralized, public authority formulated in the early eighth century.

Hired swords and franchise armies

During the Heian period most of the responsibilities connected with law-enforcement in the capital came to be exercised by an agency called the Office of Imperial Police, or *kebiishi-chō*, staffed by officers collectively known as *kebiishi* ("Investigators of Oddities").[8] This organization first appeared in the second decade of the ninth century, as a special unit within the Outer Palace Guards (*emonfu*). It was detached and given its own administrative apparatus during the 930s, but the connection with the older guard unit remained strong: for most of its history, virtually all *kebiishi-chō* personnel held concurrent posts in the *emonfu*.[9]

Originally charged with "patrolling the capital, interrogating felons, and carrying out special directives," the Office of Imperial Police saw its powers expand rapidly during its early decades. By the end of the ninth century, *kebiishi* duties "included arrest, imprisonment, and interrogation by torture. . . . as well as other functions, placing [it] in charge of investigating persons and crimes and of determining punishments."[10] By the mid-900s, Imperial Police had begun to investigate complaints of criminal activity throughout the capital region (the *Kinai*, that is, the provinces of Yamashiro, Yamato, Kawachi, Settsu and Izumi). In some instances, *kebiishi* could be sent even farther afield, to arrest fugitives wanted for crimes in Kyoto. Nevertheless, the *kebiishi-chō* was, throughout its history, primarily a police force for the capital.[11]

The principal military and law-enforcement officers in the countryside were the *ōryōshi* ("Envoy to Subdue the Territory") and *tsuibushi* ("Envoy to Pursue and Capture"). "*Ōryōshi*" appeared first, introduced during the late eighth century as a designation for officers deputized to lead *ritsuryō* provincial regiments to duty stations outside their home provinces. Early *ōryōshi* appear to have been involved in recruitment and training of troops as well, and may in fact have served as the primary officers for the companies under them. By the 930s the title had evolved into a more permanent commission used to legitimize elite provincial warriors acting in the name of the state – a device by which private military forces could officially be declared public.[12]

"*Tsuibushi*" was coined in the late ninth or early tenth century, as a temporary commission given to central nobles serving in imperial guard units. The first *tsuibushi* appointments carried jurisdiction over one or more of the old *ritsuryō* circuits (*dō*) for the duration of a particular mission that required a coordinated effort over a multi-province area.* Authority of this level could not be handed out to provincials, for reasons of status and precedent. Protocol therefore ruled out use of the *ōryōshi* title, which had already been assigned a different sort of function, was associated with men of insufficient pedigree, and, in any case, conveyed only province-wide authority. Accordingly, the court, faced with a new situation calling for a new type of officer, simply created one.[13]

But while the *tsuibushi* originally differed from the *ōryōshi* of the same period in social background, area of jurisdiction, length of service and mission, the office underwent a rapid evolution in the first two decades following its inception. By the second half of the tenth century, distinctions between *tsuibushi* and *ōryōshi* had virtually disappeared. From the 950s onward, both officers were appointed on a standing basis with jurisdiction over a single province, and held similar law-enforcement responsibilities. And both titles were now assigned to provincial warriors co-opted by the court to fight on its behalf.

Henceforth, *ōryōshi* and *tsuibushi* were involved in all aspects of provincial peacekeeping, from investigation to apprehension and even punishment. Most

---

* *Dō*, also called *michi*, represented an administrative grouping of provinces under the *ritsuryō* system. There were seven such circuits, each named for a major travel route originating in the capital and passing through each of the provinces in the circuit: the Tōkaidō, Tōsandō, Hokurikudō, San'indō, San'yōdō, Nankaidō and Saikaidō, plus the capital region (*Kinai*).

were local figures, warrior leaders serving in their home provinces, although, on occasion, provincial governors or assistant governors requested the *ōryōshi* title for themselves. Their appointments, however, came from the central, not the provincial, government. The normal process called for provincial governors to recommend suitable candidates to the Council of State, which would then consider the requests and issue edicts ordering the appointments. This process was hardly expeditious – it commonly took eight to ten months, and occasionally as long as three years, from start to finish – but it allowed the court to maintain a voice in military and police affairs in the provinces. Appointments continued to be made by the Council of State until well into the thirteenth century, when the offices faded from importance.

The conversion of "*tsuibushi*" from a temporary commission to a standing office necessitated the introduction of an additional title for officers dispatched by the court on specific missions, particularly those involving troubles in more than one province. "*Tsuitōshi*" ("Envoy to Pursue and Strike Down"), used for the first time in 941, bore a strong resemblance to the *tsuibushi* post as it had originally been conceived, except that the circuit (*dō*) was no longer designated as the formal area of jurisdiction. *Tsuitōshi* were appointed for the duration of special crises. Most were warrior members of *zuryō* houses – often the governors of provinces in which disturbances took place, or of nearby provinces.[14]

Heian provincial elites were, as has often been observed, engaged in the business of self-aggrandizement, making provincial warriors members of precisely the demographic most in need of being policed. This placed the state in the ironic position of depending on the very group most active in outlawry to preserve the peace. As one might predict, therefore, not every provincial military officer was entirely conscientious in his duties. Most were not above trading on the prestige and authority of their offices to intimidate provincial residents for their own gain; a few were even amenable to engaging in out-and-out criminal activity themselves.[15]

Nevertheless, the system, working in tandem with other centripetal sociopolitical forces, did a remarkably good job of setting thieves to catch thieves. By deputizing powerful warrior leaders, the court gave them a stake in the survival of the polity and linked their success to its own. To this were added rewards in the form of rank, office and land granted for the meritorious performance of assigned tasks.

Commissions such as *ōryōshi*, *tsuibushi*, *kebiishi* and *tsuitōshi*, though extracodal, held true to the spirit of the eighth-century military system in most respects. Appointments and compensation alike came from the center, following principles and procedures that closely paralleled those specified for comparable posts under the *ritsuryō* codes. These essential similarities enabled the court to retain exclusive authority over – and at least general control of – military affairs throughout the Heian period. But the new offices were also fundamentally different from their *ritsuryō* antecedents on one critical point: they were premised not on the existence of a publicly conscripted pool of manpower over which the officer's commission gave charge, but on the appointee's ability to recruit troops for himself.

Curiously, the court offered no statutory guidelines for drafting or otherwise raising troops after its dismantling of the provincial regiments in 792. For most of the ninth century, troop mobilizations remained grounded in public authority, but were conducted through ad hoc means. Responsibility for mustering fighting men as the need arose rested with provincial governors; the specific manner in which this was to be accomplished varied from case to case, but generally involved drafting the necessary manpower on the basis of the general corvée obligations required of all imperial subjects.[16]

This notion of public military service, and induction based on public duties, remained alive throughout the early medieval era, but by the middle of the tenth century recruitment had become largely privatized, with "government" troops enlisted and mobilized through private chains of command. The phenomenon that made this possible was the predilection of warriors to arrange themselves into bands and networks.

Warriors began forming gangs by the middle of the ninth century – perhaps even earlier. Military networks of substantial scale, centered on leading provincial warriors, appeared by the 930s.[17] Although the government initially opposed these developments, it embraced them as soon as it realized that private military organizations could be co-opted as mechanisms for conscripting troops when it needed them. Henceforth, the responsibility for mustering and organizing the forces necessary to carry out an assignment could simply be delegated to warrior leaders, who could in turn delegate much of the responsibility to their own subordinates.

Most private military organizations during the Heian period were patchwork assemblages of several types of forces.[18] Leading warriors in both the provinces and the capital maintained relatively small core bands of fighting men who were direct economic dependants of the warriors, lived in homes in or very nearby the warriors' compounds, and were at their more or less constant disposal. Manpower for these martial entourages could be drawn from a variety of sources. Some troops were simply hired mercenaries; others were sons or close relatives of the organization's leader; still others were conscripted from among the residents and cultivators of lands over which the leader exercised some degree of control.

Just *how* small these components were is difficult to ascertain, for few reliable sources record the numbers of followers under a given warrior's direct command. Those that do, moreover, indicate substantial variation from one *bushi* leader to another. At the same time, they also suggest that the range of warband sizes remained relatively constant between the mid-tenth and late thirteenth centuries. *Shōmonki* and *Konjaku monogatarishū*, for example, relate that two tenth century warrior leaders had only "less than ten" or "four or five" warriors at their disposal when they were taken by surprise in night attacks on their homes. Similarly, a 987 complaint filed with the *kebiishi-chō* describes a night attack on the residence of one Minu Kanetomo by sixteen mounted warriors and "20 or more foot soldiers" led by a handful of his kinsmen. A document from 1086 numbers Minamoto Yoriyoshi's "sons and immediate followers" at "20 men in all"; while a document from 1058 describes five notable warriors as having thirty-two followers between them – a figure that includes women and boys, as well as adult men. A roster of warriors from Izumi in 1272 lists nineteen warriors; of these, one led eighteen warrior followers, six led four to nine men each, three led three retainers, four led two, and five had only one follower each. A document from 1276 catalogs the warband of a *bushi* in Higo as consisting of three followers and a horse, in addition to the man himself. And a report "concerning the warband [*gunzei*] of Nakamura Yajirō Minamoto no Tsuzuku, a resident of Haruzuchi estate in Chikuzen province," lists "Tsuzuku, mounted and clad in ōryoroi; his younger brother, Saburō Nami, mounted and clad in haramaki; his retainer, Gorō Tarō, mounted; and his foot soldiers, Matajirō, the lay monk [*nyūdō*] Hōren, Gentōji, Gentō Jirō, Matatarō, Sūtarō, and Inujirō."[19]

It would appear, therefore, that the core units from which early medieval military forces were compiled averaged around a half-dozen or so mounted warriors, augmented by varying numbers of foot soldiers. Some were much smaller. But even the largest numbered only in the high teens or low twenties.

For major campaigns, *bushi* also mobilized the cultivators, woodsmen, fishermen, and other residents of the lands in and around the estates and districts they administered. Such men were, strictly speaking, not under the warrior's control, but they often leased land from him, borrowed tools and seed from him, and conducted trade at his compound, making his residence an important economic center for them. By exploiting whatever political and economic leverage they could bring to bear on these semi-dependants, warriors could assemble armies numbering in the hundreds. Larger armies had to be knit together through networks based on alliances of various sorts between *bushi* leaders of different socio-political status. This technique made it possible for warriors to assemble forces many times the size of their core organizations.[20]

The incentive to build or belong to military organizations of larger and larger scale was a natural consequence of the same factors that induced men to take up arms or create warrior bands in the first place, and the most obvious way for a warrior to augment his personal corps of followers was to go into partnership with his peers. Genuinely lateral alliances were, however, problematic.

A cardinal feature of political activity at all levels of the Heian polity was what Cornelius Kiley has termed "consociation between persons of disparate status."[21] Heian society was rigidly stratified. Functionally unbridgeable gulfs of station separated the top tier of court aristocrats (*kugyō*), the lower- and middle-level central nobles, and the rural elite. For each stratum in this hierarchy there were reserved certain rights of access to specific types of government posts, rights over land, and forms of income. The rights and privileges of each stratum were sealed from below, as well as from above. That is, scions of the top court families were as effectively barred from assuming district and local government posts as provincial elites were from becoming top court officials. This formed a basis for vertical cooperation between members of different strata, because neither party could effectively challenge the prerogatives of the other. That is, social disparity contributed to the solidarity of vertical factions, because each member of the alliance could aid the others in obtaining rewards for which he himself was ineligible.

But the corollary to these same principles was that the interests of men of similar station were generally at odds with one another. This tended to exercise a divisive influence, rendering lateral alliances unstable and therefore difficult to maintain for long periods, with the result that, for most of Japanese history, horizontal cooperation between coequals has tended to be an ephemeral phenomenon.[22]

Warrior leagues that were in essence alliances between coequals did come into existence during the early medieval period, most notably in the southern part of Musashi.[23] But the predominant organizational pattern for warrior cooperation was hierarchical, centering on figures whose prestige enabled them to serve as rallying points for alliances between warriors of lesser pedigree. Peer rivalries could be readily subsumed and transcended in warrior networks that were focused on men of overarching status. By the mid-tenth century, the most powerful provincial warrior leaders were exploiting this phenomenon to gather armies numbering in the thousands, and were able to terrorize whole regions.

Like their provincial counterparts, warriors in the capital had core organizations of armed retainers who lived and operated with them in Kyoto, and traveled with them to provincial posts. By the early eleventh century, warrior *zuryō* were also establishing alliances with prominent warriors in or near the areas to which they were posted. Such arrangements worked to the advantage of both parties. For provincial warriors, they were a means by which to gain a connection to the court and could provide entrance into the patron–client network of a senior court figure. Connections of this sort served to raise the prestige (military and otherwise) of the provincials, to aid them in obtaining or maintaining posts in local government or on private estates, and generally to advance their ability to compete with local rivals. For the *zuryō*, the alliances greatly expanded their efficiency as martial servants of the state – or the top nobility – when they operated in the provinces.*

Warrior aristocrats were not the only central court figures with whom provincial *bushi* established ties, but for many they were the most attractive and logical bridge to the court. For the *zuryō*'s sometime presence in the provinces

---

* On the other hand, as in all alliances, the parties tended to become embroiled in each other's quarrels. In 1091, for example, Minamoto Yoshiie and his younger brother Yoshitsuna were drawn into a dispute over land rights in Kawachi between two of their retainers, Fujiwara Sanekiyo and Kiyowara Norikiyo. The incident threatened to escalate into a major battle in the capital city between Yoshiie and Yoshitsuna, but the retired emperor was able to defuse it (*Hyakurenshō*, 1091 6/12).

not only made them accessible in a way that higher-ranked courtiers were not, both they and their provincial clients were warriors, sharing common skills and a common ethic. It is hardly surprising, then, that *bushi* in the countryside should have been drawn to men they could look up to as illustrious practitioners of their own vocation.

The cornerstones of the late Heian military system – the posts of *ōryōshi*, *tsuibushi*, and *tsuitōshi*, and the private warrior networks through which they functioned – were all in place by the mid-tenth century. But the system continued to evolve and adapt to an ever-changing socio-political reality, until the court lost the last of its governing power during the fifteenth century. Throughout the Heian period, despite considerable institutional change, the underlying principles and the basic framework of the system remained much the same as they had been in the early eighth century. Final authority and formal control over the application of physical coercion still rested with the imperial court. All major officers continued to be appointed by the central government. All but the most minor criminal problems were first reported upward, and the appropriate action decided upon and ordered by the Council of State. And, as we noted in Chapter 1, any form of military activity undertaken without a warrant (*tsuibu kampu*) was considered private warfare and subject to strict punishment.

Primary responsibility for carrying out the pursue-and-capture orders of the Council of State rested with the provincial government. In virtually all cases, even those in which *tsuitōshi* were designated, warrants were first issued to the province(s) where the disturbance took place. The ever-increasing complexity of political, economic and social conditions in the hinterlands, however, rapidly brought about a much more intricate military chain-of-command network. By the late eleventh century, Council of State instructions could result in the mobilization of provincial warriors through any of at least three additional channels.

The most intriguing complication to the system involved the development of the *tsuitōshi* office. As we have seen, those appointed *tsuitōshi* were leading warriors in the capital. Such men commanded sizeable private warrior followings, which were often scattered through several provinces. When called to government military service, they brought their own forces with them, mobilizing provincial *bushi* directly, through their personal connections. Designation as a *tsuitōshi*, which put a warrior in charge of the entire campaign, thus put him at the head of two overlapping chains of command: those warriors who followed him directly and those who were called up through the provincial governments under him.

Military and police procedures were further complicated by the development of immunity privileges for some privately held estates (*shōen*). Once government agents came to be denied access to such lands, the court found it necessary to petition the *shōen* owner for the extradition of criminals hiding within estate borders. There is a considerable body of evidence suggesting that this problem may have led to the creation of private estate versions of the *ōryōshi* and *tsuibushi* posts.[24]

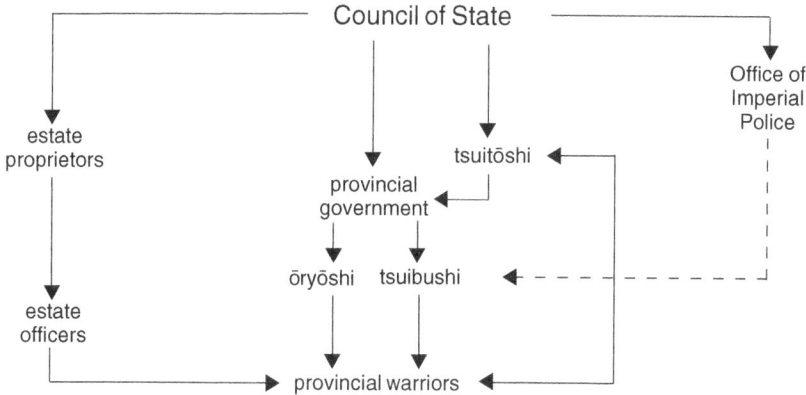

Figure 2.1 Chains of command in the provincial military and police system of the eleventh and twelfth centuries (Friday, *Hired Swords*, 164)

The three channels through which the court might mobilize provincial warriors are shown in Figure 2.1. A fourth channel sometimes came into play as well, when complaints about troubles in the Kinai or nearby provinces were handled by the Office of Imperial Police. In such instances, the *kebiishi-chō* might issue instructions to provincial *tsuibushi* to investigate the case and arrest any suspects. This does not necessarily indicate a special relationship between the Office of Imperial Police and the *tsuibushi*, however, for, although there is no evidence of *kebiishi-chō* orders addressed to *ōryōshi*, neither is there any of such orders being addressed to *tsuibushi* outside the capital region, and no *ōryōshi* is known to have been appointed in the Kinai. It is likely, in other words, that these orders came about only because the problem fell within the geographical scope of the Imperial Police's authority.[25]

Equilibrium and revolution

The late Heian military system was a curious mixture of public and private parts. It was organized and directed through centralized, public principles. But it was utterly dependent for its operations on private resources – private training and acquisition of skills, private recruitment and mobilization, and private equipment.

While historians once saw only the private elements of this mix, and equated the appearance of the *bushi* with the onset of "feudalism," more recent scholarship emphasizes the continued – indeed, the enhanced – integration of the center and peripheries during the late Heian period.[26] The government was not without armed forces in the eleventh and twelfth centuries; it had simply privatized – franchised – the mechanisms of state defense and law enforcement, delegating responsibility for the logistics and particulars of these functions to private contractors, even as it carefully preserved its rights and powers to oversee them from the center.

In most respects the organizing principles of thirteenth- and fourteenth-century armies and military campaigns remained true to this pattern. The key difference was, of course, the introduction of the shogunate, which, after 1183, stood as an intermediary between the Council of State and warriors throughout the country. But in its military capacity, if not in its judicial and managerial roles, the new institution represented less a usurpation or intrusion into the system than an adaptation or outgrowth of it. With respect to the court and state military functions, the shogun simply assumed roles and duties that had hitherto been spread among the various Minamoto and Taira warrior leaders. That is, he – or rather the institution he symbolically headed – became in effect the lone surviving warrior noble, carrying out the court's law-enforcement and national defense jobs by mobilizing personal retainers, in much the same way that Heian *bushi* leaders had. Militarily, the shogunate was in essence simply a corporate warband leader writ large.

What was new, however, was the permanence of the commission Yoritomo and his successors held, the sheer size of the vassal corps they led, and the degree to which they were able to rationalize and institutionalize both. For unlike twelfth-century *tsuitōshi*, whose command authority lasted only for the duration of a specific mission, the thirteenth-century shogunate exercised an ongoing – and more or less exclusive – jurisdiction over warfare. It also introduced new mechanisms for organizing and directing its housemen, as well as an unprecedented clarity to the reciprocal obligations that bound them.

The Kamakura vassal corps

The eastern warriors who answered Minamoto Yoritomo's call to arms in 1180 put him at the center of a military network that spanned nine provinces. His military and diplomatic efforts over the next five years expanded the scope of this organization into western Japan and Kyushu. But, as Yoritomo was well aware, inaugurating a warband of this scale was far easier than controlling or maintaining it. Astoundingly, he was able to do just that.

When Yoritomo first raised his banner in 1180, he had even less going for him than typical *bushi* leaders of his age. His father's misadventure in 1160 had denied him the career as a provincial official and warrior noble he might otherwise have expected from his heritage, and doomed him instead to an obscure existence in Izu as the son-in-law of an unremarkable provincial *bushi*. Thus Yoritomo held no government posts or titles on private estates, led no warband of his own, and controlled no lands. His one and only asset was, in fact, his tenuous claim to a rightful preeminence among his surviving kinsmen. Remarkably, he found a way to exploit the very bleakness of his circumstances to create the largest and most stable private military organization Japan had seen since the advent of the *ritsuryō* era, and – even more remarkably – successfully to prevent large-scale military lordships from forming under anyone other than himself or his successors for the next century.

Prince Michihito's call to arms against Taira Kiyomori offered Yoritomo a cause in which to cloak his personal ambitions – an excuse for reasserting what he perceived to be his patrimony. And Kiyomori's rapid defeat of Mochihito determined the means by which he would proceed. Effectively locked out of all other channels through which to raise troops or advance his own fortunes, Yoritomo instead exploited his outlaw status, declaring a martial law under himself across the eastern provinces, and promising any and all who pledged to his service confirmation (under his personal guarantee) of lands and offices. At the same time, he took pains to style himself a *righteous* outlaw, a champion of true justice breaking the law in order to rescue the institutions it was meant to serve.

In any event, the response to his invitation equipped Yoritomo with the military forces he needed both to pursue his campaign against Kiyomori and to defend his assertion of hegemonic lordship over the east. His rapprochement with the court in 1183, his victory over the Taira, and his suppression of his various rival kinsmen transformed this organization from a private warband of the sort his ancestors and rivals had directed into the principal military force of the state. By the end of the twelfth century, a great many military tasks theretofore administered by provincial and district officials, and incumbent on all *bushi*, had been converted to services provided exclusively by Kamakura vassals – the retainers of a single warlord – and overseen by the shogunate. Yoritomo was not the first to make public military duties the obligation of a specific subset of warriors – Kiyomori had done very much the same thing – but the organization and formalization of his arrangements took this principle to a new level, and deserve to be viewed as a new phenomenon.

Nevertheless, Takahashi Noriyuki rightly cautions against conceptualizing the Kamakura vassal corps as a public army. It was, he notes, first and foremost a personal network, premised on the competitions and alliances that existed among provincial warriors and landowners. Its stability and cohesion were, accordingly, rooted in these same rivalries and associations. The organization born of these exigencies derived from two parents: its mother was the military/police system of the Heian era; but it was sired by Yoritomo's mobilization of troops, and the arrangements he made to organize them and retain their support.[27] And it existed, first and foremost, to safeguard the station of Yoritomo and his successors; defense of the realm and maintenance of law and order were but a means to this end.

The success and endurance of Yoritomo's new organization owed much to his unprecedented finesse in juggling legally delegated with personally appropriated authority. At many points during the Gempei War and subsequent conflicts, the shogunate raised or directed troops under the mandate of a court-issued warrant, exploiting – and intermingling – both the emergency powers inherent in a *tsuitōshi* commission and the standing military apparatus overseen by provincial governors. But there were also times when these mechanisms were not or could not be utilized, and the shogunate simply issued calls to arms to its own vassals, on the basis of their personal ties to the Kamakura lord. Sometimes a warrant was requested, but refused, as was initially the case during the Ōshū campaign, against Fujiwara Yasuhira, in 1189. Other times Yoritomo or the shogunate were acting outside or in opposition to court directives, as in the early stages of the Gempei War, at the start of the campaign against Yoshitsune, and during the Jōkyū War. On still other occasions – and with increasing regularity during the thirteenth century – Kamakura simply laid claim to a standing authority to deal with rebellions and violent crimes.[28]

Yoritomo's adept shifts and syntheses between legal and personal authority demonstrate his grasp of an important truth about the dynamics of the late twelfth-century military system: possession of a warrant amounted to an authorization rather than a real empowerment. That is, it legalized mobilizations, but it did not compel them. In principle, *tsuibu kampu* deputized the warrior who received them, and commanded other fighting men to muster under him. In practice, however, *bushi* responded to mobilization calls in anticipation of rewards from or retaliation by the individual who called them, not because they feared the consequences of ignoring a court order to join up. Warrants really only conveyed greater surety that rewards would be forthcoming – and thus enhanced the attraction of following a warrior who held one. Their practical effect was more akin to temporarily expanding the vassal corps of the warrior deputized than to creating a public army. All of which is to say that the line between public and private authority in military mobilizations was very thin indeed. Yoritomo's genius lay in his ability to see, and to manipulate, this deceptively simple truth.

The Kamakura vassal corps of the late 1180s and the 1190s represented a stabilization and normalization of early wartime relationships. Wartime arrangements did not, of course, simply carry over into the post-war era: a number of key changes were made to adapt the system to fit peacetime conditions.

As the Gempei War wound down, Yoritomo struggled to reconcile the two competing obligations on which his chieftainship rested. On the one hand, he had a mandate from the court to restore and maintain order in the provinces, which made his regime legal and formed the basis of its national authority. On the other, his ability to carry out this mandate depended entirely on the continuing support of his followers, which in turn hinged on his support of their (mostly local) aspirations.

His solutions revolved around three ground-breaking ideas. First, he cast his key supporters and their progeny as a permanent clientage, a new coterie of Kamakura "housemen," or *gokenin*, whose status would derive from his authority alone, and would continue from one generation to the next. Second, he made himself the exclusive intermediary between his liegemen and the court, insisting that all calls to service, all rewards thereof, and all disciplinary matters pass through him. And third, he secured for his vassals the first tangible benefice

THE ORGANIZATION OF WAR

in Japanese history: confirmation as *jitō*, a title that both granted administrative rights over lands and people and was entirely controlled by Yoritomo (and his successors).[29]

With these measures, he was, in effect, establishing a kind of warriors' union, with himself at its head. By insulating an elite – albeit substantial – subgroup of the country's provincial *bushi* from direct court control or employ, Yoritomo ensured that warriors could no longer be managed by playing them against one another. Initially this merely served to vault Yoritomo (and later the shogunate) into the ranks of the *kenmon* oligarchy – although in the long run it created a mechanism for unraveling the fabric of centralized authority.

In spite of its formidable implications, however, membership in Yoritomo's warrior union was often uncertain, and recognized more by circumstance than by formalities. Yoritomo conducted no special ceremonies, extracted no oaths of homage, and issued no documents certifying vassalage per se. Even the term "*gokenin*," as a label for Kamakura vassals, did not come into common usage until the 1190s, and the first provincial registers of vassals only appeared at about the same time.[30]

The turning point for regularization of the Kamakura vassal corps came with Yoritomo's Ōshū campaign, in 1189. Before this, there was considerable ambiguity about who was liable for calls to service and eligible for Kamakura protection. Beyond the relatively small pool of men who had been confirmed in *jitō* titles lay a much larger body of warriors who had – or claimed to have – followed Yoritomo during the Gempei War years but had not yet been either granted or explicitly refused a benefice. It seems likely, in fact, that not even Yoritomo and his inner circle of advisors were entirely certain where such men stood. In 1189, Yoritomo found a means to test loyalties and an opportunity to trim and tighten his vassal corps, in the form of a punitive expedition against Fujiwara Yasuhira.

Yasuhira's father, Hidehira, and grandfather, Motohira, had established a nearly autonomous enclave of personal hegemony across much of Mutsu and Dewa, centered on their so-called northern capital of Hiraizumi, in what is now Iwate prefecture. Although courted by both the Minamoto and the Taira, Hidehira had remained neutral throughout the Gempei War. In 1187, however, he offered refuge to Yoritomo's fugitive brother, Yoshitsune, providing Yoritomo with a pretext for moving against him. Although Hidehira died in late 1187, and his heir, Yasuhira, turned on Yoshitsune and killed him in the fourth month of 1189, Yoritomo was not dissuaded from his invasion plans. He left Kamakura in the seventh month of 1189 at the head of an enormous army, and swept on into Hiraizumi in a little over a month.[31]

Kawai Yasushi points to several exceptional decisions and developments surrounding mobilization for the Ōshū campaign. First, Yoritomo led the main army himself, marking the first time that he had taken the field in person since 1180. Second, warriors were mobilized in sizeable numbers from as far away as Kyushu and Shikoku, in spite of the fact that the theatre of fighting was in

Mutsu, in the far northeast. Third, powerful *gokenin* who did not appear as called were punished with the confiscation of their lands, an unusually harsh penalty in the context of Yoritomo's judgments before that time. And fourth, Yoritomo pardoned and summoned to service even erstwhile enemies – followers of the Taira, Yoshinaka or Yoshitsune – including some who had been his prisoners. None of these measures, Kawai argues, were necessitated or justified by the military imperative of crushing the Fujiwara alone. Clearly then, while the potential threat posed by the Fujiwara, and Yoritomo's desire to deal with it were certainly real, they could not have represented the whole of Yoritomo's rationale for the war.[32]

It would seem, rather, that, with the upheavals of the Gempei War now settled, and in the face of a return to peace and order, Yoritomo used the excuse provided by a campaign to punish Yasutoki's intransigence to rationalize and solidify his nascent *gokenin* system, mobilizing everyone who had fought under his banner earlier, as well as pressing to bring in men as yet unassimilated – including those who had formerly served his adversaries. Whereas his mobilization of forces in 1180 had been cast as an invitation, the calls to service he issued in 1189 were commands, with clear undertones of ultimatum. Failure to respond was treated as disloyalty tantamount to joining the enemy, and invited termination of the recalcitrant's standing with Kamakura and confiscation of rewards previously granted.[33]

The concept of a formal *gokenin* corps, and the institutions necessary to manage it, crystallized rapidly in the 1190s. In the wake of his victory in the Ōshū campaign, Yoritomo set out to establish a countrywide presence for his authority, based on a readily identifiable cohort of vassals, with regularized privileges and obligations. Although surviving sources tell us little about how he accomplished this – or even the extent of his own role in the process – it does appear that, by Yoritomo's death in 1199, trusted Kamakura deputies posted to provinces across the country were maintaining lists of thirty to forty warrior leaders in each province recognized as *gokenin*.[34]

Even as the system matured, however, it retained inconsistencies inherent in its origins. Foremost among these was the fact that it included both enfeoffed and unenfeoffed vassals – that is, warriors who received no confirmations of lands or titles from the shogun, as well as those who had. Because of this, the defining characteristic of a *gokenin* – the badge that signified Kamakura vassal status – came to be the performance of regularized service to the shogunate: a *gokenin* was simply anyone who performed *gokenin* duties (*gokenin yaku*).

Takahashi Noriyuki's exhaustive analysis divides the various chores expected of *gokenin* into services performed directly for the shogunate (*kōreiyaku*), such as guard duty in Kamakura, repairs and other labor on Kamakura buildings and the like, and services performed for third parties, on behalf of Kamakura (*rinreiyaku*). The last-named included duties relating the shogunate's function as the court's military arm, services deriving from Kamakura's broader character as a governing body in the east (such as contributions to construction and maintenance of the

Tsurugaoka Hachiman shrine and other religious institutions), and services demanded in conjunction with the shogunate's role as a *kemmon*, which paralleled those performed by minions of temples, shrines and courtier houses. Examples of *gokenin* excused from one sort of duty in order to perform another reveal a clear hierarchy among these various services. In general, *rinreiyaku* took precedence over *kōreiyaku*, and military duties took precedence over other *rinreiyaku*. The most important – and therefore most prestigious – duty of all was guard service in the capital (*ōban'yaku*).[35]

In the twelfth century, *ōban'yaku* had been a rotating obligation administered by provincial governors and their staffs. We do not know precisely how or when Yoritomo was delegated (or seized) control of this function, but, by the mid-1190s, we find Kamakura edicts rejecting arguments from *shōen* authorities asserting the right to select men from their estates to serve guard duty at the imperial palace. Shogunate decisions and regulations issued throughout the early thirteenth century reaffirmed the principal that *ōban'yaku* was to be performed by *gokenin* – and only by *gokenin* – and forbade shifting of responsibilities over this duty to local authorities. Kamakura vassals were liable for capital guard service, irrespective of whether or not they held land titles confirmed by the shogunate. Thus, by the early 1200s, the label *gokenin* had largely become synonymous with the names on lists of those who were subject to muster for *ōban'yaku*. These lists were maintained by the shogunate's provincial deputies, the *shugo*, who were also in charge of selecting which individuals would serve, when the duty to provide guards fell – in rotation – on their provinces of appointment.[36]

Officers and the chain of command

From the 1220s onward, *shugo* functioned as general agents for the shogunate and intermediaries between the *gokenin* under their jurisdiction and Kamakura. They were also the regime's chief military officers. But this role, like the *shugo* office itself, emerged only slowly over the first four decades of the shogunate's existence.

Yoritomo's command structure was, in the main, a minimally articulated network of personal relationships. Although his stewardship over gubernatorial titles in the east and elsewhere gave him jurisdiction over *ōryōshi*, *tsuibushi* and other provincial military posts, he never made any of these offices a regular or significant part of his wartime command structure. Nor did he create any other standing military units or commands.[37] (See Figure 2.2.)

Throughout the 1180s, all of the provincial warrior leaders who comprised his vassal corps answered directly to him, and he mobilized and assigned them at first hand. Vassals did not, of course, report for duty as individuals; they brought with them the family, retainers, subordinate allies, and others that made up their own warbands. But while subaltern troops of this sort clearly represented the vast majority of Yoritomo's forces, he left tactical command of them entirely in the hands of the warriors who mustered them. Much of the time, he allowed

THE ORGANIZATION OF WAR

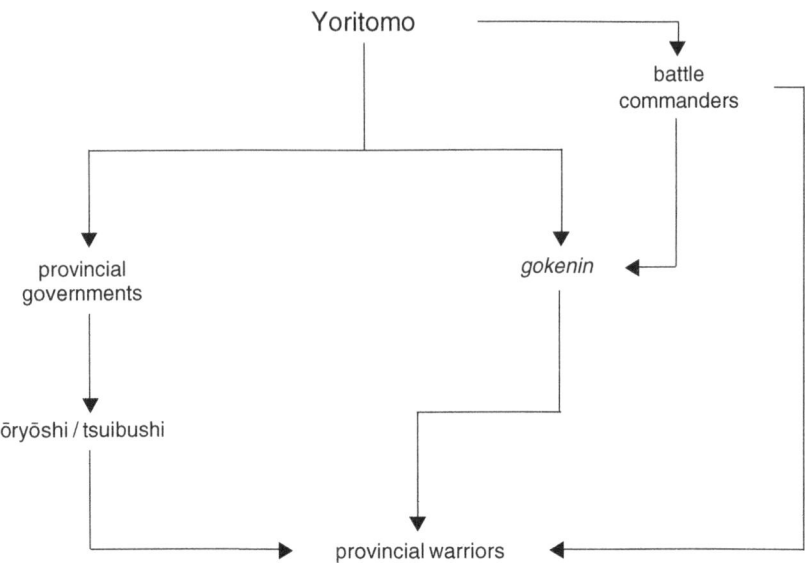

Figure 2.2 Yoritomo's chain of command

his direct vassals to operate autonomously of one another as well. And when he did interpose intermediary commanders between himself and his vassals, for large battles or campaigns, the commissions were temporary, the divisions thus created were ad hoc, and *gokenin* organized and directed their own men without interference – or assistance – from the command staff.[38]

The organization of early Kamakura armies is manifest in *Azuma kagami*'s description of the forces deployed at the battle of Ichinotani, in the second month of 1184.[39] Command of the main host was entrusted to Yoritomo's brother Noriyori, whose "accompanying troops" consisted of thirty-two named vassals and "more than 56,000 horsemen under them," while a second division, commanded by Yoshitsune, included seventeen named vassals and "more than 20,000 horsemen under them."

Three points stand out from this account. First, the text assigns no formal titles to Noriyori and Yoshitsune, describing them only as the "commanding officer for the main force" (*ōte no taishōgun*) and "commanding officer for the flanking force" (*karamete no taishōgun*).[40] Second, the identification of only three levels of warriors – divisional commanders, named vassals and "horsemen under them" – and the ratio of officers to other warriors (the improbable overall numbers notwithstanding) testifies to the lack of articulation in the army. And third, the assignment of vassals to the divisions betrays no logical pattern, beyond grouping warriors of the same surname together. Both forces included men of Taira, Minamoto and Fujiwara descent; both included men from various provinces; and men from the same provinces were split between the divisions.[41]

50

THE ORGANIZATION OF WAR

The command structure of the forces sent north against Fujiwara Yasuhira in 1189 was similarly personal and irregular. At the same time its sheer size – 280,000 men, according to *Azuma kagami* – demanded more rational organization and greater articulation.

Yoritomo divided his army into three parts. The first corps, under Chiba Tsunetane and Hatta Tomoie, was to advance up the Tōkaidō, across Sagami, Shimōsa and Hitachi. The second, under Hiki Yoshikazu and Usami Sanemasa, was to march through Kōzuke and then along the Hokurikudō through Echigo and Dewa. In the meanwhile, the main force, under Yoritomo himself, would travel up the middle, along the Tōzandō. Command of Yoritomo's vanguard fell to Hatakeyama Shigetada, with various other eastern *gokenin* acting as subalterns. Warriors were consigned to their respective divisions on the basis of instructions from Yoritomo's closest advisors, Wada Yoshimori and Kajiwara Kagetoki.

Muster and assignment were in part organized by province, but there were numerous exceptions and overlaps. Tsunetane and Tomoie were, for example, ordered to bring with them "the stalwarts of their houses and of their home provinces, Hitachi and Shimōsa," while Yoshikazu and Sanemasa were directed to "gather the residents of Takayama, Kobayashi, Ōgo and Sanuki in Kōzuke." At the same time, Yoritomo's main division comprised the warbands of some 144 leading warriors, including the Oyama and Satake of Hitachi, the Nitta of Kōzuke, the Kumagae of Musashi, and the Shimokabe of Shimōsa, as well as two other subalterns, Katō Kagekane and Kassai Kiyoshige, specifically instructed "to lead into battle . . . the fellows of the warbands in Musashi and Kōzuke."[42]

Yoritomo's first experiment with province-wide military titles, the post of *sōtsuibushi* ("*tsuibushi* in chief"), appears to have been intended mainly as a commission for peacekeeping in areas away from the main fighting, rather than for battlefield command. The earliest record of *sōtsuibushi* recounts the appointment, in 1181, of one Kashima Saburō Masamoto, who was given the task of ending depredations on lands belonging to the Kashima grand shrine. Most other references to *sōtsuibushi* similarly involve charges to suppress warrior outrages on *shōen*, suggesting that the post may have been fashioned as a unified police commission with jurisdiction over both public and estate lands, superseding the immunity privileges that had hitherto prevented *ōryōshi* and *tsuibushi* from entering some estates (and given birth to the *shōen* versions of those offices).[43]

Not until the very end of his career did Yoritomo come around to the idea of posting standing deputies with broad jurisdiction over Kamakura vassals across their provinces.[44] By the early 1200s, his Hōjō successors had made *shugo* a recurring part of the shogunate's organizational structure, and had included oversight of military tasks, such as Kyoto guard duty, among their responsibilities. Nevertheless, *shugo* remained outside Kamakura's wartime chain of command during the Jōkyū War in 1221. For this campaign, the shogunate mobilized vassals from fifteen eastern provinces, and sent them to the capital along the Tōkaidō, Tōsandō and Hokurikudō. But the muster orders were issued directly to "the heads of houses [*kachō*] to report with their kinsmen," and tactical command of the divisions was split among thirteen prominent vassals; *shugo* were not involved in either process.[45]

In the wake of the Jōkyū conflict, however, both the role of the *shugo* in the shogunate's military operations and the responsibilities of the shogunate itself in state military and police affairs broadened considerably. Kamakura's victory in that conflict effectively ended any court military ascendancy independent of the shogunate, and forced an expansion – largely unwanted – of Kamakura involvement in law enforcement to fill the resultant void, particularly in western Japan.[46] Shogunal law now unequivocally subordinated Kamakura vassals to the *shugo* of their province in military and police matters, and gave *shugo* explicit jurisdiction over control of "rebels, murderers, and also night raiding, robbery, banditry and piracy," as well as responsibility for mustering and leading warriors for *ōban'yaku*. And when Kublai Khan attempted to overrun Japan in 1274 and 1281, the shogunate centered its mobilization on vassals with land-holdings in the southwest, and assigned command of defensive operations to the *shugo* of Aki, Bungo, Buzen, Chikuzen, Chikugo, Hizen, Higo, Hyūga, Ōsumi and Satsuma. At the same time, the law limited *shugo* to acting as agents of the shogunate, forbidding them to undertake judicatory actions on their own initiative, without specific orders from Kamakura.[47]

The Mongol invasions, and the long cold war of continued vigilance that followed, further expanded Kamakura's role in state military and police affairs. In assuming complete responsibility for national defense during the crisis, the shogunate significantly enlarged the formal limits of its authority – and thereby the weight of its countrywide presence. The prolonged crisis enabled the shogunate to cross hitherto inviolate jurisdictional boundaries – feudatory, as well as geographic. Thus, by the 1280s, it was claiming the right to levy commissariat taxes on, or draft troops from, virtually any property. It was also accepting – and rewarding – military services not just from *gokenin*, but from other Kyushu warriors as well.[48]

By the 1280s, then, the shogunate had become the state's principal military and law-enforcement agency, and had gone a considerable way toward systematizing and institutionalizing its procedures for handling these functions. But the military/police system of the late Kamakura period was considerably more complex than the simple shogunate-to-*shugo*-to-*gokenin* chain of command emphasized in dealing with the Mongols.

Kamakura continued, on occasion, to make use of the older provincial government mechanisms for mustering warriors, or to mobilize important vassals directly. And while shogunal law claimed responsibility for "rebels, murderers, and also night raiding, robbery, banditry and piracy," it also reserved jurisdiction over "theft, arson, kidnapping," and other less disruptive crimes for *shōen* authorities or the police bureaus (*kebii-dokoro*) attached to the offices of provincial governors.[49] *Gokenin* and their followers, moreover, made up but a small percentage of the total warrior population of the time; substantial numbers

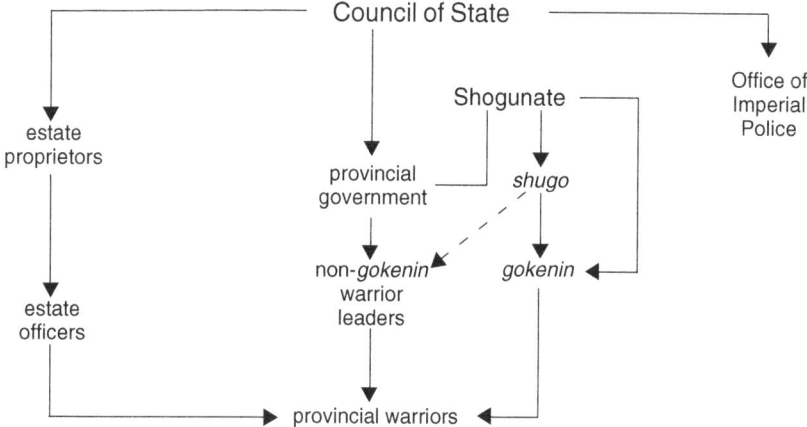

Figure 2.3 Chains of command in the late Kamakura military/police system

of *bushi* remained under the jurisdiction of estate proprietors or provincial governors. Thus the organizational structure under which late thirteenth- and early fourteenth-century warriors served looked something like the system depicted in Figure 2.3. The command structures of the Kemmu regime and the Muromachi shogunate (during the Nambokuchō era) remained essentially the same, at least in theory.

Warbands and warbonds

The remarkable admixture of public and private elements that coalesced during the tenth and eleventh centuries, and the dialectic of institutional with personal authority Yoritomo galvanized during the twelfth, continued to shape and condition warfare throughout the early medieval period. At the strategic level, military organization remained public and centralized: armies were raised, deployed, legitimated, and held together under principles that dated back to the *ritsuryō* codes. But the monadic components of those armies – the units that represented military structure at the tactical level – were configured, mustered, and led on the strength of personal relationships and familial ties, as had been the case since the mid-Heian period.

From the perspective of 800 years' hindsight, it is easy to recognize the thirteenth and fourteenth centuries as a transitional era, during which Japan was shifting from a mobile-like paradigm of authority radiating from the top down and from the center out, to a pyramid-like one of multiple power structures built from the bottom up. Warriors of the time, however – to whom the ultimate direction of progress must have been far less clear – continued to believe in the time-honored model of a unitary military authority. Thus, when the involuntarily retired Emperor Go-Daigo fled from Kyoto to Mount Kasagi and began raising troops in 1331, the shogunate had no difficulty assembling an army to send against him, through its (by then) traditional command structure. The expeditionary force that left Kamakura that year – and crushed Go-Daigo's troops – was mustered and led by *shugo*, and included contingents supplied by every noteworthy eastern warrior house.[50]

Nevertheless, the endurance of the old paradigm was only half the story. For, during the next two years, Kusanoki Masashige and Go-Daigo's son, Prince Moriyoshi, proved remarkably adept at exploiting the emergent localized power structures of the era to raise new forces. Their successes were substantial enough to shake the confidence of some of Kamakura's key housemen – and even of the Hōjō regents themselves. Accordingly, the shogunate dispatched two armies against Go-Daigo after his escape from exile in 1332. The first was conventionally raised and structured. But the second, although assembled on behalf of the shogunate, was mustered wholly from the kinsmen and followers of Ashikaga Takauji, and entirely under his personal command.[51]

To be sure, Masashige, Takauji, Nitta Yoshisada, and other great warriors of the Kemmu Restoration and Nambokuchō eras were never able to assemble or maintain sizeable armies or region-wide alliance networks without heavy reliance on delegated authority. By the same token, however, their careers would have been unthinkable just over a century earlier: their rise to national prominence was made possible by socio-economic changes in the provinces that, among other things, significantly enhanced the integrity, coherency and stability of locally based private military networks.

Thus, the great theme of thirteenth-century warrior evolution was consolidation: of rights over lands and people, of the strategic command structure under the Kamakura shogunate, and of tactical organizational patterns and authority under local warrior leaders. Developments in these three spheres sometimes conflicted, as centralized bureaucratic models of authority competed with localized personal and familial ones; but they were also mutually reinforcing.

The outstanding feature of Heian era warrior alliances was their fragility, a condition that reflected the amorphous nature of the lord–vassal bond during the period. For, unlike other forms of consociation, such as the land-commendation arrangements set forth between provincial elites and the leading courtiers and religious institutions of the capital – the process by which estates (*shōen*) were formed – alliances between warriors were not supported by legal contracts. The exchange of obligations that accompanied warrior partnerships during Heian times was far less palpable, and the nature, extent and duration of these obligations much less precise, than those attendant to the land-holding system of the period.[52]

Formal arrangements under which specified benefices were offered in return for defined military services were slow to develop in Japan, because the ability of warrior leaders to manipulate any forms of carrot or stick in order to recruit, maintain and control followers was closely circumscribed by their relatively weak political circumstances. For even the most powerful provincial *bushi* and warrior *zuryō* of the age occupied only intermediate positions in the socio-political hierarchy, and were dependent on connections with the higher echelons of the court to maintain their political and economic positions.[53] Their autonomy, in matters of governance and land-holding, was limited, which meant that they lacked the right – and therefore the means – to reward or punish their own troops directly.

In Heian times, warriors remained primarily mercenaries, offering their skills and services in exchange for long-term patronage of their careers by court powers-that-be, or for more immediate rewards. While the latter often brought perquisites over lands and peoples, and sometimes involved the transfer of properties hitherto administered by warriors on the losing side of a conflict, Heian *bushi* were rarely, if ever, able to specify the size or the particulars of rewards for themselves; and any transfers of lands were accomplished indirectly, through the agency of the court, and in accord with the niceties prescribed by the court-centered legal system.

Consequently, Heian military alliances tended to be nebulous and short-lived entities. The larger the organization, the more ephemeral it tended to be. On occasion, illustrious warriors such as Minamoto Yoshiie or Yoshitomo were able to construct martial networks that extended across multiple provinces, but until the 1180s no such organization survived the death of its founder.[54]

It was, therefore, no coincidence that the first truly enduring warrior organization – the *gokenin* system devised by Yoritomo and his successors – was also the first vassalage network validated by law and documentation. The shogunate's court-sanctioned powers to confirm vassal land rights and to confiscate properties from "rebels" reinforced the bond between Kamakura and its vassals with a direct benefice arrangement theretofore lacking in *bushi* alliances. This was, in many respects, a signal development: no warrior before Yoritomo had been able to reward followers with lands except by negotiating grants from higher authorities, on a case-by-case basis.

Be that as it may, the arrangements undergirding early medieval war bonds represented something short of a straightforward exchange of fiefs for services. During the early Gempei War years, Yoritomo offered broad protection for almost any sorts of property rights enlisting that vassals claimed were rightfully theirs, issuing confirmation documents pertaining to domains as small as a warrior's home and as large as whole estates or districts. Later, however, he backed away from such a broadly cast involvement with warrior holdings, opting instead for exclusive control over a single benefice: the *jitō* title – which was a managerial post within the land-owning hierarchy dominated by courtiers and clerics.[55]

This meant that the "fiefs" distributed by Kamakura remained intimately bound to the court-centered, hierarchical proprietary system, and that the shogunate's benefice offerings could not be imitated at the regional level by other warrior leaders. It also meant that the equation of vassalage with benefice remained incomplete, for, while there were hundreds of *jitō* posts distributed across the country, there were thousands of *gokenin*, and tens of thousands of other land titles, for which warriors could contend.

Nevertheless, shogunate policies *did* create an association of military obligations with lands. Over the course of the thirteenth and fourteenth centuries, this association deepened, becoming a force for localism and consolidation of ties between warriors on the land.

Although *gokenin* services remained, in principal, personal obligations to the Kamakura lord, in practice many – particularly *ōban'yaku* and other military duties – tended to be prorated according to the extent of the vassal's holdings.[56] This policy was complicated by other practices: *gokenin* were not, for example, expected to perform, or even supervise, all services required of them in person; they could, and frequently did, delegate others to serve in their names. Moreover, many of the shogunate's chief vassals – the great eastern warrior houses – held lands in multiple provinces, and in multiple regions, which they administered through collaterals and cadet branches of their families. At the same time, *gokenin* military services were coordinated province by province, by *shugo*. In combination, these customs encouraged delegation of control over key vassal military duties such as *ōban'yaku* to local authorities, and the participation of *gokenin* collaterals (many of whom had largely replaced the main lines as the actual holders of the lands they administered), who were not formally regarded as Kamakura vassals in their own right. All of this, then, seems to have promoted a growing identification of services with the lands, rather than with the vassals themselves.[57]

At the same time, warrior houses were proliferating all over the country, and military organizations outside Kamakura's vassal network were emerging, particularly in the west. These included both forces assembled by establishment figures – *shōen* officers and local government officials – and the anti-establishment bands cited as "evil gangs" (*akutō*) in contemporary sources. In practice, the memberships of these groups often overlapped with one another, as well as with the *gokenin* corps. Thus the new organizations transcended the labels of *gokenin* and non-vassal (*higokenin*), and challenged the validity of both constructs.[58]

By the early fourteenth century, moreover, the value, and even the meaning, of possessing *gokenin* status was changing. As we have noted, Kamakura never fully synchronized the fief/benefice awards it administered – appointments to *jitō* posts – with its vassalage network. Thus, while all *jitō* were *gokenin*, not all *gokenin* held lands confirmed by the shogunate. Initially this was a source of some discontent among unenfeoffed Kamakura housemen – it was even one of the factors behind vassal defections during the Jōkyū War.

But as the system of hierarchical proprietary rights (*shiki*) on which the *jitō* post had been premised began to unravel during the late 1200s, and *jitō* entitlements became divided among multiple holders, the attraction of *jitō* appointments waned considerably. For while the remunerations associated with *jitō* titles were diminishing, the titles still bore explicitly defined obligations toward proprietors in the capital. Recognition as a Kamakura houseman, on the other hand, carried no such formal contractual responsibilities, only a much vaguer commitment to provide services to the shogunate – obligations that were by this time being demanded of non-vassals as well – and the presumption that a feudatory buffer – the shogunate – stood between the warrior and the court.[59]

The *gokenin* label was, in other words, becoming less and less a matter of vassalage and obligation, and more and more one of license – a dispensation to ignore directions from Kyoto – and of elite status. Accordingly, warriors persisted in styling themselves "housemen" even after the collapse of the Kamakura shogunate – ostensibly the "house" toward which their services were directed – in spite of the Kemmu regime's attempts to eradicate the title.[60]

As this perceptual shift developed, the "feudal" bonds holding the Kamakura vassal corps together became frayed. The shogunate's coherency as the warband writ large it had once been waned, and it increasingly relied on its institutional identity for survival.

In the meantime, Kamakura's (generally successful) endeavors to consolidate its role in the national polity and to prevent large-scale military lordships from forming under anyone else were dovetailing with the more localized ambitions of provincial warrior leaders to produce fundamental changes in the structure of warrior houses and the integrity of provincial warbands.

Historians have long pointed to kinship ties – real or fictive – as the glue that held early Japanese warrior alliances together. And indeed, there is little doubt that, from the first, *bushi* thoroughly seized on familial relationships as a device for building and strengthening warbands. This much is clear from the frequency with which they employed terminology suggestive of familial connections – *kenin* ("houseman"), *ie no ko* ("child of the house") and the like – to designate vassals, and from their zeal in arranging marriages between their offspring or siblings and those of allies, followers or lords.[61]

During the Heian period, however, such practices were more symbolic than efficacious; for, ideology to the contrary, consanguinity was by no means a guarantee of harmony in Heian society. Conflict, even out-and-out warfare, between in-laws, cousins, uncles and nephews, and even brothers, was a near-constant theme of Heian military history, visible in dozens of famous and not so famous skirmishes throughout the period.[62]

In practical terms, cohesion existed only within the smallest kinship units, that is, within nuclear families. Although ties between parent and child were usually strong, those between siblings were relatively weak, and those between cousins, uncles and nephews, and in-laws weaker still. Thus, the Minamoto and Taira "clans" that receive so much attention in popular literature – and even the branches of these clans – amounted, as Jeffrey Mass has observed, to little more than aggregates of diffuse units that were "not in any sense the sums of their separate parts."[63]

This situation was, in part, a consequence of the laws and customs governing inheritance during the Heian period: estates were divided to provide independent means to multiple heirs; wills were probated by the authorities

– provincial governors or estate owners – who had jurisdiction over the lands and titles bequeathed, not by clan patriarchs or matriarchs; and bequests were nearly always lineal (parent to child), not lateral (sibling to sibling). All of which meant that, in legal and economic terms, cousins, and uncles and nephews (or nieces), had little or no meaningful relationship to one another.[64]

As can easily be imagined, this inheritance system often led to a geometrically progressing diffusion of family property and, with it, of familial identity, from generation to generation. While siblings might maintain a fair degree of family unity during the lifetime of their father, the various cadet houses tended to split off following his death and become independent of one another. Each new household head inherited properties and titles of his own, which he would subsequently pass on to his heirs. Each followed his own career path and maintained his own retinue or private warband. Even in cases in which fathers designated a primary heir (and they did not always do so), his residual rights over the affairs of these cadet houses were minimal at best; consociation between collateral lines usually did not extend beyond an innocuous consciousness of a shared heritage.

Accordingly, kinship ties did little to hold Heian military alliances together. Cadet houses joined, or refused to join, the military networks of more prestigious kinsmen grounded in the same considerations that might have led them to follow completely unrelated warrior leaders: based, that is, on a communality of interests, not bloodline.[65] During the thirteenth century, however, this situation began to change as the shogunate and its leading vassal houses learned to navigate around the pitfalls of the partible inheritance system, and even exploit it to their mutual advantage.

The extensive confiscations and redistributions of land rights that occurred during the Gempei and Jōkyū War eras left most important *gokenin* with generous portfolios of widely scattered properties, which could be entrusted to cadet heirs. Coparceny was thus both affordable and convenient for early Kamakura warrior houses, who, in any event, needed deputies to administer distant holdings. But it also raised the dangers of permanent alienation of cadet branches from the family's main line and an amoeba-like proliferation of *gokenin* houses.

In response, both the shogunate and the vassal houses themselves began to emphasize the notion of special rights and privileges adhering to the main line and its principal heir. The result was what became known as the *sōryō* (literally, "paramount holding") system: the formulation of a corporate center for warrior houses whereby the principal heir (*sōryō*) acted as representative and intermediary for his siblings and their progeny in all transactions with higher authority. Under this arrangement, Kamakura left all decisions regarding bequests and estate planning – including the choice of the next *sōryō* – to its vassals, but channeled all demands for service through the main heir, and placed all discharge of vassal duties by secondary heirs and their descendents under his supervision.[66]

At the same time, the *sōryō* houses themselves were engaged, by mid-century, in efforts to reallocate family resources so as to enhance the power of the main line and preserve the integrity of its holdings. Chief among these was a gradual shift from divided to unitary inheritance. To this were added such other devices as the creation of house laws and family codes detailing principles of organization and conduct for all collaterals, and the retention by the *sōryō* of all original documents pertaining to the holdings of branch lines, even those devised outright in the bequests of previous *sōryō*.[67]

The combination of shogunate and vassal efforts in these directions greatly enhanced the integrity of warrior houses and the subordination of cadet branches to the main line. But it was still not enough entirely to prevent branch lines dispatched to administer distant holdings from forming ties with other warriors in their new geographical areas, and becoming functionally independent of the main house.[68]

Consequently, military – and familial – organization was at once intensifying and deteriorating during the late Kamakura period. On the one hand, *bushi* leaders, particularly the leading *sōryō* houses of eastern Japan, were developing unprecedented levels of integration and control over kinsmen and other subalterns in and around their home bases. Thus while Yoritomo's call to arms in 1180 divided warrior families all over the Kanto, pitting kinsman against kinsmen, Go-Daigo's call 150 years later did no such thing; virtually no eastern *gokenin* houses split between the two sides that formed in 1333.[69] On the other hand, *sōryō* in the east were finding it increasingly difficult to maintain charge over far-flung kinsmen. Ties and associations, particularly military alliances and chains of command, were becoming progressively more local, and the principal casualties were the dominions of family heads over geographically separated collaterals.

In the final analysis, the integrity of Heian-, Kamakura- and Nambokuchō-era private military networks was only as strong as the adherents' perceptions that affiliation worked to their advantage. Warrior leaders could count on the services of their followers only to the extent that they were able to offer suitably attractive compensation – or, conversely, to impose suitably daunting sanctions for refusal.

The ability to reward depended on a number of factors. Some of these, such as possession of lands, government posts, or positions in the administrative structures of private estates, were relatively stable and could even be inherited. Others, such as personal military skills and reputation, or connections at court, were more elusive. Similarly, the rewards offered could take many forms, including help in securing government posts or managerial positions on private estates, division of spoils from successful campaigns, and intercession with provincial governors, the shogunate or other higher authorities on behalf of one's followers.[70]

Warrior allegiances were further circumscribed by the multi-tiered, hierarchical structure of the military networks to which they belonged. Most of the provincial warriors in the organizations of prominent *bushi* had vassals of their own, and many of the members of these, in turn, had followers. The loyalties of lower-ranking figures in this complex hierarchy to those at the top were tenuous at best, being buffered at each interceding level by the allegiances of their higher-ups.[71]

Nor were ideological constraints of much value in holding early warrior alliances together. Medieval texts such as *Heike monogatari*, which purport to describe events of the late Heian period, are filled with edifying tales attesting to the fierce loyalty displayed by the warriors of the age. But while earlier sources, closer to these events, do give some hints that the fighting men of this time were not entirely oblivious to the concept of fealty as a virtue valuable to and befitting a good warrior, the real effect of this notion on samurai behavior was minimal.[72] For the most part, early medieval warriors viewed loyalty as a commodity predicated on adequate remuneration, rather than an obligation transcending self-interest.

In the fourteenth century, expectations concerning commitments and fealty became closely bound up with distinctions between warriors of varying levels of autarchy, which, in turn, hardened into hereditary social categories. Thus *bushi* of means came to be styled *tōzama* ("outsiders"), while those who maintained strong dependent ties to greater lords were called *miuchi* ("insiders").* *Tōzama* were ideologically, as well as economically, autonomous. They chose their battles and their leaders according to narrowly defined personal interests and circumstances of the moment, and were more than ready to desert to other employers whenever they thought they might better their situation by doing so. Only warriors without substantial holdings of their own – whose fortunes were therefore inseparable from those of their lords – behaved loyally.[73]

Nevertheless, the bonds between *tōzama* and their *miuchi* vassals – and, to some extent, the categories themselves – were inherently unstable, inasmuch as they hinged on a disparity of resources that kept the vassals unable to challenge their lords. *Miuchi* were reliable only in inverse proportion to their dependence. Those with minimal holdings often displayed striking loyalty to their overlords; those who possessed, or were entrusted with, extensive lands and followers could – and did – condition their service, and compel greater rewards. Beyond a certain point, *miuchi* dependence – and therefore *tōzama* control – became nominal. Accordingly, a warrior's military forces grew less and less cohesive as his power and size increased, and his vassals also became land-holders of means.

Tōzama loyalties and military obligations to those above them were even more fluid and contingent. For while *miuchi* faithfulness might be demanded as an obligation born of dependency, *tōzama* autonomy in military affairs was normative, and *tōzama* services had to be bought. Presumption of autarchy

---

* "*Miuchi*" and "*tōzama*" originally distinguished the personal vassals of the Hōjō regents from the direct vassals of the Kamakura shogun, who were "outside" the parameters of Hōjō familial (but not bureaucratic) authority. This usage apparently remained current at least as late as 1319, when Kamakura's *Sata mirensho* legal compendium appeared (see *Sata mirensho*, p. 6). The new meanings seem, however, to have emerged quickly after the fall of the shogunate.

freed *tōzama* from any transcendent duty to fight or serve, shifting the burden of responsibility for maintaining allegiance from the warriors called to the armies that sought to hire them.[74]

Ironically, this inverted and mercenary ideological dynamic kept large military organizations not only unstable but reliant on central authority throughout the fourteenth century. For few warriors of the era were able to assemble resources of their own sufficient to purchase large numbers of followers. *Tōzama* who attempted to expand locally had to do so at the expense – and, against the opposition – of surrounding peers; and, beyond a finite level of expansion, the need to delegate administrative tasks also risked giving their vassals *de facto* autonomy of means, and therefore of action.

Rewards on a scale that would entice *tōzama* were possible only through the backing of public authority. The Ashikaga shogunate, its generals and redefined *shugo* deputies, and the Southern Court competed for *tōzama* loyalties by manipulating controls and sanctions that were as yet prerogatives of the state – powers that ostensibly derived from the throne – including the authority to confirm titles over lands, to confiscate holdings from "rebel" partisans, to adjudicate disputes, or to delegate responsibility for collecting various taxes.[75]

At the same time, such competition whittled away at the very authority it manipulated. For most of the fourteenth century, the existence of rival courts, each claiming identical – and exclusive – authority offered *tōzama* warriors a choice of customers to whom to market their support, and thereby sustained the premise that military services had to be purchased from rightfully autonomous contractors, rather than demanded of obedient subjects or vassals.

In the political realm, the long-term effects were revolutionary: central authority all but ceased to exist in other than name. In the military sphere, however, the centrifugal flow of power tended to reinforce what was, in effect, the *status quo*. Armies of the period, therefore, remained minimally articulated, short-term aggregates of comparatively small components.

★ ★ ★ ★ ★

Military *power* in Japan became private and "feudal" long before government or military *authority* did. Unlike the knights and barons of northwestern Europe, Japan's *bushi* were fashioned to serve the needs of a still-secure, still-vital centralized state. Court enfranchisement of private warrior power from very early on worked, paradoxically, to keep connections between the military and political hierarchies thin for many centuries thereafter. There was no power vacuum into which incipient warlords could rush, and little *bushi* class-consciousness to incite a warrior revolution.

Until the very end of the early medieval era, the "feudalization" of military organization was thoroughgoing only at the monadic level, between warrior leaders and small bands of direct retainers. Large forces and networks were difficult to sustain for very long, and difficult to assemble, even in the short term, without the support of state authority in some form. Hence military power was seldom a practical route to political power in Japan before the fourteenth century. Indeed, the opposite more often proved true: political power and authority were crucial to any maintenance of military power.

Minamoto Yoritomo's declaration of independence in 1180 stands, in many respects, as a glaring exception to this precept. But even his early calls to arms, which claimed – however spuriously – a mandate from Prince Mochihito to rouse the east, co-opted the authority and the framework of the imperial state. And the developments that followed from his subsequent negotiations with Go-Shirakawa integrated the feudal lordship he had initiated deeply into the court-centered polity.

In its mature form, the Kamakura power structure simplified the Heian military/police system while retaining most of its basic principles and key features. As such, it created a framework for the continued existence of the Heian polity, even as it laid the groundwork for the warrior rule that emerged under the Ashikaga regime.

On a more prosaic level, and of more direct concern to this study, the dual – and dueling – organizational principles of Heian-, Kamakura- and Nambokuchō-era military forces mitigated against extensive articulation of command and control on early medieval battlefields, with significant repercussions for tactics and the nature of warfare. We will return to this topic in Chapter 4; but first we need to explore the technological parameters of early medieval warfare.

3

THE TOOLS OF WAR

> Weapons . . . are the intermediaries between the aggressive human intelligence and its desires.
>   Harry Holbert Turney-High, *Primitive War*, 1949

> It is war that shapes peace, and armament that shapes war.
>   John Frederick Charles Fuller, *Armament and History*, 1945

In no field of human endeavor do Thomas Carlyle's famous characterization of man as "a tool-using animal" and his insistence that "without tools he is nothing, with tools he is all," have greater resonance than in regard to war.[1] Weapons and other tools shape the face of battle and the identities of those who use them.

It is, in fact, scarcely necessary to argue this premise before modern readers. Historians have long cited changes in weaponry as cause or catalyst to fundamental shifts in the nature of warfare, and even in the organization of medieval Japanese society itself.[2] Moreover, the waves of innovation in weaponry accompanying the advance of the physical sciences during the past two centuries have reified the equation of military science with technology, to the extent that few today would question an assertion that the history of warfare has been driven by inventors and shaped by efforts to acquire and maintain technological superiority. Yet this idea is neither self-evident, nor even very old. Before the technological nightmare of World War I, military historians and theoreticians seldom discussed the adoption of new weapons as a fundamental element in the evolution of warfare.[3]

One reason for this was that the pace of change in weapons design was much slower, and its impact generally much less dramatic, in the premodern era. Indeed, virtually all of the important armaments of the pre-gunpowder age were already in widespread use by the end of the second millennium BCE. Despite countless alternations and recombinations of existing weaponry, fundamental innovations were minimal during the next 2,500 years. Supremacy in the premodern military world was seldom a matter of obtaining a superior weapon, but was, rather, one of integrating existing weapons and tactics in superior combinations.[4]

Nevertheless the variety and form of weapons available to early medieval warriors, how they were used, and whence they were obtained are important questions concerning *bushi* development. These, then, are the central issues to be explored in this chapter and the one that follows.

Manufacture and procurement of weapons

The *ritsuryō* state approached the task of equipping its armed forces in much the same way it did other affairs of government: with a curious mixture of constraint and indolence. Much of the equipment was produced in the capital, under the direction of an Office of Weapons Manufacture (*Tsuwamono-zukuri no tsukasa* or *Zōhyōryō*) attached to the Ministry of Military Affairs (*Hyōbushō*) and closely affiliated with the Left and Right Arsenal Bureaus (*Hyōgoryō*). The raw materials needed – iron, wood, leather, cloth, bamboo, feathers, and the like – were collected countrywide as part of the handicraft and special products taxes (*chōyō*), requisitioned from state-managed forests, mines and pastures; or sometimes simply purchased. Artisans drawn from some 465 registered tax households (*ko*) in the capital region performed the actual work. Each household contributed one worker, who labored from the start of the tenth month of each year until the close of the second month of the next, in exchange for which the entire household was excused from all other handicraft tax (*chō*) obligations. Provincial government headquarters (*kokuga*) throughout the country also manufactured weapons, under the supervision of the governor.[5]

War-horses were culled from among those raised in state-owned pastures in the east and southwest, or received as tax or tribute, and assigned to the provincial regiments (*gundan*), where they were consigned to soldiers from "families of wealth, able to care for them." Henceforth the soldiers were expected to look after the animals, and to bring them along when their regiments were mobilized for training or war. They were also held accountable for horses that died, except under circumstances deemed unavoidable.[6]

During the early *ritsuryō* era, weapons production and storage were supposed to have been watched and regulated with an attention to detail that bordered on paranoia. The codes prohibited any trade in "bows, arrows and other weapons" with foreigners, and enjoined against even situating steel and ironworks "near the eastern or northern borders." They also dictated that "weapons shall be manufactured in accord with prescribed models. The year and month of manufacture, and the name of the artisan, shall be inscribed on each." Supplementary legislation even stipulated the materials to be used in the production of armor, swords, bows and arrows, and the time required for each step of the manufacturing process.[7]

Weapons and other military materiel produced at provincial government headquarters were placed directly in provincial arsenals or consigned to collection officers for transport to the capital, where they were warehoused by the Left and Right Arsenal Bureaus. Supervising officials prepared and filed reports at every stage of these processes. And the items in government arsenals were inventoried at regular intervals, whence they were inscribed with the name of the officer in charge.[8]

Nevertheless, not all weapons manufacture took place under government supervision. The state forbade private possession of large battlefield weapons and of devices for organizing and directing armies (that is, of "drums, ballistae, [four meter] spears, [seven meter] spears, horse armor, great horns, small horns, and military flags"), but it did not outlaw ownership of personal weapons, such as bows and swords. Indeed, it *required* each conscript soldier "to provide for himself one bow, one bow case, two spare bowstrings, fifty war arrows, one quiver, one long sword, and one short sword," which he was to bring with him on days of mobilization. It also held individual conscripts liable for "weapons or armors lost or damaged other than in battle," or other circumstances "such as fire or flood, which are beyond human control," mandating that all such equipment "be paid for at current prices or as directed by the statutes governing weapons manufacture." Clearly such demands presupposed the existence of a substantial private trade in arms.[9]

There is no direct documentation of this trade, but, during the Nara period, it must have been part and parcel of the broad commercial activity that centered on the exchange of iron, cloth, salt, and other tax items for additional goods and services. State-run markets in the capital were the hubs of a network of markets established near provincial government headquarters and regulated by provincial officials. Taxpayers pooled their resources to hire specialist artisans to produce required handicraft and special products tax goods, and traded labor, rice, produce, game, and manufactured products of their own for agricultural implements, pottery wares, and other goods – including weapons.[10]

The court experienced problems with both public and private arms production almost from the start. Even the *ritsuryō* codes themselves included an injunction that "merchants shall not engage in the sale of counterfeit merchandise. Swords, spears, saddle-trees, and lacquered goods shall bear the name of the maker."[11] By the mid-eighth century, complaints of shortfalls and the poor quality of weapons collected were beginning to mount. In 761, the Council of State found it necessary to insist anew that:

> The [duty to] manufacture weapons is the same for all provinces. Yet the provinces of the western seaboard do not make their annual quota which is all the more surprising inasmuch as they are on the frontier! Therefore . . . [these] provinces are reminded that stipulated numbers of armors, swords, bows and arrows are to be produced, and samples sent each year to the Dazaifu.[12]

Four months later shortfalls elsewhere prompted an order that soldiers in some provincial regiments be put to work making weapons.[13]

In 791, the Council of State directed that "persons of the fifth rank or higher, from the Minister of the Left on downward, shall make armor, in quantities proportionate to their status . . . and wealth."[14] This order foreshadowed a new direction of policy for arms production and procurement. Direct state participation in either would soon become superfluous, as the court turned more and more to hired swords – privately trained, privately equipped mercenaries – to act as its "claws and teeth" in military and police affairs. The new privatized and pluralized military system and the warrior order that staffed it were supported in part by a new economy emerging in both the capital and the provinces.

One facet of this new economy was an increased commercialization of the production of weapons and other manufactured goods. By the late ninth century, the changes to the tax system discussed in Chapter 2 had led provincial governors, who were now free to explore more efficient methods of extracting goods and revenues from their bailiwicks, to commute handicraft taxes to payments in rice, and to use the proceeds to purchase the required products in the market, or to pay artisans to manufacture them, at workshops supervised by provincial or local officials.[15]

In all probability, government-supervised production of armaments had always been largely a matter of the state setting prices for goods purchased from specialist artisans. Under the early *ritsuryō* system, this effectively made the artisans employees of the court or the provincial government. But the multi-polar structure of power and authority that emerged during the Heian period helped turn blacksmiths, armorers, bowyers, and other weapons makers into free agents providing goods and services directly to local elites, powerful court houses, provincial governors and members of their staffs, and religious institutions, as well as to the state. This situation was sufficiently common by the end of the ninth century to prompt legislation proscribing the making of arms for the private market (*shiki*) and for the government on the same days.[16]

In the countryside, artisans gradually came under the protection of the provincial elites who managed private estates and administered provincial and district governments. Under the auspices of figures such as the *Utsubo monogatari* character Kaminabi Tanematsu, whose home in Kii is supposed to have included a *sake* brewery, a carpentry shop, a foundry (*imoji dokoro*), a forge (*kajiya*), a pottery shop, a kiln, a silk-fulling house (*uchimono no dokoro*), a sewing shop and a spinning shop, craftsmen produced goods for both the local authority and the absentee proprietor of the lands he oversaw.[17] Their efforts included the manufacture of numerous finished products, but by and large they centered on small-scale production of semi-processed materials and components for a growing, and increasingly integrated, market network. Archeological excavations of ironworks and other manufacturing sites, like the one discovered in 1987 at Nishiotani, near Yokohama, reveal that pots, pans, kettles, dishes, nails, arrowheads, knives, sickles, metal shears, branding irons, iron lamellae (the components of medieval armors; see below) and parts of horse bridles were being produced all over the hinterlands. But they do not show evidence that more complex products were being fabricated there.[18]

Early medieval warriors appear to have obtained some of their weapons and military goods from local artisans in their private employ, but items such as swords, or armor and saddles, which require high levels of skill to make, were manufactured primarily in and around the capital. By the middle of the Heian period, consumer demand, led by the great houses and religious institutions of the capital, increasingly concentrated in Kyoto and the capital region, inducing the best artisans from throughout the country to congregate there.

The center of weapons-making, throughout the early medieval period, was the Shichijō-chō section of the Eastern Market, just to the north of what is now Kyoto station. An early tenth-century legal compendium records swords, bows, arrows, armor, helmets, stirrups, saddle-trees, and other equestrian gear among the principal merchandise offered for sale there. The Shichijō-chō area, which was very near the homes of many of the prominent Taira and Minamoto warrior houses, was both the workplace and the residence of arms craftsmen, such as the metal-worker described in a thirteenth-century tale collection, who returned unexpectedly to his home there and caught his wife in bed with a mountain ascetic (*yamabushi*)![19]

Artisans specialized broadly by the materials they worked, rather than in specific products, until at least the mid-Kamakura period, when sword-smithing and bow-making began to emerge as distinctive trades. Thus saddle-trees were made by carpenters – as were "knick-knack boxes, inkstone cases, box pillows, makeup cases, cabinets, Chinese chests, room dividers, folding screen frames, lamp stands, Buddhist altars, flowered desks, sutra shelves, high stools, daises, platters, tables, armrests . . . fan ribs, quivers, sword stands, Chinese umbrellas, artificial flowers," and other items – while "short swords, long swords, spears, razors, and arrowheads with blades like ice in winter" were produced by metal-smiths who also made "stirrups, bits, locks, saws, planes, hatchets, broad axes, sickles, axes, plowshares, hoes, nails, clamps, augers, tweezers, scissors, and other metal goods; as well as pots, cook pots, kettles, large mouth kettles, three-legged cook pots, bowls, tubs, stoves, mirrors, water jars, flower vases, arghya vessels, comb boxes, incense burners, priest's staves, cymbals, single emery pestles, triple emery pestles, quintuple emery pestles, hand bells, temple bells, metal drums, and the like."[20]

Warriors in the capital and the countryside purchased their weapons and gear through markets operated by traveling merchants. A twelfth-century literary work relates the nasty habit of a warrior named Fujiwara Yasusuke of robbing vendors of "swords, saddles, armor, helmets, silk, cloth and various sundry goods" when they visited his residence in Kyoto.[21] And an eleventh-century text describes the archetypical merchant:

> He values profit but knows not his wife and children. He esteems himself but pays not a second look to others. If he has one of anything, he turns it into ten thousand. If he strikes dirt, he turns it to gold. He is a master, who deceives the hearts of others with his words; and steals their eyes with his cunning. His travels range east to the lands of the barbarians and cross the islands of the devils in the west. The goods he trades, and the varieties he buys and sells, cannot be counted.[22]

THE TOOLS OF WAR

Projectile weapons

While their Tokugawa-era progeny would revere the sword as "the soul of the samurai," the tools that produced the *bushi* – and defined them throughout the early medieval era – were the horse and the long bow. Both had venerable histories in Japan.

Stone arrowheads unearthed by archeologists suggest that bows and arrows have been used in Japan from as far back as 10,000 BCE. During the Jōmon era (*c*.8,000–300 BCE), the bow appears to have been only a hunting tool, but skeletal remains make it clear that it was being trained on more sapient game by the Yayoi period (*c*.300 BCE–300 CE), when fighting and war became frequent and widespread. Slings, used to hurl fist-sized rocks or spheres of clay shaped roughly like miniature rugby balls, also appeared during the Yayoi age, distributed in a geographic pattern that suggests mutually exclusive regional preferences for the sling or the bow.[23]

Compound or composite bows of the sort favored on the Asian continent – made by laminating together layers of wood, animal tendon and horn – were known in Japan by the late ninth century, but never widely adopted.[24] Instead, without ready access to supplies of bone and horn, the Japanese fashioned their bows from wood or from laminates of wood and bamboo.

The earliest designs were of plain wood – usually catalpa, zelkova, sandalwood or mulberry – made from the trunk of a single sapling of appropriate girth (*marugi yumi*) or from staves split from the trunks of larger trees (*kiyumi*), and sometimes lacquered or wrapped with bark thongs. Most were straight when unstrung, but some were steam-bent into arc shapes and strung against their curves, an innovation that greatly enhanced their power.* Simple wood bows of this sort were limited in range and penetrating force, but they were also easy to draw, and therefore well suited to repetitive shooting at short distances. For this reason they continued to be used for ceremonial and competitive archery, for hunting, for some kinds of training, and even on the battlefield throughout the medieval period and beyond.[25]

The earliest clear reference to a composite bow in Japan is a poem by Minamoto Yorimasa (1104–80), Prince Mochihito's co-conspirator against Taira Kiyomori in 1180:

---

* Picture scrolls depicting warriors and weaponry suggest that recurved bows were popularized during the Nambokuchō era. Scrolls created during the late thirteenth century show warriors using bows that were either straight or recurved only very slightly at the ends (see, for example, *Obusama Saburō ekotoba*, *Ban dainagon ekotoba*, or *Zenkūnen kassen ekotoba*). The *Mōko shūrai ekotoba*, compiled sometime between 1293 and 1324, shows the Japanese using straight or nearly straight bows, while the Mongols shoot dramatically recurved ones. The bows depicted in the late fourteenth or early fifteenth century *Taiheiki emaki*, on the other hand, are all recurved.

THE TOOLS OF WAR

Omowazu ya   Unthinkable!
Tanarasu yumi ni   That I should forsake you even for a night
fusu take no   would be like separating a bamboo slat
ichi yo mo kimi ni   from a familiar bow.
hanaru beshi to wa.*

These first compound bows, called *fusetake yumi*, featured a single strip of bamboo laminated to the outside face of the wood, using a paste (called *nibe*) made from fish bladders. Sometime around the turn of the thirteenth century, a second bamboo laminate was added to the inside face of the bow, to create the *sammai uchi yumi*. In the fifteenth century, two additional bamboo slats were added to the sides, so that the wooden core was now completely encased, producing the *shihōchiku yumi*. The *higo yumi* used for traditional Japanese archery today appeared sometime during the seventeenth century. It features a core of three to five bamboo slats, with additional bamboo facings laminated to the front and back edges, and strips of wood laminated to the sides (see Figure 3.1). To protect the glued joints from moisture, which could cause the bow staves to delaminate or lose springiness, *takefuse yumi* and later composite bows were lacquered – usually in black or vermilion – and bound with thongs of rattan, birch bark or silk.[26]

Simple wood bows will not bend very deeply without breaking, and overflexing composites of wood and bamboo stresses the adhesive and makes the laminations separate. To achieve significant power, therefore, wood or wood and bamboo bows must be long.[†] And medieval Japanese bows were long – some over 2.5 meters – which would have made them impossibly awkward to use from horseback but for their unique shape, with the grip placed a third of the way up from the bottom, rather than in the middle in the manner of European longbows.

Some historians have speculated that this unusual grip was adopted to facilitate the use of the weapon by mounted warriors, but there is evidence that the shape of the bow predates its use from horseback. Reports by Chinese envoys to Japan, recorded in the chronicles of the Wei dynasty, for example, indicate

---

* The poem, which appears in *Genjū sanmi Yorimasa kyōshū* (quoted in Takahashi Masaaki, *Bushi no seiritsu*, 266, and Fujimoto Masayuki, "Bugu to rekishi II," 63), turns on the phrase "*ichi yo*," which alternatively means "one night" or "one slat," and the verb "*hanaru*," which means both "to separate" and "to forsake."

† The strength of medieval bows was sometimes rated in terms of the number of men required to bend and string them. The late Kamakura-period *Obusama Saburō ekotoba* includes a famous illustration of three men stringing a bow against a tree (p. 22). While texts such as *Heike monogatari* include references to five- and six-man bows, it seems unlikely that such weapons existed outside the realm of literary imagination. Not only would a bow this strong have been difficult to shoot, it would have been ridiculously impractical to string under combat conditions.

THE TOOLS OF WAR

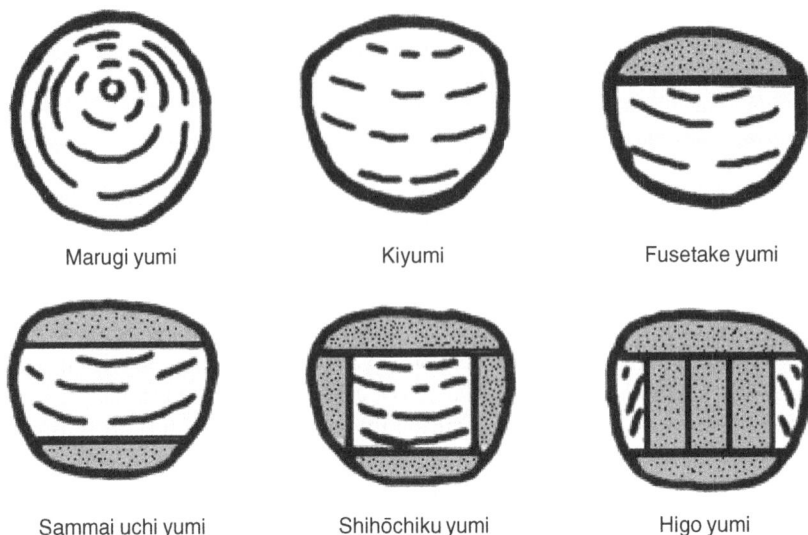

Figure 3.1 Japanese bow designs in cross-section

that the Japanese were using "wooden bows made with shorter lower part and longer upper part" by the mid-third century, while making no mention at all of equestrian culture in Japan at that time.[27]

Other scholars argue that the lopsided proportions were originally necessary to balance the bending characteristics of the wood: simple bows, produced from a single piece of wood, were made from young trees, using the root end of the tree for the lower part of the bow stave. The branch end of the tree is, however, springier than the root end. Thus the grip needed to be located closer to the bottom of the bow – the stiffer end of the wood – in order to balance out the elasticity of the weapon, so that it would draw evenly, without over-stressing either end.[28]

Whatever the initial reason for its adoption, gripping the bow two-thirds of the way down its length maximizes its rebound power and minimizes fatigue to the archer far better than the more familiar centered grip. Careful analysis of the mechanics of a bow pulled to full draw and released shows that the Japanese grip places the archer's hand at one of two nodes of oscillation during the shooting movement, which means that little shock is imparted to the left (gripping) hand and arm when the string is released (see Figure 3.2). In contrast, locating the grip at the center of the bow stave puts the gripping hand at a point of maximal oscillation, and thereby imparts significant shock to the arm when the string is released.[29]

The arrows in use during the Nara period averaged around 71 cm and were relatively thin. Those favored by the *bushi*, from the mid-Heian period

THE TOOLS OF WAR

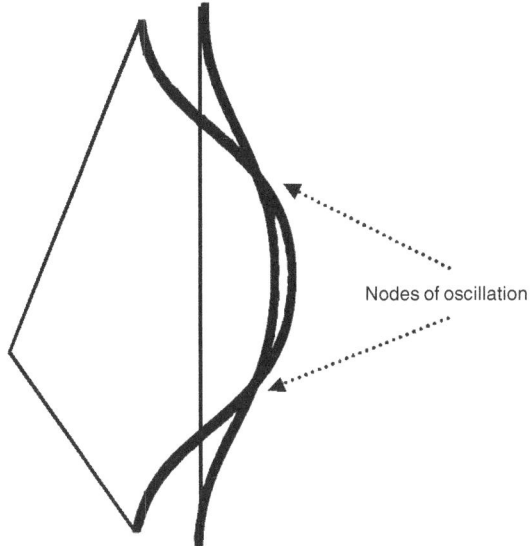

Figure 3.2 Bow oscillation (adapted from Irie Kōhei, "Kyūjutsu")

onward, were much thicker and markedly longer, averaging between 86 and 96 cm.* The shafts were usually made of bamboo, but in ancient times they were also sometimes made from willow or cane. The bamboo was cut during the early winter, shaved to remove the joints and outer skin, and straightened by softening it in hot sand. The nock for the bowstring was usually placed just above a joint, and at the end farthest from the root of the growing plant, so that the shaft tapered toward the nock. Arrowheads were mounted into the shafts by long, slender tangs, in the same manner as sword blades were mounted into hilts, and assumed a bewildering variety of shapes and sizes (see Figure 3.3): narrow, four-sided heads; flat, leaf-shaped broadheads; forked heads; blunt, wooden heads (used for practice); and whistling heads (used for signaling). Fletchings were made from the tail or wing feathers of a variety of birds, with those of hawks or eagles preferred, primarily for aesthetic reasons. Most arrows sported three fletchings, but some – particularly those designed for use with very large arrowheads – featured four. Arrow shafts were often marked with the name of the owner, so that kills could be identified.[30]

Heian- and Kamakura-period warriors carried their shafts on their right hips, in devices called *ebira*, which resembled small wicker chairs (see Figure 3.4). The

---

* Arrows were measured in fists and fingers, a system known as *yatsuka*. The most common length for arrows cited in written texts is twelve fists, but some literary war tales speak of arrows as long as fifteen fists.

71

THE TOOLS OF WAR

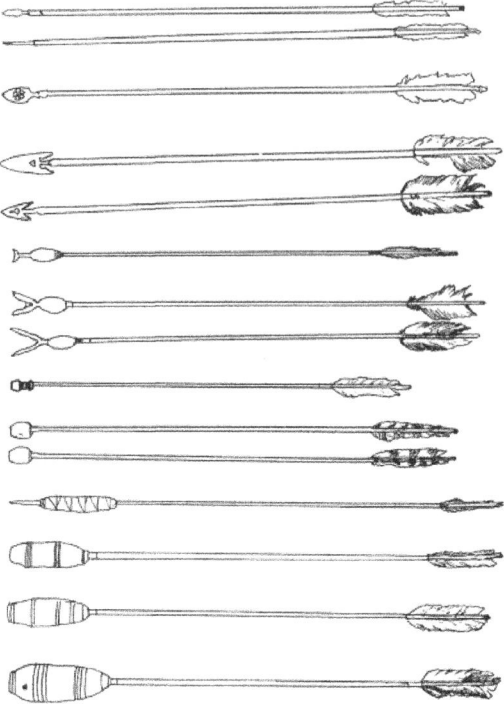

Figure 3.3 Early medieval arrows

lower section of this apparatus was box-shaped, with a grid of leather or bamboo strips across the top. Arrows were thrust through this grid, and then bound by a loose cord to the top of an openwork frame that rose from the back of the box. To draw them, the archer grasped the shaft just above the head, lifted it free of the grid, and then pulled it downward and outward until it cleared the cord. During the Muromachi era, *ebira* were gradually replaced on the battlefield by fur-covered quivers, called *utsubo*, worn across the back. *Utsubo* were used only for hunting until late Kamakura times, but came into common military usage from the fourteenth century onward, while *ebira* were increasingly relegated to use only when traveling.[31]

Next to the bow and arrow, the most important projectile weapon of the classical and early medieval era was a somewhat mysterious artillery piece called an *ōyumi*, or *do*. "Among the weapons of this court," wrote the tenth-century courtier Miyoshi Kiyoyuki, in a famous memorial to Emperor Daigo, "the *ōyumi* is god.... The old tales tell us how the Empress-Regent Jingū had it fabricated following a wondrous inspiration."[32] The plausibility of such a fabulous origin notwithstanding, the weapon enjoyed a long history in Japan. The earliest written reference to *ōyumi* records an unspecified number of the devices being

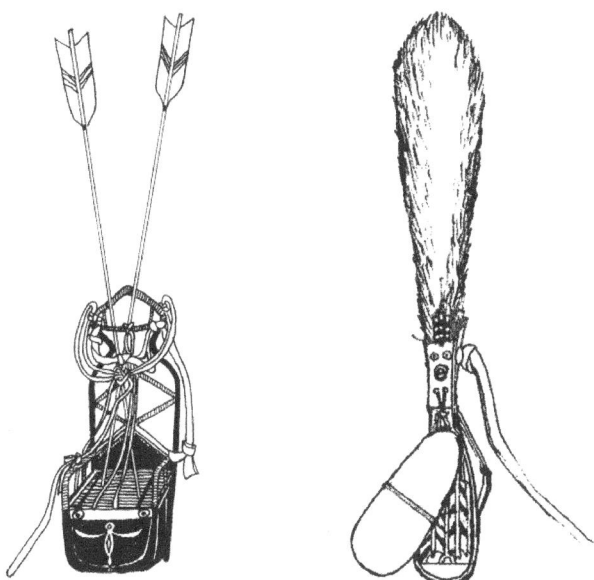

Figure 3.4 Ebira (left) and *utsubo* (right)

presented to the court in 618 by envoys from the Korean kingdom of Koryō, but it was clearly in general service by the late 600s, and deployed under the *ritsuryō* military system by both the provincial regiments and the various guard units in the capital through the early tenth century. There is some evidence that it continued to be used at least occasionally as late as the twelfth century.[33]

The form of the *ōyumi* is not actually known, as no contemporaneous drawings or detailed descriptions of the Japanese version survive, and no examples have been found in archeological sites. The same character (read *nu* in Mandarin) was used in China to name several types of crossbow, but the Japanese weapon does not seem to have been the same as any of these.[34] It appears, in fact, to have been some sort of platform-mounted, crossbow-style catapult, on the order of the Greek *oxybeles* or *lithobolos*, the Roman *ballista*, and similar devices, perhaps capable of launching volleys of arrows or stones in a single shooting. A chronicle entry from 835 notes the existence of a "new *ōyumi*" (*shindo*), invented by Shimagi Fubito Makoto, that was supposed to have been able to rotate freely, shoot in all directions, and be easier to discharge than the existing design. The text remarks that, when the weapon was demonstrated, the assembled courtiers could "hear the sound of it being set off, but could not see even the shadows of the arrows as they passed."[35]

One source described the *ōyumi* as "short on offense and long on defense," but it must, in any case, have been formidable. An 837 petition to the court from Mutsu province declared that, "when *ōyumi* are brought into the fighting, even tens of thousands of barbarians cannot bear up to the arrows of a single machine; the savages stand in awe of its power."[36]

Redoubtable as it may have been, the weapon also appears to have been a very complex machine to operate. This seems, in fact, to have proved its undoing. Between 814 and 901, the court received requests for ōyumi instructors from no fewer than seventeen provinces. All had the same complaint: regrettably, the weapons in their armories were going to waste because no one knew how to use them.[37] In his 914 memorial, Miyoshi Kiyoyuki went further, complaining of the incompetence of even the teachers:

> Ōyumi instructors today are permitted to buy their offices. Only the price is negotiated with no questions as to the candidate's ability. At the time of their appointments, those named do not know even of the existence of the weapon called the ōyumi, still less how to use the springs and bowstrings. Although the realm is now at peace and we fear nothing from any direction, we must each day be cautious, never forgetting danger. For, however unlikely, what if there should come invading neighbors who challenge us with death? The weapon has become empty nostalgia; who can use it [in our defense]?[38]

The hand-held crossbow, a mainstay of Chinese armies from the fourth century BCE onward, was also known and used in Japan, but neither the ritsuryō armies nor the bushi appear to have developed much interest in it, preferring to rely instead on the long bow. The ritsuryō military statutes provided for only two soldiers from each fifty-man company to be trained as ōyumi operators, and no later source indicates that this ratio was ever increased. Hand-held crossbows and crossbowmen are not mentioned in the statutes at all.[39] It is, of course, possible that the term "ōyumi" in the ritsuryō codes and other sources referred to hand-crossbows, as well as ballista-like ones, but this is improbable, for several reasons.

First, while source references to crossbows of any form are scant, two documents do clearly distinguish ōyumi from "hand-crossbows" (shudo). The first, a report concerning a bandit raid on the Dewa provincial office in 878, discloses that among the items destroyed or stolen were "29 ōyumi" and "100 shudo." The second, an inventory from the Kōzuke provincial office compiled around 1030, lists "25 shudo" (apparently its entire stock) as missing. The specific identification of "hand-crossbows" in these documents strongly suggests that the term "ōyumi" here and in earlier sources referred to something else. The reading "ōyumi" ("great bow") itself is also evocative of a large, rather than a hand-held, weapon.[40]

Second, hand-crossbows require very little skill to operate – in fact this is their principal advantage over the long bow. And yet more than two-thirds of the extant sources that mention ōyumi (indeed, virtually all such references from the ninth century) complain of the dearth of men capable of using the weapon or training others to use it.[41]

Third, archeologists have, to date, unearthed only one trigger mechanism for a hand-crossbow, despite more than a century of efforts.[42] That more have not been discovered, and that none had been discovered at all until the late 1990s, is strong testimony to the rarity of the weapon in Japan.

And finally, positing more than an incidental presence for hand-held crossbows in early military forces necessitates an explanation for their virtual disappearance during the early tenth century. William Wayne Farris, the only scholar to date to argue that hand-crossbows once played a significant role in Japanese warfare, attributes their decline to "high technological requirements" and other difficulties involved in manufacturing the weapons, which made them prohibitively expensive for private ownership.[43] This thesis, however, rests on an exaggeration of the relative difficulty involved in making the weapons.

Crossbows are ingenious devices, but they are not particularly complex. The simplest designs require only two moving parts in addition to the stock and the bow itself. The trigger mechanism recently discovered in Miyagi prefecture, and nearly identical to those used in Han China, had three moving parts.

Chinese craftsmen cast the parts for the trigger in bronze, and then carefully filed and worked them to the precise fit necessary to make the mechanism function smoothly. Japanese trigger mechanisms appear to have been similarly made. This process required an impressive level of workmanship and a considerable investment in labor, but it was no more difficult or expensive than the methods applied to produce swords, arrowheads, armor and other manufactured goods that continued to find a market long after enthusiasm for crossbows of any sort evaporated.[44]

The technological problem that would have most vexed Japanese artisans concerned not the trigger but the bow stave, an issue not of craftsmanship but of available materials, and one that would not have been affected one way or another by the withdrawal of direct government involvement in the manufacturing process. For the same limited choices of construction materials that determined the development of the distinctive Japanese long bow would have complicated the design and manufacture of hand-crossbows as well.

The bow staves of Chinese crossbows were composites of wood, bone, sinew and glue, constructed in much the same manner as the ordinary Chinese bow.[45] But, as we have observed, the Japanese lacked supplies of animal products, and fashioned their bows from wood and bamboo instead, which required that the weapons be long. Manufacturing crossbows with composite bow staves of wood and bamboo comparable in length to those of regular bows would have resulted in a weapon too unwieldy to be practical: not merely extraordinarily wide – and not readily usable by troops standing in close ranks – but also extraordinarily long, as it would have been necessary to lengthen the stock to permit a sufficient draw. Crossbows made with either short wood or wood and bamboo bow staves would have been considerably weaker, and more prone to breaking or delaminating, than the regular bows already in use.

The remaining alternative open to the Japanese would, of course, have been to import crossbows manufactured on the Asian continent. Although there is no direct evidence to support such a conjecture, this may in fact have been what the Japanese did. Written and archeological sources can confirm the existence of only 125 hand-crossbows, in Dewa and Kōzuke provinces. The only specimen uncovered to date, the trigger mechanism found in Miyagi, is made of bronze, and the Japanese are not believed to have ever produced bronze armaments on their own – all other bronze weapons discovered in Japan are thought to have been imports.[46]

In any event, in light of what the privately armed warriors of later centuries *were* able to purchase from artisans in the capital, it is hard to accept the notion that production difficulties could have precluded *bushi* ownership of hand-crossbows, had they wished to acquire them. European knights were, after all, able to obtain crossbows under conditions far less favorable to the manufacture of sophisticated, high technology machinery than those faced by Heian warriors. *Bushi* do, in fact, appear to have made sporadic use of *ōyumi* as late as the eleventh and twelfth centuries. And while the court prohibited private ownership of *ōyumi*, it was not entirely successful in enforcing this ban. A report from the Dazaifu in 866, for example, complains of a resident of Hizen province having traveled to Korea and brought back "the art of manufacturing military *ōyumi* devices."[47]

It would seem, therefore, that early medieval warriors lacked interest in using hand-crossbows, not potential sources for obtaining them. And if technological difficulties did not preclude continued use of the weapon, we are left with the thorny problem of explaining why the Japanese suddenly abandoned crossbows between the mid-ninth and the early tenth centuries. The simplest answer to this riddle, and the one indicated by the preponderance of available evidence, is that they did no such thing. That is, indifference toward hand-held crossbows predated the *bushi*, having been shared by the *ritsuryō* military apparatus as well. This apathy is easy to fathom when one considers the technological benefits and limitations of the weapon.

A crossbow is, fundamentally, a bow attached to a stock, so that it can be kept drawn and ready for shooting without continuing effort from the archer. This arrangement, coupled with a mechanical release, enables the use of a bow otherwise too strong for an archer to draw and hold. Crossbows also have an advantage in accuracy over regular bows, because a crossbowman can sight directly along the top of his arrows, using the fletchings like the sights of a modern firearm, and because the rigid stock holds the bowstring absolutely stable relative to the bow stave during aiming and release, eliminating the errors introduced by otherwise inevitable oscillation between the archer's hands. Crossbows enjoy the further advantage of being able to use shorter bolts, or quarrels, than are needed in the case of an ordinary bow, because the projectile rests on the stock and does not need to span the entire gap between the string and the bow stave. This not only makes crossbow bolts cheaper and easier to manufacture than regular arrows, it means that, in the words of a twelfth-century Chinese text, "if the crossbow bolts are picked up by the barbarians, they have no way of making use of them" – at least insofar as the enemy is not also equipped with crossbows![48]

But crossbows also have serious limitations. Most designs are difficult or impossible to cock and reload while walking, running or riding on horseback. This makes them better suited to defense, siegecraft and naval warfare than to offensive tactics on land. Crossbows are, moreover, much slower to reload and shoot than ordinary bows, resulting in a reduced volume of missiles that can be directed at a charging – or fleeing – enemy host while it is within effective range. Nor does the greater power of crossbows always translate into range longer than that obtainable by ordinary bows, because, while a regular bow can be angled upward, and shot to its maximum range with reasonable accuracy, a crossbow cannot be elevated very far without the stock obscuring the archer's aim. In practice, this renders the crossbow largely a line-of-sight weapon.

Advantageous use of crossbowmen therefore requires that they be carefully deployed and drilled. As an early eleventh-century Chinese author explained:

> ... the crossbow cannot be mixed up with hand-to-hand weapons, and it is beneficial when shot from high ground facing downward. It needs to be used so that the men within the formation are loading while the men in the front line of the formation are shooting ... each in their turn they draw their crossbows and come up; then as soon as they have shot bolts they return again into the formation.[49]

Maintaining this degree of order would have been difficult for *ritsuryō*-era Japanese armies, which were composed of militia units filled by conscripts who served only thirty or forty days a year on active duty. It would have been impossible for the privatized warriors of the Heian and Kamakura periods.[50]

Shock weapons

Although early medieval warriors were first and foremost "men of the way of bow and horse," swords occupy a special place in Japanese military history. The elegantly curved, two-handed *Nihontō* was born about the same time as the *bushi* order itself, and came, during the early modern era, to be identified as "the soul of the samurai." An estimated three million of these weapons survive today, and many times that number must have been produced since the Heian period. By contrast, only a tiny number of bows, arrows, and other weapons manufactured before the Tokugawa period survive today. Simple durability was no doubt one factor explaining this discrepancy, inasmuch as bows and arrows were made from materials easily destroyed by time. Construction was another, for it was usually easier and cheaper to replace a damaged bow than to repair one. Manner of usage was yet another factor: while a warrior was likely to possess only a very few swords, he would have owned dozens of arrows, and would essentially throw them away in combat. But neither durability nor construction, nor the weapon's actual importance on the battlefield, can fully explain the survival of so many swords. After all, other weapons – spears, glaives, firearms and the like – were also made of steel and retained by their original wielders throughout the battle, yet medieval specimens of these armaments are rare.[51]

In Japan, as elsewhere in the premodern world, the sword held a special symbolic identity. More adaptable and more subtle than axes or clubs, more easily carried on or off the battlefield than polearms, and yet less easily concealed – and thus seemingly more honorable – than daggers, swords achieved a singular status as heirlooms and symbols of power, war, military skill and warrior identity. In the words of Sir Richard Burton:

> The history of the sword is the history of humanity.... Uniformly and persistently personal, the Sword became no longer an abstraction but a Personage, endowed with human as well as superhuman qualities. He was a sentient being who spoke, and sang, and joyed, and grieved. Identified with his wearer he was an object of affection, and was pompously named as a well-beloved son and heir. To surrender the Sword was submission; to break the Sword was degradation. To kiss the Sword was... the highest form of oath and homage.... The Sword was the symbol of justice and of martyrdom, and accompanied the wearer to the tomb as well as to the feast and the fight.[52]

Swords, as emblems of power, appear in the earliest Japanese mythology, and were regularly presented by medieval warrior leaders as gifts or rewards to their followers. By the Muromachi period, expressions such as "clash of swords" (*tachi uchi*, *katana uchi*, or *uchi tachi*), or "wield a sword" (*tachi tsukamatsurare*) were recognized as generic appellations for combat, irrespective of the actual weapons employed.[53] Mystique and symbolic value notwithstanding, however, swords were never a key battlefield armament in medieval Japan. They were, rather, supplementary weapons, analogous to the sidearms worn by modern soldiers. While they were sometimes employed in combat, they were used far more often in street fights, robberies, assassinations and other (off-battlefield) civil disturbances.

Contemporary aficionados classify Japanese swords as *tachi*, *katana*, *wakizashi* and *tantō*, but this is an entirely modern typology, designed for evaluating swords and sword furniture as art objects rather than as weapons. The term "*tantō*," for example, written with a pair of characters that mean "short sword," is now a technical description applied to blades less than one *shaku* (approximately 30 cm) long, but during the Heian period the same compound was read "*nodachi*," and indicated any sort of smallish sword or long knife. Similarly, "*wakizashi*," which modern sword collectors use to designate intermediate-length blades (between one and two *shaku*), was originally an abbreviation of "*wakizashi no katana*" ("sword thrust at one's side"), and applied to companion swords of any length. Interpreting references to any of these terms in early medieval sources in the context of the modern classification system, therefore, invites serious problems of anachronism.[54]

In early medieval usage, single-edged long swords were most commonly called "*tachi*," written with any of several characters or compounds, while the term "*katana*" referred to what was later called a *tantō* or *wakizashi* – that is, a short blade worn thrust through one's belt.[*] Companion swords of this sort were also known as "*sayamaki*" ("wound case"), because of the wrapped design of their scabbards, or "*koshi-gatana*" ("hip sword"), because of the way they were carried.[55]

The *tachi* was a warrior's principal sidearm, employed when he ran out of arrows or was otherwise unable to bring his bow into play. *Katana* were used for grappling and other very close combat, as well as for removing the heads of slain opponents, and for committing suicide. Kondō Yoshikazu notes that these differing functions are clearly reflected in the vocabulary associated with the two types of swords: with very few exceptions, in literary and more prosaic sources alike, warriors are depicted using *tachi* to "cut" (*kaku* or *kiru*) or "strike" (*utsu*) and the *katana* to "stab" (*sasu*) or "thrust" (*tsuku*).[56]

Sometime around the turn of the twelfth century, the Japanese also began to use a different sort of sword, called an *uchi-gatana* or *tsuba-gatana*. As these names suggest, the new weapon was furnished with a hand guard (*tsuba*) like a *tachi*, and used primarily for cutting rather than stabbing (as was a *tachi*), but it was carried like the theretofore short *katana*, thrust through the belt, with the cutting edge upward (rather than slung with the cutting edge downward, as a *tachi* was). It was also longer than earlier *katana*, but a few centimeters shorter than most *tachi*.[57]

Uchi-gatana probably originated as poor men's *tachi*. The early sources show them used by messengers, monks, low-ranked personnel of various police agencies, children, and the like – people who, because of circumstances, social status or economic resources, were unable to possess *tachi*. But, from about the end of the fourteenth century, *uchi-gatana* began to supplant *tachi* as the sword of preference carried by warriors both on and off the battlefield.[†] This change

---

[*] A tenth-century lexicon distinguishes between single-edged and double-edged blades, assigning the latter meaning to either of two characters commonly read as "*tsurugi*" (劍 or 劔; also read as "*ken*," as in the compound, "*kendō*"), but does not specify the contemporary reading. The former, written with the character 刀, read as "*katana*" in medieval and later lexicons, is assigned no reading when used alone, but glossed as "*tachi*" when paired with the character for "big" (大刀) and as "*katana*" when paired with the character for "small" (小刀). *Wamyō ruijūshō*, p. 254.

[†] A lack of clear documentary evidence, and the fact that the difference between *uchi-gatana* and *tachi* was really just a matter of how the sword was mounted and carried – the same blade can be used as either a *tachi* or an *uchi-gatana* – makes it difficult to be precise about when the transformation from *tachi* to *uchi-gatana* began. But the first blades that were manufactured specifically to be long *katana* (as revealed by the location of the maker's signature on the tang: on the left side of the hilt in the case of the *katana* and on the right in the case of the *tachi*, so that it would face outward when the blade was worn) date back to the Ōei (1394–1427) era. The earliest pictorial evidence of long swords carried blade upward in the wearer's belt appears to be a scene in the *Ban dainagon ekotoba* (p. 90).

appears to have been a response to a number of factors that centered on the greater convenience of a slightly shorter weapon carried in one's belt, rather than slung below it: wearing a sword in this manner was more stable, and therefore more convenient when venturing about in civilian garb, and it kept the sidearm better out of one's way when using a polearm in battle. Moreover, the adoption of new, closer-fitting forms of armor (discussed later in this chapter) and the increased frequency with which *bushi* fought on foot, rather than on horseback, made it easier to draw swords carried in the new fashion.*

The history of the curved *tachi* favored by early medieval warriors is the subject of lively debate and speculation but little consensus, spurred on by evidence that is not only incomplete but equivocating. Medieval *tachi* combine elements from several earlier types of sword, but the sequential relationship – if any – between these ancestral blades is far from clear. And efforts to put together a complete picture of sword evolution are further complicated by the dearth of surviving examples of swords from the early and middle Heian period.

Kofun-era "*tachi*" were straight-bladed, and about 70 to 80 cm in length. Some were forged with the hilt and the cutting blade as a single piece (*tomotetsu-zukuri*), and featured any of several sorts of ring-shaped pommels (*watō tachi*), while others were made with tangs that fit into separate hilts (*kukishiki-zukuri*) that ended in round (*entō*), square (*hōtō*), bulb-shaped (*kabuuchi*) or jade-shaped (*keitō*) pommels. By the Nara period, the one-piece, ring-pommeled blades had disappeared, and the elaborate *entō*, *kabuuchi* and *keitō* hilts had been supplanted by simpler designs. Straight swords of this type – called *tachi* in contemporaneous sources, but dubbed "*chokutō*" by modern scholars – continued to be manufactured until at least the late tenth century.[58]

The first curved Japanese sword was the *warabite katana*, so-named by archeologists for the shape of its hilt, which resembles a young bracken (*warabi*). *Warabite katana* hilts, forged in a single piece with the blade, are curved and offset to the outside, away from the cutting edge of the blade.[59] Some late examples of *warabite katana*, called *kenuki-gata* or *kenuki-dōshi warabite katana*, feature rectangular openings in the hilts. The reason for this opening is unknown: some scholars believe its purpose to have been shock absorption, while others contend that it served simply to reduce the overall weight of the weapon. In any case a similar open-hilted design is also the key feature of a slightly longer and heavier sword (the *kenuki-gata katana*) found in ninth-century tombs in the far northeast, and of a much longer, slimmer weapon, the *kenuki-gata tachi*, which

---

* Kondō Yoshikazu, *Chūsei-teki bugu*, 59–62, 70–73; Suzuki Masaya, *Katana to kubi-tori*, 86–105. During the medieval period, quite a number of older *tachi* were shortened for use as *uchi-gatana*, a process known as "*suriage*." Because this shortening was generally done from the tang end, the signature on the blade was often chopped off in the process, resulting in what are called "*ōsuriage mumeitō*." The large percentage of medieval swords that are of this category is probably the result of the transition from *tachi* to *uchi-gatana*.

THE TOOLS OF WAR

appeared around the mid-tenth century and became the standard sidearm of the officers commanding the various court guard units. *Kenuki-gata tachi*, also called *eifu tachi*, were named for the peculiar bone-shaped opening in their hilts, which resembled a device used by court ladies for plucking eyebrows and other unwanted body hair.*

The medieval *tachi* is distinguished by two principal features: a blade (*tōshin*) that curves away from its cutting edge, and a separate hilt (*tsuka*) composed of wood wrapped in leather and silk or bark, fitted over a tang extending from the blade. In length and shape, it closely resembles the *kenuki-gata tachi*, while the hilt of the latter looks much like that of the *kenuki-gata katana*. And the *kenuki-gata katana* is similar in overall length and shape to the *kenuki-dōshi warabite katana*, differing only in its squared-off, rather than bracken-shaped, hilt (see Figure 3.5).

Surmising from the foregoing, some historians have postulated that the *warabite katana* evolved into the *kenuki-gata katana*, which then evolved into the *kenuki-gata tachi*. Others have argued that the *kenuki-gata tachi* was the direct ancestor of the medieval *tachi*. Combining the two theories leads, then, to the conclusion that the curved *tachi* favored by the early medieval *bushi* evolved in

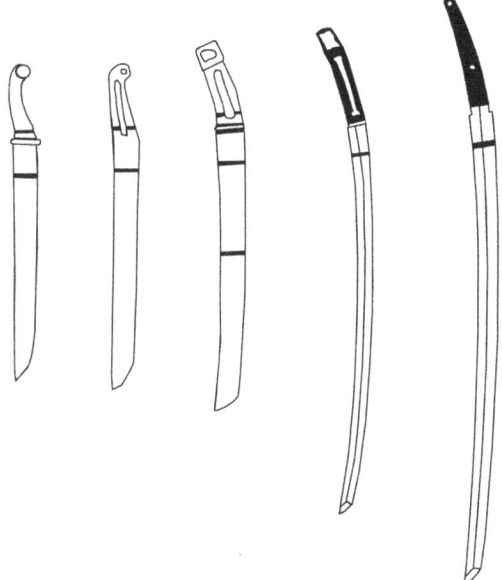

Figure 3.5 (left to right) *Warabite katana, kenuki-gata warabite katana, kenuki-gata katana, kenuki-gata tachi* and *tachi*

---

* Among the names used to distinguish these various sword types, only "*kenuki-gata tachi*" was actually used historically. "*Kenuki-gata warabite katana*," "*kenuki-dōshi warabite katana*" and "*kenuki-gata katana*" were all coined by modern scholars.

stages from the *warabite katana*. But there are difficulties and complications with all three conclusions.

First, the curve (*sori*) of the *warabite katana* was almost entirely in the hilt; the blade was virtually straight. The blade of the *kenuki-gata katana* was similarly straight, but set at a more pronounced angle to the hilt. But even the oldest *kenuki-gata tachi* discovered to date, found in Nagano prefecture, has curvature in the blade as well as the hilt. It is also considerably longer and slimmer than the *kenuki-gata katana*.

Second, the *kenuki-gata tachi* and the curved *tachi* both appeared at about the same time, during the late 900s. It seems more likely, therefore, that the two weapons evolved simultaneously, rather than one from the other.

And third, while the medieval *tachi* and the *kenuki-gata tachi* look similar in profile, they are fundamentally different in construction. The latter is made with the hilt and blade all of one piece, while the former utilizes a hilt-and-tang design. The blades are also different when viewed in cross-section: all but a few very late *kenuki-gata tachi* have a simple, triangular shape (*hirazukuri*), while both the straight *tachi* of the Nara and early Heian periods and the curved ones of the medieval era present five-faceted (*kiriha-zukuri*) or six-faceted (*shinogi-zukuri*) profiles (see Figure 3.6).

Except for the curve, then, medieval *tachi* are much more like Nara and early Heian *chokutō* than *kenuki-gata tachi*. It seems likely, therefore, that these straight swords, not the *kenuki-gata tachi*, were the direct ancestors of the medieval *tachi*, while the *kenuki-gata tachi* developed (in a parallel line of evolution) from the ring-pommeled *tachi* of the Kofun period and/or from the *warabite katana*.[60]

Whatever its sequence of evolution might have been, the curved blade undoubtedly enhanced the sword's cutting ability. A blade curved backward, away from its cutting edge, promotes a smooth, slicing cut and distributes impact more evenly along the whole of the weapon than a straight blade, reducing the

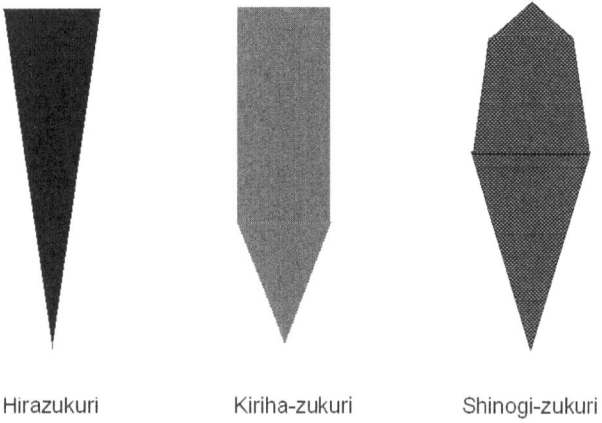

Hirazukuri   Kiriha-zukuri   Shinogi-zukuri

Figure 3.6 Sword shapes in cross-section

shock transmitted back to the wielder. Offsetting the hilt away from the blade also augments wrist movement and power when using the sword one-handed.

These considerations, combined with the timing of the curved *tachi*'s appearance – coinciding with the emergence of the *bushi*, who were mounted warriors – have led many scholars to link the shape of the early medieval *tachi* to the demands of cavalry warfare. The straight-bladed *tachi* of the Nara and early Heian periods, goes this argument, were developed for infantry usage and intended primarily as thrusting weapons. Swordplay from horseback, however, calls for slashing and cutting, rather than stabbing. Thus the curved *tachi* was introduced in response to a new style of fighting favored by a new order of warriors.[61]

But the hypothesis that the medieval *tachi* was designed as a cavalryman's weapon ignores more evidence than it embraces. To begin with, it is premised on an inflated dichotomy between the style of warfare favored by the *bushi* of the late tenth and eleventh centuries and those of their forebears. There was no sudden change in the importance of mounted warriors in the decades immediately preceding the adoption of the curved sword. Cavalry did not suddenly become fashionable during the mid-tenth century; court military policy had been increasing its tactical focus on mounted warriors – and trimming back the infantry component of its armed forces – since the 700s. By the mid-ninth century this process was already near complete: fighting men on horseback were the predominant force on Japanese battlefields. Thus the straight (*chokutō*) *tachi* of the Nara and early Heian periods must have been as much cavalrymen's weapons as were the curved *tachi* of the later Heian and Kamakura periods.

Reasoning from technological evidence leads to the same conclusion. Curved blades are inherently stronger and easier to cut with than straight ones. They are also easier to draw, and can therefore be made slightly longer. But these advantages are of as much value to swordsmen on foot as to mounted warriors. The construction of the *chokutō*, moreover, testifies that it, too, was meant to be used as much for hacking and slashing as for stabbing.

The ideal design for a thrusting blade is straight, with both edges sharpened – the form of ancient and medieval Japanese spear blades. But Nara and Heian *chokutō tachi* were single-edged, a design better suited to cutting and chopping than to thrusting. The five-faceted cross-sectional shape of the *chokutō* also marks it as a cutting weapon. The simplest shape for a single-edged sword blade is triangular, tapering evenly from the back to the cutting edge. This design (*hirazukuri*) is an excellent silhouette for a stabbing blade – and was in fact the form applied to early medieval *katana* – but it puts a great deal of stress on the edge if the weapon is used to cut or chop. Japanese swordsmiths soon found, however, that the strength of the blade could be increased without losing sharpness if it was forged such that the back four-fifths was shaped like a rectangle, with only the cutting edge shaped like a triangle (*kiriha-zukuri*). This was the design utilized in most Nara- and Heian-period *chokutō* and in the earliest curved *tachi*. Still later it was discovered that the addition of ridges to the side and back, resulting in a six-sided cross-sectional silhouette (*shinogi-zukuri*), produced a lighter, more wieldy blade without sacrifice of strength or sharpness.[62]

Even more to the point, the written and pictorial record shows that, while both the *chokutō* and the curved *tachi* may indeed have been cavalrymen's weapons, neither were *cavalry* weapons: there is not a single example, in any document, text or drawing produced before the thirteenth century, that depicts warriors wielding swords from horseback.[63] Throughout the Heian and Kamakura periods, *bushi* employed swords in street fights, and when unhorsed or otherwise forced to fight on foot, but seldom while mounted – an argument to which I will return in the next chapter.

Clearly, then, cavalry warfare could not have been the impetus behind the transition from straight to curved swords during the middle Heian period. The curved blade may, in fact, originally have been simply a fortuitous by-product of the solution to a different engineering problem.

A key difficulty in forging an efficient sword stems from the mutually exclusive nature of hardness and resiliency in steel. A proper sword requires a blade that is hard enough to take and hold a sharp cutting edge, yet resilient enough not to be easily broken by impact. These properties are a function of the interaction of the iron and the carbon that make up the steel, as the metal is heated, worked and cooled.[64]

In Europe, the most common solution to this dilemma was to produce tempered blades, first made hard and brittle, and then reheated to allow some of the hardness to dissipate, resulting in a compromise steel that was tough, but still hard enough to hold a reasonable edge. Middle Eastern swordsmiths forged high-carbon steel together with almost pure iron to form a mixture of hard and soft metals. Japanese craftsmen sometimes used a similar method, but they employed other solutions as well.

We actually know surprisingly little about the techniques used for forging swords during the Heian and early Kamakura periods, for the simple reason that very few blades from this era survive, and those that do are too precious to be dissected for study. Nonetheless, during the Kamakura era, five distinct schools of sword-making techniques emerged, which came, by the early modern period, to be called the "Five Traditions" (*gokaden*). Presumably each of these had its own forging technique, although no one really knows for sure. In any case, scholars have identified seven distinct forging methods, which resulted in five basic constructions of blade (see Figure 3.7).

The simplest was *maru kitae*, in which slats of high- and low-carbon steel were stacked together and hammered out to produce a blade of more-or-less uniform hardness throughout. A slightly more sophisticated approach was *wariha kitae*, in which a cutting edge made from a thin strip of hardened, high-carbon steel was welded into a lower-carbon steel back. The third and fourth methods were *makuri kitae* and *kōbuse kitae*, which produced cores of low-carbon steel surrounded on three sides by layers of higher-carbon steel. Two other techniques, *honsammai kitae* and *oriawase kitae*, resulted in a similar blade, albeit with the cutting edge

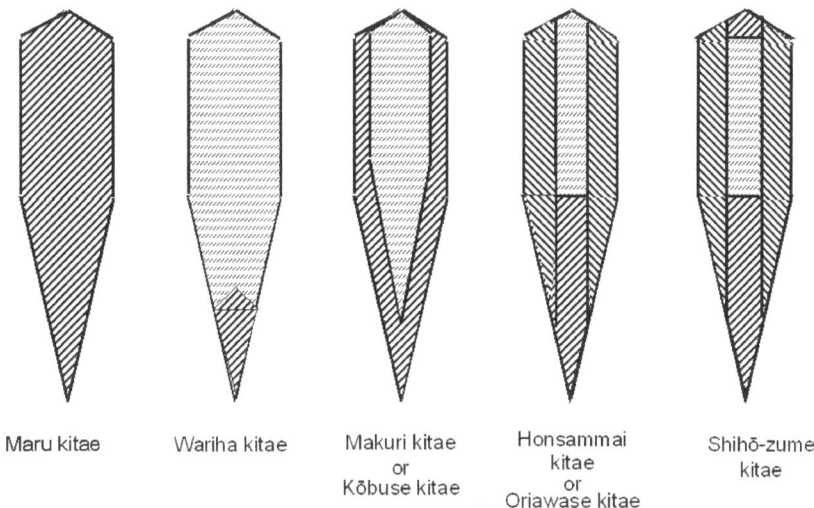

Figure 3.7 Methods of forging Japanese swords

and sides made from distinct pieces. And the seventh method, *shihō-zume kitae*, added a fourth slat of high-carbon steel to the back of the blade, completely surrounding the softer core.

When a blade forged using any of these methods is heated, the thinner edge reaches a higher temperature, and expands slightly further, than the back. If the heating process is then followed by a rapid quenching in cool water, the edge of the blade cools quickly, becoming much harder, and retaining most of the expansion brought about by the heating. But the back, both because of its thickness and because of special techniques developed by trial and error, cools much more slowly, preventing it from hardening as much, and allowing it to contract back to its original size, thereby causing the blade to bend into a curve.

In any event, while swords were primarily a back-up weapon on early medieval battlefields, the Japanese did deploy other shock weapons (see Figure 3.8). The oldest of these was the *hoko*, a straight spear fashioned from a round, wooden shaft fitted into a socketed metal head. *Hoko* were used from Yayoi times until at least the end of the Heian period, becoming longer and heavier in both shaft and blade over time. Yayoi *hoko* ran about 2 to 3 meters in overall length, while those that survive in the collection of the Shōsōin in Nara feature heads averaging around 36 cm, mounted onto 4-meter hafts. Most of the latter have flat, double-edged blades, but a few sport halberd-like secondary blades protruding at a right angle from the base of the main blade, and curving back toward the haft.[65]

Both the design of the blade and the descriptions in written sources of warriors using them indicate that the *hoko* was principally a one-directional stabbing weapon. This sort of polearm is most suitable for use by troops in close,

THE TOOLS OF WAR

Figure 3.8 Naginata and kumade (Mōko shūrai ekotoba)

organized ranks, rendering the *hoko* a fine weapon for the *ritsuryō* armies but less than ideal for the early *bushi*, who therefore gradually abandoned it for a new form of polearm, called the *naginata*.[66]

Often described in English sources as "halberds," *naginata* were in fact more like glaives, featuring a long (up to 85–100 cm) curved blade mounted to an oval haft of about 120 to about 150 cm in length, by means of a lengthy tang inserted into a slot in the haft, and held in place by pegs. Unlike the unidirectional *hoko*, a *naginata* can be used to sweep, cut or strike, as well as to thrust, and can even be twirled like a baton to keep opponents at bay! It is, in other words, a personal weapon, designed to be used by a warrior fighting largely as an individual, and to maximize his ability to deal with multiple opponents at once. On the other hand, a *naginata* is a poor weapon for use by troops fighting in rank or in large numbers on a crowded battlefield. Accordingly, during the fifteenth and sixteenth centuries, it was in turn displaced by a new form of straight, thrusting spear called the *yari*.[67]

Exactly when *naginata* first appeared is difficult to ascertain. There are almost no extant examples of *naginata* blades that predate the mid-Kamakura period, and none that can be reliably dated to Heian times. The earliest clear reference to a *naginata* in the written record is a chronicle entry from 1146, which describes a warrior being startled by thunder and reaching for a weapon "commonly called a *naginata*." A document dated three months later reports the investigation of a raid on an estate in Kawachi province, in which the perpetrators carried off "20 head of good oxen, 3,000 sheaves of cut rice, 20 *haramaki* armors, 100 swords [*tachi*], and 10,000 [*sic*] *naginata*." Both sources write the word "*naginata*" phonetically, leaving little doubt that the weapon must have been around by this time. On the other hand, as Kondō Yoshikazu points out, the phrase, "commonly called" (*zoku ni gō su*) in the first entry suggests that the term "*naginata*" was not yet widely known, supporting the conclusion that the weapon was relatively new in the late twelfth century.[68]

Nevertheless, there are earlier, albeit somewhat more ambiguous, references to *naginata* in the sources. A diary entry from 1040, for example, mentions what may be a *naginata* carried by a warrior in the capital. In this case, "*naginata*" is written with characters that mean "long sword" (長刀), which was the standard orthography until the fifteenth century. Similarly, a diary entry from 1097 speaks of what may be a *naginata*, using a similar orthography (長劔); a document from 1124 depicts a police official "drawing a naginata"; and a diary entry from 1110 describes foot soldiers parading through the capital bearing "*uchimono*," an alternative term for *naginata* in later sources. But it is difficult to be sure whether any of these are indeed early references to *naginata* or simply literal allusions to very long swords. The phrase "drawing a *naginata*" in the 1124 document raises additional questions in this regard, inasmuch as the verb used in later medieval sources to describe unsheathing a *naginata* is "remove" (*hazusu*), rather than "draw" (*nuku*), which is normally associated with swords. Similar ambiguities arise with respect to appearances of "*hoko*" in later Heian- and early Kamakura-period sources. Some clearly distinguish *hoko* from *naginata*, while others use the term "*hoko*" metaphorically, as in the case of the 1201 chronicle entry that tells of warriors from Echigo, Sanuki and Shinano provinces "racing to assemble and align their *hoko*." But later medieval sources sometimes confused *naginata* with *hoko*, giving rise to the possibility that some of the "*hoko*" appearing in eleventh- and twelfth-century texts may actually have been *naginata*.[69]

"*Yari*," written phonetically, appears for the first time in a report on battlefield casualties filed in 1334, and there are scattered references to the weapon in fourteenth-century battle records, but the new spear did not really catch on until the late 1400s.[70] It differed from the earlier *hoko* both in the way the blade was attached to the haft, and in the construction of the haft itself. *Hoko* blades form sockets into which the hafts are inserted, while *yari* blades have tangs that are inserted into slots in the hafts. This design, which *yari* share with medieval swords, *naginata* and arrowheads (see Figure 3.9), reflects mainly the period in which *yari* were invented. But the most important difference between the two types of spear was a matter of function and usage, reflected in the architecture of the haft. The shafts of *yari* were round, like those of *hoko* (and unlike the oval hafts of the *naginata*), but *hoko* hafts were also wrapped with bands of thread or metal. This reinforced the shaft, which was often made of laminates of wood and bamboo, but its principal function was to prevent the user's hands from slipping about. That is, *hoko* were designed for thrusting with both hands kept pretty much in place, in a manner similar to the way modern riflemen stab with bayonets. *Yari*, by contrast, have smooth shafts, to facilitate sliding the weapon through one hand, like a pool cue, which was the standard thrusting technique for this type of spear.[71]

In addition to *hoko*, *naginata* and *yari*, one finds references in pictorial and literary sources from the early medieval period to a handful of other polearms.

THE TOOLS OF WAR

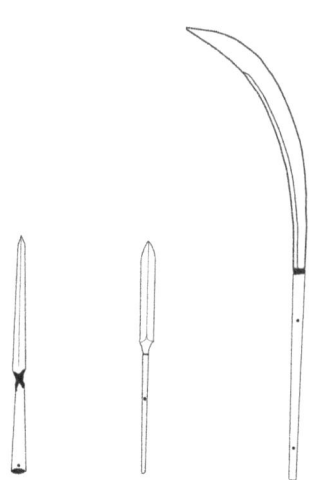

Figure 3.9 (left to right) *Hoko*, *yari* and *naginata* blades

The most interesting of these is the *kumade* (literally, "bear paw"), a three- or four-clawed rake attached to a long pole, used to pull on things or drag an opponent to the ground (see Figure 3.8). In most examples depicted in the sources, there is a chain attached to the claw and wound around the haft, presumably so that, if the shaft were to be cut or broken, the wielder could still pull on the chain, or use the claw as a swinging missile. *Kumade* were probably intended primarily for sieges and naval battles, but some picture scrolls even depict the weapon being used from horseback![72]

Medieval literary accounts of battles also contain scattered references to "hand spears" (*teboko*) and "small glaives" (*konaginata*). Kondō Yoshikazu's exhaustive analysis of appearances of both terms, and of the verbs associated with them, demonstrates that "*teboko*" and "*konaginata*" were used virtually interchangeably in medieval sources, indicating that the two words almost certainly referred to the same weapon. Although the exact nature of this weapon – or weapons – is hard to determine, inasmuch as there are no extant examples of blades identified as *teboko* or *konaginata*, it appears to have been about a meter to a meter and a half in overall length, with a short, straight blade.[73]

From the late Kamakura period, warriors also began to use extremely long swords, called *nodachi* or *ōdachi*, which feature prominently in fourteenth-century literary and pictorial sources. Because such weapons, with their short hilts relative to their blade lengths, were difficult to handle, it became common practice to wrap the lower part of the blade with thin cord, effectively extending the grip. Later, the hilt itself was simply made longer, to produce yet another polearm, the *nagamaki*, which consisted of a sword-like blade about a meter in length, mounted in an equally long hilt that was usually wrapped in leather or silk cord, like the hilt of an ordinary *tachi* or *uchi-gatana*.[74]

88

THE TOOLS OF WAR

Protective weapons

The most basic, and quite probably the oldest, form of protective armament is the shield. Descriptions in Chinese dynastic records indicate shields in use in Japan at least as far back as the third century CE, and a plethora of evidence – including pictures, *haniwa* figurines, and surviving examples unearthed from tumuli – informs us about shields of the fourth, fifth and sixth centuries. The latter assumed various shapes, but most were essentially rectangular, 100 to 150 cm in length, and approximately 50 cm wide. Most appear to have been made from multiple layers of leather covered in lacquer, although at least two examples of iron shields, said to date from this period, survive in the collection of the Ishinogami grand shrine in Nara.[75]

The shields deployed by *ritsuryō*-era armies and by early medieval *bushi* resembled the mantlets sometimes used by medieval European archers and crossbowmen: self-standing wooden barriers approximately eye-level in height and about the width of a man's shoulders (see Figure 3.10). They were made to stand by means of a pole, or foot, attached to the back by hinges that allowed it to be folded against the shield for transport or storage. The best were constructed from a single board, but most were made from two, three, or even four planks, about 3 cm thick. Shields were usually not lacquered on either front or back, although by the late Kamakura period it was common to decorate them with family crests (*mon*).[76]

Figure 3.10 Japanese shields (*Taiheiki emaki*)

89

Typically, shields of this sort were lined up, sometimes overlapping like roof tiles, to form a portable wall that protected archers on foot. They were also placed atop the walls of fortifications and hung from the sides of boats. On occasion, they served as substitutes for other tools, such as benches or ladders.[77]

Japanese warriors never, on the other hand, appear to have developed much interest in hand-held shields, probably because of the incompatibility of this sort of armament with mounted archery. There are, in fact, only two appearances of hand-held shields in early medieval sources, both in thirteenth-century picture scrolls. One depicts a lightly armored foot soldier wielding a sword in his right hand and a rectangular wooden shield about 60 cm by 40 cm in his left, as he participates in an attack on a warrior's home. The other shows a warrior on horseback carrying what appears to be an ordinary, free-standing shield.[78]

In lieu of hand-held shields, *bushi* adopted heavy body armor specifically devised for fighting with bow and arrow from horseback. There were five principal styles of armor to be seen on early medieval battlefields (*ōyoroi*, *haramaki*, *haramaki-yoroi*, *dōmaru* and *hara-ate*), but all five were constructed from the same fundamental components.

The monadic constituents of Japanese armors were tiny plates, or lamellae, called *sane*. Most were trapezoidal in shape, with curved, diagonal top edges and flat bottoms (see Figure 3.11). The size of the lamellae decreased over time; during the Heian–Kamakura age, they were usually about 7 or 8 by 3 or 4 cm. Each was perforated with thirteen or nineteen holes, arranged in two or three columns. Individual lamellae were stacked with each overlapping the one to its right, and laced together with leather or braided silk cords through the bottom three holes to form plates, called *saneita*. The *saneita* were lacquered, to protect them from moisture, and then laced together in rows that overlapped downward, like shingles on an upside-down roof. The laces connected the third row of holes in the upper plate to the first two rows of holes in the plate below, so that the lower plates hung down outside the upper ones, on cords roughly half the length of the *saneita* themselves. This arrangement made the resulting armor collapsible, allowing the upper part to fold into the lower part like a telescope, for transport and storage.[79]

Sane could be made from either iron or rawhide. Iron, of course, offered better protection, but was also heavier, less comfortable, and more expensive. Accordingly, while the earliest Japanese lamellar armors were made exclusively from iron, leather became the dominant material by the early ninth century.[80] Most medieval armors utilized a mixture of iron and leather lamellae, particularly in the *saneita* that covered the most critical parts of the wearer's body. In some armors, these sections were made entirely from iron lamellae, but more commonly iron and leather *sane* were alternated, in a pattern known as *ichimai maze*. The preferred type of leather was cowhide, and the preferred part of the hide was the animal's back, as this was the thickest. But because it was uneconomical to waste the rest of the hide, craftsmen also made *sane* from the belly leather, which was thinner and softer. This meant that the lamellae in most armors were of uneven

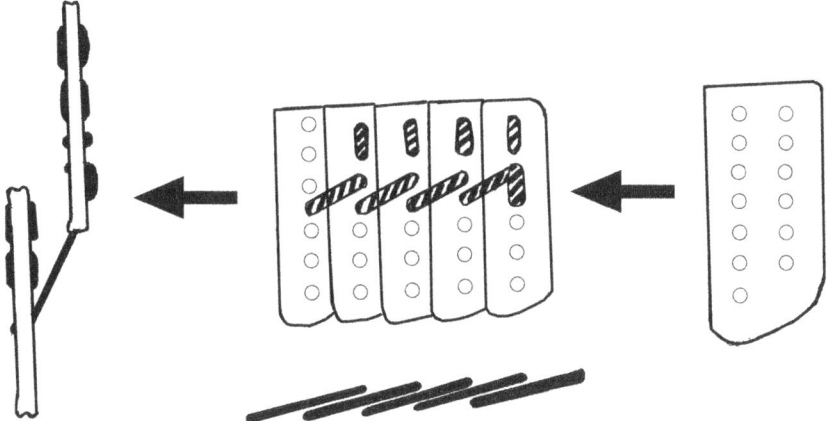

Figure 3.11 The components of Japanese armors

quality, necessitating the development of various techniques for testing them for strength.[81]

Lamellar armor, widely used across Asia and the Middle East, is more flexible, easier to move in, easier to store and transport, and requires less customization for fit than plate armor; and it offers better protection than chain mail. Its principal defensive advantage over other types of armor is its capacity to absorb shock, by diffusing the energy of blows landing against it through the layers formed by the overlapping scales and lacings.[82]

Contemporaneous European mail, by contrast, was readily pierced by arrows and lances, and, once pierced, the fractured links could become shrapnel that would exacerbate or infect the wound. Chain mail offered even less real protection against bladed weapons, which did not actually need to penetrate the armor to be deadly: hemorrhaging or brain damage due to blunt trauma could kill just as readily as lacerations or incisions.[83]

Japanese armor had the further advantage of ease of repair, which could be undertaken by warriors in the field. Individual lamellae could even be recycled into new armors, a process called *shigaeshi*.

The premier armor of the early medieval era, the *ōyoroi* ("great armor"), appeared sometime between the mid-tenth and the early eleventh centuries.[84] Its boxy cuirass wrapped around the left, front and back of the wearer's chest, while a separate piece, called the *waidate*, protected his right side (see Figure 3.12). An Edo-period legend speculated that the *waidate* was originally fused to the rest of the cuirass, and that it was removed to accommodate the Empress-Regent Jingū, who became pregnant during one of her campaigns in Korea, and could not fit into her armor. But inasmuch as Jingū lived and died half a millennium before *ōyoroi* was devised, it seems more likely that the open right side was a vestige of the *ryōtō-shiki keikō* out of which the *ōyoroi* is thought to have been developed.

THE TOOLS OF WAR

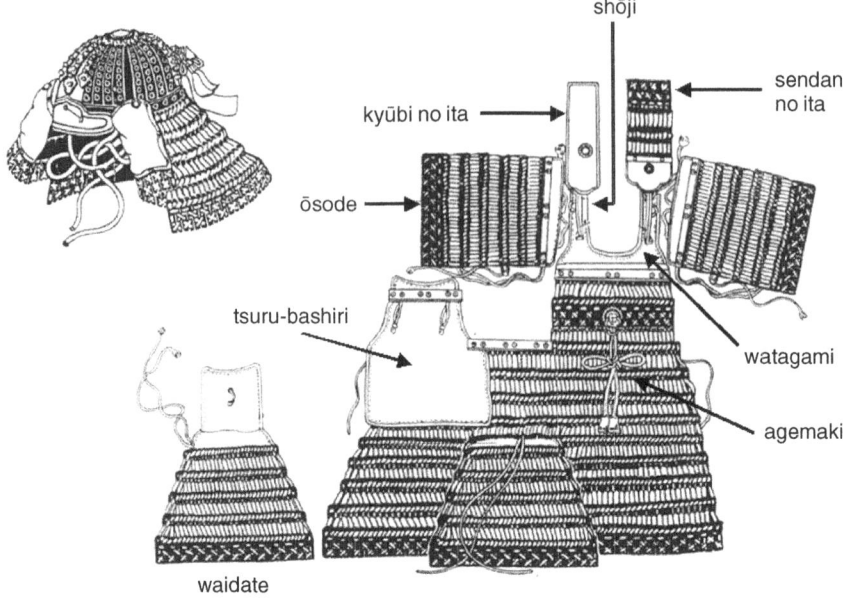

Figure 3.12 Construction of ōyoroi (Kondō Yoshikazu, *Chūsei-teki bugu*)

Ryōtō-shiki keikō (also called *ryōtō-kei keikō*), the style of armor adopted by the capital guard units of the late *ritsuryō* military, was a four-piece armor consisting of wide front and back panels of lamellae that hung from the shoulders like sandwich-board signs, worn over separate, narrower panels that protected the sides of the soldier's torso. *Ōyoroi* improved on this design by joining three of the panels to eliminate the openings on the side that faced the enemy when shooting a bow, but retained the one on the right, perhaps for ease of donning and doffing the armor, in order to permit minor adjustments in the girth of the cuirass, or to make the armor easier to fold and transport.

In any event, unlike the rest of the cuirass, the *waidate* was a solid plate, not a lamellar one. Experts disagree on the reasons for this, but it was probably to prevent the side piece from bunching up and creating gaps when pinched by the other parts of the armor.

The front of the cuirass was often covered with a facing of smooth deerskin – or sometimes silk – called a *tsuru-bashiri*, which kept the lamellae on the upper part of the chest from snagging the bowstring or the sleeves of the wearer's undergarment when he shot. Heavily padded leather shoulder straps (*watagami*) extended from the back of the cuirass, and were connected by cords to another solid leather plate at the top of the chest piece. A four-piece lamellar skirt hung below the *waidate* and cuirass, to protect the wearer's hips, abdomen and thighs.[85]

In some earlier Japanese lamellar armors, the parts protecting the wearer's shoulders, neck and torso were made all of one piece.[86] But this design restricted shoulder and arm movement, hindering easy use of the bow and arrow. To maximize freedom of motion for archers, the cuirass of the *ōyoroi* was cut away around the shoulders and armpits, and the resulting gaps were covered by free-hanging accessory pieces (collectively called *kogusoku*).

Large, flat, rectangular plates of lamellae, called *ōsode*, which were easily the most recognizable feature of early medieval armors, afforded protection for the shoulders and upper arms. About 30 cm square, *ōsode* served mounted archers (who needed both hands to ride and shoot) as substitutes for hand shields. They were fastened to the body of the armor by cords such that they fell back and out of the archer's way when he drew his bow, but could be slung forward to cover most of his face and upper body between shots. Most warriors wore *ōsode* on both sides, but those of low status or financial means sometimes wore only one – on the left, where they were most likely to be struck when facing an enemy.

The main weight of each *ōsode* was borne by a single cord connecting the middle of the plate to the top of the shoulder straps. To prevent the plates from twisting around, additional cords attached on either side connected to the front of the straps, and to a large silk bow-knot (*agemaki*) hung from a copper ring on the back of the cuirass. Yet another cord connected the back edges of the plates to this same knot, to keep the *ōsode* from shifting too far forward. The underside of the right plate featured an extra piece of leather intended to avoid pinching and catching arrows carried in the *ebira* (on the warrior's hip) between the lamellae.[87]

The tops of the shoulder straps were fitted with small, ridge-like plates, called *shōji*, to guard the wearer's neck against attacks from the side, and to stop the *ōsode* from riding up too high. To cover the gaps left at the shoulders when the *ōsode* fell back during the draw, two additional plates were hung on the front of the armor. The plate on the left, the *kyūbi no ita*, was smaller and made from a solid piece. But the plate for the right, the *sendan no ita*, was wider – to protect the larger gap that opened on that side as the bow was drawn – and made of lamellae, so that it would flex and stay close to the chest, rather than jutting out to snag the bowstring when the wearer's chest puffed forward during his draw.[88] To protect his left arm (which faced the enemy when shooting), and to keep the bowstring from snagging on the sleeves of the warrior's under-robe, he wore a close-fitting, armored over-sleeve (*kote*).

Ōyoroi were initially worn without leg armor, but plated shin guards (*suneate*) were introduced during the late twelfth century, and lower-cut fur shoes replaced the calf-high bearskin boots thitherto favored by mounted warriors. By the late Nambokuchō era, the *suneate* had grown to cover the warrior's knees, and the shoes had been discarded in favor of straw sandals.

Early medieval helmets were slightly conical bowls of overlapping iron plates, fitted with a shallow visor of the same material (making this part of the helmet look not unlike the headgear worn by modern jockeys!), and augmented by a sweeping skirt made from five rows of lamellae that extended nearly to the wearer's shoulders. The front edges of the skirt were curled back, to shield the face from arrows. Some helmets were decorated with a pair of flat, metal antlers, called *kuwagata*, that resembled the antennae of large beetles.[89]

Kuwagata, tsuru-bashiri and other decorations provided early medieval *bushi* with opportunities for individual or familial expression, as well as a convenient tool for identifying one another. So too, did the lacings that held the lamellar armor together. This appears, in fact, to be a principal reason behind the preference for braided silk, rather than leather, for the cords. Both the color and the pattern of the lacings could be varied, making it possible to distinguish individuals even at quite some distance. By the late Kamakura period, it had become common practice for *bushi* to incorporate family crests (*monshō* or *kamon*) into the designs produced by the lacings or coverings of their armor. The color of the lacquer applied to the *saneita* added additional variety. One medieval text even claims that the color of a warrior's armor reflected his surname – black for the Minamoto, purple for the Taira, chartreuse for the Fujiwara, and yellow for the Tachibana – although there is no other documentary or pictorial evidence to corroborate any such custom.[90]

Ōyoroi offered warriors formidable protection, but that protection came only at a considerable price. An early tenth-century legal compendium indicates that the production of a *keikō*-style armor – composed of only 800 lamellae, while *ōyoroi* comprised 2,000 or more – required between 192 and 265 days (depending on the season and the length of the day). Modern craftsmen normally need ten months to two years of full-time labor to construct replica *ōyoroi*. A complete armor must, therefore, have involved a substantial investment: one document from 1107 gives the value of an *ōyoroi* as 80 *hiki*, a sum equal to the cost of eight short swords (*uchi-gatana*), and to several months' wages for an ordinary worker of the period.[91]

Moreover, while *ōyoroi* were excellent armors for mounted *bushi*, particularly in short skirmishes involving relatively small numbers of combatants, they posed problems for warriors fighting on foot. For one thing, at around 30 kilograms, and nearly a full centimeter thick, *ōyoroi* were heavy. On horseback, this was of small consequence, as much of the load was borne by the saddle, but on foot this much weight was a significant burden. Similarly, the boxy, loose-fitting shape of the *ōyoroi* served a mounted warrior well, permitting the plates of the skirt to hang over the saddle (see Figure 3.13) without pushing up to expose his thighs, and creating a space between the armor and his body that prevented arrows just piercing the lamellar plates from inflicting deep wounds. But, for foot troops, the loose fit exacerbated the problem of the armor's weight, putting most of the burden on the warrior's shoulders, and rendered *ōyoroi* unbalanced and awkward to move in.[92]

Consequently, early medieval foot soldiers were often outfitted with simpler forms of armor that were better suited to their needs. The oldest of these was the *haramaki*, which appeared at about the same time as the *ōyoroi*. Although constructed from precisely the same kind of lamellae and *saneita* as the *ōyoroi*,

Figure 3.13 Mounted warrior in ōyoroi (*Mōko shūrai ekotoba*)

the cuirass of the *haramaki* was designed as a single piece that wrapped around the wearer's chest and back and overlapped under the right arm, eliminating the *waidate*. To make them easier to run or walk in, *haramaki* fitted more closely at the waist, thereby dividing the weight of the armor between the wearer's shoulders and hips, and featured an eight-piece skirt. In place of the *ōsode*, *haramaki* were fitted with much smaller, leaf-shaped iron shoulder pieces, called *gyōyō*.[93]

Originally developed for low-ranked, auxiliary troops, by the thirteenth century *haramaki* were also becoming popular among elite warriors, who added *ōsode*, *suneate*, *kote*, and other key ornaments of the *ōyoroi* to produce hybrid armors sometimes called *haramaki yoroi*. Most scholars explain this as a result of increased fighting on foot, but it seems more likely that economy was a bigger factor here than comfort. Numerous sources indicate that *haramaki yoroi*, which could be obtained for a quarter of the price of an *ōyoroi*, were worn by mounted *bushi*, as well as by warriors on foot.[94]

The fourth, and simplest, type of early medieval armor, the *hara-ate*, was a lamellar torso protector with a very short, three-piece skirt. Covering the wearer's chest and sides, but leaving his back exposed, it resembled the *dō* pieces worn by modern *kendō* players, and was sometimes used when standing guard duty or engaged in other activities that did not demand the full protection of an *ōyoroi* or a *haramaki yoroi*. *Hara-ate* are thought to have been around from the late Heian period, but the earliest pictorial and documentary evidence of them is from the late Kamakura era, and the oldest surviving example dates from the Muromachi period.[95]

The *dōmaru*, introduced near the end of the Kamakura period, was very similar in construction to the *haramaki*, except that it wrapped around the front and both sides of the chest, leaving a small gap at the back, rather than closing on the right side. It was, in fact, essentially a *hara-ate* on which the sides, and the length of the skirt, had been extended. Intriguingly, modern application of the names "*haramaki*" and "*dōmaru*" precisely reverses their medieval usage: today, armors that overlap on the right side are called "*dōmaru*" while armors that open in back are called "*haramaki*." This swap appears to have taken place sometime during the Sengoku era, for reasons that have not yet been satisfactorily explained. In this volume, I have followed the early medieval conventions.[96]

Analyses of battle casualties expose few surprises concerning the protective value of medieval armors. One study, by Shakadō Mitsuhiro, for example, reveals that approximately 70 percent of wounds cited in casualty reports were sustained on the arms and legs, the areas least protected by either the *ōyoroi* or the *haramaki*. Most wounds to the chest and head, moreover, occurred in areas left uncovered by the heavy helmets and cuirasses – the face, lower neck and underarms – while wounds to the arms were considerably more common among lower-ranked warriors than among the elite *bushi*, who more often wore *kote* on both arms (rather than on the bow arm alone, a practice widespread among less affluent warriors). Wounds to the thighs and calves, which were largely unprotected by medieval armors, were the most common of all – some 41 percent of the casualties reported.[97]

Horses and tack

Mobility in, to or from early medieval battles was synonymous with feet, human or animal, with those of horses commanding the greater attention. Horsemanship was central to *bushi* identity, distinguishing the professional warrior from those who served him – and fought beside him, on foot. As we have seen, the horse was one of the two tools that defined the "way of bow and horse," which defined the samurai. Fighting men on foot, wielding bows, swords or polearms, also played important parts in a great many early medieval battles, but the mounted warriors overshadowed them – both in the fighting itself and in the consciousness of those who participated in or recounted it. Indeed, both documentary and literary sources often counted armed forces in numbers of horsemen alone.[98]

But the coursers that dashed about early medieval battlefields bore scant resemblance to the great chargers that carried European knights into the fray, or even to the thundering, graceful thoroughbreds ridden by samurai in movies and television programs. Early medieval Japanese war-horses were much smaller, and much slower, than either of these. Most were the descendants of animals imported from China and Korea, interbred with broncos that had been in Japan since the stone age. Their bloodlines mingled those of the wild ponies of the Mongolian steppes with those of Arabians, which had reached China by the second century CE, and other horses that had diffused northward from southern

China in prehistoric times. The mounts favored by early medieval *bushi* were stallions raised in eastern Japan and selected for their size and fierce temperament. They were stout, short-legged, shaggy, short-nosed beasts, tough, unruly and difficult to control.[99]

Hayashida Shigeyuki's analysis of skeletons found in the mass grave discovered in 1953 at Zaimokuza, near Kamakura (thought to contain the remains of men and horses killed during Nitta Yoshisada's attack on the city in 1333), shows that the horses of the period ranged in height from 109 to 140 cm at the shoulder, with the average height being 129.5 cm, and the height of most falling between 126 and 136 cm. Modern Japanese ponies of about the same size as the Kamakura skeletons average around 280 kilograms in weight. Modern thoroughbreds, by contrast, average around 160 to 65 cm in height and weigh about 450 to 550 kilograms.[100]

In general, a horse can carry only about a third of its own weight without severely compromising its running speed. A saddle plus a rider dressed in *ōyoroi*, and his weapons could easily exceed that limit for early medieval ponies. A horse at full gallop, moreover, places nearly eight times its normal weight on its hooves, and cannot, therefore, sustain this effort for very long. Even modern racing horses can only run full out for 200 to 300 meters; and medieval ponies were unshod, compounding their difficulties.*

An intriguing experiment, conducted in 1990 by NHK, the Japanese public television network, demonstrated the running prowess of medieval war-horses. A pony standing 130 cm tall and weighing 350 kilograms – larger than average for early medieval horses – was timed while carrying a 50 kilogram rider and bags of sand totaling 45 kilograms (to simulate the weight of armor and weapons). The poor beast dropped from a gallop to a trot almost immediately, and never exceeded 9 kilometers per hour. After running for ten minutes, the horse was visibly exhausted. To put these numbers in perspective: unladen thoroughbreds can gallop at up to 60 kilometers per hour, while the standard prescribed during the Meiji period for cavalry mounts carrying (unarmored) riders was 300 meters per minute – about 18 kilometers per hour.[101]

Early medieval Japanese tack, moreover, gave *bushi* a rugged, stable, and comfortable platform from which to shoot, but it was heavy, and not particularly well designed for high speed or long-distance riding. The saddle-trees (*kurabane*) of medieval Japanese saddles consisted of four pieces of lacquered wood: an arched burr-plate (*maewa*) and cantle (*shizuwa*), connected by two contoured bands (*igi*), which rested on either side of the horse's spine and served as the

---

* Steel horseshoes were not used in Japan until modern times. But, from the late Muromachi period, horses were sometimes fitted with straw sandals (*umagutsu*) very much like the *waraji* worn by humans, to protect their feet during long marches. Kawai, *Gempei kassen*, 53; Takahashi Masaaki, "Nihon chūsei no sentō," 197–9; Kuroda Hideo, *Sugata to shigusa no chūseishi*, 22–8; Sasama, *Nihon kassen bugu jiten*, 352.

under frame for the seat (see Figure 3.14). This frame was mounted on a two-layered padded leather under-saddle (*shita-gura*) to which it was tightly bound by hemp cords, and overlaid with a padded leather seat (*basen*), held in place by the stirrup leathers (*chikaragawa* or *gekiso*), which passed through matching slots in the seat and bands. The burr-plates and cantles of military saddles were heavy and thick, and rose high above the bands, providing riders with additional protection against their opponents' blades and arrows, and against sliding forward or backward out of the saddle when they stood in the stirrups to shoot.[102]

Stirrups, known in China by the first century CE, were used in Japan from the very beginnings of equestrian culture there. The earliest ones, unearthed from fifth-century tombs, were flat-bottomed rings of metal-covered wood, similar to European stirrups; but, by historical times, these had been supplanted by cup-shaped stirrups (*tsuba abumi*), which enclosed the front half of the rider's foot. During the Nara period, the base of the stirrup, the part supporting the sole of the rider's foot, was elongated a few centimeters beyond the cup. This half-tongued style of stirrup (*hanshita abumi*) remained popular at court until the late Heian period, by which time it had in turn been supplanted by a new model (the *fukuro abumi* or *Musashi abumi*) in which the base extended to the full length of the rider's foot, while the left and right sides of the toe cup had disappeared. The military stirrup (*shitanaga abumi*), standard in Japan from the middle Heian period until the reintroduction of ring stirrups from the West in the late nineteenth century, was thinner than the ordinary version, and featured a deeper toe pocket and an even longer, flatter foot shelf.

Lacking direct evidence, we can do little more than speculate about the rationale underlying this odd, uniquely Japanese design. Nevertheless, by spreading the rider's weight more evenly across the whole of his foot, it does

Figure 3.14 Medieval Japanese saddle and tack (*Obusuma Saburō ekotoba*)

appear to have offered a more stable platform for a warrior rising in his stirrups to shoot than a ring-shaped stirrup, which forces the rider to balance on his arches. The open sides also ensured that a rider unhorsed would not catch a foot in the stirrup and be dragged – a significant danger in the case of Western stirrups.[103]

Saddles were held in place by three braided-cord straps. The main anchor was the girth-strap (*harubi*), which wrapped completely around the horse's belly, passed through openings in the under-saddle, and then between the under-saddle and the saddle-tree, to be secured with a knot between the bands of the seat. A breast strap (*munagai*) and a crupper (*shirigai*), attached to the saddle-tree by rings on the burr-plate and cantle, provided additional stability, preventing the saddle from slipping forward or backward.[104]

Riders and grooms controlled their mounts by means of a bridle and a whip. Whips, made from bamboo or willow (*kumayanagi*), were about the same length as a short arrow. They were normally used with the right hand, and secured by a wrist strap, which allowed the warrior simply to drop the whip and let it dangle from his wrist while shooting. Bridles, comprising a headstall (*omogai*), bit (*kutsuwa*) and reins (*tezuna*), were very similar in form and function to their European counterparts, except that they were usually constructed of folded fabric – most commonly silk – rather than of leather. The headstall consisted of a head band (*omozura*) running across the horse's forehead, a head piece (*kashira-gake*) running behind its ears, and a throat last (*omogai*) running under the jaw. The headpiece extended down the horse's face in cheek bands, connecting to the bit.

Japanese bits were made from six pieces of steel. A pair of rods with rings at either end, linked together like a chain, formed the *hami*, the piece that went into the horse's mouth. The other ends of the *hami* connected to twin cheek pieces (*kagami*), which fitted closely at the sides of the horse's mouth and connected the bit to the cheek bands of the headstall. The reins were attached to the bit by a pair of rods (*mizu tsuki* or *hikite*), ringed at both ends, and connected in link fashion to the cheek pieces. From the Heian period onward, most Japanese bridles also featured a second set of reins, the *sashinawa*, used when leading the horse on foot. When the horse was ridden (without someone leading it) the *sashinawa* were tied to the front of the saddle.[105]

★ ★ ★ ★ ★

Among the most important lessons to be gleaned from examining early *bushi* weapons, armor and horses – the tools of war – is that warriors, and the culture of warfare, were largely the same all over the country. Horses may have been raised predominantly in the eastern provinces, but equestrian culture was countrywide, with horses included in tax levies – and sent to the capital and western provinces – from the start of the *ritsuryō* era. Weapons and armor were also developed, manufactured and distributed in national networks of trade and exchange of information. While the raw materials came from all over the country, and production of these tools took place in multiple locations, the capital remained central to the process, serving as the principal marketplace and point of exchange, as well as a key manufacturing location. Thus we note that, with the exception of subtle variations in sword construction, there are utterly no regional differences to be found in the armor, equestrian tack, or other weapons of the early medieval period.[106] Warrior leaders, particularly during the Heian period, when *bushi* military traditions were forged, were as much a part of the world of the capital and the country as a whole as of their home provinces; they were part of a national socio-economic structure, not just a local one.

Even more fundamentally, a survey of the shape, strengths and limitations of early medieval Japanese weaponry is an essential prelude to the chapters that follow, on the science and culture of war. For knowing what warriors fought with is as crucial to comprehension of how they fought as is discerning why they fought or how fighting men were mobilized and organized. Weapons set the parameters of war and battles, within the boundaries established by the purpose of the conflict. They determine what is and is not possible.

At the same time, understanding the tools of war is not the same thing as understanding war. Weapons are not so important, nor their form so determinate of the conduct or outcome of war, as is commonly assumed. War is a sociological phenomenon, and weapons are merely tools facilitating its practice. Moreover, as Martin van Crevald reminds us, the evolution of weapons and other tools of war is rarely governed solely by rational considerations pertaining to their technical utility, capabilities or effectiveness. Inasmuch as warfare itself is irrational – dominated by passions like courage, honor, duty, loyalty or self-sacrifice – the design and employment of arms has always been intertwined with multiple, interacting anthropological, psychological and cultural factors. Identical tools can be used – and understood – in entirely different ways by different societies.[107]

"Superior technology" in warfare is not always what it seems. To acquire superior mobility, superior destructive power, or superior protection to that of one's enemies can be advantageous in the pursuit of victory. But what is ultimately far more important is achieving a symbiosis between one's own tactics and weaponry and those utilized by the enemy. The best military technology is not one that is superior in some absolute sense, but one that neutralizes an opponent's strengths and exploits his weaknesses. The weapons of a people tend to conform to those of their traditional enemies, to the missions for which they fight, and to the terrain on which they meet.[108]

Thus while the acuity of historical hindsight often makes the adoption of particular weapons seem alternatively inevitable or quixotic, the correlation between technology, war and societal evolution is far more nuanced than is sometimes appreciated. Science and technology, notes van Crevald, operate on a logic that is different from, even opposed to, that which governs human conflict and war. The former is linear, predicated on efficiency and repeatability; the latter is paradoxical, demanding uniqueness within convention and deliberately embracing redundancy and slack. The former can sometimes be timeless and mono-dimensional; but the latter is the dynamic product of interplay between the structures of political power, the goals of conflict, the composition of military forces, and the equipment at hand.[109]

In this and the preceding chapters, we have surveyed the political, organizational and technological parameters of early medieval warfare. In the following two chapters, we turn to the conduct of battle itself.

4

THE SCIENCE OF WAR

The military arts are far from the human realm; an activity close to the bestial and of no interest or profit to those not born of warrior houses.

Yoshida Kenkō, *Tsurezuregusa*, c.1330

Of all the theories on the art of war, the only reasonable one is that which, founded upon the study of military history, admits a certain number of regulating principals but leaves to natural genius the greatest part of the general conduct of a war without trammeling it with exclusive rules.... War in its ensemble is not a science, but an art.

Antoine Henri de Jomini, *Précis of the Art of War*, 1838

Early medieval warriors went to battle clad in heavy armors, bearing at least two swords, and regularly employing a variety of polearms and auxiliary weapons. But the technology that cast the broadest shadows across early medieval Japanese battlefields was archery from horseback. Indeed, phrases like "the way of the bow and arrow" (*yumiya no michi* or *kyūsen no michi*) and "the way of bow and horse" (*kyūba no michi*) became synonymous with military skills and the profession of arms from the ninth through the fourteenth centuries.[1]

Viewed from a world-historical perspective, however, this seems incongruous, for the way of horse and bow was first and foremost a technology of the steppe – the open expanses of northern, central and western Asia. It was pioneered by charioteering pastoral peoples – the Hyskos, Hurrians, Kassites, Hittites and Aryans in the West and the as yet unidentified founders of the Shang dynasty in the East – and refined by horse-riding nomads like the Scythians, Cimmerians, Huns, Turks, Hsiung-nu, Mongols and Manchus. In China and in Europe, where the climate, topography and geological resources gave rise to metal-working, agrarian-based civilizations, warfare was, during most periods, dominated by foot soldiers wielding metal-bladed weapons and wearing heavy armor. Cavalry – particularly light cavalry – was regarded as an auxiliary arm – although it could be an important, and even a decisive, one.[2]

Culturally and geographically, classical and medieval Japan were far more akin to Europe or China than to the steppe. Certainly nothing like the herding, equestrian existence that characterized life on the steppe ever emerged on the Japanese archipelago. Indeed, horses, although present in Japan as far back as the Jōmon period, played little or no role in early Japanese agriculture, do not appear to have been domesticated until reintroduced from China and Korea in the fourth century, and were kept only by governments and socio-political elites before the middle part of the Heian period. Moreover, while some scholars believe the ancient state to have been founded by horse-riding invaders from the continent, *haniwa* figurines of warriors (wearing head-to-toe iron or leather armor, and bearing swords rather than bow and arrow) make it apparent that the cavalry technology they brought with them differed considerably from the light cavalry of the steppe, and in fact drew closely on Chinese shock cavalry models.[3] Indeed, long before the birth of the samurai, the Japanese were already well acquainted with more sophisticated technologies, such as crossbows, drilled infantry, and coordinated, mixed-forces tactics.

And yet, horse-borne archers emerged as the period-defining military technology of Japan's early medieval era. Mounted archery gave birth to the *bushi* and shaped Japanese tactical thinking from the eighth through the late fourteenth centuries. To understand why this should have been the case, we need to look at a matrix of social, political, strategic and technological factors that affected military decision-making across this formidable span of time.[4]

The way of the horse and bow

Takahashi Masaaki has argued that early medieval warriors took to the bow and horse principally as a kind of status symbol and expression of ritual continuity between themselves and the imperial state (*ritsuryō*) military. *Bushi* weaponry and skills, he observes, continued traditions established early on by imperial court guards, who valued the bow for its spiritual power and utilized it in various ceremonial functions, including exorcisms. Thus, he contends, mounted archery – practiced in Japan with feeble bows and puny horses – had a symbolic appeal for early medieval warriors that transcended its practical military value.[5]

This thesis misjudges the practical value of light cavalry to the pre-samurai military establishment, and underplays its domination of early medieval warfare.[6] Nevertheless, Takahashi's emphasis on historical precedent and the symbolic status of mounted archery is well placed.

The military apparatus of the *ritsuryō* state – the milieu from which the *bushi* sprang – was modeled on that of T'ang China, but the Japanese system was neither technologically nor organizationally a duplicate of the Chinese one. The Japanese showed little interest, for example, in adopting hand-held crossbows, a key weapon of Chinese armies. And even at the peak of Chinese influence, in the seventh and eighth centuries, horse-borne archery remained a key factor in Japanese tactical thinking. It was cavalry, not infantry, that proved the decisive element when Emperor Temmu swept to victory in the Jinshin War of 672–3;

horsemen carried the day for the court in Fujiwara Hirotsugu's rebellion in 740 and in the revolt of Fujiwara Nakamaro in 764; and special contingents assembled as shows of force for ceremonies attendant to the arrival of foreign emissaries were invariably cavalry.[7]

Nevertheless, like its T'ang archetype, the *ritsuryō* military was a mixed weapons-system force: predominantly an infantry drawn from peasant conscripts, augmented by heavily armored missile cavalry. Unlike those of the T'ang, however, Japanese cavalrymen were a class apart from their foot soldier comrades, for the imperial state overcame the logistical difficulties of training peasant conscripts to fight from horseback through the simple expedient of staffing its cavalry units only with men who had acquired the basic skills of mounted archery on their own – the upper echelon of provincial society and the lower-ranked members of the central aristocracy. One, perhaps unintended, result of this policy was to institutionalize the identification of mounted archery as the weapons system of the elite.

From the mid-eighth century, both the prominence and the tactical importance of this elite technology expanded exponentially, as the court restructured its armed forces. The regiments that formed the core of the military institutions laid down in the *ritsuryō* codes were first augmented with special cavalry corps and then discontinued entirely, in favor of a more flexible system centered on elites. By the tenth century, arms-bearing and law-enforcement in the capital and the countryside had become the exclusive preserve of an emerging order of professional warriors, defined by skills they cultivated on their own, using personal (and family) resources.

This privatization and professionalization of armed forces had important consequences for the manner in which warfare would – could – be conducted. It meant, for one thing, that early medieval warfare would be shaped by mercenaries whose careers were determined by reputations built on individual prowess.

Such men were, like modern professional basketball players, more apt to think of themselves as highly talented individuals playing *for* a team, than as the component parts *of* a team: the success of the team was always to the benefit of each of its members, but a distinguishing individual performance could bring its own rewards, even in the face of team failure. This situation favored arms and tactics that presented maximal opportunities to showcase the skills and prowess of individuals or small groups.

More importantly, however, early medieval armies and warbands were patchwork conglomerations, assembled for specific campaigns and demobilized immediately thereafter. This arrangement offered commanders few, if any, opportunities to drill with their troops in large-scale group tactics, and mitigated against fielding integrated, well-articulated armies. Instead, the hosts that clashed on early medieval battlefields tended to be arrays of skillful individuals, heavily dependent on the prowess of their components.

Cavalry can be effective in relatively small numbers, and without extensive large group drill, while the superior mobility of cavalry, both on and off the battlefield, makes it the natural arm of attack and pursuit – an important consideration for Heian warriors, whose functions centered on law-enforcement rather than border defense. At the same time, the expense and the long, individual training needed to produce a competent horseman distinguishes cavalry as a fighting method for elite warriors.[8]

The missile cavalry tradition the *bushi* inherited from their *ritsuryō* forebears was, in other words, exceedingly well matched to the social and political circumstances of the Heian age. Already long associated with elite socio-economic status, mounted archery put a premium on professional – personal – skills and training, while minimizing the liabilities and constraints imposed by the organizational structure of early *bushi* forces.

For skirmishes in the capital and other situations that circumscribed the arena of combat, *bushi* often fought on foot. They also conscripted or hired foot soldiers, armed them with bows or polearms, and deployed them in most sorts of battles.[9] Such troops were active combatants, not just grooms and attendants to the mounted warriors (as they have often been portrayed in standard accounts of early medieval warfare).[10] At the same time, they were considerably less than an infantry.

Early medieval foot soldiers fought side by side with mounted warriors, in mixed units, rather than in distinct companies of infantry. Infantry units, which could neither run away from pursuing horsemen nor run down cavalry in flight, would have been of limited worth in early medieval Japanese warfare. On open ground, where mounted warriors had adequate room to maneuver, horsemen could easily stay out of range and pelt foot soldiers bearing swords or polearms with arrows. Even missile infantry posed no decisive threat to mounted *bushi*, who, unlike European knights, could shoot back. While archers on foot enjoy a higher rate of shooting and greater accuracy than mounted bowmen, in Japan these advantages were largely, if not completely, offset by the short effective killing range of the bows and the protection afforded by the horsemen's heavy armor, which was specifically designed to shield them from arrows. Unless protected by fortifications, standing archers therefore fared little better than other infantrymen against the cavalry.

On open ground, infantry can stand against a cavalry charge only when it can form up with sufficient density and depth to force horses to refuse to collide with it, and only when it also has sufficient morale and courage to stand and face the terrifying charge. This requires that infantry units have ample numbers, as well as enough practice and experience fighting together to be able to trust their fellows to stand with them, rather than break and run. Moreover, without extensive training, infantrymen fighting together in dense formation risk killing or wounding their own comrades, crowded in around them. Effective infantry can, therefore, be deployed only by a command authority strong enough to gather sufficient troops, and rich enough to maintain them while they train or fight together long enough to develop the needed unit cohesion.[11] Samurai commanders lacked the resources to accomplish this until well into the sixteenth century.

In early medieval battles, therefore, the principal value of foot soldiers lay in their ability to harass and distract *bushi* on horseback, whose attention could otherwise be fully directed at allied horsemen. On the other hand, while infantrymen were clearly an auxiliary presence on early medieval battlefields, they should not be dismissed too lightly – as reports of illustrious warriors having been killed by "stray arrows" attest.*

Mounted archery tactics in Japan were fundamentally different from those of other celebrated light cavalry traditions, such as the horse-riding peoples of the continent. While huge expanses of time and geography separate Scythians from Huns from Turks from Manchus, and gave rise to considerable diversity of technology, political organization and military practices, one can, with only a moderate degree of over-simplification, identify among the range of pastoralist civilizations a characteristic pattern of warfare. John Keegan argues that steppe tactics probably developed out of and were honed by the skills required for working herds of livestock. From techniques originating in the need to break flocks into smaller, more manageable parts, to round up scattered animals, to cut off lines of retreat by circling and flanking, to compress herds into compact areas, to isolate flock leaders, to kill specific animals without panicking the rest of the herd, and to dominate superior numbers by threat and intimidation, steppe nomads developed a classic order of battle that confounded and terrified the agriculturist societies who faced them.[12]

Steppe warfare centered on sweeping, fluid, coordinated cavalry maneuvers that managed enemy troops like animals hunted or herded. Armies advanced in loose, far-flung formations that encircled their enemy on both flanks and forced him to bunch together, where he could be harried and intimidated by volleys of arrows, launched either from long range or from close-up by waves of riders coming in at full gallop and then breaking off to regroup at the rear for another charge. When too strongly resisted, they pulled back, hoping to draw the enemy into a pursuit that would break his ranks and leave him vulnerable to further hit-and-run counter-charges. Finally, when the enemy had been thoroughly worn down and thrown into confusion, they would close and drive him from the field with swords and polearms.

The weapon that made such tactics possible was the composite reflex bow, constructed by laminating together layers of wood, animal tendon, and horn. Bows of this sort were short – about the length of a man's torso when strung –

---

* See, for example, *Sandai jitsuroku* 878 6/7, *Fusō ryakki* 1057 8/10, *Chūyūki* 1095 10/23, or *Azuma kagami* 1213 5/3. Arrows used by ranking warriors usually bore the name of the arrow's owner on the shaft, so that kills could be identified, while those carried by foot soldiers were unmarked. When renowned warriors were killed by unmarked arrows, sources record the deaths as having been by "stray arrows" (*nagere-ya*). See Mori Toshio, "Yumiya no iryoku (1)."

and powerful enough to shoot accurately to 300 meters or more, or to penetrate armor at up to a hundred meters. They shot light arrows (each weighing just under 30 grams), which allowed every warrior to carry as many as fifty in his quiver.[13]

Japanese *bushi* confronted very different technological, as well as geographical and organizational circumstances. To begin with, they were forced to make do with bows distinctly inferior to those used by horsemen on the continent. The *kiyumi* and *fusetake-yumi* of the tenth to twelfth centuries were particularly weak and, used in conjunction with the heavy ōyoroi armors favored by early medieval samurai, forced warriors to shoot only at very close range – usually 10 meters or less – and to target with precision the gaps and weak points in the armor of specific opponents.[14]

Japanese ponies were also much less dependable than their continental cousins. Incapable of carrying more than about 90 kilograms – including rider, saddle and weapons – and unshod, so that their hooves could not take heavy pounding, they could gallop long distances only with great difficulty and lacked the endurance to run about continuously for entire battles – which is precisely why troops on foot were able to mingle with the horsemen. They were also unruly and difficult to control – especially when both the rider's hands were occupied with a task like archery.

The combination of puny mounts, weighty armor, and the rarity of open terrain would have precluded the sweeping charges and feigned retreats favored by the steppe warriors, even if the Japanese had wished to fight that way. Instead, therefore, the *bushi* developed a distinctive, somewhat peculiar form of light cavalry tactics that involved individuals and small groups circling and maneuvering around one another in a manner that bore an intriguing resemblance to dogfighting aviators.

Among the most famous descriptions of warriors fighting in this fashion is an account from the *Konjaku monogatarishū* of a duel between two tenth-century *bushi*, Minamoto Mitsuru and Taira Yoshifumi:

> They fitted forked arrows to their bows and charged, firing their first shots together. Thinking that the next arrow would surely strike home, each drew his bow and released a shaft as they galloped past one another. They pulled up their horses and returned for another pass, again drawing bow but this time releasing no arrows as they rode by. Again they reined in their horses and turned. Again they drew their bows and aimed. Yoshifumi shot at Mitsuru's midsection, but, moving as if falling from his mount, Mitsuru dodged the arrow, which struck the scabbard of his long sword. He then once again turned his horse and took aim at Yoshifumi's midsection. But Yoshifumi twisted his body, so that the arrow only struck his sword belt. Once more quickly reining in and turning their horses, they again notched arrows and charged...[15]

As vivid as this account is, however, it describes a duel, not a battle, and as such it gives only a partial picture of early medieval mounted archery tactics. In the heat of battle, warriors seldom had the luxury of concentrating on one adversary at a time. They also had to contend with double-teaming by allied opponents, stray arrows from nearby skirmishes and archers on foot, and the polearms wielded by enemy foot soldiers.

Bushi further had to deal with complications introduced by their own equipment. Ōyoroi was not perfectly symmetrical, leaving it unevenly balanced between its right and left sides. And, because it fit loosely, rather than snugly at the waist (so that it could hang over the saddle and cover the wearer's thighs), it shifted readily from front to back and side to side, like a bell around its clapper, rendering the warrior's balance unsteady.[16]

Boxy, stiff ōyoroi also left gaps, which were necessary for movement. In order to shoot, the warrior had to raise his head, spread his arms, and let his shoulder plates (ōsode) fall back out of his way. This posture exposed his throat and the sides of his upper chest. Thus Kumagae Naozane's principal counsel to his son, Naoie, at the battle of Ichinotani in 1184, was to:

> Stay calm as the enemy approaches. Keep the shoulder plate that faces incoming arrows opposite your helmet. Close the gaps in your armor – keep shaking and hiking it up so that you do not let an arrow through. Do not let your armor open as you move.[17]

Similar considerations are reflected in the guidance offered a young Wada Yoshimori, when he sought advice from the veteran Miura Sanemitsu, on the eve of a skirmish in 1180:

> Try to meet the enemy with your left side facing his. Do not get caught with your bowstring slack. Be mindful of the gaps in your armor: adjust it constantly. Guard, especially, your face. Keep dear your arrows – do not shoot wild or waste them. As soon as you loose one shaft, quickly fit another to your bowstring. Aim at the opponent's face. In the old days one did not shoot at horses, but recently it has become common practice to shoot first at the belly of the enemy's mount, so that he will be thrown down and left on foot.[18]

In this sort of fighting, horsemanship counted for as much as marksmanship. The angle at which warriors closed with opponents was crucial, because they could shoot comfortably only to their left sides, along an arc of roughly 45 degrees, from the ten or eleven o'clock to about the nine o'clock position. Attempting to shoot at a sharper angle to the front would have resulted in either bumping the horse's neck with the bow or bowstring, or spooking the mount when the arrow was released and flew too close to its face. Attempting to shoot at a sharper angle to the rear would have twisted the archer right out of his saddle. And shooting the lengthy Japanese bow to the right of the horse's neck demanded the flexibility of a contortionist.[19]

Bushi could not, therefore, easily target opponents to their right. Accordingly, "left" and "right" came to be described in early medieval texts as the warrior's "bow hand" (*yunde*) and "rein hand" (*mede*, literally, "horse hand") sides. Early medieval thinking on the importance of positioning relative to one's opponent is entertainingly – if fancifully – underscored by a story about two brothers recounted in the *Konjaku monogatarishū*.

One evening, goes the tale, the elder brother was hunting deer just after dusk, when he heard a gruff voice call his name from somewhere to his right. Not recognizing the voice, but not liking its tone, the warrior wheeled his mount, to put whomever the voice belonged to on his left, or bow, side. At this, the calling stopped, only to start up again as soon as the warrior returned to his original course. But when the warrior turned again, hoping to get a shot at his antagonist, the voice once more fell silent. This pattern was repeated for the rest of the evening: each time the warrior attempted to put the voice on his bow side, it disappeared; and each time he turned back, it resumed calling his name.

Later, the warrior's younger brother encountered the same mysterious voice, following the same pattern: calling to him when it was on his rein-hand side and falling silent whenever he turned to place it on his left. The brother, however, was apparently a somewhat more creative tactician than his sibling. Quietly dismounting, in the dark, he removed and reversed his saddle, and then remounted, riding his horse backward. The ruse worked: the trickster, believing himself to be safely on the warrior's right side, called out, whereupon the warrior shot in the direction of the sound. Hearing a shriek, followed by silence, the warrior returned home. The next morning the two brothers went to the woods to investigate, and discovered a large boar perched in a tree, dead from an arrow wound![20]

The boar's fate in this tale notwithstanding, getting to an opponent's right side was an excellent defensive tactic. At a dinner party in 1191, an elder warrior named Oba Kageyoshi recounted how he had once taken advantage of this, when he found himself bow-to-bow with the illustrious Minamoto Tametomo during the Hōgen Conflict of 1156:

> Tametomo was an archer without peer in our realm. . . . For this reason when . . . I found myself facing his left side and he began to draw his bow . . . I galloped across to his right and rode past him, below his sights. Thus the arrow he meant for my body struck my knee instead. Had I not known this trick, I surely would have lost my life. A stalwart needs only to be expert at horsemanship![21]

The tactic that Kageyoshi describes here may, indeed, have saved his life, but it was also purely a defensive maneuver: by cutting across Tameyoshi's path and escaping to his right side, Kageyoshi prevented Tameyoshi from getting a clean

THE SCIENCE OF WAR

shot at him, but he also prevented himself from shooting at Tameyoshi. For Kageyoshi, who was clearly outmatched in this encounter, such discretion was perhaps the wiser part of valor; but, in order to fight back, a warrior needed to keep his opponent to his left.

Canny warriors, then, attempted to maneuver so as to approach the enemy from his right, where he could not return fire, while keeping him on their own left. The most advantageous angle of attack would therefore have been to slip in behind an opponent, on his right side, either overtaking him on a parallel course (as Figure 4.1a), approaching more or less broadside from his right and veering off again (as in Figure 4.1b), or cutting across his path behind him (as in Figure 4.1c). Of these alternatives, the third would likely have been the easiest to accomplish, as well as the safest. The first, by contrast would have been the trickiest and the riskiest, inasmuch as the warrior would either have to topple his opponent with his first shot, or maintain pace and course precisely beside him for subsequent shots: failure to do so risked allowing the opponent to slip behind him to *his* right side (as in Figure 4.1d).

All three tactics, however, required the rider to come up on his opponent unawares. For, unlike Kageyoshi or the boar, enemy warriors would usually have been looking to shoot back, and could be expected to come about to bring their own bows to bear on an attacker once they detected his approach. Warriors

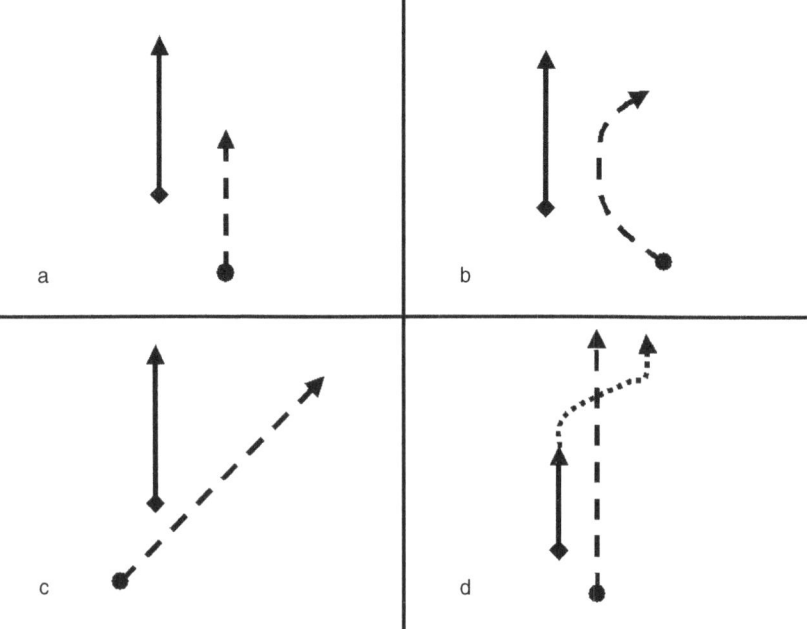

Figure 4.1 Possible angles of attack for mounted archery encounters

THE SCIENCE OF WAR

riding straight at one another, each closing to the left of the other, in the manner Miura Sanemitsu advised, must, therefore, have represented a common pattern of attack.

If the first shot did not topple the opponent (which was probably the norm), the rider could circle to his right, before coming about for a second pass. This would, however, have been a risky maneuver: if the opponent maintained a straight course or also turned to his right, the warrior might get off a second shot to the rear (Figure 4.2a); but if the opponent instead circled to his left, he could easily come up on the warrior's vulnerable, rein-hand side (Figure 4.2b).

The safest alternative would therefore have been to circle to one's left. Should the opponent then fail to come about quickly enough, the warrior could slip behind him on his right (Figure 4.2c). And if the opponent also circled to his left, the two would either end up circling one another (Figure 4.2d) or wheeling about completely for another head-on charge, as Yoshifumi and Mitsuru are depicted doing in the tale cited earlier (Figure 4.2e).[22]

All of this maneuvering was, of course, further complicated by the presence of other horsemen and foot soldiers, and by the terrain and other circumstances of the battle site. Japanese ponies, moreover, lacked stamina, making a *bushi*'s ability to judge when and for how long to run his mount full out as important a skill as knowing where to point it.

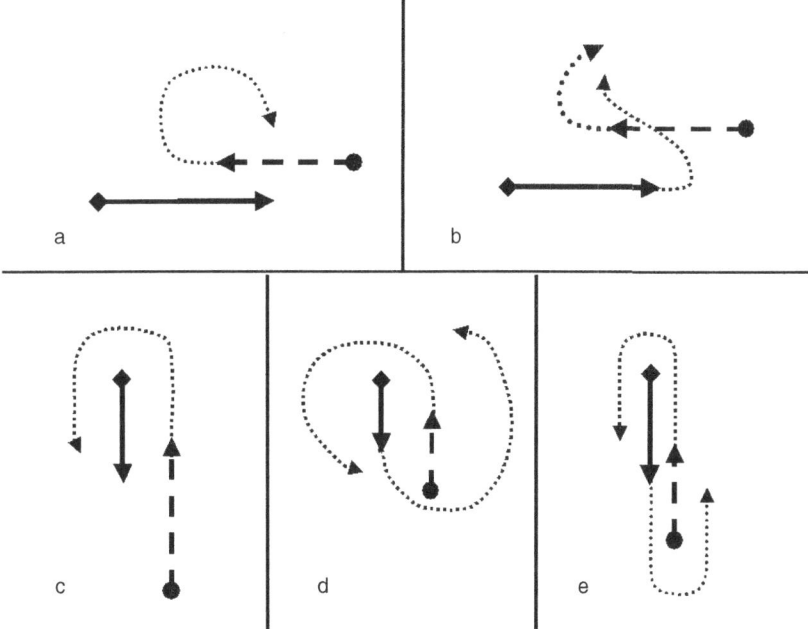

Figure 4.2 Maneuver options for subsequent passes

111

Shaping battle

Early medieval armies carried on with little or no direction from their commanders once the enemy had been engaged. Even senior officers usually fought in the ranks themselves, and were seldom able to exercise much control over the contest beyond orchestrating the initial attack or defensive position. But if the warriors of the age seldom attempted large-scale tactical maneuver, neither did they fight as individuals, independent of their comrades. Instead, tactical cooperation devolved to smaller units and components, with troops working together in small teams of varying numbers and makeup. Battles, therefore, tended to be aggregates of lesser combats: mêlées of archery duels and brawls between small groups, punctuated by general advances and retreats, and by volleys of arrows launched by bowmen on foot, protected by portable walls of shields. This, too, was a consequence of early medieval military organization.

As we have seen, *bushi* leaders knit together needed forces through complex networks, calling on a variety of relationships and public, as well as personal, forms of authority. Early medieval warriors were not solitary free agents recruited for campaigns as individuals. Many of those who answered calls to arms brought with them followers and allies belonging to their own private military organizations. In some cases these followers and allies had followers and allies of their own. Thus, while *armies* were temporary, irregular assemblages, unable to drill together and therefore unresponsive to large-scale command and control, they were made up of smaller components, which were in turn made up of even smaller units that *were* able to fight and train together regularly and therefore *were* able to coordinate and cooperate on the battlefield.[23]

The fighting men who comprised these monadic organizations lived and trained in close proximity to one another, honing their skills through a variety of regimens and competitive games. By training together in this fashion, *bushi* were able to harmonize their actions with those of close associates with a degree of discipline and fluidity that struck their civilian contemporaries as positively eerie.

In one celebrated story, a ranking cleric of Miidera sent on a late-night errand was escorted by a warrior named Taira Munetsune and some of his men. Munetsune first raised the monk's curiosity when he reported for duty on foot, even though his charge would be traveling on horseback. The two had trekked only a few hundred meters, however, when they met two other warriors waiting in the road with a horse for Munetsune. When the latter had mounted, his retainers fell in behind him and the cleric, and the four of them proceeded another few hundred meters, where they were joined by another pair of warriors. This drama continued: as the entourage rode along, every two or three hundred meters warriors appeared and silently fell in at the end of the line, so that by the time they all reached the outskirts of the capital, the party numbered more than thirty men. On the return trip, the pattern was reversed, each of the retainers silently dropping out at the very spot at which they had joined the group, until at length only the monk and Munetsune – once again on foot – arrived back at their point of debarkation. After this, Munetsune returned to his quarters, leaving the cleric to marvel at the extraordinary display of group discipline and coordination he had just witnessed.[24]

Another anecdote, related in the same text, recounts how Minamoto Yorinobu and his son Yoriyoshi tracked down and killed a horse thief. Awakened in the middle of the night by the shouts of stable hands, both men set off in pursuit of the thief. Each armed himself and rode out independently of the other, but each was confident that the other was also giving chase close by, even though they could not see one another and did not communicate verbally. Eventually they caught up with the thief, who, though still unseen, could be heard walking his horse through a pool of water:

> Yorinobu heard [the sound of the water] and, though it was dark and he could not yet know if Yoriyoshi was there or not, called out "Shoot him down!" just as if the two had agreed on this spot beforehand. Before the words had faded away, a bow-string twanged. Yorinobu heard the arrow strike home, followed by the sound of a horse running off without a rider. He called once again, "You have already shot down the thief. Now run quickly after the horse and fetch it back." Then, without waiting for Yoriyoshi to bring the horse, Yorinobu returned to his home.

As Yoriyoshi brought the animal back to his father's house, he was joined on the road by several of his men, who came to meet him in twos and threes. By the time he arrived home, he had an entourage of some thirty men. He dismissed them, returned the horse to the stable, and went to bed, without checking on his father. The next morning neither Yorinobu nor Yoriyoshi discussed the incident, apparently taking adventures of this sort as a matter of course.[25]

Tales like these are, of course, fictional, and cannot be taken literally. Nevertheless, they reflect a clear belief on the part of the court figures who recorded them that *bushi* were capable of considerable organization and teamwork – a belief that must have had at least some basis in fact. Less fanciful sources, moreover, confirm that collaboration among small units, rather than single combat, was the norm.

Takezaki Suenaga, for example, described one of his encounters with Mongol forces in 1274 as follows:

> I attacked. At this, [my retainer] Tō Genta Sukemitsu called to me, "Our allies continue to arrive; would it not be better to wait and do battle when there are witnesses?" I replied, "In the Way of the Bow and Arrow, it is normal to steal a march [even on one's allies]. Let us then charge!" and galloped forward shouting. . . . My bannerman's horse was shot, and he was thrown. Then I was wounded, as were three of my mounted retainers. My horse was hit as well, but just as I sprang from

it, Shiroishi Rokurō Michiyasu, a shogunal vassal from Hizen province, came galloping in from the rear, with a sizeable force. The Mongol warband retreated toward Sohara. Michiyasu, whose mount was not yet wounded, plunged into the enemy ranks again and again. Had it not been for him, I would surely have perished. Amazingly, we both survived, and could act as witnesses for one another.[26]

Accounts of battles in *Azuma kagami*, such as the following description of the battle of Azugashiyama, during Minamoto Yoritomo's Ōshū campaign in 1189, also depict warriors fighting in teams:

Amid the defenders who remained to fight was Kasuo Tarō Hidekata (thirteen years old), a son of Kongō the Intendant [*bettō*]. He rode forth on a black-dappled horse and, turning its bangs to the enemy, took his place in the lines; his countenance was striking. He galloped toward Kudō Jirō Yukimitsu, but as he drew near Yukimitsu's retainer, Tō Gonan, rode between them and engaged him. . . . Gonan thereby killed Hidekata, yet the youth's strength was out of proportion to his years, and it is said that they fought for some time. Oyama Shichirō Tomomitsu also struck down Kongō the Intendant. . . .

Among those pursuing [the fleeing enemy troops] rode Wada Kotarō Yoshimori, who galloped ahead of the vanguard and by dark arrived near Ōtakamiya in the Shibata district. Nishikido Tarō Kunihira was attempting to cross into Ōzekiyama along the Dewa road, racing at that time across the dikes in the paddies to the right of a road that ran in front of the shrine. Yoshimori pursued him, calling for Kunihira to turn and face him. Kunihira wheeled his horse about, called out his name, and the two rode at one another, each approaching from the other's left. Kunihira nocked an arrow fourteen hand-breadths long, but before he could even draw his bow, Yoshimori let fly a thirteen hand-breadth arrow, which pierced Kunihira's left shoulder plate and struck his upper arm. In pain from this wound, Kunihira turned to flee. Meanwhile, his head filled with thoughts of shooting down an especially important [enemy] commander, Yoshimori readied a second arrow and rode after him.

At this time, [Hatakeyama] Shigetada came galloping up, leading a large force, which rode between Yoshimori and Kunihira, cutting off Yoshimori from his prey. Shigetada's houseman, Ōkuji Jirō, engaged Kunihira. Fearing Yoshimori's second arrow, and startled by Shigetada and his large force, Kunihira plunged his mount off the road and into the deep paddies around it. Now, Kunihira's mount was among the best in Mutsu, standing nearly fifteen hands [that is, 49 *sun*, about 247 cm] tall. Its name was Takadateguro, and, although Kunihira, who was very fat, galloped this animal up Mt. Taka in Hirazumi at least three times every day, it never broke a sweat. Nevertheless, on this occasion it could not climb back to dry land, even when Kunihira whipped it many times. Thus Ōkuji and his men had all the more the advantage, and quickly took his head.[27]

Ambushes and raids

Early medieval Japanese warriors, it should be recalled, legitimately took to the saddle only to chastise lawbreakers – as agents of the court or of the *kenmon* powers that comprised it. Their right to "self-help" – to the pursuit of private ends through violence – was closely circumscribed under law and precedent. While the Kamakura and Muromachi shogunates were, in practice, unable fully to control private feuds and struggles between warriors, they never dropped their pretense that such activities were criminal. Moreover, early medieval warrior titles over lands they claimed to own or administer were still subject to the confirmation and approval of central authority, in contrast to later ages, in which military might became the ultimate – indeed the primary – arbitrator of political and economic right. In the 1180s, the Kamakura regime first seized, and then won legal endorsement for, the right to bypass the court and reward its troops directly. It also dramatically expanded the practice of confiscation of lands from the defeated for redistribution to the victors. But such spoils still came to warriors indirectly, from the shogunate as payment for service, not as plunder seized in the course of the fighting itself; and only a minority of Kamakura vassals ever received landed titles as rewards for their performances in battle.

Consequently, early medieval military campaigns – even private ones – focused on the destruction or apprehension of opposing warriors, not on the capture of territory. The objective – the definition of victory – entailed eliminating the enemy, rather than simply occupying his lands or driving him off them.[28]

Because of this, warriors on the offensive faced a thorny tactical problem: an army in retreat can almost always move faster than a similar army in pursuit, because the latter needs to remain in ranks and ready to fight, should it overtake its quarry. Thus, when opposing hosts are composed of essentially the same weapons systems or similar combinations of systems – as was the case in Japan – it is difficult for either to force battle on the other. All things being equal, combat can take place only when both sides think it to their advantage to stand and fight.[29]

The severity of this impasse depends, of course, on the strategic objectives of the offensive army; some goals – the occupation of enemy territory, for example – can be accomplished without a decisive confrontation. But for early medieval *bushi*, whose missions were complete only with the capture or death of their opponents, the challenge of running an elusive foe to ground must have proved a particular source of frustration.

The simplest solution to this problem, and the one favored by tenth- and eleventh-century warriors, in particular, was to catch the opponent off-guard

– in an ambush or surprise attack. Written sources, other than literary texts, from the Heian period tend to be terse in their accounts of battles, making it difficult to assemble meaningful statistics on strategy and tactics. Nevertheless, the majority of the battles fought during the period appear to have involved some form of surprise attack: out of fifty-eight episodes recounted by various sources in sufficient detail to permit judgments concerning the order of battle, forty-one involved ambushes and/or surprise attacks of one form or another.[30]

Ambush is, however, an effective tactic only if the enemy's whereabouts can be reliably predicted. For early medieval *bushi*, this was most easily accomplished by attacking his home. Night attacks were especially effectual – and particularly favored – for this purpose.

The best-known skirmish of this sort is doubtless Minamoto Yoshitomo's attack on Sanjō Palace in 1159, vividly illustrated in eleven panels of the *Heiji monogatari ekotoba*; but, as Fujimoto Masayuki observes, a late Kamakura-era depiction of a night raid on the home of Uruma Tokikuni, father of the future priest Hōnen, in 1141 offers a better glimpse at the actions and ambiance surrounding what was probably a more typical example of such fights. The armor-clad attackers have smashed open the screens of the Uruma home, and storm across the veranda, overpowering the defenders who, taken unawares, fight only in casual robes and skirts. A severed arm, still clutching a sword, lays on the floor, next to its dying former owner. Women in the adjoining room dart about in panic, while the nine-year-old Hōnen (then called Seishi) brandishes a bow and arrow in the doorway. Meanwhile two warriors, one wearing *ōyoroi* and the other *haramaki*, stand guard at the gates to the compound to prevent reinforcements from entering or occupants of the house from escaping.[31]

Raiding warbands seldom confined their attentions to the home of the principal quarry himself. More often, they laid waste to surrounding fields and to the homes of his allies and dependants as well. The raiders targeted not the real estate itself, but the humans whose livelihoods were tied to it, burning fields, plundering houses and killing residents. Capturing an opponent's lands was not yet possible within the political framework of the time; attacks on his home or economic base, on the other hand, threatened his ability to continue the fight.

Shōmonki, the chronicle of Taira Masakado's exploits in the mid-tenth century, offers several vibrant descriptions of raiding tactics.[32] It relates, for example, that early in the second month of 935, Masakado was ambushed by Minamoto Tasuku at a place called Nomoto, near the convergence of Hitachi, Shimozuke, Musashi and Shimōsa provinces. Taken by surprise, Masakado and his men nevertheless carried that day, prevailing on a combination of luck and determination. Then they struck back, burning and plundering the homes and property of Tasuku's supporters across southeastern Hitachi, and slaughtering "thousands of residents" thereof. *Shōmonki* paints a terrifying picture of Masakado's counter-strike:

> He went about burning the homes of Nomoto, Shida, Ōgushi and Motoki, from the compounds of the wealthy to the tiny houses of

those who abetted them. Those who ran out to escape the flames were surprised with arrows and forced back into the fires. . . . Then he burned more than 500 homes in the three districts of Tsukuba, Makabe and Niihari belonging to allies [of Minamoto Tasuku and his kin], obliterating each and every one of them. How sad it was! Men and women became fuel for the fires, and rare treasures were divided among strangers. . . . That day the voice of the flames contended with the thunder as it echoed; that hour the color of the smoke battled with the clouds as it covered the sky. . . . People s homes became ashes scattered before the winds. Provincial officials and common folk witnessed this in anguish; relatives from near and far heard of this and grieved.[33]

Two years later, Masakado's uncle and father-in-law, Yoshikane, managed to catch and surround him near the border between Hitachi and Shimōsa. Outnumbered and unprepared for combat, Masakado and his men fled. While they attempted to regroup, Yoshikane raided homes and pasture lands around Masakado's home at Kamawa, in the Toyota district of Shimōsa. Nine days later, Masakado and Yoshikane squared off once again at Horikoshi Ford, on the Kinu River a few kilometers northwest of Masakado's home. The battle was a shattering defeat for Masakado. His men broke and ran, while the enemy troops continued to raid and burn in the area. Yoshikane spent ten days raiding and hunting for Masakado, before dispersing his men and returning to Kazusa. Masakado waited him out, and then set out in pursuit, at the head of a sizeable force. At this point, however, Yoshikane elected to retreat and evade rather than risk a decisive fight. Masakado chased him about the valleys and foothills between Mount Tsukuba and Mount Kaba for a week, but was unable to force battle on him, and at length returned to his base "empty-handed." But Yoshikane's decision not to stand and fight proved an expensive choice of tactics, for it was late autumn and the year's harvest was still in the fields. Unable to engage his inimical father-in-law directly, Masakado turned his efforts to burning and pillaging homes and crops belonging to Yoshikane and his men, destroying "thousands of houses" and "tens of thousands" of rice and grain fields.[34]

The breadth of Masakado's rampage in these incidents – the razing of not just the compounds of warrior leaders but the villages in the general area as well – was not a simple matter of cruelty. It was, rather, a calculated attempt to destroy his enemies' capacity to raise additional troops and strike again, as well as to bait them into standing and fighting. On occasion, the scale of destruction wrought by such tactics could be staggering.

Taira Naokata's two-year long attempt to run Taira Tadatsune to ground is a dramatic case in point. In 1031, when the fighting ended, the governor of Shimōsa warned the court that Awa, Kazusa and Shimōsa were "already dead provinces [bōkoku]," and that, "because of the pursuit of Tadatsune, Shimōsa was in extreme distress . . . on the verge of starvation," with "wives and daughters grieving on the roadways."[35] Three and a half years later the governor of Kazusa reported that, while things were at last looking up – owing in considerable measure to his own merits and efforts – the scale of devastation had been horrendous:

> Following the pursuit of Tadatsune, there are now none in the Bandō who refuse to pay their taxes or who resist authority. After the rebellion, however, there was much death and loss, particularly to this province, which was Tadatsune's home. The emissary Naokata and the warriors of the province absorbed [all] taxes for three years. In the year in which his term expired, the previous governor, Koretoki, reported total paddy lands in production to have been no more than 36 acres. . . . whereas there had originally been more than 45,960 acres under cultivation in the province. While there was great destruction during the time of Masakado's rebellion, nothing like this had yet been seen.[36]

In the event, it required more than half a century for eastern Japan to recover from a loss of population and farmlands of this magnitude. As late as 1095, Awa, Shimōsa, Kazusa, Hitachi and Sagami were still petitioning for tax relief on grounds of the "singular expenses of the rebellion."[37]

The horrific destruction of the Taira Tadatsune affair was a direct consequence of the inability of either side to inflict a decisive defeat on the other. Tadatsune, who did not need to crush Naokata, only to hold him off and to survive, appears to have concentrated on keeping the enemy perpetually at bay – denying him both a base of operations anywhere in Awa, Kazusa or Shimōsa and a decisive confrontation – while Naokata spent a good part of his time and energy burning crops and homes belonging to Tadatsune's supporters, in an effort to force his elusive foe to stand and fight.*

By the mid-eleventh century, both tactics had featured prominently in Japanese warfare for longer than anyone could remember; but the costs attendant on employing them were becoming less and less bearable, as the scale of *bushi* military resources and socio-economic influence grew. In the late 930s, Taira Masakado, a relatively powerful warrior and provincial magnate for his day, had stalked about a bailiwick that spanned two districts in Shimōsa. By the late 1020s, however, warriors such as Tadatsune were able to hold lands and exercise influence across three provinces. The result was that, although the military campaign against Tadatsune lasted ten times as long as the (successful) one against Masakado, it produced only widespread destruction.[38]

---

* Fukuda Toyohiko reminds us that the sources explicitly attribute the devastation of the Bōsō provinces resulting from the conflict to the subjugation effort, not Tadatsune's activities (*Tōgoku heiran*, 64).

Fortifications and strongholds

Fortunately for the economic survival of Japan, in subsequent decades defensive strategies, particularly in large-scale campaigns, began to center on entrenchments and fortifications, rather than on evasion and refusal of battle. Whether *bushi* perceived a problem and responded directly to it, or simply stumbled onto a solution for other reasons, is difficult to assess. Whatever their genesis, however, in the event, the new tactics helped prevent recurrences of devastation on the level of the Tadatsune episode.[39]

The first significant campaign in which fortifications played a major role appears to have been Minamoto Yoriyoshi's so-called Former Nine Years' War against Abe Yoritoki and his sons, waged from 1055 to 1062. This contest took place in Mutsu, in the northeast, a region where warriors were heir to a three-century-old tradition of establishing stockades as bases from which to control the local population.[40] The Abe's strategy throughout the conflict centered on ensconcing themselves and their followers behind bulwarks and palisades, in an effort to outlast Yoriyoshi's patience and resolve. Such tactics played on the eagerness of Yoriyoshi's troops to get back as soon as possible to their own lands and affairs. As Yoriyoshi's lieutenant Kiyowara Takenori warned him:

> Our government army is made up of mercenaries, and they are short of food. They want a decisive fight. If the rebels were to defend their strongholds and refuse to come out, these exhausted mercenaries could never maintain an offensive for long. Some would desert; others might attack us. I have always feared this.[41]

If the *Mutsuwaki*, a nearly-contemporaneous literary account of the war, is to be believed, the forts the Abe manned, and the defenses they employed, could be elaborate:

> On the north and east sides of the stockade there was a great swamp; the other two sides were protected by a river, the banks of which were more than three *jō* [about 10 meters] high and as unscalable as a wall. It was on such a site that the stockade had been built. Above the stockade the defenders stood towers, manned by fierce warriors. Between the stockade and the river, they dug a trench. At the bottom of the trench they placed upturned knives and above the ground they strew caltrops. Attackers at a distance they shot down with ōyumi; at those who drew close they hurled stones. When, intermittently, an attacker reached the base of the stockade wall, they scalded him with boiling water and then brandished sharp swords and killed him. Warriors in the towers jeered the besieging army as it approached, calling for it to come forth and fight. Dozens of servant women climbed the towers to taunt the attackers with songs. . . .

Yoriyoshi's tactics against this stockade were equally elaborate – and ruthless as well:

> The attack began on at the hour of the hare [5:00–7:00 am] on the following day. The assembled ōyumi shot throughout the day and night, the arrows and stones falling like rain. But the stockade was defended tenaciously and the besieging army sacrificed hundreds of men without taking it. The following day at the hour of the sheep [1:00–3:00 pm] the besieging commander ordered his troops to enter the nearby village, demolish the houses, and heap the wood in the dry moat around the stockade. He further told them to cut thatch and reeds and pile these along the river banks. Accordingly much was demolished and carried, cut and piled, until at length the stacks towered high as a mountain. . . . The commander then took up a torch himself and threw it on the pyre. . . . A fierce wind suddenly sprang up and the smoke and flames seemed to leap at the stockade. The arrows previously fired by the besieging army blanketed the outer walls and towers of the stockade like the hairs of a raincoat. Now the flames, borne by the wind, leaped to the feathers of these arrows and the towers and buildings of the stockade caught fire at once. In the fortress thousands of men and women wept and cried out as with one voice. The defenders became frantic; some hurling themselves into the blue abyss, others losing their heads to naked blades.
>
> The besieging forces crossed the river and attacked. At this time several hundred defenders put on their armor and brandished their swords in an attempt to break through the encirclement. Since they were certain of death and had no thought of living, they inflicted many casualties upon the besieging troops, until [the deputy commander of the besieging army] ordered his men to open the cordon to let the defenders escape. When the warriors opened the encirclement, the defenders immediately broke for the outside; they did not fight, but ran. The besiegers then attacked their flanks and killed them all. . . . In the stockade dozens of beautiful women all dressed in silk and damask, minutely adorned in green and gold, wept miserably amidst the smoke. Every one of them was dragged out and given to the warriors, who raped them.[42]

Yoriyoshi's experiences with the Abe may have become the inspiration for increasingly widespread use of fortifications elsewhere in the country; nevertheless defensive works as elaborate or permanent as those Yoritoki and his sons occupied remained rare outside the northeast until the fourteenth century. Most Heian- and Kamakura-period fortresses were comparatively simple structures erected for a single battle or campaign.

Unlike the castle homes – protected by deep moats, wooden palisades and earthworks – of Sengoku-era warlords, early medieval *bushi* residences were scarcely distinguishable from those of other rural elites, and differed only in size and opulence from the dwellings of nobles in the capital.[43]

Heian, Kamakura and Nambokuchō warriors built their homes on level ground, usually on relatively high points in or very near the alluvial lowlands of rivers, and immediately adjacent to paddies and other agricultural fields. The main houses, stables and other key buildings were surrounded by water-filled ditches and hedges or fences, and accessed through wooden- or thatch-roofed gates (see Figure 4.3). None of these features, however, appear to have been designed for military expediency.

Ditches were narrow and shallow – less than a meter wide and 30 cm deep – and enclosed areas of 150 by 150 meters or more, presenting an impractically long line to defend with the small number of men normally available to early medieval landowners. They seem, therefore, to have served primarily as components of irrigation works, used to warm water and as a safeguard against droughts. Similarly, fences depicted in medieval artwork are low – a meter or so in height – and constructed of wood, thatch or natural vegetation, making them more suitable for controlling wandering animals than for keeping out marauding warriors. Careful archeological studies indicate that deeper moats and earthworks did not appear around warrior homes until the fourteenth century, and did not become widespread until the fifteenth.[44]

The terms "*shiro*" or "*jōkaku*" (usually translated as "castle" in later medieval contexts) appear frequently in diaries, chronicles, documents and literary accounts of late twelfth- and thirteenth-century warfare, but only in wartime situations, and nearly always in reference to field fortifications, erected for a particular battle.[45] Such breastworks were intended to be temporary, and were rudimentary in comparison to the castles of the later medieval period, but they were not always small in scale. Some, like the famous Taira defense works erected in 1184 at Ichinotani, near Naniwa on the Harima border of Settsu province, could be quite impressive:

Figure 4.3 A mid-twelfth-century warrior residence (*Hōnen jōnin eden*)

The entrance to Ichinotani was narrow; the interior was broad. To the south was the sea; to the north were mountains – high cliffs like a folding screen. There seemed not even a small space through which horses or men could pass. It was truly a monumental fortress. Red banners in unknown numbers unfurled, blowing toward heaven in the spring wind like leaping flames. . . . The enemy would surely lose its spirit when it looked upon this.[46]

From the mountain cliffs to the shallows of the sea they had piled up large boulders, and over these stacked thick logs, on top of which they positioned two rows of shields and erected double turrets, with narrow openings through which to shoot. Warriors stood with bows strung and arrows at the ready. Below this, they covered the tops of the boulders with brush fences. Vassals and their underlings waited, grasping bear-claw rakes and long-handled sickles, ready to charge forth when given the word. Behind the walls stood countless saddled horses in twenty or thirty rows. . . . In the shallows of the sea to the south were large boats ready to be put to oars instantly and head to the deeper water, where tens of thousands of ships floated, like wild geese scattered across the sky. On the high ground they readied rocks and logs to roll down upon attackers. On the low ground they dug trenches and planted sharp stakes.[47]

These descriptions, drawn from later literary accounts of the Gempei War, doubtless incorporate considerable exaggeration, but they nevertheless offer important clues about the nature of late twelfth-century fortifications. Two points, in particular, merit special attention. First, the preparations for battle involved provisions for escape – "countless saddled horses in twenty or thirty rows" and "large boats ready to be put to oars instantly," to ferry troops to "tens of thousands of ships" waiting in deeper water – in addition to the defensive works. And second, as formidable as Ichinotani was, it was neither a complete enclosure nor fortified in all directions. In fact, the Taira defeat there was brought about, in part, by Minamoto Yoshitsune's attack from the hills behind it. Similar tactics decided other key battles of the age as well.[48]

Late Heian and early Kamakura "*jōkaku*" were defensive lines, not castles or forts intended to provide long-term safe haven for armies ensconced within. Many were simply barricades erected across important roads or mountain passes. Others were transient wartime modifications to temples, shrines or warrior residences. Their purpose, in either case, was to concentrate campaigns and battles: to slow enemy advances, thwart raiding tactics, control selection of the battleground, restrict cavalry maneuver, and enhance the ability of foot soldiers (who could be recruited in much larger numbers) to compete with skilled horsemen. And they were expendable, as well as expedient; they were never the sites of sustained sieges or – by choice – of heroic final stands. Contingency

THE SCIENCE OF WAR

planning normally provided for withdrawal and reestablishment of new defensive lines elsewhere.[49]

Picture scrolls indicate that most of the defense features cataloged in the descriptions of Ichinotani were commonly deployed by the late thirteenth century, and most appear in descriptions of other Gempei War-era fortifications in *Heike monogatari* and its sister texts. Curiously, however, some of the simplest devices – brush barricades (*sakamogi*) and shield walls (*kaidate*) – cannot be corroborated in more reliable sources for the 1180s.[50]

Shield walls were exactly what the name implies: rows of standing shields erected behind or on top of other defense works (see Figure 4.5). Standing shields had been used as portable field fortifications since the *ritsuryō* era, and were also deployed as counter-fortifications by besieging armies. *Kaidate* were used on boats as well, to convert what were otherwise fishing vessels to warships.

Sakamogi (literally, "stacked wood") appear to have been essentially piles or hedges of thorny branches placed in front of the principal defensive palisade (see Figure 4.4). They served as an application of what is sometimes called "the principle of the curtain": a light barrier designed to break the momentum of an enemy charge, dissipating its shock power and holding the enemy under fire before he can bring force against the main walls. Brush fences of this sort were architecturally simple, yet extremely effective for the task: Martin Brice notes

Figure 4.4 Sakamogi (Hōnen jōnin eden)

that, during World War I, thorn enclosures, called *boma* or *zareba*, built by the Masai of Tanzania and Kenya proved as difficult to cross, and as resistant to high explosive bombardment, as barbed wire![51]

Masai thorn fences represented a wartime application of a device normally used to contain and protect livestock. Japanese *sakamogi* may have had similar origins.[52] Such a military adaptation of a technology developed for animal control was entirely apropos for early medieval warriors, whose main concern was restricting the movement of enemy horsemen. Brush curtains are, however, vulnerable to fire, which, as we have seen, was a favorite weapon of early *bushi*.

Ditches and moats, another tool borrowed from horse and cattle breeders, offered twelfth-century military architects a more durable curtaining wall for their field fortifications. Because they were intended to halt or hinder the advance of mounted troops, rather than keep hordes of attacking infantry at bay, such ditches needed to be only a few meters wide or deep, and were usually dry. Many were topped on the inner side with earthen ramparts constructed from the dirt removed to dig the trench.[53]

Among the most remarkable examples of early medieval military ditches is the massive defensive line Fujiwara Yasuhira prepared when he learned of Yoritomo's invasion plans in 1189. This barrier, the remains of which can still be seen today, effectively blocked the whole of the Tōsandō, the only route into Mutsu. Stretching some 3 kilometers between Azukashiyama and Kunimishuku, on the northeast end of the Fukushima plain, it was about 15 meters wide and 3 meters deep, featuring steep ramparts of packed earth, augmented here and there with stone. Yasuhira also set up a secondary line some 20 kilometers behind this, and stretched ropes across the Natori and Hirose rivers to form a tertiary line 30 kilometers behind that.[54]

The line of walls constructed along the coastline of northern Kyushu, as a defense against the Mongol invasions of the late thirteenth century, was even grander. Composed of earth, granite and sandstone, and standing 2 to 3 meters high and equally wide, it stretched nearly 10 kilometers.[55]

Fortifications of this scale required enormous labor resources. Manpower costs for Yasuhira's Azukashiyama ditch have, for example, been calculated at more than 20,000 working days. Thus, even mobilizing the entire adult peasant population of the neighboring three districts – at the time, about 5,000 men – the project would have taken forty days or more to complete.[56] Workers for military construction projects were usually conscripted locally, on the basis of various tax obligations.[57]

Ditches and dry moats, augmented with *sakamogi* or earthen ramparts, were more than adequate barriers against Japanese ponies. Unlike European or later medieval Japanese castles, moreover, twelfth-century *jōkaku* did not trap the defenders inside, and therefore constituted only a part of the strategy underlying the battles and campaigns in which they were deployed. Indeed, the construction and use of barricades was intimately bound up with the question of how and when to throw one's own mounted troops at the enemy. Warriors waited behind the walls for the right moment to charge out and counter-attack, or to withdraw to secondary or tertiary lines.

Wooden gates (*kido* or *kidoguchi*), through which defenders on horseback could rush forth to assault besieging forces, constitute the one ubiquitous feature of late twelfth- and early thirteenth-century fortifications. As the only points at which mounted warriors – of either side – could readily cross the barricades, they were usually the nodal points of battle.[58] Consequently, they were the most heavily defended parts of the line, flanked by one or more shielded platforms (*yagura*, literally, "arrow stores") from which archers could shoot down at approaching troops (see Figure 4.5).[59]

On occasion, attacking armies mobilized laborers to build counter-fortifications or dismantle enemy barricades. In the Mutsu campaign, for example, Yoritomo set eighty men, under Hatakeyama Shigetada, to hauling rocks and earth with plows and hoes in order to fill in parts of the Azukashiyama ditch, so that his horsemen could cross.[60] But while the sheer size of the Azukashiyama ditch, and of Yoritomo's army, made counter-mining operations practical and necessary, against less extensive – and more densely defended – fortifications this tactic would have exposed the workers and their supervisors to rocks and arrows launched from the ramparts. Similarly, *bushi* who dismounted to scale the

Figure 4.5 A *yagura* and *kaidate* (*Go-sannen kassen ekotoba*)

walls of the trench made themselves vulnerable to horse-borne counter-offenses, or made it easier for the defenders to withdraw and escape. More commonly, therefore, warriors confronting fortifications focused on storming the entrances and on flanking attacks.[61]

The architectural features, and the tactical considerations, that governed Kamakura-period fortifications continued to dominate the fortresses and skirmishes of the Nambokuchō era as well.[62] But the battles of the 1330s also introduced a new role for warrior strongholds, new kinds of fortresses, and new forms of siege warfare.

During the eighth month of 1331, Go-Daigo fled the capital and "reestablished his imperial abode" in Kasagi temple, on the border between Yamato and Yamashiro. There he speedily erected fortifications and began sending out calls to arms. In response, the shogunate dispatched Sasaki Tokinobu, in command of troops from Ōmi and reinforced by 800 horsemen under the Kuge and Nakazawa families of Tamba, to capture him. On the first day of the ninth month, as 300 outriders from this force, under Takahashi Matashirō, approached the foot of Mount Kasagi, they were ambushed and routed by the castle garrison. Concerned that "should rumors spread of how [the shogunate's men] lost this first battle, and how the castle was victorious, warriors of the various provinces would gallop to assemble there," Kamakura promptly sent a massive army – nearly 75,000 men, according to *Taiheiki* – to invest the castle.[63]

At dawn, on the third day of the ninth month, this force assaulted Kasagi "from all directions." But the castle defenders fought back fiercely, showering the attacking troops with rocks and arrows such that:

> Men and horses tumbled down one upon another from the eastern and western slopes surrounding the castle, filling the deep valleys and choking the roads with corpses. The Kozu River ran with blood, as if its waters reflected the crimson of autumn leaves. After this, though the besieging forces swarmed like clouds and mist, none dared assail the castle.[64]

While the shogunal leaders stood at bay in front of Kasagi castle, "which held strong, and did not fall even when attacked day and night by great forces from many provinces," to their rear other imperial loyalists were "raising large numbers of rebels, and messengers rushed to shogunal headquarters daily":

> On the eleventh day of that month, a courier was dispatched from Kawachi, reporting that, "Ever since the one called Kusanoki Hyōe Masashige raised his banner in service of the Emperor, those with ambitions have joined him, while those without ambition have fled to the east and west. Kusanoki has impressed the subjects of his province, and built a fortress on Akasaka mountain above his home, which he has stocked with as many provisions as he could transport, and manned with

more than 500 horsemen. Should our response lag, this must become a troublesome matter indeed. We must direct our forces toward him at once!"...

Meanwhile, on the thirteenth day of that month a courier was dispatched from Bingo, with the message that, "The lay monk Sakurayama Shirō and his kinsmen have raised imperial banners, and have fortified [Kibitsu] shrine of this province. Since they have ensconced themselves within it, rebels of nearby provinces have been galloping to join them. Their numbers are now more than 700 horsemen.... If we do not strike them quickly, before night gives way to day, this will become an immense problem."[65]

Go-Daigo's loyalist followers looked to fortifications not just as tactical barricades – devices for focusing battles, delimiting campaigns, or trammeling enemy horsemen – but as rallying points, sanctuaries, and symbols of resistance. Thus, while most twelfth- and thirteenth-century defense works had been constructed across or adjacent to roads, beachheads and other travel arteries, Kusanoki Masashige and his allies ensconced themselves in remote mountain citadels, whose purpose and presence defied Kamakura authority, and served as a beacon to other recruits.*

Descriptions in *Taiheiki* and other texts, and depictions of fortifications in fourteenth-century scroll paintings, indicate that fortresses of the period were architecturally similar to those of the early Kamakura era, albeit now fully enclosed and often reinforced with wooden palisades and additional *yagura* erected at various points along the walls between, as well as adjacent to, the gates. The latter two innovations were a necessary consequence of the first. For, unlike the easily abandoned defensive lines favored by twelfth- and thirteenth-century warriors, the citadels Kusanoki and his compatriots occupied allowed the defenders no rapid means of escape or retreat. Indeed, they invited encirclement and siege, beckoning enemy horsemen – hitherto stymied by trenches and simple earthworks – to dismount and assault the walls directly.[66]

Compact enough to be easily defended on all exposures, and located on terrain sufficiently treacherous to render them difficult to approach quickly or in large numbers, such citadels were not readily taken by direct onslaught – even if besieging forces did not really have to contend with the collapsing sham walls, decoy armies of mannequins, and other imaginative slight-of-hand tactics *Taiheiki* attributes to Kusanoki Masashige. More often, it seems, mountain castles fell to attrition – sometimes hastened by cutting off the garrison's water or food supplies. Others were captured by infiltration or stealth.[67]

---

* Even mountain castles of the Heian and Kamakura periods guarded passes, roads or waterways. Some, such as the famous Kinugasa-jō erected in Sagami by the Miura, fronted on inlets or rivers that are no longer apparent. For more on this, see Nakazawa, "Chūsei jōkaku-shi shikiron," 39–41.

In this way, relatively small numbers of warriors could tie up sizeable enemy forces for long periods, buying time and credibility for Go-Daigo's cause, and whittling away at the morale of Kamakura's troops. Kusanoki's garrison of "more than 500 warriors" on Mount Akasaka in 1331 held "what looked to be a hastily-devised" fort "less than one or two hundred meters across" for nearly three weeks, against a shogunal army allegedly comprising "more than 20,000 horsemen." In 1333, he held Chihaya castle near Mount Kongō in Kawachi for more than two months, while a besieging force "rumored to have been over 800,000 horsemen at the beginning" of the siege dwindled to "scarcely 100,000 riders."[68]

New wine in old bottles

The Gempei War and the Nambokuchō wars were momentous events that ushered in profound changes to the place of warriors in Japan's social, political and economic order. Both, moreover, are celebrated in epic wartales whose vivid descriptions of battle have shaped the imaginations of scholars and popular audiences alike for centuries. Given all this, it seems only natural that these two great conflicts should have marked watersheds in the nature of combat and war as well; and, indeed, a veritable legion of historians have identified fundamental shifts of strategy and tactics during one or both struggles.

Among the most influential of these was Ishii Susumu, in the early 1960s. Basing his analysis primarily on the battle accounts in *Heike monogatari* and related literary works, Ishii argued that, while late twelfth-century warriors continued to fight as individuals and on horseback, they no longer engaged in the galloping archery duels favored by their forebears. Instead, they confronted one another at more intimate range, using swords or even grappling techniques to unseat opponents, whom they would then finish off on the ground, with daggers.[69]

A decade later, Satō Shin'ichi, Amino Yoshihiko and others ascribed a similar sea change to the structure and tactics of Nambokuchō-era armies. The mounted professional warriors, fighting as individuals with bow and arrow that had dominated Heian- and Kamakura-era battlefields were, they maintained, superseded from the fourteenth century onward by spear-wielding peasant infantries, deployed in close-ordered formations.[70]

More recent studies have challenged Ishii's, Satō's and Amino's conclusions, identifying instead other sorts of fundamental shifts in tactics introduced in one or both eras. Kawai Yasushi, for example, cites the use of fortifications as a new and dominant pattern of fighting during the 1180s. Abe Takeshi maintains that, from the Gempei War onward, horses were more generally used for transport than for riding, and that mounted troops rarely actually clashed on horseback, preferring instead to dismount just outside arrow range and close on foot, to fight with swords. Okada Seiichi and Futaki Ken'ichi see fourteenth-century warfare as centering on guerrilla tactics, conducted by new types of military forces that appeared during the late Kamakura period. Kondō Yoshikazu contends that the introduction of more powerful bows in the late twelfth century enabled warriors to shoot from longer distances, eliminating the need to gallop close to opponents, while the advent of lighter, less awkward armor in the fourteenth century permitted *bushi* greater freedom of movement when on horseback, and greater comfort when fighting on foot. Accordingly, he maintains, the prevailing tactic of the Gempei War was to shoot from horseback, with the animal standing at rest rather than at a gallop, while by the Nambokuchō era horse-borne warriors fought mainly with bladed weapons, and archers plied their trade on foot. Imai Seinosuke, however, argues that what stands out most about fourteenth-century armies is the degree of cooperation between cavalry and infantry, and the degree to which both horsemen and infantrymen became specialists in the use of either the bow or the blade. In other words, he says, by the Nambokuchō period, military forces had evolved into true armies, whereas during the Gempei era they had still been mostly arrays of individual warriors.[71]

The sheer variety of "sea changes" identified in this cornucopia of theories in and of itself casts doubt on the notion that either the Gempei or the Nambokuchō wars gave rise to *any* sort of truly fundamental transformation of warfare. And indeed, neither did.

The underlying conditions and strategic priorities, and thus the central fighting methods, of war remained predominantly the same throughout the early medieval era. Thirteenth- and fourteenth-century warriors continued, by and large, to perceive themselves as followers of "the way of horse and bow"; and thirteenth- and fourteenth-century commanders continued, by and large, to look to mounted *bushi* as their primary weapons.

Nevertheless, if the Gempei and Nambokuchō wars witnessed no epoch-making transfigurations of warfare, neither did they leave the lineaments of battle unchanged. There were, as we have already noted, significant innovations in weaponry and military organization introduced during and between both conflicts. The socio-political structure was also evolving rapidly. In combination, these factors led to substantial tactical innovation and restyling as well. The most important military vicissitude of the era, and the catalyst to all other changes, was the expanding scale of war and the size of armies.

Appraising the numbers of troops involved in early medieval conflicts is an exceedingly woolly task. Few records specify the size of forces; many of those that do are literary accounts, prone to hyperbole; and different sources often give vastly different numbers for the same armies and battles. Moreover, as Hans Delbrück reminds us, even the most dependable records are shaped by the prejudices and foibles of their authors, including "the general tendency to hyperbolic concepts, a lack of feel for numbers, boastfulness, fear, apology, or other similar human weaknesses," over and above the simple reality that "it is very hard, even for a practiced eye, to estimate accurately rather large masses" of men. Thus even prosaic sources like personal diaries are prone to overestimation – and to understatement as well. Nevertheless, in assessments recorded at or very close to the time of the events recounted, "even underestimates and exaggerations must still take into account the prevailing contemporary notions," and commanders or observers compiling battle reports could not offer up numbers so distorted that contemporaries would immediately have recognized them as such.[72] Within these limitations, then, it does seem possible to reckon the scale of forces with enough precision to support the conclusion that the battles and armies of the Gempei War were an order of magnitude larger than anything experienced in earlier *bushi* conflicts.[73]

The vast majority of Heian skirmishes were localized and *very* small-scale. The most trustworthy sources for the period – legal documents, court records, diaries and the like – describe forces numbering in single or double digits.[74] Even melodramatically hyperbolic literary accounts (and court records demonstrably based on them) of major struggles, such as the campaign against Taira Masakado, recount "surprisingly large armies" as consisting of "more than a thousand men," "a few thousand troops," or "more than 4,000 warriors."[75] For the Gempei War, discrepancies between the numbers given in courtier diaries such as *Gokuyō*, official chronicles such as *Azuma kagami*, and literary texts such as *Heike monogatari* are sometimes dramatic. Nevertheless, even the former describe armies of 5,000, 6,000, "several tens of thousands," "seven or eight thousand," and even 20,000 or 40,000 clashing in some battles.[76]

The relatively sudden appearance of armies of this magnitude – a product of the countrywide scope of the Gempei conflict – introduced new tactical problems, which were intensified by the use of field fortifications. Kawai Yasushi suggests such challenges may have been further exacerbated by a decline in quality of troops that accompanied efforts to enlarge the ranks. While, he argues, it is impossible to calculate with even reasonable precision the total number of warriors in Japan during any part of the Heian or Kamakura periods, it is unlikely that there were, before 1180, vast numbers of skillful, but hitherto unemployed, mounted bowmen waiting in the hinterlands for a call to arms and new lives as *bushi*. This being the case, the majority of even the cavalrymen who filled out the Gempei armies must have been relatively new recruits to military life. Commanders would, therefore, have been faced with finding ways to compensate for the lack of proficiency of many of their troops at combat in the classical, archery-at-a-gallop style.[77]

In any event, defense works enhanced the role and value of foot soldiers in the fighting. More importantly, the combination of fortifications with larger forces concentrated battles and battlefields, rendering the former longer and the latter more crowded. These factors, in turn, limited the mobility of both attacking and defending troops, mitigating some of the shortcomings of warriors inexperienced at mounted archery. The inability of Japanese horses to continue to run about for the entire duration of long battles, and the inability of the *bushi* to carry sufficient numbers of arrows to last through the entire skirmish, moreover, forced even seasoned veterans to make adaptations. Thus in the accounts of Gempei battles we see warriors shooting from stationary mounts, engaging in swordplay and grappling from horseback, and even using their horses to ram opponents.

THE SCIENCE OF WAR

Nevertheless, it is clear that the new tactics *augmented* traditional ones; they did not supplant them. Warriors engaged in archery at a gallop still took the forefront in Gempei War battles. They also featured prominently in later Kamakura conflicts, including the Ōshū campaign, the Wada rebellion, the Jōkyū War, and the Mongol invasions.[78] Swords, by contrast, were rarely employed except under circumstances in which warriors could not use their bows.

As I noted in Chapter 3, there is not a single example in any Heian-period document, text or drawing of warriors wielding bladed weapons from horseback. This is scarcely surprising, when one considers how ill-suited early medieval *tachi* and *ōyoroi* were to mounted swordplay. It would, to begin with, have been no easy task to close to sword range on horseback against a mounted adversary armed with bow and arrows. Cutting or stabbing through *ōyoroi* with the slender, short-hilted *tachi* of the era – or even walloping an antagonist with sufficient force to unhorse him – presented a still more formidable challenge, particularly for a warrior whose balance, striking power and freedom of movement were impeded by the rigid, boxy cuirass and loose-hanging shoulder plates of his own armor.* Simply knocking the opponent to the ground would not, moreover, have concluded the contest; the warrior would have had to dismount himself, to finish him off with sword or dagger. But repetition of that sort of tactic – which Ishii Susumu envisioned as the prevailing form of combat in Gempei battles – would have rapidly exhausted even the hardiest warrior, for his armor added nearly half again to his own body weight. It would also have given the warrior's horse ample opportunity to scamper off, converting him to a foot soldier for the duration of the battle.

Grappling on horseback was fraught with similar problems – as are scholarly speculations that Kamakura warriors preferred to fight that way. To be sure, wrestling skills were fundamental components of a warrior's bag of tricks, and notable contributors to his reputation and identity. In fact the phrase "master of bow, horse and grappling" (*kyūba sumō no tatsusha*) was a common appellation for illustrious *bushi*.[79] Medieval wartales, moreover, intone that "warriors of the East . . . ride after their foes, and overtaking them, decide the contest by grappling – this is their war art," or "how, indeed, the young bands of Musashi and Sagami excel at pushing and wrestling on horseback!"[80] They also feature quite a number of episodes in which contending samurai grappled with one another, first on horseback and then on the ground.

---

* Even expert swordsmen under optimal conditions cannot readily cut through Japanese armor. Sword techniques developed during the late medieval and early modern periods for use against armored opponents target gaps and weak spots in the armor, but this requires considerable precision and skill, even fighting on foot and wielding the sword with both hands. It would have been doubly hard to accomplish one-handed on the back of a bouncing horse. Suzuki Masaya makes a strong case for the conclusion that swords continued to play only a minor role, even in late medieval battles. See *Teppō to Nihonjin* or *Katana to kubi-tori*.

All such incidents, however, occur during the final stages of large battles, at points when the warriors involved had exhausted their arrow supplies and one side or the other was in retreat.[81] Swordfights took place at similar times, or under other circumstances in which *bushi* did not have recourse to their bows. One searches in vain for a single battlefield example of warriors voluntarily forsaking bow and arrow to fight one another hand-to-hand. All *bushi* carried long swords (*tachi*), as well as shorter, companion blades (*katana*), and trained at grappling; but they viewed these weapons as supplements to their bows and arrows, never as replacements for them. Kamakura warriors were still, by preference and for good reason, first and foremost bowmen on horseback. *Azuma kagami* makes this point explicitly in an entry from 1180:

> While [Matano] Kagehisa and his retainers camped in the hills north of Mt. Fuji, rats gnawed and ruined over a hundred of their heavy-duty bowstrings. At this inopportune time, Yasuda Saburō Yoshihisa; Kudō Kagemitsu; his son, Kojirō Yukimitsu; and the Ichikawa Intendent, Yukifusa, having heard of the battle at Ishibashi, had set forth from Kai to join it, when they met up with Kagehisa and his men at Mt. Hashida. Wheeling their mounts and letting fly arrows, they attacked Kagehisa. The hour of the fray had come! Their bowstrings severed, Kagehisa and his men unsheathed their swords and brandished them, but they could not thus contend against arrows and stones. Many were shot. . . . Kagehisa cast away his pride and fled like lightning.[82]

Mounted archers remained central to Nambokuchō warfare as well. Recent studies by Thomas Conlan, Shakadō Mitsuhiro, Suzuki Masaya, Imai Seinosuke and others have persuasively undermined long-cherished presumptions that the fourteenth century marked the advent of a new age of infantry supremacy. The most compelling evidence on this point comes from analyses of statistics on wounds, compiled from battle reports. Conlan looked at 1,302 such documents, cataloging 721 identifiable wounds. Of these, some 73 percent were caused by arrows, while only 25 percent were the result of sword strokes, and fewer than 2 percent involved spears. Suzuki examined 175 such documents, and found that nearly 87 percent of the 554 identifiable casualties reported therein came from arrows, 8 percent were caused by swords or *naginata*, just under 3 percent were the result of troops having been struck by rocks, and 1 percent were caused by spears. Shakadō's less extensive survey of some thirty battle reports indicates that 82 percent of the wounds were caused by arrows.[83]

Moreover, pictorial, narrative and documentary records alike indicate that ratios of horsemen to foot soldiers in field battles remained similar to those of Heian and Gempei conflicts; and that troops on foot fought in scattered groups, shooting, whenever possible, from the cover of rocks, trees, buildings, or standing shields.[84] Clearly then, Nambokuchō battles continued to revolve around skirmishes between mixed clusters of mounted warriors and foot soldiers.

If bowmen on horseback no longer dominated the battlefield quite as thoroughly as they had during previous centuries, neither were they superseded by massed formations of spear-wielding peasant infantrymen – as Satō Shin'ichi, Amino Yoshihiko and others have contended.

There was no fourteenth-century military revolution comparable to the upheavals sweeping through the political, social and economic structures during the period. Significant innovations in weaponry and military organization notwithstanding, strategic and tactical thinking continued along predominantly the same lines they had followed since the waning of the *ritsuryō* regiments.

★ ★ ★ ★ ★

The science of war in early medieval Japan was shaped by a complex and multifarious confluence of geography, available resources, ideology, polity, technology, goals and mission. Some of these factors stood immutable – or nearly so – throughout the six centuries on which this study focuses. Others evolved steadily, or even dramatically. The early medieval period was an age in which struggles between competing political centers at once spawned and masked the rise of new socio-economic structures on the land. Certainly a warrior somehow transported from the mid-tenth century to the mid-1300s would have encountered much that would have been nigh unrecognizable to him. And yet the battlefield would have remained one place where he felt comfortably at home. By and large, while warfare changed a great deal in terms of scale, duration and frequency, it changed little in terms of strategies and tactics. Early medieval Japan remained, throughout, the age of horse and bow.

The pertinacity of hoary tactical paradigms reflects the survival of key socio-cultural imperatives at the eye of a swirling maelstrom of change. Foremost among these were the *bushi*'s identity and self-image as a professional mercenary, and the belief in the existence of a centralized, national power structure. Together, these ideological constructs stayed warriors from fully exploring the possibilities being opened by advances in weapons technology and military organization.

Between the late twelfth and late fourteenth centuries, *bushi* political power progressively displaced that of the imperial court, but the idea that a center existed continued to dominate political – and therefore strategic – thinking. The evolving realities of power on the land notwithstanding, warrior leaders persistently clung to status defined in terms of hierarchies averring possession of countrywide authority. Early medieval *bushi* were not yet warlords.

Nor were they soldiers. Having come into being as hired swords for the state and for the *kenmon* powers that dominated the court, the *bushi* of the Heian era represented an order of professional mercenaries defined by their mastery of a unique style of mounted archery. Indeed, this technology *created* the *bushi*, and determined the form of their armor and other equipment – and this, in turn, circumscribed what they could and could not do in combat. The peculiar tactics they developed in response to political, strategic and technological circumstances, moreover, maximized opportunities for individual warriors to distinguish themselves in the field, and thereby advance their careers.

During the thirteenth and fourteenth centuries, the broadly cast warrior order of Heian times evolved rapidly into the provincially based warrior class of the later medieval period. Nevertheless, the survival of central government, and the success of the court and shogunate in keeping notions of *droit de guerre* bound to concepts of law enforcement and service to public authority, mitigated against fundamental changes to definitions of military success. The early medieval era was, moreover, a time when – with the exception of the very small-scale Jurchen invasion in the eleventh century and the Mongol invasions of the 1270s and 1280s – Japan faced no foreign enemies and *bushi* only fought one another. Such circumstances provided little incentive to seek out new tactical paradigms.

Tactics – in the narrow sense of techniques of combat – are, however, but one element in the larger construct of early medieval warfare. In war, irrespective of time and place, how one fights is determined not just by why one fights and how one *can* fight, but also by how one *may* fight and how one *should* fight. Historians and philosophers have, in fact, directed considerable attention to this proposition, in the process formulating two kinds of rules of war: those governing the reasons for fighting (Just War or *jus ad bellum*); and those governing the way wars are fought (Just Warfare or *jus in bello*).

Early medieval Japanese warriors forged a body of custom – a culture of war – that continued to provide a framework for Japanese thoughts on *jus in bello* well into modern times. This, then, forms the subject of the next (and final) chapter of this study.

5

THE CULTURE OF WAR

> You may be obliged to wage war, but you are not obliged to use poisoned arrows.
> Baltasar Gracian y Morales, *The Art of Worldly Wisdom*, 1647

> War is a social creation.
> Michael Walzer, *Just and Unjust Wars*, 1977

In one of the most intriguing analyses of early medieval military culture to date, William Wayne Farris applied extrapolations from sociobiology and anthropology to early samurai battlefield behavior. Building on Robert O'Connell's musings on the evolution of animal weaponry and its relationship to human arms development, Farris likened early *bushi* warfare to the intraspecific combat of stags and rams contesting with rivals over mates, or wolves sparring to secure dominance within their packs, and contrasted it with the predatory conflict that occurs between animals of differing species, such as when lions prey on antelopes. The latter – practiced for survival – tends to be ruthless and to involve prosaic weaponry, while the former tends toward ritual, individual combat and elaborate armaments. In human terms, he argued, predatory warfare usually occurs between distinct political or ethnic groups, such as kingdoms and states, while intraspecific combat holds within a group, such as a family, region or class.[1]

This hypothesis is imaginative and tantalizing, but the analogy on which it turns breaks down at both ends. In the animal, as well as the human world, intraspecificity is a necessary condition of ritual combat, but it is far from a sufficient condition. Clearly, rules limiting the weapons, targets, and other conditions of warfare can evolve only for conflicts between constituent groups or individuals within a larger society whose members share and agree on the values underlying the rules. But neither the creation nor the observance of such rules can be expected unless the objectives – what can be gained from victory – are overshadowed by the consequences of winning by illegitimate means. In practice, ritual combat occurs when and only when the *purpose* of the combat is ritual.*

Farris's analogy was a valiant attempt to explain a key tenet of the received wisdom on early samurai warfare, one that was largely unchallenged at the time he wrote. Indeed, the terms "ritual" and "formalism" were, until recently, nearly ubiquitous in standard treatments of this topic. In the mid-1980s, for example, Ishii Shirō enumerated six fundamental rules of engagement for the period:

- fixing of the time and place for battles
- guarantees for the safety of messengers exchanged at the start of battles
- fighting centered on one-to-one duels (*ikki uchi*)
- selection of suitable or worthy opponents by self-introductions (*nanori*)
- honorable treatment for surrendered or captured enemy troops
- guarantees for the safety of non-combatants on the field.

He noted that none of these rules were absolute – that there were more than a few exceptions to any of them – but argued that the rules existed nonetheless.[2] And he was far from alone in this conclusion. Early medieval battles have long been portrayed as set pieces, governed by gentlemanly norms and conventions, and following an elaborate choreography in which the conduct of the fighting seemed as important as the result. Eiko Ikegami's characterization of early medieval warfare as "a complex social ritual of death, honor and calculation, and actual combats on the medieval battlefield" as "colorful rites of violence, death and honor," is a recent case in point.[3]

---

* Not all intraspecific combat in the animal kingdom is ritualized and non-lethal. Chimpanzees and ants, for example, regularly stage lethal group attacks on others of their species. Stylized, low-casualty fights between animals occur only when the ends of the conflict mitigate against maiming or killing the opponent. Wolves contesting for leadership of the pack or rams butting heads over females would lose far more than they gained if they crippled or killed the other males: the alpha wolf would have no pack to lead, and the alpha ram would permanently eliminate from his herd's gene pool the best of the younger rams before they could reach their prime.

  Similarly, in the case of human beings, all ritual combat is intraspecific, but not all intraspecific combat is ritualized. Farris cites the battles of Homeric heroes over Helen of Troy and the jousts of medieval knights to win the admiration of their ladies as examples of highly ritualized warfare. But the heroic, individual combats of the Trojan War took place on the pages of the *Iliad*, not on the battlefields of Troy; and even there, they were ultimately trumped by the cunning and perfidy of the Greeks who built the Trojan Horse. The joust was ritualized for and in tournaments – knightly sporting events. Actual warfare in medieval Europe was far more freewheeling, and far more lethal. John Keegan, *A History of Warfare*, 240–54; John Warry, *Warfare in the Classical World*, 10–23; and Bernard Knox, "Trojan War," 479–80, offer concise discussions of the historicity of Homer's portrait of ancient Greek warfare. J. F. Verbruggen, *The Art of Warfare*; Malcolm Vale, *War and Chivalry*; and Matthew Strickland, *War & Chivalry*, are among the best overviews of warfare in medieval Europe.

But, as I suggested in the introduction to this volume, the early medieval period thus envisioned is more epic than epoch, arising not from the battlefield exploits of the *bushi* themselves, but from the imaginations of later litterateurs and *jongleurs* who recounted them. Such creative nostalgia found its most eloquent expression on the pages of the *Hōgen*, *Heiji* and *Heike monogatari*, which were, until very recently, the principal sources for studies of early *bushi* culture.

Analyses and descriptions of the gentlemanly rules alleged to have governed early samurai warfare all begin from the premise that such rules did in fact exist. Historians who have identified and endeavored to explain ritual and formality on early medieval battlefields have done so because they *expected* to find it there. The blinders imposed by preconceptions have restricted these scholars' views of their sources, and precluded consideration of alternative interpretations.

Closer scrutiny of the sources, even the most familiar ones, indicates that Heian and Kamakura *bushi* were a good deal less gentlemanly in their battlefield antics than was once believed. At least two of Ishii's rules of engagement – the notion that battles were usually fought at times and places agreed upon in advance, and the idea that they centered on one-on-one duels – can already be rejected on the basis of the discussion of strategy and tactics, in the previous chapter. The others, as we shall see, fare no better under careful inquiry.

This chapter, then, examines the military culture of the early *bushi*, contrasting it with the received wisdom on warfare in early medieval Japan. It analyzes behavior in war and battle, as well as the judgments of both warriors and others who observed them, to identify the norms and expectations concerning the conduct of war.

Reputation, honor and warrior personality

In early medieval Japan, honor and reputation lay at the heart of a warrior's self-perception, and provide the context within which the conventions of war must be evaluated. A samurai's reputation, honor and pride were almost tangible entities that took precedence over all other obligations. As a thirteenth-century commentary enumerating the "seven virtues of a warrior" concludes, "To go forth to the field of battle and miss death by an inch; to leave behind one's name for myriad generations; all in all, this is the way." Slights to reputation or honor were often catalysts to belligerence and bloodshed. Warriors might refuse orders from their superiors, risk the loss of valuable retainers, and even murder men to whom they owed their lives, all for the sake of their reputations.[4]

Honor – or conversely, shame – could reach beyond the warrior himself, and even beyond his lifespan. *Bushi* could prosper through the inherited glory of their ancestors or suffer the stigma of their disgrace. Thus, even a warrior's life could be of less consequence to him than his name and image, and we find in accounts of battles numerous sketches of warriors choosing to sacrifice themselves in order to enhance their reputations or those of their families.[5]

One must, however, be careful not to make anachronistic or ethnocentric assumptions about the nature of honor, or about the sort of battlefield conduct it might be expected to have engendered. For, while honor and shame were central to the self-perception of early *bushi*, honor turned on a warrior's military reputation, which turned first and foremost on his record of victories. Early medieval Japanese concepts of honor and of honorable conduct in battle were flexible enough to permit successful warriors to rationalize almost any sort behavior. Expediency, self-interest, and tactical, strategic or political advantage proved to be much more powerful determinants of early medieval Japanese military conventions than abstractions such as honor.[6]

Stolid pragmatism and a detached, professional approach to their calling seem, in fact, to have been the dominant tenets of *bushi* personality. Warriors in the sources appear as unruffled, realistic men with powerful forces of will and equally powerful egos. A report presented to the Iwashimizu Hachiman shrine in 1046 by Minamoto Yorinobu showcases this point nicely:

> Recently, in the fourth year of *Manjū* [1027] that rat of wolf-like greed, Taira Tadatsune of Kazusa, strode about the East. He defied the governors of the eastern provinces, spread his own influence, and oppressed the collection of taxes. He embraced a treacherous, wild heart. He turned the structure of the court upside down, collecting taxes and tax goods for himself, and ignoring imperial orders. Although the nobles repeatedly summoned men of valor that he should be apprehended, he firmed up his stronghold and fled into it. . . . I was then chosen by the court and appointed to pacify the East. In 1029, I was named governor of Kai. Without rousing the people, without extending my jurisdiction, without beating any drums, without flying any banners, without pulling a bow, without releasing an arrow, without deliberation, without attacking, I captured the rebel where I sat.[7]

Warriors were not callous or emotionless robots. There is ample evidence that they also valued tenderness and compassion, particularly as qualities appropriate to warrior leaders. One text, for example, reports Abe Yoritoki deciding to defy his provincial governor's summons for his son, Sadatō, with the explanation that, "It is for the sake of their wives and children that men exist in this world. While Sadatō may be a fool, a father loves his son – he cannot abandon and forget him. How could I bear it if he were executed?"[8] The same text speaks even more poignantly of Minamoto Yoriyoshi's behavior in the aftermath of a victory:

> He provided his men a feast, and saw to their weapons and armor. He personally circulated through the army, tending to the wounded. Deeply moved, the warriors declared, "With our bodies we shall repay this debt; our lives are made light by loyalty. Now we feel no aversion even toward dying for our commander."[9]

Nevertheless, where conflicts arose between emotionally and rationally inspired courses of action, pragmatism nearly always prevailed. In fact early literary depictions of warriors go out of their way to demonstrate that important decisions were always buttressed by rational contemplation. Yoritoki's decision to ignore the governor's orders, for example, although purportedly made out of fatherly affection, was also a reasoned and deliberate one. The passage quoted above goes on to show Yoritoki qualifying his emotional declaration with the codicil "We shall pretend that we did not hear the summons. I doubt that [provincial Governor Minamoto] Yoriyoshi will come to attack me, but should he come, we can resist him. We do not yet have cause for grief."[10]

Warrior relationships with the supernatural were similarly matter-of-fact. The need to bolster morale and courage make actively seeking divine aid in the pursuit of victory a natural and obvious concern for military men of any time and place. And there are, of course, pressing political – as well as moral – reasons for commanders to be conscious of the dictates of religion in order to justify and legitimize their wars. But *bushi* interaction with the divine ran much deeper than this. As Thomas Conlan observes, the medieval battlefield was "a realm where gods and buddhas mingled with men."[11]

A key feature of the medieval Japanese worldview, formed at the nexus of Buddhist, Taoist, Confucian and nativist ("Shintō") beliefs, was its monistic, or unitary, world of meaning. In this conceptualization, the phenomenal realm – the natural or manifest world – was synonymous with the sacred realm. The cosmos was a unitary whole, permeated throughout by sacred, or *kami*, nature.[12] Medieval Japanese saw the hands of their gods everywhere: every success and every failure was the result of divine approval or displeasure. Men lived or died, prospered or declined, at the whim of divinities, who were tangible, accessible and open to influence.

Medieval warriors were no more estranged from the superhuman forces around them than were other Japanese of their age. They regularly consulted oracles, and attributed military triumphs to the assistance of guardian deities and setbacks to the exhaustion of divine grace.[13]

An anecdote concerning a retainer of Fujiwara Yasumasa, and recorded in a twelfth-century tale collection, is particularly revealing in this regard: Yasumasa, who, "although not of a warrior house," was "of fierce courage and a master of the way of the bow and arrow," was serving at the time as governor of Tango, and had gotten into the habit of holding regular deer hunts. On the night before one such hunt, an exceptionally skillful retainer dreams of his mother appearing to him to reveal that she has been reincarnated as a deer, and to implore him to watch out for her when he hunts. The next morning, the retainer approaches Yasumasa, attempting to beg out of the day's hunt by claiming illness. Yasumasa, however, is unconvinced and insists the retainer participate. Later, in the excitement of the hunt, the warrior forgets his dream and shoots down a large doe that bounds across his path. But when he approaches it, he is shocked to discover that the deer has his mother's face. Grief stricken, he cuts his hair and renounces the world on the spot. When Yasumasa, puzzled by this action and by the man's obvious distress, inquires why he is behaving this way, the retainer relates the whole story. Whereupon Yasumasa scolds him, saying that, had he known the truth, he would certainly not have forced him to go on the hunt.[14]

It would, therefore, be a mistake to discount the reality or the depth of warrior religious concerns and beliefs. At the same time, early medieval relationships with the supramundane were immediate and functional, and warriors were sometimes content to rationalize away apparent conflicts between religious and practical imperatives. Thus we find accounts like the following, related about Minamoto Yoriyoshi's attack on Abe Sadatō at Komatsu stockade, in 1062:

> Since it was evening, and the date was inauspicious, Yoriyoshi did not intend to attack. But while [Kiyowara] Takesada, [Tachibana] Yorisada and others scouted nearby, their foot soldiers set fire to some buildings and reeds outside the enemy palisade. Responding to this, those inside the fort shouted and sent forth a haphazard shower of rocks and arrows. [Yoriyoshi's] government army answered in kind, each man competing to be the first to reach the stockade. [Yoriyoshi] then said to [his deputy commander,] Takenori, "Our reckoning for tomorrow is suddenly skewed. The battle has already erupted at this hour. Still, a warrior waits for opportunity; he cannot always choose the time and day. Sung Wu-ti did not avoid the *wang-wang* and in so-doing achieved merit. When a warrior sees an opportunity, he must follow it quickly, before it is too late."*

Deception, guile and surprise

Early medieval warriors were, as Yoriyoshi suggests, highly in tune to seizing, to exploiting and, especially, to creating favorable opportunities. Although *bushi* did sometimes issue challenges and even set times and places for battle, such promises were honored far more often in the breach than in the event. In fact, the preferred stratagem of early *bushi* was to catch opponents off-guard; the preference for this sort of fighting is reflected even in the later medieval wartales.

Indeed, one of the most striking passages in the *Hōgen monogatari* relates the council of war held by forces of the retired emperor, Sutoku, on the eve of battle. When asked by Fujiwara Yorinaga, the Minister of the Left, how he

---

* "Mutsuwaki," p. 27. Sung Wu-ti (356–422) was the founder of the Liu Sung dynasty in China. According to tradition, he was preparing for an attack on an enemy fortress one day in 410, when someone objected that it was the *wang-wang* (Japanese: *ōbō*; literally "go forth and die"), a day considered inauspicious for leaving a military headquarters. Wu-ti is said to have replied, "I will go forth; they will die" (Helen McCullough, "Tale of Mutsu," 209n.).

recommended conducting the coming hostilities, Minamoto Tametomo is purported to have replied:

> According to my experience, there is nothing so advantageous in striking down enemies as a night attack. Let Tametomo go now, while the heavens are not yet light, and press down upon Takamatsu Palace[, the residence of Emperor Go-Shirakawa]. If we set fire to three sides and secure the fourth, those fleeing the flames will be struck down by arrows, and for those who seek to avoid the arrows, there will be no escape from the flames.

Yorinaga was, however, unpersuaded:

> Tametomo's plan is crude; it lacks wisdom. This is the effect of his youth. Night attacks and such are suitable to private fights involving ten or twenty men, but when the Emperor and Retired Emperor contend for a whole nation, a night attack is unthinkable.[15]

Concerns for matters of propriety in warfare such as Yorinaga expresses in this passage are notably absent from any text written before the fourteenth century. It is significant that even here the words are placed in the mouth of Yorinaga – a courtier, not a military man – rather than attributed to any warrior.[16] Heian-period audiences considered surprise attacks so normal that an early eleventh-century text begins a description of the archetypical *bushi*, "the greatest warrior in the land," by informing us that "he was highly skilled in the conduct of battles, *night attacks*, archery duels on horseback, and *ambushes*" [emphasis added].[17]

Among the most famous apologues of early samurai behavior is the *Konjaku monogatarishū* story about Minamoto Mitsuru and Taira Yoshifumi that I introduced in the previous chapter. After describing how gossip carried between the two sparked a quarrel that resulted in a challenge to combat, the text relates that:

> The two sides exchanged documents agreeing to meet on the field on a specified day. After this both put their troops in order and prepared to fight. On the agreed upon day, the two war bands set forth, coming to face each other across the designated field at the hour of the serpent [9:00–11:00 am]. Both were forces of five or six hundred men. While all prepared their hearts, readying to cast aside their bodies and disregard their lives, they planted their shields in rows, facing each other at a distance of about one *chō* [approx. 110 meters].
>
> Each side then sent forth a warrior to exchange documents. As those stalwarts returned to their ranks, there began, as was customary, a flurry of arrows. The warriors did not look back or even hurry their horses forward, but returned quietly – thus displaying their bravery. After this, both sides moved their shields closer together and were about to

begin shooting, when Yoshifumi called to Mitsuru, "To simply set our respective troops discharging arrows at one another does not serve the interest of today's battle. Let only you and I learn of each other's skill. Instead of having our troops engage, how about if only the two of us ride at one another and take our best shots?"

Mitsuru concurs and, after cautioning his men to stay out of the fight, even should he lose, rides out to engage Yoshifumi alone. The two make several passes at one another, but neither is able to land a decisive shot. At length they agree to call the matter a draw and, having settled their quarrel, spend the remainder of their lives amicably.[18]

The behavior of Mitsuru and Yoshifumi in this tale accords well with the eidolon of the received wisdom, and is, in fact, the principal source cited in support of several key points, such as the conventions regarding messengers. But it contrasts vividly with another account, in the same text, about two later tenth-century warriors, Taira Koremochi and Fujiwara Morotō.[19]

A dispute over a piece of land festers, fueled by gossip, until at length a challenge is issued and date and place agreed upon. As the day of battle approaches, Morotō finds himself outnumbered nearly three to one and, apparently deciding discretion to be the better part of valor, flees instead to a neighboring province. The text that records the tale informs us that "those who spoke between the two warriors pronounced favorably on this."

Koremochi, upon receiving this news, determines things to be safe and demobilizes his men, who have been pestering him to allow them to return to their homes. But shortly thereafter, Morotō, approaching with a sizeable force, startles Koremochi and his household from their sleep. Morotō's men surround Koremochi's compound, set fire to the buildings, and shoot down anyone who emerges. When the fire has burned itself out, they search the ashes, "discovering men of high and low rank, children and the like – all told more than 80 persons – burned to death."

En route home, Morotō stops near the home of his brother-in-law, Tachibana Yoshinori, to give his troops a rest, whereupon the men celebrate their victory by gorging themselves on food and *sake*, until they pass out.[20] Unbeknownst to them, however, Koremochi is not dead. He had escaped by seizing a robe from one of his serving women, and slipping past the attackers under the cover of the smoke.*

"Dropping into the depths of a stream to the west, he carefully approached a place far from the bank where reeds and such grew thickly, and clung to the roots of a willow," where he hid until the fighting was over and Morotō's troops had

---

* *Azuma kagami* 1184 4/21 recounts a similar incident involving a warrior escaping danger disguised as a woman, and even getting a friend to impersonate him and draw off pursuers.

withdrawn. Some of his own troops who had not been in the house later find him, and resupply him with clothing, weapons and a horse, while he explains what happened, adding that he had chosen not to flee into the mountains at the beginning of the attack because he feared that "this would leave behind the reputation of one who had run away." His men counsel him to wait and reassemble his forces before going after Morotō, whose troops outnumber them five or six to one. But Koremoto shakes off this advice, arguing:

> Had I been burned to death inside my house last night, would my life exist now? I escaped in this manner at great cost, yet I do not live. To show myself to you for even one day is extremely shameful. Therefore, I will not be stingy with this dew-like life. You may assemble an army and fight later. As for myself, I will go [on to attack] alone. . . . No doubt I will send off [only] a single arrow and then die, but to choose otherwise would be a limitless shame for my descendants. . . . Those of you who begrudge your lives need not come with me; I will go alone.

Koremochi and his men then fall upon Morotō's troops, taking them completely by surprise. Drunk and sated, Morotō's side is able to offer only a half-hearted defense, and is soon utterly destroyed. After taking Morotō's head, Koremochi moves on to his home, which he puts to the torch.

In spite of very similar beginnings, the conflicts between Yoshifumi and Mitsuru, and between Morotō and Koremochi, proceed in such stark contrast to one another that readers are left wondering if perhaps there could have been two competing ethics of battlefield conduct during the tenth century. But while at least one scholar has concluded that there was in fact a "dichotomy about confrontation" at work among Heian warriors, Ishii Susumu offers a simpler explanation. The confrontation between Yoshifumi and Mitsuru, he observes, would have had to have occurred about 150 years before the text that records it was compiled. The text's editorial comment, that "the warriors of old were like this," suggests that the actions portrayed represent an idealized image of earlier *bushi* – creative nostalgia on the part of twelfth-century litterateurs – in the same way that the medieval wartales represent an idealized image of twelfth-century warrior behavior.[21]

Even if one accepts the account of Yoshifumi's duel with Mitsuru at more-or-less face value, the conclusion that the warriors' behavior therein was exceptional – or unique – seems inescapable. In other sources, the aplomb with which the early samurai engaged in deceit and subterfuge is striking. The acceptance of both warrior and non-warrior audiences of this sort of behavior is still more so.

Another incident related in the same text, for example, describes the illustrious Taira Sadamichi's tactics in carrying out an order to hunt down and kill another warrior. Sadamichi first befriends the man and wins his confidence, then rides out of sight to don his armor and prepare himself, only to return minutes later to catch his hapless victim unarmored and riding along on a spare horse, shooting him down before he can even reach his weapons. In yet another tale from that text, a samurai slays the man who killed his father by disguising himself as a servant bearing food, sneaking into the man's room (while he rested in the home of the samurai's lord), and slitting his throat while he slept. *Azuma kagami*, the Kamakura shogunate's own didactic record of its history, recounts how Minamoto Yoritomo had one of his men executed for treason by summoning him to his quarters and entertaining him with food and drink, in the midst of which another of the shogun's men, Amano Tōkage, stepped forward with a sword to lop off the unfortunate man's head. In none of these accounts is there any suggestion that this sort of conduct is improper.[22]

A fondness for surprise attacks and artifice can be seen as far back in Japanese history as the *Kojiki*, in the exploits of Yamato Takeru-no-Mikoto, and at least as recently as the Pacific War.[23] Indeed, this is perhaps one of the dominant themes of Japan's martial legacy. The idea that a warrior must be ever on guard, always prepared for, always expecting, an attack is expressed frequently in early modern commentaries on Japanese martial art or *bushidō*; it may be this sort of philosophy that is responsible for the apparent lack of sportsmanship in Japanese warfare. For if a warrior is expected to be always on his guard, to take him by surprise – to catch him unprepared – is no more taking unfair advantage than is attacking an opponent through an opening in his guard during a formal fencing match or duel.

This sort of thinking was not, of course, by any means unique to Japan. Medieval European lords also happily built on tactics of betrayal and deception to secure victory. Matthew Strickland points, for example, to the 1118–19 campaigns between Henry I and Louis VI, fought principally in Normandy, which demonstrated the repeated use of guile in almost every aspect of the fighting. And yet, argues Strickland, few of these acts provoked reproach from the pens of those who chronicled them. On the contrary, knights applauded cunning, guile and surprise, even in tournaments, and acknowledged them as fundamental and ubiquitous elements of war.[24]

Even so, the Japanese attitude toward this issue stands out. For in Europe during this same period, betrayal and deception were acceptable only within limits, restricted by conventions of war that sought to regulate fighting to the mutual benefit of both sides in any struggle. They were legitimate only because of legalistic loopholes arising from formalized conventions of oaths, truces, declarations and challenges. Knights could exploit surprise and guile without setting precedents that undermined the conventions only when their actions violated no specific promises or agreements. And such tactics were successful mainly when careless enemies failed to take note of the absence of any such prior agreements.*

---

* Strickland, *War & Chivalry*, 42–3, 128–31. Otto Brunner, *Land and Lordship*, 65, notes that "The *Summa legum* of Raymond of Wiener Neustadt contended that to kill someone 'without a challenge, without open enmity' (*sine diffidacione et sine manifesta inimicitia*) was just murder." But Strickland qualifies, "Where no prior agreement was

Japanese custom lacked all such qualifications. Promises and truces were violated with impunity, as Minamoto Yoritomo demonstrated in his destruction of Satake Yoshimasa in 1184. Using Taira Hirotsune, a relative of the Satake, as an intermediary, Yoritomo persuaded Yoshimasa to meet him alone, at the center of a bridge leading to Yoshimasa's home. When Yoshimasa arrived at the meeting point, however, Hirotsune abruptly cut him down, causing many of Yoshimasa's followers to surrender and others to turn and flee.[25]

If the foregoing seems reminiscent of James Murdoch's famous allegation that the fourteenth century was "a golden age, not merely of turncoats, but of mediocrities," however, we need to bear in mind the degree to which such judgments reflect ethnocentric or anachronistic standards for behavior.[26] Measured against the war conventions of their own time and place, early medieval *bushi* tactics were no less noble or heroic, and no more treacherous or underhanded, than those of their European contemporaries. Early medieval Japanese rules of engagement demanded that warriors concern themselves only with the most efficient means to bring about the desired result, with the ends justifying almost any means. The notion that certain sorts of tactics might be "fair" while others were "unfair" was not only inapposite to such deliberations, it was all but extraneous to *bushi* culture. The whole concept of "unfair tactics" is, in fact, meaningless to analyses of early samurai warfare, because, for the principals involved, it simply did not exist at the time.

Battle cries and self-introduction

Perhaps the most colorful and ritualistic of all the customs associated with early medieval Japanese warfare is the practice called *nanori*, or "name-announcing," which Ishii Shirō and numerous others have characterized as a means for sorting out potential adversaries and selecting opponents of appropriate reputation and stature. As depicted in *Heike monogatari* and related works, *nanori* involved warriors, prior to engaging the enemy, reciting not just their names, but their resumes and pedigrees as well:

> I am Kajiwara Heizō Kagetoki, a resident of Sagami and a descendent of Kamakura no Gogorō Taira no Kagemasa, a follower of Lord Hachiman [Tarō Minamoto Yoshiie] who, during the fighting in Mutsu province was struck in his right eye by an arrow and, plucking it out, shot down his adversary with that same shaft, thereby leaving his name to posterity. I, his descendant, am a warrior to match a thousand. My son, Kagesue, has repeatedly entered your ranks and I know not whither he has gone.

---

involved, however, surprise and guile might be considered perfectly legitimate. Low cunning was not itself dishonourable; what brought shame was perjury of an oath promising to abstain from such acts" (p. 128).

Let any commander or warrior who thinks himself my equal come forth and engage me. Come forth and engage me![27]

Stirring orations of this sort are literally the stuff of which legends are made; but it is unlikely that they were the stuff of which history was made. Careful analysis of *nanori*, as it appears in various sources, casts considerable doubt on the received wisdom with respect to this practice.

Recitations like Kagetoki's pepper the pages of *Heike monogatari* and its sister texts, but one searches in vain for a single example in earlier sources – even literary works. *Shōmonki* depicts Taira Masakado "shouting his name" (*na o tonaeru*) as he gallops into his final battle, and several entries in *Azuma kagami* tell of warriors "calling out their names" (*na o noru*) as they charge.[28] These phrases have habitually been read as short-hand allusions to more elaborate declarations.[29] But such conjecture is warranted only if one first presumes speeches like Kagetoki's to have had a solid base in reality. Certainly nothing in the passages themselves indicates anything beyond a literal shouting of the warriors' names – a far cry from the stirring orations of the later epics.

Even in later medieval literary accounts, instances of *nanori* are far less common than customary reconstructions of early medieval warfare would lead one to believe. In the *Kakuichi-bon Heike monogatari* (generally considered the most elaborately embellished version of the text), for example, there are only nineteen *nanori* incidents, thirteen of which appear in the same chapter, during the battle at Ichinotani, and three of which are by the same individual, delivered within minutes of one another.[30]

There is, moreover, little beyond pure conjecture, bolstered by long repetition, to associate the practice of *nanori* with the goal of identifying worthy opponents. For while it is certainly reasonable to speculate that warriors might have preferred to focus their attention on high-ranking enemies, whose heads would bring them greater bounties, the assumption that *nanori* could have served this purpose simply does not stand up to analysis.

In the first place, warriors selecting opponents on the basis of name-announcing would have needed to hear their antagonist's recitals – and to be heard – above the noise and confusion of battle, with dozens of warriors shouting at once. This calls to mind an image of battlefields reminiscent of the trading floor of the New York Stock Exchange – albeit with the addition of braying horses, flames and smoke, and flying rocks and arrows.

More fundamentally, in any given pairing of warriors, one of the challengers would *always* have been a worthwhile adversary for the other, even if reverse were not true. A famous or high-ranking *bushi* may well have seen little potential glory for himself in contesting with a nobody, but it is clear, even in the most romantic of the wartales, that rank-and-file warriors eagerly sought the heads of illustrious enemies. And inasmuch as lesser figures could not, therefore, have been expected to withdraw gracefully from confrontations with their betters, name-announcing could not have offered much utility in screening suitable opponents. To whatever extent early *bushi* did sift through enemies in search of worthy targets, they must have done so primarily by means of appearance, not dialogue.[31]

A careful look at the sources themselves casts further doubt on the association of *nanori* with ritualized, one-on-one combat and the selection of suitable opponents. Among the most tantalizing pieces of evidence in this regard is a passage in an account of the Mongol attack on northeastern Kyushu in 1274:

> Calling our names to one another, as in Japanese warfare, we expected fame or ignominy to be found in contesting against individuals; but in this battle the hosts closed as one.[32]

Certainly the phrase "contesting against individuals" (*hitori ate no shōbu*) could be interpreted as a reference to one-on-one dueling, but it more likely simply indicates the Japanese habit of homing in on individual *targets* – of conceptualizing enemy forces as conglomerations of individuals and small groups, rather than as synergetic units – that I discussed in the previous chapter. The entire account in which the passage appears is a hyperbolic attempt to contrast the power of the Mongols and Mongol tactics with the inefficacy of the Japanese. But that it exaggerates both is clear from other sources, such as Takezaki Suenaga's illustrated chronicle of his exploits during the invasions. In any case, the allusion to *nanori* here is once again literal and unadorned: "calling our names to one another" (*aitagai ni na o noriau*).[33]

The *Azuma kagami* and *Shōmonki* passages cited above, moreover, depict warriors calling out their names in mid-charge. The majority of the examples of *nanori* in the later medieval epics also occur while warriors charge, or as shouts of defiance at enemy troops behind fortifications or lined up to attack. The remaining examples take place as *bushi* give chase to fleeing enemies, or after warriors have clashed and one has subdued the other. In one instance, a warrior performs his oratory while standing astride the body of an enemy he has just beheaded! In most cases the declaration is one-sided only, but there are also instances in which warriors refuse to answer, acknowledge the name announcement but refuse to identify themselves, or even lie about their identities.[34]

While there *are* examples of warriors declaring themselves to be "suitable foes" (*yoki kataki*) or opponents to be "unworthy adversaries" (*awanu teki*), the very texts in which these appear also record speeches by *bushi* disparaging others who refuse to fight them. In one, a warrior declares that "the custom of battle distains neither the high nor the low; to close with whatever opponent one faces: that is the imperative." Elsewhere, a warrior taunts a fleeing enemy by demanding, "if, when armies clash, vassals refuse to engage commanders, how is there to be any sort of battle?"[35]

All these considerations point to the conclusion that *nanori* were intended as general, rather than specific, challenges. Taunts and insults hurled at the enemy have been an integral part of the psychology of war in many times and places.

They function to relieve fear, bolster morale, express defiance, and call attention to oneself and one's deeds. Given the emphasis of the *bushi* on personal glory and honor, it is only to be expected that some would have chosen to use their own names as battle cries.[36]

But the notion that warriors might have paused in mid-skirmish to introduce themselves and sort out appropriate opponents requires a considerable leap of romantic imagination. *Nanori*, as it is characterized in standard accounts of early *bushi* warfare, is simply not credible battlefield behavior, and it does not square well with the demonstrated preference of early medieval fighting men for subterfuge and ambush.[37]

It is, however, a very natural literary embellishment, common in epic literature throughout the world. Having heroes boast of their pedigrees and accomplishments at the onset of combat, a narrative device known as "naming one's name," is one of several classic motifs utilized by oral tale singers worldwide to create the aura of drama and authenticity that gives warrior epics their special power.[38]

The probability that elaborate *nanori* were simply a literary device is reinforced by the observation that, throughout *Heike monogatari*, it is only Yoritomo's Genji – never the Heike or even Yoshinaka's Genji – who are depicted performing *nanori*. That is, in the wartales, elaborate *nanori* are reserved for those on the winning side of battles.[39]

The degree to which the speeches themselves, if not the entire custom, were manufactured by the tale authors is clear from the way the orations change from version to version, growing more elaborate over time. Kagetoki's speech, for example, was far simpler in the *Engyōbon* version of the *Heike monogatari*: "I am Kajiwara Heizō Kagetoki, a resident of Sagami and a descendant of Kamakura no Gogorō Taira no Kagemasa – a man worth a thousand. Let someone come forth to face me."[40]

An even more dramatic example can be found in the speech of Kumagae Naozane, before the gates of the Taira fortress at Ichinotani. In an early version, his *nanori* is austere: "We are Kumagae no Jirō Naozane, a resident of Musashi, and his heir Naoie, a youth of 16 years. Those who hear me: if you think yourselves a match for us, come out from behind your shields." But in a later version he begins, "We are Kumagae no Jirō Naozane, a resident of Musashi, and Naoie of the same name, a youth of 16 years. Those who hear me, those who see me now: I am the strongest in all Japan. If you think yourselves a match for us, come out from behind your shields." And then, receiving no response, he adds, "Is there no one in this fortress with a sense of shame? This father and son are formidable opponents. Where are Etchū no Jirō Hyōe or Aku Shichibyōe, who earned such renown in the battles at Muroyama and Mizushima? Is Lord Noto, who is said to have fought and won in battles here and there, not among you? A great reputation is something one gets from one's enemies. Such shameless folk as yourselves are probably no match for this Naozane father and son. How long will you begrudge your lives? Come out! Engage us! Come out! Engage us!"[41]

From the foregoing, then, it seems clear that Ishii's fourth premise concerning early medieval rules of engagement – that warriors selected suitable or worthy opponents by means of self-introductions – is something less than tenable. The *nanori* actually practiced by early medieval warriors were, more likely, literally just that: the shouting of their names in order to prop up their own courage, rally their confederates, intimidate or badger opponents, or call attention to themselves, with an eye toward later reward.

Prisoners of war

Ishii's contention that the rules of engagement provided for honorable treatment for surrendered or captured enemy troops is similarly problematic. For early *bushi* customs and expectations concerning prisoners of war were considerably less consistent than the received wisdom on this issue would suggest.

Japanese warriors developed no equivalent to the curious practice of ransoming captured knights back to their families, in exchange for payments in cash or arms, that evolved in medieval Europe. The latter had precedents in ancient Greek hoplite battle and reappeared in early Frankish warfare, becoming well established by the mid-eleventh century. During this age, knights primarily faced other Christian knights, which reinforced nascent ideas of brotherhood in a common profession of arms. These factors were further buttressed by the rapidly changing political alliances that characterized the period, by which today's foe could be tomorrow's friend, and by contraction in both the geographic and logistical scale of fighting, which diminished opportunities for extensive plunder and tribute, necessitating the discovery of other means to make war pay for itself. The result was the emergence of a convention whereby knights focused on capturing, rather than slaughtering, one another. Knights were not supposed to kill other knights unless it was absolutely necessary. The code of chivalry demanded instead that a beaten enemy be given quarter and that prisoners be treated as gentlemen to be ransomed for sums not beyond their means to pay. Captivity came to be a form of contract, originally established orally on the field but recorded in writing once the battle was over.[42]

Political, social and technological circumstances in medieval Japan were substantially different from those in Europe, however, with the result that Japanese warriors developed no comparable canon of ethics and procedures for dealing with prisoners, and no comparable customs of quarter, capture and ransom. Instead, the fate of a captured *bushi* depended entirely on the particulars of his case. A pair of incidents that followed Minamoto Yoriyoshi's loss to Abe Sadatō at the battle of Kinomi, in 1057, highlight the degree to which the treatment of prisoners varied with their circumstances:

> Fujiwara Kagesue was the eldest son of Kagemichi. At 20 years of age, he was a man of few words, skilled at mounted archery. During the battle, he faced death and returned undaunted. Seven or eight times he

galloped into the rebel lines, killed an enemy leader, and emerged. But his horse stumbled and he was captured. His valor moved the rebels, but at length they executed him, because he was a cherished retainer of Yoriyoshi.[43]

In addition, there was a man of Dewa province, San'i Taira Kunitada. He fought with strength, courage and skill, always defeating many with only a few. Until this time he had never met defeat, thus people called him Taira the Unbeaten [Heifufu] (a revision of his formal sobriquet, Heidaifu). Yoriyoshi had made him a commander in his vanguard, but his horse fell and the rebels took him captive. Now this Kunitada was a brother-in-law to the rebel commander Tsunkiyo. For this reason he was pardoned. The warriors regarded this as shameful.[44]

In point of fact, capture was unusual in early medieval Japanese battles. Most prisoners mentioned in the sources were taken into custody as the result of surrender, rather than seizure. One reason for this was probably the nature of the weapons employed by the early *bushi*, inasmuch as it is difficult to use a bow in a manner designed to capture rather than kill.[45]

More fundamentally, the political circumstances of the Heian and Kamakura periods ensured that early *bushi* warfare was always legitimized under the rubric of criminal law-enforcement. While the court, and later the shogunate, were forced, with increasing frequency, to look the other way during private squabbles between warriors, they never dignified such activities with the veneer of legal respectability. One side in any conflict was, therefore, by definition, acting in the name of the state, while those on the other side were cast as rebels or outlaws. In practice, these labels could shift back and forth over the course of a long-drawn struggle – as they did during the Gempei War and the Nambokuchō wars – but in the end the winners could justify their victory only in terms of law-enforcement and defense of the polity. This characterization of the purpose of warfare not only made winning the only real imperative (and thereby justified any actions taken toward that end), it defined captured or surrendered enemy warriors as criminals or accomplices, and set the parameters for dealing with them accordingly.

From the foregoing – and from ideas about medieval samurai values popularized by World War II-era propaganda – one might expect capture to have been regarded as a matter of great shame.[46] And indeed, this conclusion is supported by some passages in medieval literary works.

One of the most interesting tells of the pursuit by a warrior named Shō Shirō Takaie of one Taira Tsunemasa, in the aftermath of the battle of Ichinotani, in 1184. Takaie calls to Tsunemasa to return and fight him, but Tsunemasa simply looks back, replies, "I'm not running away, I disdain you," and hurries his horse onward. An enraged Takaie declares his intention to "shame him by capturing him alive." He calls to two retainers, and all three take up the chase. But just as they catch up with him, Tsunemasa leaps from his horse and cuts open his own belly.[47]

Other sources, however, give a completely different impression – and address the issue more directly. One particularly interesting case in point occurred in 1189, during Minamoto Yoritomo's campaign against Fujiwara Yasuhira. Usami Heiji Sanemasa, a member of Yoritomo's army, captured Yuri Korehira, one of Yasuhira's senior retainers, and brought him to Yoritomo's camp. But another warrior, Amano Norikage, disputed Sanemasa's account, claiming instead that he had made the capture. Yoritomo thereby directed Kajiwara Kagetoki to ask the prisoner who caught him. Nevertheless, when Kagetoki attempted to do so, Korehira responded, "Your tone goes too far . . . To exhaust one's luck and a become a prisoner is an ordinary thing for a warrior. You have no call for insolence."

Kagetoki, now furious, reported this to Yoritomo, who agreed that Kagetoki had behaved badly, and directed another retainer, Hatakeyama Shigetada, to take over the questioning. Shigetada took an entirely different tack, kneeling before Korehira, bowing, and arguing that:

> To those who deal in bow and horse, becoming the prisoner of an enemy is ordained everywhere, in China as well as our homeland. It is not necessarily to be called shameful . . .. You, sir, now bear the status of prisoner, but ought you create a deep and lasting enmity? I have heard that you are praised in the six districts of Mutsu province as a great warrior leader; need we dispute between us that it was because of your meritorious service as a valiant that you were captured? You must speak now of . . . the man who captured you.

A much placated Korehira readily answered Shigetada's questions. Following a brief conversation, Yoritomo then entrusted Korehira to Shigetada's care, specifying that he be treated with respect and consideration. Six days later, Yoritomo ordered Korehira pardoned and freed, although he also directed that he not be given back his weapons or armor.[48]

Up through the early 1200s the disposition of prisoners varied from case to case, but largely reflected tenets of criminal law. The central figures of enemy armies – those deemed responsible for the conflict – were sometimes severely punished, but the majority of the warriors on the losing side were usually pardoned.[49]

It does appear, however, that treatment of captured or surrendered enemy troops hardened over the course of the thirteenth and fourteenth centuries. During the Nambokuchō era, as war became more pervasive, more frequent and more open-ended, commanders displayed an increased willingness to embrace deserters and turncoats. Warriors, particularly powerful ones, who capitulated or otherwise changed sides before any actual fighting could expect generous treatment and confirmation by their new lord of all or part of their lands. On the other hand, commanders became much less willing than they might once have been to deal with less illustrious enemy troops captured in battle, perhaps fearing that pardoned troops would simply return to the fight later. Prisoners were viewed as liabilities. Most were summarily executed. The rest were imprisoned, interrogated and (in most cases) executed later.[50]

Head-hunting

Japanese warriors found the profits of battle not in ransoms for prisoners captured alive, but in the rewards their employers – the government or private lieges – paid for energetic service. Recompense, however, demanded proof of success, which was, as we have seen, defined primarily in terms of enemies slain. Careful accounting and confirmation of one's kills was thus of considerable importance. Toward this end, warriors concocted numerous devices, ranging from the marking of arrows with their names to the commissioning of illustrated accounts of their exploits. But the cardinal warrior trophies throughout the premodern epoch were the heads of those they were commissioned to run down.

The rather gruesome practice of gathering enemy heads (*buntori*, literally, "taking one's share") dates back at least to the *ritsuryō* codes, which laid out a flexible point-based system for assessing battlefield merit and awarding promotion in rank. The relationship between performance and points varied with the scale of individual campaigns. "Points," explained the Statute on Military Defense (*Gumbōryō*), "have no fixed meaning. In one year's battles the taking of ten heads may constitute a point, while in another year's fighting five heads may make a point."[51]

Japanese custom, which equated military actions with law-enforcement, similarly equated the taking of heads with the arrest of criminals. Heads substituted for live prisoners when capture or transport of the latter was impractical. Reports from commanders in the field, and accounts of officers returning after successful missions, often refer to heads and prisoners in the same breath: "We have taken 457 heads and 150 live prisoners"; "Minamoto Tadayoshi, *tsuitōshi* to subdue the pirates of Awa, displayed the heads of 16 pirates and brought in more than 20 prisoners"; or "Mutsu Governor Minamoto Yoshitsuna entered the capital leading prisoners and bearing heads."[52] Other sources speak directly of the heads of criminals or enemy commanders killed in the course of apprehension being brought in in lieu of their owners. In one particularly revealing incident, recorded in a pair of complaints filed by the Tōdaiji in 1056, warriors acting on behalf of the Office of Imperial Police invaded the temple complex and seized a fugitive hiding there. After taking the man's head, they bound his body with rope – as they would a prisoner – dragged it from the temple, and discarded it.[53]

Heads were severed during the heat, as well as the aftermath, of battle, usually by means of the warriors' short swords (*katana*). They were then assembled, identified, and marked with red tags bearing the names of their former owners (see Figure 5.1). During the Heian period, heads collected in accord with

Figure 5.1 Heads collected and displayed on the battlefield (*Go-sannen kassen ekotoba*)

Warrants of Pursuit and Capture were impaled on, or tied to the hafts of, polearms and brought to the capital. There, they were received by agents of the Office of Imperial Police and paraded through the city streets to the gates of the prison, where they were hung from trees for exhibition.[54]

Kamakura warriors had other purposes for captured heads as well, including putting them on local display, to intimidate potential enemies. *Azuma kagami*, for example, reports that Yoritomo's men exhibited the heads of nineteen enemy warriors on a nearby hilltop, following the battle of Azukashiyama, in 1189, while a late thirteenth-century picture scroll describes a country warrior named Obusuma Saburō ordering his men to keep a steady supply of fresh heads (*namakubi*) hanging on the fence surrounding the riding grounds of his home.[55] Kuroda Hideo believes that Obusuma's alleged habits reflect the use of enemy heads as offerings to war deities – such as those of the Kashima, Katori, Shuo and Tsurugaoka shrines – in celebration of victory or prayer for success and fame, a practice which, he contends, accounted for considerably more of the head-hunting that accompanied medieval battles than the quest for proof of military accomplishments did. In this regard, he calls our attention to an entry in the records of the Utsunomiya shrine that depicts Yoritomo "making a sacrifice of the prisoner, Hizume Gorō Hidehira," as part of the celebration of his victory in the Ōshū campaign; and to an episode in *Heike monogatari* in which Yoshitsune "struck off the heads of more than 20 enemy bowmen and offered them to the deities of war (*ikusa no kami*)."[56]

Scenes in late thirteenth-century picture scrolls indicate that the presentation of heads to a warrior's superior remained simple and informal during the Heian

THE CULTURE OF WAR

and Kamakura eras. Takezaki Suenaga's *Mōko shūrai ekotoba*, for example, shows Suenaga delivering two recently captured heads to Adachi Morimune (see Figure 5.2a). Both warriors sit comfortably on the open ground, while Morimune examines the heads, placed, still bleeding, directly on the ground before him, and a scribe takes notes. In the somewhat more stylized *Heiji monogatari ekotoba*, Izumo no Zenji Mitsuyasu presents the head of the monk Shinzei (Fujiwara Michinori) to Fujiwara Yorinobu. Mitsuyasu and his entourage kneel or stand in the street, before the gates of Mitsuyasu's house, while Yorinobu inspects the head, tied to the blade of a *naginata*, from his ox cart (see Figure 5.2b).

Manuals on warrior etiquette (*buke kojitsu*), which began appearing in the late fourteenth century, however, contain sections detailing much more elaborate protocols for presenting and viewing heads in the field.[57] This ceremony, generically termed *kubi jikken* ("scrutinizing heads"), was also called *taimen* ("confronting faces") when the heads inspected had formerly belonged to generals, court nobles and other persons of high rank, or *kenchi* ("investigating knowledge") in the case of heads taken from rank-and-file troops.[58]

Most often, the inspections were conducted within the walls of temples, shrines or other compounds near the battle site, in order to provide some measure of protection against enemy survivors attempting to recapture the heads of comrades. Where no suitable walled compound was available, the ceremony was held inside tent walls. Heads were transported from the field to the inspection site tied to the saddles of mounted retainers; those of ranking or

5.2a

5.2b

Figure 5.2 Presentation of heads (a: *Mōko shūrai ekotoba*; b: *Heiji monogatari ekotoba*)

illustrious warriors were carried on the right side of the saddle, those of the less exalted on the left. Prior to inspection, the heads were washed, and the hair was combed and dressed in a proper top-knot. Facial wounds were repaired with rice paste, and make-up – white foundation, lipstick and tooth-blackening – was applied as appropriate to the rank and customs of the former owner.

Warriors assembled to view or present heads dressed out in full battle armor and weaponry, as a measure of respect toward the dead. The heads of ordinary troops were simply hung outside the inspection tent, and viewed as a group by the lord on horseback. But the heads of ranking warriors were brought, one at a time, before the inspecting officer, carried on trays by the warriors who captured them. Each presenting warrior would kneel, place the tray on the ground, and raise the head, grasping it by the hair with his right hand while his left hand supported the neck. Care was taken that the victim's eyes faced slightly to the left of the inspecting officer, rather than directly at him. After announcing his own name, and the name of the man from whom the head had been taken, the warrior placed the head back on its tray, and withdrew with it. After inspection, the heads were either returned to the families of the dead, or placed on permanent display near the gates of prisons and other appropriate sites.

Ironically, during the very period in which such elaborate ceremonies for handling captured heads were being codified, military commanders were attempting to discourage warriors from taking heads. Head-hunting – which had little direct relationship to battlefield victory – exposed troops so engaged to unnecessary risk and slowed the pace of battle. It also weakened an army's battle lines, inasmuch as, once heads had been taken, they had to be carried to the rear for safe-keeping, and placed under guard there. Moreover, the increasingly common practice of compiling battle reports (*gunchūjō*) based on witnessed accounts and testimony, which began in the early Kamakura era, rendered the actual collection of enemy heads superfluous to the process of accounting merit and rewards. Accordingly, by the fourteenth century, commanders were issuing orders *against* collecting heads.[59]

Directives of this sort did not, however, end the practice of *buntori*, in part because commanders continued to reward warriors for bringing in heads, even as they instructed them not to.[60] Head-hunting remained ubiquitous throughout the medieval era and well into early modern times. It was even practiced sporadically as late as World War II.

Non-combatants

The last of Ishii's six rules of engagement – that early *bushi* vouchsafed the lives of women, children, old men, and others who could not or did not participate in battle – is the most incongruous of the lot. For there is little evidence to suggest that medieval Japanese warriors ever troubled themselves to separate non-combatants from proper belligerents.

Non-combatants can be defined in terms of their social function – those who by virtue of their occupation cannot or do not make war – or by their circumstances – those who cannot or are not bearing arms at any given time. Medieval and later European notions of who can and cannot be a morally acceptable target or casualty of military action embrace both definitions, being rooted in the medieval Church's efforts to establish immunity for its property and its personnel, and in knightly condescension, born of pride of class, which dictated that knights should defend rather than harm the weak and innocent. But the socio-political structure of early medieval Japan mitigated against the emergence of strong imperatives for non-combatant immunity based on either sort of definition, with the predictable result that warrior treatment of those not directly involved in a particular fight was shaped largely by circumstances of the moment.

In contrast to the monolithic dominion of the Church in Europe, ecclesiastical authority in Japan was fragmented between a half-dozen or so autonomous institutions representing different schools and sects, and maintaining a consciously controlled religious balance among themselves that one historian terms a "doctrinal multitude." The great temples and shrines, moreover, not only competed with one another for patrons and followers, they also contended for secular power with the elite noble houses of the court and (from the late twelfth century) with the shogunate. By the eleventh century, the larger religious institutions had organized themselves along lines parallel to those of the great court houses. Each had its own private administrative headquarters (*mandokoro*), portfolio of rights and perquisites (*shiki*) over private estates (*shōen*), and head abbot, usually of noble or imperial birth, who represented the institution and served as a channel of communication to the other *kemmon*. Many also maintained sizeable private military forces to police their lands, defend the grounds and personnel of the main temple, and enhance their political clout within the capital. Thus the medieval Japanese religious establishment lacked a unified voice through which to dictate military ethics to warriors, and was insufficiently separate from the secular realm to make compelling claims that its lands and its clergy deserved immunity and shelter from warrior activities.[61]

At the same time, early medieval warriors could scarcely have looked upon all non-warriors as inferiors in need of mercy and protection. Defined more by craft than by pedigree, and drawn from lower and middle ranks of the court nobility and the upper tiers of rural society, they were servants and officers of the powers-that-were, not a ruling order unto themselves. And their responsibilities were delimited accordingly.

A description recounted in a thirteenth-century Japanese anthology – and paraphrased in part from the ancient Chinese classic *Spring and Autumn Annals* – observes that "the functions of warriors are: to caution against violence, to suppress weapons, to preserve the great, to determine merit, to soothe the people, to pacify the masses, and to enrich assets." It is noteworthy that, while this passage enjoins warriors to serve their rulers by controlling the rest of the population, it says nothing about *defending* or *protecting* the people.[62]

Intriguingly, there *is* some evidence of elite warriors moved to largesse and clemency toward adversaries they saw as otherwise beneath their contempt. The *Konjaku monogatarishū* offers two anecdotes that point in this direction.

The first relates an incident ascribed to Minamoto Yorinobu. When the six-year-old son of his retainer, Fujiwara Chikataka, is kidnapped and held hostage by a desperate thief, Yorinobu confronts the fugitive, demanding that he

> Throw away that sword! This much the great Yorinobu says to you: You cannot but throw it away. I will not watch and allow you to stab the child. You may have heard rumors somewhere of my temperament. Throw the sword away without fail, you scoundrel!

In awe of Yorinobu, and thoroughly cowed, the thief readily agrees to surrender his hostage. Afterward, when Chikataka wants to execute the felon, Yorinobu intervenes and scolds him:

> This scoundrel very commendably let the hostage go. As he is poor, he steals. To save his life, he took a hostage; one cannot hate him for that. Moreover, when I told him to release the boy, he released him. He is a scoundrel that knows reason.

Yorinobu thereupon not only frees the thief, he outfits him with an inexpensive horse, saddle, bow and arrows, and ten days' food before sending him on his way.[63]

The second incident involves Fujiwara Yasumasa, husband of the famous poet and diarist Izumi Shikibu. The text describes Yasumasa as "Not heir to an ancestral warrior legacy . . . but nonetheless inferior to no scion of a hereditary warrior house, being stout of heart, skilled of hand, and strong," with "powers of judgment that were subtle, such that when called to the service of the court in the way of the warrior, he gave no ground for ill ease. Those around him bent to his will and feared him without limit." One evening, while strolling alone along an empty highway, Yasumasa is accosted by a bandit with a sword, who hopes to steal his clothing. Yasumasa, however, stops the robber in his tracks by merely turning to face him and demanding his name. He then continues along his way, ordering the bandit to accompany him. When they arrive at his home, Yasumasa goes inside and returns with a thickly padded silk robe, which he hands to the bandit, instructing, "In the future when you need something like this, come to me and speak up. When you assault someone you do not know, you may find it a dangerous error."[64]

The didactic point of both tales is obviously that great warriors possessed strong senses of compassion, as well as powerful and intimidating forces of will. Both, however, relate rather special conditions, under which it was perfectly safe for the warriors to be merciful. In each case, the victims were either the warrior himself or someone in his household. Both Yasumasa and Yorinobu were acting entirely within the parameters of their own authority, rather than on the orders of the government or a patron. And both adversaries were social and martial inferiors, easily defeated. In both stories, in other words, the warriors were in complete control of the situation and the opponent, leaving mercy and compassion as practical options.

Under normal military circumstances, warriors were much less prone to worry about largesse or non-combatants. Women, children and other innocents in the proximity of early medieval battles were usually slaughtered indiscriminately along with the warriors. Raiding, which entailed burning the fields, plundering the houses, and killing the inhabitants of an enemy's lands, was a common tactic. So were sieges of enemy strongholds, which often involved surrounding the compound, setting fire to its buildings, and shooting down any and all occupants who attempted to escape the flames. In at least one case, warriors demolished the houses of a nearby village for use as kindling for the fire! Women who somehow survived raids, sieges and other battles – even women of status, such as the wives and daughters of enemy officers – might be handed over to victorious troops to be robbed of their clothing or raped. Those who wished to avoid this fate sometimes committed suicide.[65]

In the rare instances in which *bushi* did take care to distinguish non-combatants, there were specific reasons for doing so. The account of Taira Koremochi's attack on Fujiwara Morotō's home discussed earlier, for example, notes that,

> When fire had been put to all the buildings, Koremochi said, "Lay not a hand on the women, high or low. As for those you might call men, shoot them down as you see them." Standing outside the flames, they shot them all dead.

It is abundantly clear, however, that Koremochi's motive was not mercy or chivalry, but the very practical desire to avoid creating trouble with Morotō's brother-in-law, Ōkimi:

> After the fire had burned out, Koremochi and his troops returned in the twilight. Approaching the gate to Ōkimi's house, Koremochi sent in the message, "I cannot come in person. We have shown no shame to the wife of Lord Koremochi. As she is your younger sister, I have respectfully refrained from any such actions and present her to you now."

Koremochi's orders safeguarding all the women in the household were necessary to avoid the possibility that Ōkimi's sister might have been accidentally or mistakenly harmed.

This appears to have been a wise precaution. A few decades earlier, two of Taira Masakado's commanders captured the wives of two of his principal opponents. When Masakado heard about this, he issued orders that they "not be shamed," but he was too late; some low-ranking troops (*fuhei*) had already assaulted them, stripping one of the wives naked. In apology, Masakado wrote her a poem and presented her with a set of clothing.[66]

On or off the battlefield, early medieval Japanese warriors appear to have held little concern for the lives of others, or for distinctions between warriors and non-combatants. Neither the warriors themselves, nor those who chronicled their exploits, seem to have attached much impropriety to killing, except under extraordinary circumstances. Just how far circumstances had to go to be extraordinary can be gleaned from a story concerning Taira Sadamori, the warrior who defeated Taira Masakado in 940.[67]

This account, which the text says was originally reported by the wife of one of Sadamori's retainers, tells of how an aging Sadamori, suffering from an old arrow wound, is informed by a renowned physician from the capital that his best hope is a medicine made from the kidney of a male fetus. Recalling that his daughter-in-law is pregnant, Sadamori instructs his son Saemon to secure the fetus and its kidneys for him, but is later dissuaded from this course of action by the physician, who explains, "a blood relative cannot become medicine," because the resultant tonic would be ineffectual. A frustrated Sadamori then orders a survey of his household that turns up a kitchen maid six months' pregnant. Unfortunately, the text reports, "when they opened up her belly and looked, it was a female fetus, and so they threw it away. However, another was found elsewhere. The Governor [Sadamori] survived."

Later, Sadamori grows concerned that his reputation may suffer, should the doctor spread around the capital the news that he had been debilitated by an old battle injury. Rather than risk this, he orders Saemon to kill the physician. But Saemon, who has not forgotten the doctor's kindness, once again goes instead to the doctor and instructs him to dismount and walk as he crosses a certain mountain, while letting the officer assigned to accompany him ride his horse. The doctor does as he is told and, sure enough, on the mountain a "bandit" appears and shoots down the man on the horse. Saemon reports that he has killed the doctor but that the officer with him has escaped. Later, when Sadamori discovers that the doctor is in fact still alive, Saemon explains that he must have picked the wrong target, but that it was a natural error, for how could he have known "that the doctor would travel on foot like a servant?" The text concludes, "That Sadamori . . . thought to open the belly of his pregnant daughter-in-law to take out the fetal kidney shows his cruel and shameless heart."

The casual disregard displayed for human life in this tale is striking. The text condemns the "cruel and shameless" manner in which Sadamori was prepared to kill his own daughter-in-law and unborn grandchild, yet it says nothing about his unconcerned and, as it turns out, completely pointless murder of his kitchen maid. Nor does it offer any sympathy for the unfortunate – and unidentified – servant who actually provided the needed kidney. Sadamori blithely orders the murder of the physician who saved his life, and later just as blithely accepts Saemon's failure to do so. Saemon is upset over the prospect of losing his wife and child and, out of gratitude, endeavors to save the doctor. But in doing so he casually kills the man's innocent bodyguard.

Obusuma Saburō, the protagonist of a Kamakura-era picture scroll who kept fresh human heads hanging on his fence, is also said to have had a habit of abducting beggars and travelers who passed his gate for use as targets for "chasing archery games" using blunted arrows.[68]

Such stories are, of course, most likely apocryphal, but they say a great deal about the light in which their contemporaries viewed early medieval warriors. A famous petition addressed to the court in 988, from the "peasants and district officials" of Owari province, further details the brutality provincial residents ascribed to *bushi*:

> For the sake of their own honor and reputations, they willfully pluck out people's eyes. Arriving at people's homes, they do not dismount from their horses but enter. Retainers on horseback tear down the wooden shade-screens that hang outside homes and carry off tax goods. Those who dare to complain that this is unjust are meted punishment.... [These warriors] are no different from barbarians. They are like wild wolves. They butcher human meat and use this as ornaments for their bodies.[69]

As shocking and brutal as this sort of behavior appears, it is important to evaluate it in the context and manner in which it was reported. Petitions like the one from Owari were written in the name of the victims of warrior depredations (although probably not by the peasants themselves) and were produced specifically to make the warriors (and their employer) out to be wanton.

The account of Obusuma Saburō, by contrast, is not particularly censorious of his customs and instead focuses on drawing a contrast between Saburō, the rough-and-tumble provincial *bushi*, and his elder brother, Yoshimi no Jirō, who, although also a warrior, is portrayed as enthralled with the culture of the court and the capital. Saburō is said to have been so fully devoted to his warrior calling that he despised as pointless pursuits like reading poetry or playing music, saying,

> "When you face an army, do you draw a brush or blow a flute?" ... All the residents of his household, including women and children, were made to follow this path of the warrior: to ride spirited horses, and to love great arrows and strong bows.

In contrast to Jirō, who married the daughter of a capital nobleman, Saburō is said to have believed it to be improper for a warrior to take a beautiful wife; and so he searched the eastern provinces for the ugliest woman he could find, settling at last on a daughter of a provincial landowner named Kumeda no Shirō. She was quite a prize, standing over 7 feet tall, with a face "on which one saw naught but her nose" and a mouth "drawn up like the character *he* (へ)." Significantly, Jirō is eventually ambushed and killed by bandits so in awe of Saburō's martial reputation that they had earlier let him pass their stronghold unmolested.[70]

Similarly, while the account of Sadamori's efforts to cure his infection is found in volume 29 of the *Konjaku monogatarishū*, the volume devoted to "Evil Deeds," rather than in volume 25, which focuses on warriors, it clearly shows that the act of killing in and of itself was a matter of no great concern for either the characters or the compilers of the tale. To the contrary, it suggests that the ethics attached to killing were highly circumstantial; that the taking of life was a matter of rebuke only under specific conditions. The "cruel and shameless" character of Sadamori s decision to murder his daughter-in-law was not the killing itself, but his disregard for Saemon's feelings and those feelings that he himself might have been expected to have as her father-in-law. Similarly, it would have been wrong for Sadamori or Saemon to kill the physician, because both owed him a debt of gratitude. But the kitchen maid, the other woman, and the doctor's bodyguard had no such ties of obligation or affection to either protagonist, and thus, insofar as their deaths served a purpose, the warriors are not censured for killing them.

Nevertheless, medieval *bushi* disregard for the lives and property of non-combatants arose from detachment, professionalism and practicality, rather than savagery or cruelty. Their willingness to kill seems at least in part related to their willingness to die. In the anecdote involving Minamoto Yorinobu and the thief related above, Yorinobu expresses this sentiment dramatically when he admonishes the child's distraught father – who was also the son of Yorinobu's wet nurse – for losing his composure over the matter:

> Is this a thing to cry about? You must think you have taken on a devil or a deity or some such thing! To cry like a child is a foolish thing. Only one small child – let him be stabbed to death. With this sort of heart does a warrior stand! To think of yourself, to think of wife and children, is to abandon all that is proper to a warrior and his honor. To speak of fearing nothing is to speak of thinking naught of oneself, of thinking naught of wife and child.[71]

Even more fundamentally, however, *bushi* indifference to the fate of third parties stemmed from a single-minded focus on the ends of their actions, with little attention to the moral character of the means. This in turn was at least in part a consequence of *bushi* tactics and ethics having evolved in an age in which military force was mostly employed either in pursuit of criminals or in pursuit of criminal activity. Non-combatants were thus viewed either as accomplices to the criminal or simply as "collateral damage" (to borrow a term from the modern US military).

Catholic moral theology promotes a doctrine known as the law of double effect, which holds that it is permissible knowingly to bring about a result that is a side effect of one's actions, but which would be utterly impermissible to bring about as an end or means. In application to war, this principle permits such things as the killing of civilians when the deaths are incidental to attacks on enemy troops or other primary military targets, but only if the cost is not too great to be otherwise justified by one's objectives.[72] It is likely that a similar sort of principle underlay *bushi* behavior toward non-combatants.

★ ★ ★ ★ ★

The *bushi* of the Heian and Kamakura periods were the ancestors – both institutionally and genetically – of the samurai who shaped and dominated medieval and early modern Japan. Their weapons and armor were the antecedents of the tools that reigned over Sengoku-era battlefields. And their battles were the crucibles in which the samurai culture of war was forged. Curiously, however, while few would dispute the first two points, the third has seldom been thoroughly considered.

Serious students of literature and history have known since the late 1960s that the romantic battle accounts of the *Heike monogatari* and other medieval war chronicles are not reliable – that the quaint, chivalrous customs they relate were given life not by real warriors but by the imaginations of fourteenth- and fifteenth-century troubadours. Nor should the discovery of this romanticization have come as any great shock: from the campaigns of Alexander the Great to those of the Vietnam War, soldiers and citizens of one era have always looked back on the battles of bygone times as somehow having been better conducted – more just, more honorable, less confusing – than those of their own time. The problem, however, has been that scholars have shown a maddening reluctance to let go of hoary images and stereotypes of early *bushi*, clinging to what should have been untenable phantasms concerning battle mores while directing their revisionist energies elsewhere.

The old view of things implicitly posited the Heian and Kamakura periods as a chivalrous hiatus between the "anything goes" fighting depicted in the ancient legends of the *Kojiki* and *Nihon shoki*, and the equally unapologetic warfare of later medieval times, dominated by treachery and Machiavellianism. But a growing body of scholarship, which includes studies by Kondō Yoshikazu, Kawai Yasushi, Fujimoto Masayuki, Yamamoto Kōji, Gomi Fumihiko, Thomas Conlan and myself, rejects the idea of early samurai warfare as ritualized or formalistic. It argues instead for a battle culture that fits much more comfortably within the Japanese military tradition, as it stretches from ancient times to the twentieth century.

The view that has emerged over the past decade and a half is perhaps a bit less poignant and less heroic – less fun – than the popular image. But it makes clear that there was no mysterious degeneration of warrior values and standards of behavior between the late twelfth and mid-fourteenth century – that *bushi* approached their craft with substantially the same attitudes in both eras. Military technology evolved, of course, and with it evolved tactics and methods of fighting. Heian *bushi* made do with weak bows that were effective only when targeting the gaps of an opponent's armor from close range; fifteenth-century and later archers were able to shoot en masse, from much farther away. Early medieval armies were unable to rise above the sum of their parts; *Sengoku daimyō* commanded disciplined, well-articulated corps. Nevertheless, within the constraints imposed on them by the times in which they lived and fought, tenth-, eleventh- and twelfth-century warriors practiced the art of war in a manner just as rational, just as calculated, and just as sophisticated as did those of the fourteenth, fifteenth and sixteenth centuries. Early medieval *bushi* were not (as Archer Jones said of their European contemporaries) men with hearts of oak who often behaved as though their heads were made of the same substance. They were professionals; no more, no less.[73]

EPILOG

> The military student does not seek to learn from history the minutiae of method and technique. In every age these are influenced by the characteristics of weapons currently available and the means at hand for maneuvering, supplying, and controlling combat forces. But research does bring to light those fundamental principles, and their combinations and applications, which, in the past have produced results. These principles know no limitation of time.
>
> Douglas MacArthur, 1935

> The only thing harder than getting a new idea into the military mind is to get an old one out.
>
> Basil Henry Liddell-Hart, *Thoughts on War*, 1944

The peculiar style of warfare practiced by the early samurai was in every respect a product of its times. It arose apace with the warrior order itself, and waned with the changing circumstances of the late medieval age, owing both its ascendancy and its decline to a complex of interacting political, social, strategic and technological factors.

Before the invention of cannon and mechanized transportation, warriors around the globe had available to them essentially two types of weaponry and two means for deploying them: troops could be armed with missile weapons – bows, javelins, slings, and the like – or with shock weapons, such as swords, clubs, lances, or other polearms. And they could be set upon the enemy either on foot or on horseback, leaving ancient and medieval armies four principal weapons systems among which to choose: light (that is, missile-wielding) cavalry, light (missile) infantry, heavy (shock) cavalry, and heavy (shock) infantry.

At the tactical level, the superiority – or inferiority – of any of these systems was a function of purpose and circumstance. Each system displayed specific advantages and disadvantages relative to the others. Mounted troops enjoy greater mobility and a consequent capacity to force or refuse battle with infantry, which can neither run away from pursuing horsemen nor run down cavalry in flight. At the same time, missile-bearing troops, whether mounted or on foot, could attack their blade-wielding counterparts with a fair degree of impunity, owing to their ability to kill at distances that kept them well outside the range of shock weapons.*

Consequently when, as was the case in early medieval Japan, the primary objective of warfare was the apprehension or the killing of an individual or group of individuals (or the prevention thereof) rather than the occupation or defense of territory, light (missile) cavalry is in many respects superior to any of the other weapons systems technologically feasible in the premodern era.

The forerunners of the Heian *bushi* were members of select units created to deal with raiding bandits. Their missions were thus defined in terms of the pursuit and capture – or destruction – of men, goals best served by the speed and mobility of cavalry and the range advantages of missile weapons over bladed ones. The utilitarian appeal of light cavalry was, moreover, buttressed by the elite status accorded mounted bowmen under the imperial state military system.

As the economic and political structure of the country evolved over the ninth to fourteenth centuries, the central objectives of warfare remained human, rather than geographic: in function, if not necessarily in personality, status or equipment, Heian and Kamakura samurai were more constables or sheriffs than soldiers or warlords. Throughout the Heian and Kamkura eras, a warrior who tried to add to his holdings through the expedient of capturing territory directly by force only invited the censure and punishment of the state, usually visited at the hands of a rival commissioned to chastise him. During the Heian period, no one successfully challenged these rules, although there were a few – most notably Taira Masakado and Taira Tadatsune – who tried. Even in Kamakura times very little warrior expansion was accomplished by direct military action alone.

To be sure, raids on an enemy's homes or fields were common throughout the era, but the purpose was destruction, not seizure: raiders burned fields, plundered houses, killed inhabitants, and then moved on. Raids were *tactical* expedients whose underlying *strategic* objectives were not the real estate itself, but the humans whose livelihoods were tied to it. Attacks on an opponent's home or economic base threatened his ability to continue to fight. They could also force an elusive foe to stand and accept battle (or risk the destruction of his property and the lives of his family), thereby simplifying the task of running him to ground. For warriors who found themselves the objects of pursuits, on the other hand, entrenching themselves behind fortifications offered at least some measure of control over the place, if not the time, of battle, and could even be an effective way to thwart armies made up of temporarily mobilized troops who were eager to get back as soon as possible to attend to their own lands and affairs.

---

* In practice, of course, the four categories of weapons systems were not absolute. Cavalry could dismount to fight on foot, infantrymen could be put on horseback for transport, and horsemen could be armed with both missile and shock weapons to form a mixed, or general-purpose, cavalry. Nevertheless, the basic tactical considerations outlined here applied. My treatment summarizes those of Jones (*Art of War*, 39–45, 145–7) and Keegan (*The Face of Battle*, 92–106).

Political circumstances, furthermore, precluded warriors from assembling extensive, well-articulated armies and pushed them instead to rely on agglomerations of individuals and small groups. The technological limitations imposed by Japanese armor, bows and horses required warriors to shoot at very close range, putting an additional premium on individual skills and small group tactics. And *bushi* personality, coupled with the mercenary arrangements that defined the Heian military/police system, further reinforced the appeal of this style of combat. The combined effect of political, social and technological circumstance, then, was to turn early *bushi* battles into loosely coordinated mêlées centering on dogfighting between small teams of mounted bowmen and foot soldiers.

Most Heian-period warfare was localized and small-scale, involving just a few dozen troops on either side. Even conflicts of major event – the rebellions of Taira Masakado (935–41) and Taira Tadatsune (1028–31), the Former Nine Years' and Latter Three Years' Wars (1051–62; 1083–7), the Heiji Incident (1160), and the like – were contested by forces numbering only in the hundreds. But the Gempei War, in the late twelfth century, represented a significant departure from even the very recent past, with troops involved in individual battles ranging into the thousands.

The dramatically expanded dimensions of the fighting during the Gempei War introduced new logistical considerations to Japanese warfare and forced *bushi* to employ new kinds of tactics. The changes, however, proved neither fundamental nor long-lived. By the time the dust raised by the war had settled in the early 1200s, the political and economic structure of the country had assumed a shape that resembled that of the late Heian polity as much as it departed from it, and the classic pattern of combat hung on, braced by the power of more than two centuries of tradition. The Mongol invasions introduced *bushi* to a foreign enemy, an alien style of fighting, and a strategic concern for holding ground, but they do not seem to have altered subsequent patterns of warfare.

Nevertheless, the polity was evolving, and so was the technology of Japanese weaponry. The sixty-year Nambokuchō conflict that broke out in the 1300s, and the century-and-a-half long Age of the Country at War that commenced in the late 1400s, drove both processes into high gear.

The fourteenth century was an era of thoroughgoing social and political change, with attendant consequences for the conduct of war. The old order cracked, broke up, and all but disappeared as the seeds of a new, medieval world first sown in the 1180s at last sprouted into foliage that overgrew the understructure of the classical state. At the center of all the changes stood the 500-year-old *modus vivendi* between the court nobility and provincial warriors – questioned, adjusted, but never renounced during the Kamakura age – which dissolved, leaving both practical and formal control of the country in the hands of warriors.

In point of fact, the ongoing state of war that persisted for nearly three-quarters of this century was itself the cause and catalyst for much of the broader institutional evolution. For while the skirmishes of the period appear, in the main, to have involved smaller numbers of troops than those of the Gempei era, fighting was general and endemic throughout most of this sixty-year span, with battles fought in every region, engaging warriors from every province in the country. The need to prosecute this enduring conflict translated into an imperative toward enhanced ability to control and extract surplus from the countryside, in order better to raise, equip, feed, transport, and direct soldiers and armies. Over time, provincial warrior leaders were able to expand ostensibly temporary, commissariat rights and powers into a more comprehensive local political authority than had existed in Japan since the advent of the *ritsuryō* state at the turn of the seventh century.[1]

Weapons technology was changing as well. By the late 1300s the Japanese had evolved new types of polearms, heavier and more durable swords that were easier to wield, stronger bows that could shoot accurately at much greater range, and new kinds of armor that allowed greater freedom of movement to cavalry and infantrymen alike. One consequence of these developments was an enhanced ability for horsemen to function as shock cavalry, using swords and other bladed weapons, as well as for archers to ply their trade on foot and at longer ranges than before.

By the fifteenth century, substantial numbers of warriors were even forsaking the "Way of Horse and Bow" entirely, and riding into battle armed with multiple striking weapons instead. Rapid attenuation of the political center, intensified local control of lands and peoples, increasing specialization by individual warriors in either the bow or the blade, and a concomitant increase in the degree of cooperation between cavalry and infantry presaged important changes in the conduct of war. Late medieval military forces would come to employ both light and heavy cavalry together with light, as well as heavy, infantry, and were rendered more effective by better organization and the use of integrated, multiple weapons-systems tactics.

During the Nambokuchō era, the transformation was still largely incipient; the real revolution yet to come. For while fourteenth-century *bushi* were developing new tools for pursuing their wars, war itself remained pretty much what it had always been.

In the course of the Nambokuchō upheavals, warrior power and authority displaced and supplanted all but the last vestiges of rule by the imperial court; but the center itself continued to hold. Under Ashikaga Takauji, Yoshiakira and Yoshimitsu, the new shogunate was able to establish itself as executive and mediator at the apex of what one recent author aptly labeled a "complex corporatist state."[2] The realities and dynamics of local power were changing rapidly, but until the early 1400s, at least, warrior leaders across the realm – the *shugo-daimyō* – still perceived their identities in terms of the country as a whole.

Accordingly, the battle lines between the sides that clashed in the Nambokuchō wars were drawn not geographically, but between competing hierarchies of allegiance that both claimed nationwide jurisdiction; and the strategic objectives of warfare continued to focus on men, not land – on the elimination of enemy forces, not the control of territory. These circumstances provided military commanders little incentive to seek out new tactical paradigms. Thus while the weaponry, recruitment, deployment, organization and articulation of fourteenth-century armies advanced in sophistication, their goals and tactics did not change in any fundamental way.

In the end, however, the Ashikaga-led polity did not endure. Power continued to devolve steadily and decisively from the capital to the countryside until, in the aftermath of the Ōnin War (1467–77), only the thinnest pretext of local rule drawing its legitimacy from a central governing authority remained. The province-wide jurisdictions of the *shugo-daimyō* broke apart into smaller territories controlled by a new class of local hegemon. These *Sengoku daimyō* ruled all-but autonomous satrapies whose borders coincided with the area that they – and the lesser warriors whose loyalties they commanded – could dominate by force.

One effect of this new political reality was a shift in the underlying purpose of war. For the first time in the history of the samurai the primary strategic objective of warfare became the capture or defense of territory. At the same time, the armies fielded by the emerging hegemons were increasingly composed of contingents of fighting men bound to their commanders by standing obligations to service, rather than by short-term contractual promises of rewards. These developments transformed *bushi* from mercenaries to soldiers and refocused their attention on contributing to the success of the group rather than on distinguishing themselves as individuals.[3] The changing makeup and goals of late medieval armies in turn concomitantly made possible and demanded increased specialization of individuals to particular weapons systems, increasingly disciplined group tactical maneuver, and an enhanced role for infantry, which is better suited than cavalry for holding ground.

Faced with a new strategic imperative to capture or defend specific geographic areas, and armed with a growing ability to drill and discipline troops and therefore to field versatile, articulated armies, Japanese commanders soon discovered that archers – and later gunners – on foot were just as effective at harassing and breaking the formations of infantry armed with swords and polearms – and far more amenable to coordinated maneuver – than were their mounted counterparts. Light infantry was also superior to light cavalry on the defense. Protected by well-drilled pikemen, moreover, they could even stand their ground against shock cavalry. In other words, the effective coordination of light and heavy infantry with heavy cavalry rendered light cavalry essentially superfluous, and mounted archery ceased to play a significant role in Japanese battles.

And so it was that, armed with new tools and enhanced organizational powers, and embracing a new paradigm concerning the purpose of war and the meaning of victory, Japanese warlords gravitated toward more sophisticated mixed weapons-system forces and tactics, and ended the identification of the *bushi* as "Men of Horse and Bow."

NOTES

INTRODUCTION

1 *Azuma kagami* 1213 5/2. The chronicle describes Yoshimori's initial troop strength as consisting of "150 warbands" (*gunsei*).
2 See, for example, *Azuma kagami* 1185 3/9, 1189 8/10, 1203 9/5.
3 *Azuma kagami* 1213 2/16, 3/19, 4/2, 5/2. My account of the background to the Wada rebellion follows that of Paul Varley, "The Hōjō Family and Succession to Power," 154–5. For more on this incident, see Niita Hideharu, "Bakufu seiji no tenkai," 67–70.
4 *Azuma kagami* 1213 5/2.
5 *Azuma kagami* 1213 5/2.
6 *Azuma kagami* 1213 5/2.
7 *Azuma kagami* 1213 5/3.
8 *Azuma kagami* 1213 5/5, 5/6, 5/7, 5/8.
9 Karl Friday, *Hired Swords: The Rise of Private Warrior Power in Early Japan*, offers a detailed discussion of the evolution of Japanese military institutions between the late seventh and late twelfth centuries. Wm. Wayne Farris, *Heavenly Warriors: The Evolution of Japan's Military, 500–1300*, provides an alternative treatment of the subject.
10 For more on this phenomenon, see Takahashi Masaaki, *Bushi no seiritsu: bushizō no sōshutsu*, 13–20; or John W. Hall, *Government and Local Power in Japan 500–1700: A Study Based on Bizen Province*, 116–28.
11 G. Cameron Hurst III, *Insei: Abdicated Sovereigns in the Politics of Late Heian Japan 1086–1185*, 19–35, discusses this system in detail.
12 Friday, *Hired Swords*, 56–69.
13 Japanese historians refer to the differences between the Heian and Nara polities as a transformation from the *ritsuryō kokka* to the *ōchō kokka*. Morita Tei, *Ōchō seiji*, offers an excellent overview of this transformation. For a survey of Japanese historiography on this subject, see Morita, *Kenkyūshi ōchō kokka*. For English-language treatments of the changing relationship between the center and the provinces, see Dana Morris, "Peasant Economy in Early Japan, 650–950"; Morris, "Land and Society"; Cornelius Kiley, "Provincial Administration and Land Tenure in Early Heian"; Kiley, "Estate and Property in the Late Heian Period"; and Bruce Batten, "State and Frontier in Early Japan: The Imperial Court and Northern Kyushu, 645–1185"; or Batten, "Provincial Administration in Early Japan: From Ritsuryo kokka to Ocho kokka."
14 Morris, "Peasant Economy," 163–205; Yoneda Yōsuke, *Kodai kokka to chihō gōzoku*, 145–6.
15 *Ruijū sandaikyaku* 2: 614 (867 3/24 daijōkanpu), 2: 623–24 (835 10/18 daijōkanpu,

quoted in 867 12/20 daijōkanpu; 894 7/16 daijōkanpu); *Chōya gunsai*, p. 525; *Heian ibun* doc. 339.

16 The court issued repeated prohibitions against *zuryō* establishing residential bases in their provinces, in areas as far apart as Kyushu and Kazusa. See, for example, *Ruijū sandaikyaku* 2: 619–21 (797 4/29 daijōkanpu, quoted in 891 9/11 daijōkanpu; 842 8/15 daijōkanpu, quoted in 895 11/7 daijōkanpu; 891 9/11 daijōkanpu; 895 11/17 daijōkanpu; *Sandai jitsuroku* 884 8/4.)

17 *Chōya gunsai*, 525; *Heian ibun* doc. 339; *Konjaku monogatari shū* #19.4, 28.2. For details, see Friday, *Hired Swords*, 81–5.

18 Jeffrey Mass, "The Kamakura Bakufu," 49. Yasuda Motohisa, *Bushi seikai no jōmaku*, 6; Morita Tei, *Zuryō*, 139–43; Takahashi Masaaki, *Kiyomori izen*, 14; Hodate Michihisa, "Kodai makki no tōgoku to ryūjū kizoku," 7–12.

19 Friday, *Hired Swords*, 98–9; Farris, *Heavenly Warriors*, 188–9; Ishii Susumu, *Kamakura bushi no jitsuzō*, 64; Yasuda Motohisa, *Bushi sekai*, 34; Fukuda Toyohiko, *Tōgoku heiran to mononofu-tachi*, 6–7. For more on Heian marriages and family structure, see William McCullough, "Japanese Marriage Institutions in the Heian Period"; Peter Nickerson, "The Meaning of Matrilocality: Kinship, Property, and Politics in Mid-Heian"; Wakita Haruko, "Marriage and Property in Premodern Japan from the Perspective of Women's History"; Hattō Sanae, "Kodai ni okeru kazoku to kyōdōtai"; Hattō, "Sekkanki ni okeru zuryō no ie to kazoku keitai"; Sekiguchi Hiroko, "Kodai kazoku to kon'in keitai"; or Tabata Yasuko, "Kodai, chūsei no 'ie' to kazoku: yōshi o chūshin to shite."

20 See Friday, *Hired Swords*; and Farris, *Heavenly Warriors*, especially pp. 367–80.

21 Tournaments, which brought together knights from differing principalities in an artificial and controlled environment that emphasized the social as much as the martial, gave knights on different sides of shifting political alliances and animosities the chance to get to know one another, as well as to display their prowess and win glory and ransoms. This was an ideal setting for fostering class-consciousness. For more on this point, see R. Allen Brown, *Origins of English Feudalism*, 23–7; Matthew Strickland, *War & Chivalry: The Conduct and Perception of War in England and Normandy, 1066–1217*, 149–53; James Turner Johnson, *Just War Tradition and the Restraint of War*, 131–50; Robert C. Stacey, "The Age of Chivalry," 36–8. Yoritomo's use of the hunts and archery competitions toward the same ends is discussed in Takahashi, *Bushi no seiritsu*, 130–4, 144–8, 210–26; Nakazawa Katsuaki, *Chūsei no buryoku to jōkaku*, 99–107; Noguchi Minoru, *Buke no tōryō no jōken: chūsei bushi o minaosu*, 56–64.

22 My treatment of the developments of 1180–5 follows those of Jeffrey Mass, *Yoritomo and the Founding of the First Bakufu*, and G. Cameron Hurst III, "The Kōbu Polity: Court–Bakufu Relations in Kamakura Japan."

23 Detailed treatments of the Masakado and Tadatsune rebellions, and fuller development of this thesis, can be found in Karl Friday, "Futile Warlords: Provincial Rebellion in the Mid-Heian Age," and "Lordship Interdicted: Taira Tadatsune and the Limited Horizons of Warrior Ambition."

24 Jeffrey Mass, "Jitō Land Possession in the Thirteenth Century: The Case of Shitaji Chūbun," and *The Development of Kamakura Rule 1180–1250: A History With Documents*, discuss this process in detail.

25 For details, see Andrew Goble, *Kenmu: Go-Daigo's Revolution*.

26 For details, see Thomas Conlan, "State of War: The Violent Order of Fourteenth Century Japan."

27 Kenneth D. Butler, "The Textual Evolution of the *Heike Monogatari*"; "The *Heike Monogatari* and the Japanese Warrior Ethic"; and "The *Heike Monogatari* and Theories of Oral Epic Literature"; Hasegawa Tadashi, "The Early Stages of the Heike Monogatari"; H. Paul Varley, *Warriors of Japan as Portrayed in the War Tales*, describes in depth the origins of the best-known *gunkimono*. A detailed discussion of the textual

evolution of the *Hōgen monogatari* appears in William R. Wilson, *Hōgen Monogatari: A Tale of the Disorder of Hogen*, 109–30. The two best-known English translations of *Heike monogatari* (Hiroshi Kitagawa and Bruce Tsuchida, trans., *The Tale of the Heike*, and Helen McCullough, *The Tale of the Heike*, are both based on the Kakuichi-bon version of the text.
28 Kawai Yasushi, "Chūsei bushi no bugei to sensō: Gempei kassen o chūshin ni," 75–7; Kawai, "Jishō · Jūei no sensō to *Heike monogatari*"; Takahashi, *Bushi no seiritsu*, 1–66.
29 Translation by Helen McCullough, *The Taiheiki: A Chronicle of Medieval Japan*, 89.
30 Kume Kunitaka, "*Taiheiki* wa shigaku ni eki nashi," 152–3. Kawai, "Chūsei bushi no bugei," 73, also cites and discusses this example.
31 Kaizu Ichirō, "Kassen teioi chūmon no seiritsu"; Urushibara Tōru, "Gunchūjō ni kansuru jakkan no kōsatsu"; Gomi Fumihiko, *Azuma kagami no hōhō: jijitsu to shinwa ni miru chūsei*, 64–85.
32 Kuroda Hideo, *Nazo kaki Nihon shi: ega shiryō o yomu*, provides an easily accessible introduction to *emaki*.
33 *Konjaku monogatarishū* 28.2; *Heian ibun* doc. 339.

1 THE MEANING OF WAR

1 Clausewitz, *On War*, 75, 87; John Keegan, *A History of Warfare*, 3.
2 Roland H. Bainton, *Christian Attitudes Toward War and Peace: A Historical Survey and Critical Re-evaluation*, 33–43; James Turner Johnson, *Just War Tradition and the Restraint of War*, xxi–xxxv; Frederick H. Russell, *The Just War in the Middle Ages*, 3–7; Robert C. Stacey, "The Age of Chivalry," 27–8.
3 Johnson, *Just War Tradition*, xxi–xxxv; Bainton, *Christian Attitudes Toward War and Peace*, 53–100; Russell, *Just War*, 10–12, 292–6.
4 Tien, Chen-Ya, *Chinese Military Theory*, 21–2. General discussions of Chinese thoughts on warfare can also be found in Frank A. Kierman, Jr., and John K. Fairbank, eds., *Chinese Ways in Warfare*; Robin D. S. Yates, "Early China"; David A. Graff, *Medieval Chinese Warfare, 300–900*; Futomaru Nobuaki, *Senryaku senjutsu heiki jiten Chūgoku kodai hen*; and Futomaru Nobuaki, *Senryaku senjutsu heiki jiten Chūgoku chūsei/kindai hen*.
5 There is evidence that more specific treatises on military science and philosophy also found their way to Japan by the mid-Heian period, if not earlier. For example: a catalog of books in an imperial library included several such texts, among them *Sun Tzu ping fa* (*Sonshi heihō*) *Ssu-ma fa* (*shiba hō*) and *Huang Shih-kuang san lue* (*Kōsekikō sanryaku*). *Nihonkoku genzaisho mokuroku*, p. 27; Alexander R. Bay, "Bugei and Heihō: Military Skills and Strategy in Japan from the Eighth to Eleventh Centuries," 48.

The *emishi* wars were the only offensive "foreign" campaigns conducted between the late seventh century, when Japan withdrew from active participation in political and military affairs on the Korean peninsula, and the late sixteenth, when Toyotomi Hideyoshi attempted to march through Korea to invade China. For more information on the *emishi* pacification efforts, see Karl Friday, "Pushing Beyond the Pale: The Yamato Conquest of the *Emishi* and Northern Japan"; Wm. Wayne Farris, *Heavenly Warriors: The Evolution of Japan's Military, 500–1300*; Takahashi Tomio, "Kodai kokka to henkyō"; Hirakawa Minami, "Tōhoku daisensō jidai"; Haga Noboru, "Emishi to henkyō"; Kudō Masaki, "Kodai emishi no shakai: kōeki to shakai soshiki"; Kudō Masaki, *Jōsaku to emishi*; Takahashi Takashi, "Kodai kokka to emishi," *Kodai bunka* 38, no. 2 (1986): 13–24; Matsumoto Masaharu, "Seiishi to seitōshi"; and Tanaka Katsuya, *Emishi kenkyū*.

Japanese defensive military encounters with foreigners during the Heian and Kamakura periods included scattered and inconsequential troubles with the Korean

NOTES

kingdom of Silla during the ninth and early tenth centuries (which climaxed with landings in Hizen and Tsushima in 893 and 894), an attack by Jurchen forces in 1019, and the Mongol invasions of 1274 and 1281. *Nihon kiryaku* 812 1/5, 893 5/3; *Ruijū sandaikyaku* 838 7/25; *Sandai jitsuroku* 880 5/23; *Honchō monzui* 914 4/28. For information on the Jurchen invasion, see Fukuda Toyohiko, "Senshi to sono shūdan"; or Morita Tei, *Ōchō seiji*, 142–4. For the Mongol wars, see Thomas Conlan, *In Little Need of Divine Intervention: Scrolls of the Mongol Invasions of Japan*; Hori Kyotsu, "Economic and Political Effects of the Mongol Wars"; Aida Jirō, *Mōko shūrai no kenkyū*; Hatada Takashi, *Genkō*; Ōta Kōki, *Mōko shūrai: sono gunji shiteki kenkyū*; or Kaizu Ichirō, *Mōko shūrai: taigai sensō no shakaishi*.
6   *Shoku Nihongi* 774 7/23.
7   *Shoku Nihongi* 780 2/11.
8   John Haldon argues that the Byzantine state made a similar equation of defense of the polity with Holy War. See *Warfare, State and Society in the Byzantine World, 565–1204*, 13–34.
9   *Ryō no gige*, pp. 186, 194–5; *Ryō no shūge*, 1: 98–104, 164–5. Friday, *Hired Swords*, 8–32.
10 *Ryō no shūge*, 1: 99.
11 For more on these developments, see Chapter 2.
12 Bainton, *Christian Attitudes Toward War and Peace*, 101–21.
13 Stacey, "Age of Chivalry," 31–3.
14 *Ryō no gige*, pp. 186, 311–12.
15 Such warrants were alternatively called *tsuibu senji*, *tsuitō kanpu* or *tsuitō senji*. For an example of such a document, see *Heian ibun* doc. 4573.
16 *Chūyūki* 1104 6/24; *Heian ibun* doc. 1627. The injunction against raising more than twenty troops without a court order dates back to the *ritsuryō* codes (*Gunbōryō sahei no jō*, in *Ryō no gige*, p. 186).
17 Friday, *Hired Swords*, 160–2. The powers granted by *tsuibu kampu* are discussed in detail in Shimomukai Tatsuhiko, "Ōchō kokka gunsei kenkyū," 308–19.
18 "Goseibai shikimoku", 357. An English translation of the entire code appears in John Cary Hall, "Japanese Feudal Law: The Institutes of Judicature: Being a Translation of 'Go Seibai Shikimoku'; the Magisterial Code of the Hojo Power-Holders (A.D. 1932)."
19 "Kemmu shikimoku tsuika-hō," pp. 366–406. An alternative translation appears in Kenneth A. Grossberg, *The Laws of the Muromachi Bakufu*, 40.
20 The classic statement of Kuroda's *kemmon* theory is his "Chūsei kokka to tennō." Fuller expositions can be found in Kuroda's *Nihon chūsei no kokka to shūkyō* and *Jisha seiryoku*. In English, see Mikael Adolphson, "Enryakuji: An Old Power in a New Era"; Adolphson, *The Gates of Power: Monks, Courtiers and Warriors in Premodern Japan*; and G. Cameron Hurst III, *Insei: Abdicated Sovereigns in the Politics of Late Heian Japan 1086–1185*.
21 See, for example, *Ruijū sandaikyaku* 896 4/2, 905 8/25, 905 11/03; *Honchō seiki* 941 9/19; *Nihon kiryaku* 969 2/7; *Shōyūki* 985 3/22, 996 1/16; *Heian ibun* doc. 372; *Gonki* 1000 11/3; *Midō kampakki* 1016 5/25, 1017 3/11; *Chūyūki* 1113 4/30, 1114 5/27.
22 *Shoku Nihongi* 707 7/17, 717 11/17. Morita Tei, "Heian zenki o chūshin shita kizoku no shiteki buryoku ni"; Sasayama Haruo, *Nihon kodai efu seido no kenkyū*, 96–7; Friday, *Hired Swords*, 32–69, 78–92.
23 *Kojidan*, #317.
24 *Konjaku monogatarishū* 25.4, 25.10; *Nihon kiryaku* 989 11/23; *Azuma kagami* 1241 11/29.
25 See, for example, *Konjaku monogatarishū* 23.13, 25.3 and 25.5.
26 "Goseibai shikimoku," 358–9.

NOTES

27 See, for example, *Suisaki* 1079 8/30; *Shōmonki*, p. 65; "Mutsuwaki," p. 23; *Heian ibun* doc. 2467; *Konjaku monogatarishū* 25.4, 25.9; *Shōyūki* 989 4/4; *Azuma kagami* 1219 1/27.
28 "Goseibai shikimoku," 358.
29 For discussions of the phenomenon of warrior self-aggrandizement by armed force, see Friday, *Hired Swords*, 78–88, 155–6; Oyama Yasunori, "Kodai makki no tōgoku to saigoku"; Endō Motō, "Shuba no tō no kōdō to seikaku"; Okuno Nakahiko, "Heian ji no guntō ni tsuite," 5–27; Jeffrey P. Mass, *Warrior Government in Medieval Japan: A Study of the Kamakura Bakufu, Shugo and Jitō*; Mass, *The Development of Kamakura Rule 1180–1250: A History With Documents*; Mass, *Lordship and Inheritance in Early Medieval Japan: A Study of the Kamakura Sōryō System*; Loraine F. Harrington, "Social Control and the Significance of the Akutō"; Arai Takashige, *Chūsei akutō no kenkyū*; Kaizu Ichirō, "Chūsei kokka kenryoku to akutō"; Amino Yoshihiko, *Akutō to kaizoku: Nihon chūsei no shakai to seiji*; Thomas Conlan, "State of War: The Violent Order of Fourteenth Century Japan," 203–43; David L. Davis, "Ikki in Late Medieval Japan."
30 *Hyakurenshō* 1091 6/12; *Gonijō Moromichi ki* 1091 6/11, 6/12, 1092 5/12. Summary histories in English of the Masakado affair appear in Friday, *Hired Swords*, 144–7; and Farris, *Heavenly Warriors*, 131–42.
31 *Fusō ryakki* 1049 12/28, 1050/1/25; *Konjaku monogatarishū* 23.13; *Kojidan* #330.
32 Friday, *Hired Swords*, 109, 175–6; Farris, *Heavenly Warriors*, 233–41; *Fusō ryakki* 1079 8/17.
33 *Kamakura ibun* docs. 12699, 12762, 12859, 12860, 12861, 12884, 12885, 12929, 13050, 13051, 13069, 13070, 13075, 13076, 13150, 13808.
34 See, for example, *Kamakura ibun* docs. 169, 2231, 2946, 2973, 6254, 6721, or 7354; *Azuma kagami* 1200 11/1–11/4, 1201 2/3, 1201 4/2–4/6, 1205 6/22, 1205 8/7, 1207 9/24, 1218 1/12, 1241 11/29, 1247 5/21–6/22. The workings of the Kamakura judicial system are discussed in detail in Mass, *Development of Kamakura Rule*. In the late thirteenth century, Kamakura did make an attempt to rejuvenate its enforcement of centrally dictated law with respect to the right to fight, but by then it was too late, was widely perceived as tyrannical, and proved the catalyst to rapidly growing vassal hatred of the shogunate. For details, see Conlan, "State of War," 208–20.
35 Conlan, "State of War," 203–42.
36 Otto Brunner, *Land and Lordship: Structures of Governance in Medieval Austria*, 8–81.
37 Johnson, *Just War Tradition*, 41–9; Brunner, *Land and Lordship*, 34; Stacey, "The Age of Chivalry," 38–9.
38 Stacey, "The Age of Chivalry" 38–9.
39 The pioneering work on this subject has been done by Takahashi Masaaki, "Bushi to ōken," 8–14; and *Bushi no seiritsu: bushizō no sōshutsu*, 190–207. My treatment largely follows his.
40 Waida Manabu, "Sacred Kingship in Early Japan"; Joan R. Piggott, *The Emergence of Japanese Kinship*; Takahashi Masaaki, "Bushi to ōken," 8–14.
41 Takahashi Masaaki, *Bushi no seiritsu*, 189.
42 Yoshimura Shigeki, "Takiguchi no kenkyū"; Noguchi Minoru, *Buke no tōryō no jōken: chūsei bushi o minaosu*, 37–42.
43 Noguchi, *Buke no tōryō*, 41–3; Takahashi Masaaki, "Bushi to ōken," 10; Helen C. McCullough, *Genji & Heike: Selections from The Tale of Genji and The Tale of the Heike*, 72–3.
44 Takahashi Masaaki, *Bushi no seiritsu*, 202; Noguchi, *Buke no tōryō*, 36–53. For more on the spiritual power of the bow and its place in Japanese religious ritual, see Carmen Blacker, *The Catalpa Bow: A Study of Shamanistic Practices in Japan*. For detailed descriptions of court archery and wrestling rites, see G. Cameron Hurst III, *Armed Martial Arts of Japan: Swordsmanship & Archery*, 105–12; Takahashi Masaaki,

NOTES

"Bushi to ōken," 10–15; *Bushi no seiritsu*, 190–9; Ōbinata Katsumi, *Kodai kokka to nenjū gyōji*, 7–131; Noguchi Minoru, "Sumōbito to bushi"; Wada Tsuyoshi, ed., *Sumō no rekishi*; Nitta Ichirō, *Sumō no rekishi*. Stephen Selby, *Chinese Archery*, 27–86, discusses archery rituals and the magical power of the bow in ancient China.

2 THE ORGANIZATION OF WAR

1 For more on the Yamato military system and its evolution into the *ritsuryō* army, see Naoki Kōjirō, *Nihon kodai heiseishi no kenkyū*, 172–92; and Sasayama Haruo, *Kodai kokka to guntai*, 12–74.
2 *Ryō no gige*, p. 192.
3 Karl Friday, *Hired Swords: The Rise of Private Warrior Power in Early Japan*, 33–69.
4 The state did try to maintain as large a cavalry component as possible, but the effort ran afoul of major logistical problems – in particular the formidable time and expense required to train recruits in the extremely complex skill of manipulating bow and arrow while on horseback. It was simply not practical to develop large numbers of cavalrymen out of short-term, peasant conscripts. The *ritsuryō* authors' solution to these problems was to draw cavalry troops from among elites who acquired the necessary equestrian and archery skills on their own, stipulating that, when new conscripts were assigned to companies and squads, "those skilled with bow and horse were to be placed in cavalry companies; the remainder were to be placed in infantry companies" (*Ryō no gige*, p. 183). A detailed discussion of the shortcomings of the *ritsuryō* military system appears in Friday, *Hired Swords*, 34–45.
5 Friday, *Hired Swords*, 43–5.
6 Friday, *Hired Swords*, 45–68.
7 One week after the Council of State abolished the provincial regiments, it issued an edict establishing a nationwide system of *kondei*, or "stalwart youth," to be selected from among the "sons and younger brothers" of district officials. The close timing of the two edicts, and a reference in the second to the dissolution of the regiments, have led many scholars to conclude that the *kondei* were intended as the new, more select military that was to replace the regiments. This view, pioneered by Nishioka Toranosuke in 1928, long remained the accepted explanation for historians on both sides of the Pacific and has been reaffirmed in English-language publications as recently as 1992. Nevertheless, most scholars today believe that *kondei* neither were, nor were intended to be, more than watchmen for provincial government storehouses. See Friday, *Hired Swords*, 52–6; Yamanouchi Kunio, "Kondei o meguru shomondai"; Hirano Tomohiko, "Kondeisei seiritsu no haikei to sono yakuwari"; Inoue Mitsuo, *Heian jidai no gunji seido no kenkyū*, 29–54; or Nagai Hajime, "Kondeisei ni tsuite no saikentō: Heianki kondei o chūshin to shite." For the earlier view of things, see Nishioka Toranosuke, "Bushi kaikyū kessei no ichiyoin to shite no 'maku' no hatten"; John W. Hall, *Government and Local Power in Japan 500–1700: A Study Based on Bizen Province*, 132–3; or Wm. Wayne Farris, *Heavenly Warriors: The Evolution of Japan's Military, 500–1300*, 107–13. The influence of Nishioka's thesis on later scholarship is discussed in Seki Yukihiko, *Bushidan kenkyū no ayumi: gakusetsu shiteki tenkai*, 1: 170–2.
8 Among the most helpful studies of the *kebiishi-chō* are Uwayokote Masataka, "Heian chūki no keisatsu jōtai"; Inoue Mitsuo, *Heian jidai no gunji seido*, 104–31; Watanabe Naohiko, "Kebiishi no kenkyū"; Ōae Akira, *Ritsuryō seika no shihō to keisatsu: kebiishi seido o chūshin to shite*; and Morita Tei, "Kebiishi no kenkyū." The only detailed Western-language treatments of *kebiishi* to date are Francine Herail, *Fonctions et fonctionnaires japonais au debut du XIeme siecle*, 480–97; and Friday, *Hired Swords*, 128–36.
9 Satō Shin'ichi, *Nihon no chūsei kokka*, 18–19.

NOTES

10 *Ruijū sandaikyaku* 2: 645 (820 11[?]/25 kebiishi ge, quoted in 832 daijōkanpu); *Seiji yōryaku*, p. 689 (kebiishi bettō ge, quoted in 895 12/22 daijōkanpu).
11 *Heian ibun* docs. 372, 374, *ho* 7, 520, 682; *Chōya gunsai*, pp. 262–3 (1025 Ubenkan kudashibumi, and 1025 Sabenkan kudashibumi). The actual investigation of incidents occurring outside the capital was usually handed by provincial *tsuibushi*, rather than by the *kebiishi* themselves. But the officers and personnel of the Office of Imperial Police were not the only figures to be called *kebiishi* during the Heian period. A second species of *kebiishi*, dubbed "provincial *kebiishi*" (*kuni kebiishi*) by modern scholars, began to appear in the provinces around the middle of the ninth century. By the end of that century, however, this post had become a minor office under the control of the provincial government, and no longer played a significant role in military/police activities. For more on provincial *kebiishi*, see Friday, *Hired Swords*, 136–40.
12 Friday, *Hired Swords*, 141–8; Friday, "Teeth and Claws: Provincial Warriors and the Heian Court," 163–70. The earliest extant occurrence of the term *ōryōshi* is in an edict issued by the Council of State in 795 (*Ruijū sandaikyaku* 2: 548 [795 11/22 daijōkanpu]) but the phrase "in accordance with precedent" in the document suggests that the office did not originate with this order.
13 Friday, *Hired Swords*, 148–53; "Teeth and Claws," 170–3.
14 Friday, *Hired Swords*, 159–60.
15 Friday, *Hired Swords*, 147, 153–9. *Heian ibun* doc. 374; *Chōya gunsai*, pp. 513–14 (952 3/2 Echizen kokushi ge).
16 See, for example, *Sandai jitsuroku* 862 5/20, or 883 2/9.
17 Friday, *Hired Swords*, 70–97. The warrior alliances of the Heian and Kamakura periods are commonly referred to by Japanese historians as *bushidan* (literally, "warrior groups"), but, for several reasons, I find it advisable to avoid the use of the term. For details, see *Hired Swords*, 93–5.
18 During the Heian period, private martial entourages were assembled by retired emperors and top courtiers, by monastic institutions, by career provincial officials, and by provincial residents of many levels of status. Although all such organizations shared an obvious similarity of purpose, and warrior groupings at various levels were knit together into networks of alliances, both the networks and their component groups varied considerably in scale, complexity and cohesiveness from place to place and from time to time. For this reason, historians attempting to generalize about Heian military organizations must be careful not to lose sight of the fact that they are dealing with a variety of interactive but diverse entities.
19 *Shōmonki* p. 83; *Konjaku monogatarishū* 25.5; *Heian ibun* docs. 372 and 4652; *Kamakura ibun* docs. 11115, 12275 (see Thomas Conlan, *In Little Need of Divine Intervention: Scrolls of the Mongol Invasions of Japan*, 216, for a translation of this document) and 12276. Both Farris, *Heavenly Warriors*, 335–43 and Conlan, *Divine Intervention*, 261–4, offer illuminating discussions of the sizes of early medieval fighting forces.
20 See, for example, *Honchō seiki* 941 11/5 or *Fusō ryakki* 940 2/8. The following discussion of early warrior bands and networks is condensed from Friday, *Hired Swords*, 98–101.
21 Cornelius J. Kiley, "Estate and Property in the Late Heian Period," 110.
22 This basic issue has been discussed in other contexts by Endō Motō, "Shuba no tō no kōdō to seikaku," 13–15; and by Miyagawa Mitsuru with Cornelius J. Kiley, "From Shōen to Chigyō: Proprietary Lordship and the Structure of Local Power."
23 The so-called seven leagues of Musashi are discussed in detail by Yasuda Motohisa, in *Bushi sekai no jōmaku*, 28–38; and by Ishii Susumu, in *Kamakura bushi no jitsuzo*, 91–4.
24 For details, see Shimomukai Tatsuhiko, "Ōryōshi · Tsuibushi no shoruikei," 26–7, and Inoue Mitsuo, *Heian jidai no gunji seido*, 167–8.
25 Friday, *Hired Swords*, 160–4.

26 See the articles in *Centers and Peripheries in Heian Japan*, ed. Edward Kamens and Mikael Adolphson.
27 Takahashi Noriyuki, "Buke seiken to sensō · gunyaku," 50–2.
28 See, for example, *Heian ibun* docs. 4130–4135, 4175, 4177, 4178; *Azuma kagami* 1180 9/1, 1184 3/1, 1184 5/1, 1185 2/5, 1186 intercalary 7/2, 1186 8/6, 1189 7/16. Miyata Keizō, "Kamakura bakufu ni yoru Minamoto Yuitsune tsuitō," 3–6.
29 Jeffrey P. Mass, "Of Hierarchy and Authority at the End of the Kamakura," 17–18.
30 Yasuda Motohisa, "Gokeninsei seritsu ni kansuru isshiki ron"; Tanaka Minoru, "Kamakura shoki no seiji katei: kenkyū nenkan o chūshin ni shite"; Jeffrey P. Mass, "The Early Bakufu and Feudalism," 131–3. Mass notes that "*Azuma kagami* contains numerous usages of the term [*gokenin*] beginning in 1180, which helps to explain why scholars have always equated Yoritomo's first recruiting efforts with an offer of something more formal. But there exists no document actually referring to gokenin until the end of 1183, and the authenticity of this record and even later citations can now be seriously questioned. Yoritomo was demonstrably a military chieftain who extended his influence by inviting membership into his movement, by confirming or rewarding meritorious (or essential) followers, and by exercising indirect governance over the territory or offices his followers controlled. Yet (before 1192) he seems to have accomplished this feudal program without the benefit of a clearly defined apparatus of vassalage."
31 For more on the northern Fujiwara and the Ōshū campaign, see Takahashi Tomio, *Hiraizumi no seikai: Fujiwara Kiyohira*; or Ōya Kuninori, *Ōshū Fujiwara godai: Michinoku ga hitotsu ni natta jidai*. In English, see Mimi Hall Yiengpruksawan, *Hiraizumi: Buddhist Art and Regional Politics in Twelfth-Century Japan*; or Jeffrey P. Mass, *Yoritomo and the Founding of the First Bakufu*, 133–47.
32 Kawai Yasushi, *Gempei kassen no kyozō o hagu*, 197–210.
33 Kawai Yasushi, "Ōshū kassen nōto"; Mass, *Founding*, 141–5.
34 Mass, *Founding*, 151–67.
35 Takahashi Noriyuki, "Sensō · gunyaku," 50–5.
36 *Kamakura ibun* docs. 794, 934, 2182, 2131, 2182; "Goseibai shikimoku," p. 357; "Gosebai shikimoku tsuikahō" # 68, # 210; Gomi Yoshio, "Kamakura bakufu no gokenin taisei: Kyōtō ōbanyaku no tōsei o chūshin ni"; Takahashi Noriyuki, "Kamakura bakufu gunsei no kōzō to tenkai," 6–11; Mass, *Founding*, 197–207.
37 Yoritomo did occasionally appoint *gokenin* to or confirm them in *ōryōshi* or *tsuibushi* titles, and sometimes used the posts for recruiting or directing warriors (see, for example, *Heian ibun* docs. 4175, 4177, 4178; or *Kamakura ibun* docs. 262, 3827, 6240, 12271); but incidents of this sort appear to have been exceptional. The *ōryōshi* title appears in just seven *Azuma kagami* entries (1186 intercalary 7/2; 1186 8/6; 1187 9/13; 1186 1187 10/29; 1189 9/3; 1209 12/15; 1235 1236 1/17), only one of which refers to the officer in question acting in a military capacity on behalf of Kamakura. The others simply cite titles held by ancestors of *gokenin* or by enemies of the shogunate. One entry (1235 1/17) describes "*ōryōshi*" as a nickname for a boil or some other disease appearing on a man's groin and knees!
38 Yoritomo's attack on Taira Kanetaka in 1180 is a case in point. See *Azuma kagami* 1180 8/4, 8/6, 8/12, 8/13, 8/16, 8/17.
39 *Azuma kagami* 1184 2/5.
40 Comparative analysis of appearances of the term throughout the text clearly indicates that *Azuma kagami* used "*taishōgun*" in the informal, generic sense of "general" or "commanding officer," rather than as a proper title. Its entry for 1189 7/17, for example, describes Chiba Tsunetane and Hatta Tomoie as "the so-called *Tōkaidō* commanders" (*iwayuru Tōkaidō no taishōgun*) and Hiki Yoshikazu and Usami Sanemasa as "the *Hokurikudō* commanders" (*Hokurikudō no taishōgun*), while the 1189 9/4 entry styles Hiki and Usami the "*Hokurikudō tsuitōshi*."

NOTES

41 Noriyori's force included, for example, Oyama Tomomasa (of Hitachi and Shimozuke), Takeda Ariyoshi (Kai and Shinano), Chiba Tsunetane, Shigetomo and Kagetaka (Shimōsa), Chichibu Yukitsuna and Tadaie (Musashi), Sanuki Hirotsuna (Kazusa) and Kajiwara Kagetoki (Sagami); while Yoshitsune's contingent listed Doi Sanehira (Sagami), Miura Yoshitsura (Sagami), Yamada Shigezumi (Ise) and Kumagae Naozane (Musashi).

42 *Azuma kagami* 1189 7/17, 7/19, 9/4, 12/23, 1190 1/6, 1/7, 1/8 1/13, 1/24, 1/29. Uwayokote Masataka, *Nihon chūsei kokka shi ronkō*, 423–9; Jeffrey P. Mass, *Warrior Government in Medieval Japan: A Study of the Kamakura Bakufu, Shugo and Jitō*, 146–7. Miyata Keizō, "Kamakura bakufu seiritsuki no gunji taisei," 8–11, argues that the three divisions were based on the old imperial circuits (*dō*). Both *Azuma kagami*'s account of the marching orders given the army and closer analysis of the composition of the divisions, however, indicate that the Tōkaidō and Hokurikudō labels attached to the two secondary armies refer primarily to the routes along which the divisions were to advance, rather than to the composition of their forces. The division under "Hokurikidō no taishōgun, Hiki Yoshikazu and Usami Sanemasa," for example, included troops from Kōzuke, in the Tōzandō, while Yoritomo's central division took in warriors from all over the country, among them the Tōkaidō and Hokurikudō.

43 *Azuma kagami* 1181 3/12, 1185 4/26, 1186 1/11, 1186 3/1, 1186 3/2, 1186 3/7, 1199 3/23, 1200 2/20; *Heian ibun* docs. 4083, 5079, 5080. For more on *sōtsuibushi*, see Yasuda Motohisa, *Shugo to jitō*, 27–36; Inoue Mitsuo, *Heian jidai no gunji seido*, 207–15; Mass, *Founding*, 103–9; or Friday, "Teeth and Claws," 179 n. 118. *Shōen ōryōshi* and *tsuibushi* are discussed in more detail in Inoue Mitsuo, *Heian jidai no gunji seido*, 167–8; Shimomukai Tatsuhiko, "Ōryōshi," 26–7; or Friday, "Teeth and Claws," 182 n. 136.

In 1960 Ishimoda Shō asserted that Yoritomo also experimented briefly with a province-wide version of the *jitō* title (dubbed *kuni-jitō* or *ikkoku jitō* by historians). This post, he argued, was essentially a tax commission, tested in seven provinces for a few months in late 1185 and quickly abandoned. While Ishimoda's theory has been extensively debated by subsequent scholars, it has not found broad acceptance. For more on this controversy, see Ishimoda Shō, "Kamakura bakufu ikkoku jitō-shiki no seiritsu"; Yasuda Motohisa, *Shugo to jitō*, 31, 115–19; Kawai Yasushi, *Gempei kassen*; or Mass, *Founding*, 194–6.

44 Yoritomo's preference for handling criminal activities that did not threaten his own leadership was to relegate responsibility for most law-enforcement to local authorities: the *kebiishi-chō* in the capital; the police bureaus (*kebii-dokoro*) attached to the offices of provincial governors, in cases of crimes committed on public (*kokugaryō*) lands; or the estate managers (*jitō, gesu* or *azukari dokoro*) in cases of crimes committed on *shōen*. In exceptional instances, however, such as when felons operated across proprietary boundaries – and therefore across multiple local jurisdictions – Yoritomo and his successors dispatched special agents, known as *shisetsu*, to oversee the investigation and capture of the criminals. See Nishida Tomohiro, "Kamakura bakufu kendan taisei no kōzō to tenkai," 6–7. For examples of *shisetsu* in action, see *Azuma kagami* 1185 2/5, 3/3, 3/4, 1186 8/19, 8/27, 8/30, 1199 7/10, 7/16, 8/18, 10/24, 1213 6/25.

45 *Azuma kagami* 1221 5/19, 5/25. Uwayokote Masataka, *Chūsei kokka shi*, 423–9. Gomi Katsuo ("Kamakura gokenin no ban'yaku kinshi ni tsuite [2]", 29–34) and Uwayokote Masataka (*Chūsei kokka shi*, 423–9) cite the chains of command followed during the Gempei War, the Ōshū campaign and the Jōkyū War to argue that *shugo* only acted as military commanders for *gokenin* residing in the western provinces, and that eastern vassals were mustered and organized directly by the shogunate, as family units. The problem with this reasoning, however, is that, as Uwayokote

NOTES

acknowledges, eastern warriors *were* placed under the command of Kyushu *shugo* during the Mongol invasions (see below). This would seem to suggest that time, rather than geography, distinguished the organizational principles underlying Kamakura armies. My treatment, therefore, generally concurs with those of Satō Shin'ichi (*Zōtei Kamakura bakufu shugo sido no kenkyū*, 58–69, 257–8; *Nihon chūsei shi ronshū*, 14–20) and Ishimoda Shō (*Kodai makki seijishi jōsetsu*, 403–42).

46 Nishida Tomohiro reaches similar conclusions. See "Bakufu kendan taisei," especially pp. 8–13.

47 "Goseibai shikimoku," 357–8; *Azuma kagami* 1227 4/3, 7/12, 1230 11/6, 1232 4/21; *Kamakura ibun* docs. 10873, 10874, 10964, 11741, 11743, 11771, 11805, 12022, 13906, 14207, 14389, 14583, 15182, 16082, 18131.

48 Andrew E. Goble, *Kenmu: Go-Daigo's Revolution*, 111–12; Hori Kyotsu, "Economic and Political Effects of the Mongol Wars," 192, 196–8; Conlan, *Divine Intervention*, 269–71; Ishii Susumu, "The Decline of the Kamakura Bakufu," 141–50.

49 *Kamakura ibun* docs. 917, 2173, 2953, 3145, 3364, 3574, 3830, 3844, 4099, 6204, 6327, 12271; "Goseibai shikimoku," 361. For more on the *kebii-dokoro*, see Friday, *Hired Swords*, 136–40. Nishida Tomohiro observes that Kamakura law and actions still recognized some properties – including some to which *jitō* had been posted – as possessing immunity from entrance by the *shugo* or his agents. When dealing with criminals hiding or operating on such lands, *shugo* were required to petition the *jitō* or the estate proprietor for extradition. *Jitō* failing to comply with such requests were subject to dismissal. Uncooperative proprietors risked having *jitō* appointed to the properties in question. See "Bakufu kendan taisei," 9–12; see also *Azuma kagami* 1236 2/19, 1238 10/11, 1248 10/27, 1263 10/10; *Kamakura ibun* doc. 9305.

50 For details, see Goble, *Kenmu*, 121–5.

51 Goble, *Kenmu*, 127–35.

52 Friday, *Hired Swords*, 112–13. Some scholars have described warrior alliances as analogous to land-commendation agreements (see, for example, Yasuda Motohisa, "Bushidan no keisei," 127–8), but the absence of legal paperwork in the former represents a crucial – and fundamental – difference between the two phenomena. Commendation instruments exist in abundance, but one searches in vain for a single document formalizing a military alliance before the agreements issued by Minamoto Yoritomo in the 1180s. As in the case of patron–client relationships between court nobles, a warrior entering the service of another presented his new master with his name placard (*myōbu*). There is, however, no evidence that the junior party to the arrangement ever received any written confirmation in exchange. For examples of warriors offering *myōbu* as gestures of submission, see *Heian ibun* doc. 2467 or *Konjaku monogatarishū* 25.9.

53 On this point, see Mass, *Warrior Government*, 33–5, 45–54.

54 Mass, *Founding*, 13–62, discusses the vicissitudes of Taira and Minamoto efforts at creating lasting warrior networks.

55 See, for example, *Heian ibun* docs. 5073, 3972, 3973, 3975, 4110, 4187; *Azuma kagami* 1180 10/23, 1182 12/30. Mass, *Founding*, 174–87, offers a detailed treatment of Yoritomo's retrenchment.

56 *Kamakura ibun* doc. 11115, a roster of warriors from Izumi called for *ōban'yaku* in 1272, for example, dictated that one man's service for up to four months was owed for each 2.5 *chō* of land held.

57 By the end of the thirteenth century, generations of warrior encroachments on the prerogatives of others in the land-holding hierarchy, and the compromises generated by resultant litigation, gave rise to the construct of "warrior lands" (*bukeryō*) existing in juxtaposition to "proprietor's lands" (*honjo ichien-chi*), with one of the key distinctions between the two being the presence or absence of attendant obligations – including military service – to the shogunate. See Takahashi Noriyuki, "Kamakura

bakufu gunsei," 11–24; Jeffrey P. Mass, "Jitō Land Possession in the Thirteenth Century: The Case of Shitaji Chūbun."
58 Takahashi Noriyuki, "Sensō · gunyaku," 52–5. *Akutō* rank among the most celebrated phenomena in recent historiography. Among the most important studies are Amino Yoshihiko, *Akutō to kaizoku: Nihon chūsei no shakai to seiji*; Akutō kenkyūkai, ed., *Akutō no chūsei*; Arai Takashige, *Chūsei akutō no kenkyū*; Nakazawa Shin'ichi, *Akutōteki shikō*; and Kobayashi Kazuoka, "Akutō to nambokuchō no 'sensō'." The most extensive treatment in English is Loraine F. Harrington, "Social Control and the Significance of the Akutō."
59 Mass, "Hierarchy and Authority," 28–9. On the breakdown of the *shiki* system, see Thomas E. Kierstad, *The Geography of Power in Medieval Japan*.
60 Thomas Conlan, "Largesse and the Limits of Loyalty in the Fourteenth Century," 46–7.
61 Friday, *Hired Swords*, 113–16.
62 Famous incidents include the Taira Masakado and Taira Tadatsune insurrections of the mid-tenth and mid-eleventh centuries, and the Hōgen incident and Gempei War of the late twelfth century. For examples of less well-known incidents, see *Denryaku* 1101 7/3; *Hyakurenshō* 1091 6/12; or *Shōyūki* 1005 8/5.
63 Jeffrey P. Mass, *Lordship and Inheritance in Early Medieval Japan: A Study of the Kamakura Sōryō System*, 26.
64 Mass, *Lordship*, 9–37.
65 Noguchi Minoru, *Bandō bushidan no seiritsu to hatten*, 86–101. Mass, *Warrior Government*, 59–123, details a number of cases in which related houses fought on opposite sides during the Gempei War.
66 The definitive study of the *sōryō* system and Kamakura inheritance practices is Mass, *Lordship*.
67 Toyoda Takeshi, *Bushidan to sonraku*, 133–229; Hitomi Tonomura, "Women and Inheritance in Japan's Early Warrior Society"; Mass, *Lordship*, 42–108; Goble, *Kenmu*, 119–21.
68 Cadet houses could sometimes even find support for their ambitions from Kamakura and its *shugo* deputies. As we have seen, the shogunate never fully defined the parameters of membership in its vassal corps. Instead, *gokenin* status simply came to be tantamount to inclusion among those who rendered vassal services (*gokenin-yaku*). During the late thirteenth century, the most important – and the most visible – of these chores were guard duty in the capital (*ōban'yaku*) and participation in coastal watches and other activities relating to the Mongol crises. One problem with identifying *gokenin* status with performance of such duties, however, was that oversight of both *ōban'yaku* and the coastal defense efforts, including the selection of which warriors were to be mustered, rested with the *shugo*. This effectively made *shugo* the arbiters of who was and was not a *gokenin*. That is, warriors seeking recognition as Kamakura housemen – for the prestige, insulation from court proprietary authority, and other sundry benefits that came with such identification – could achieve considerable support for their case by arranging to be listed on *ōban'yaku* duty rosters, which was largely a matter of convincing the *shugo* to include them. Establishing a close relationship with the *shugo* of one's home province thus became an expedient route to *gokenin* status and therefore independence from the *sōryō* house. (See Takahashi Noriyuki, "Sensō · gunyaku," 52–5.) Conlan, *Divine Intervention*, 269, discusses attempts by warriors to use service under *shugo* as an excuse for ignoring commands from their *sōryō* and for seeking direct recognition from Kamakura.

Warrior aspirations of this sort were, to be sure, directed mainly at achieving recognition from Kamakura as direct vassals – peers of their erstwhile *sōryō* chiefs. They were, therefore, essentially central in orientation, which is, perhaps, a key reason why they did not become ready vehicles for enhancing and localizing *shugo* power. *Shugo*, and *shugo* deputies, who might logically have been expected to exploit their influence over who did and did not appear on rosters of provincial *gokenin* to extort homage from ambitious warriors under their jurisdiction, were unable to do so, because such vassalage arrangements would have been paradoxical to the very ambitions on which they would have depended. At the same time, to the extent that they were aimed at establishing new house centers and severing subordinating links with absentee holders of titular rights, the efforts of branch lines to achieve autonomy from their main lines represented moves toward localism.

69 On the former, see Mass, *Founding*, 65–86; on the latter, see Goble, *Kenmu*, 120–1.
70 See, for example, *Heian ibun* doc. 1663, 1682, 4652; *Denryaku* 113 3/13; *Chūyūki* 1114 5/16, 5/17, 6/8, 6/30, 7/18, 7/22, 8/13, 8/16, 8/21, 9/3, 9/4; *Shōmonki* pp. 95–7; *Fusō ryakki* 939 11/21; *Nihon kiryaku* 939 12/2.
71 Friday, *Hired Swords*, 118–19. One of the best illustrations of this point is an incident related in "Mutsuwaki," pp. 25–6.
72 See, for example, *Shōmonki*, pp. 79, 125–9; *Konjaku monogatarishū* 25.9; "Mutsuwaki" pp. 23–4; *Chōya gunsai*, p. 284 (1058 3/29 daijōkanpu); or *Chūyūki* 114 5/6. A fuller discussion of these points can be found in Karl Friday, "Mononofu: The Warrior of Heian Japan," 106–9.
73 Conlan, "Largesse," 42–4.
74 Conlan, "Largesse," 46–8.
75 Discussions of the devices through which the competing Muromachi regimes cajoled and dominated provincial warriors can be found in Peter J. Arnesen, "The Provincial Vassals of the Muromachi Shoguns"; Conlan, "State of War"; Conlan, "Largesse"; David L. Davis, "Ikki in Late Medieval Japan"; Goble, *Kenmu*; Kenneth A. Grossberg, *Japan's Renaissance: Politics of the Muromachi Bakufu*; John W. Hall, "Muromachi Power Structure"; Miyagawa Mitsuru with Kiley, "Shōen to Chigyō"; Thomas Nelson, "Bakufu and Shugo under the Early Ashikaga"; and Prescott B. Wintersteen, Jr., "Muromachi Shugo and Hanzei."

3 THE TOOLS OF WAR

1 Thomas Carlyle, *Sartor resartus*, quoted in *The Columbia Dictionary of Quotations* (Microsoft Bookshelf 98 edition, 1998).
2 See, for example, Satō Shin'ichi, *Nambokuchō no dōran*; Amino Yoshihiko, *Akutō to kaizoku: Nihon chūsei no shakai to seiji*; or Amino Yoshihiko, *Mōko shūrai*. Edwin Reischauer, Jackson Bailey and John W. Hall's choice of "The Cross and the Gun" (University of Mid-America, 1978) as the title for their video on the late Sengoku period is a trenchant example of this view.
3 Martin van Crevald, *Technology and War*, 5–6, 321–3, *passim*; Thomas Conlan, "Innovation or Application? The Role of Technology in War."
4 van Crevald, *Technology and War*, 14–23.
5 *Ryō no shūge* 1: 102–3; *Ryō no gige*, p. 44; *Engi shiki*, pp. 709–11, 794–5, 990–1; *Shoku Nihongi* 715 5/15, 724 4/1. For a detailed analysis and discussion of weapons production, see Inoue Mitsuo, *Heian jidai no gunji seido no kenkyū*, 82–7. Dana Robert Morris, in "Land and Society," 206–8, or "Peasant Economy in Early Japan, 650–950," 42–64, offers excellent overviews of the handicraft and special products tax system.
6 *Ryō no gige*, pp. 183–4, 274; *Engi shiki*, pp. 708–9; Karl Friday, *Hired Swords: The Rise of Private Warrior Power in Early Japan*, 39–40. Nishioka Toranosuke, "Bushi kaikyū kessei no ichiyoin to shite no 'maku' no hatten," remains the definitive examination of the system of state operated pastures.
7 *Ryō no gige*, pp. 221–2, 298; *Engi shiki*, pp. 989–90. Bows, arrows and other items "that cannot be engraved" were exempted from the labeling requirements.

NOTES

8 *Ryō no gige*, pp. 194–5; *Engi shiki*, pp. 709–11. Weapons manufactured at provincial headquarters in Kyushu were delivered to the Dazaifu for storage in its arsenal.
9 *Nihon shoki* 685 11/4; *Ryō no gige*, pp. 184, 194.
10 Aoki Kazuo, "Ritsuryō zaisei"; Torao Toshiya, "Nara Economic and Social Institutions," 434–6; Morris, "Land and Society," 206.
11 *Ryō no gige*, p. 301.
12 *Shoku Nihongi* 761 7/2.
13 *Shoku Nihongi* 761 11/17. See *Shoku Nihongi* 785 5/24, 785 7/28; or *Ruijū sandaikyaku* 1: 330 (797 4/16 *daijō kanpu*) for other examples of problems with weapons procurement.
14 *Shoku Nihongi* 791 3/17.
15 Morris, "Land and Society," 207.
16 *Engi shiki*, p. 711; Nakamura Ken, "Chūsei no daiku · tōkō · imonoshi to gijutsu," 262–3.
17 Kaminabi Tanematsu and his lifestyle are the subject of the *Fukiage jō* chapter of the *Utsubō monogatari* (1: 307–59).
18 Sakamoto Akira, "Tōgoku bushi no sōbi kōjō o horu: Yokohama-shi Nishinotani iseki no chōsa seika"; Fukuda Toyohiko, *Chūsei seiritsuki no gunsei to nairan*, 35–40; Fukuda Toyohiko, "Rekishigaku kara mita Nishinotani kiseki no igi"; Itō Kaoru, "Nishinotani iseki shutsudo ibutsu no kinzokugakuteki kaiseki"; Kondō Yoshikazu, "Ōyoroi no seiritsu: yūshoku kojitsu no kenchi kara"; "Buki · bugu no shōsan: Nishotani iseki no hatten"; Kozo Yamamura, "The Growth of Commerce in Medieval Japan," 345–66; Amino Yoshihiko, "Commerce and Finance in the Middle Ages: the Beginnings of 'Capitalism'."
19 *Engi shiki*, pp. 228–9; *Ujishūi monogatari* 1.5; *Azuma kagami* 1186 2/25, 1186 2/26, 1186 9/25; Nakamura, "Chūsei no daiku," 262–4; Noguchi Minoru, "Ikusa to girei," 144–6; Kawai Yasushi, *Gempei kassen no kyozō o hagu*, 28–30; Seki Yukihiko, "'Bu' no kōgen: kōchū to yumiya," 29–30. Dewa and Mutsu were second centers, respectively, of medieval arms manufacture, and of raw materials for arms manufacture in the capital; see Noguchi Minoru, *Buke no tōryō no jōken: chūsei bushi o minaosu*, 8–16; Noguchi Minoru, "Bandō bushi to uma," 55.
20 "Shin sarugakki," pp. 139, 148; Sasaki Minoru, "Tetsu to Nihon-tō," 41–57; Takahashi Masaaki, *Bushi no seiritsu: bushizō no sōshutsu*, 265–8.
21 *Ujishūi monogatari* 11.2.
22 "Shin sarugakki," pp. 150–1. The perception of vendors as both greedy and efficient is echoed in Fujiwara Atsumitsu's 1135 missive to the court: "Not only that, but there are among those resident in the capital great merchants without fixed employers. They acquire one thing near the capital, and crave a threefold profit for it in distant provinces" (*Kanjin*, p. 181).
23 Fujio Shin'ichirō, "Yayoi jidai no tatakai ni kansuru shomondai: tetsu · tetsusōzai no jittai to tatakai," 15; Sasayama Haruo, "Bunken ni mirareru senjutsu to buki," 125–8; Fujimoto Masayuki, "Bugu to rekishi II: Yumiya," 58–9; Kamiya Satoshi, "Yayoi jidai no yumiya: kinōgawa kara mita yajiri no jūryōka 1" and "Yayoi jidai no yumiya: kinōgawa kara mita yajiri no jūryōka 2."
24 *Wamyō ruijushō*, an early tenth-century lexicon, lists "horn bows" (*tsuno yumi*) among the types of weapons used in Japan at the time.
25 Kondō Yoshikazu, "Nihon no yumiya: sono katachi to hataraki"; Fujimoto Masayuki, "Bugu to rekishi II," 58–65.
26 Irie Kōhei, "Kyūjutsu ni okeru waza to kokoro: Nihon no kyūsha bunka no tokusei," 61–2; Kondō, "Nihon no yumiya," 42–3; Futaki Ken'ichi, *Chūsei buke no sakuhō*, 9–10; Fujimoto, "Bugu to rekishi II," 58–65; Takahashi Masaaki, *Bushi no seiritsu*, 265–8; Mori Toshio, "Yumiya no hattatsu."
27 "Wei chih"; Karl Friday, "Valorous Butchers: The Art of War during the Golden

NOTES

Age of the Samurai," 3; Sasayama Haruo, "Senjutsu to buki," 131; I. Bottomly and A. P. Hopson, *Arms and Armour of the Samurai: The History of Weaponry in Ancient Japan*, 26–7.

28 Kondō Yoshikazu, *Yumiya to tōken: chūsei kassen no jitsuzō*, 42–55; Mori, "Yumi no hattatsu"; Fujimoto, "Bugu to rekishi II," 58–64.

29 Irie, "Kyūjutsu ni okeru waza to kokoro," 65; Kobayashi Kazutoshi, "Iru: kyūdō ni okeru te no uchi no rikigaku."

30 Suzuki Keizō, "Ya no kōsei: Yūshoku kojitsu no kenkyū"; Bottomly and Hopson, *Arms and Armour*, 28; Mori, "Yumi no hattatsu"; Futaki, *Chūsei buke no sakuhō*, 9–12.

31 Futaki, *Chūsei buke no sakuhō*, 11–12.

32 *Honchō monzui*, p. 51 (914 4/28 Miyoshi Kiyoyuki *iken fuji*).

33 *Nihon shoki* 618 8/1, 672 7/22; *Ryō no gige*, p. 185; *Shoku Nihongi* 740 9/24, 10/9; *Ruijū sandaikyaku* 2: 553 (753 10/21 *daijōkanpu*); *Shoku Nihon kōki* 837 2/8; *Nihon kiryaku* 893 5/22; *Fusō ryakki* 933 12/17; "Mutsuwaki," p. 30; *Gempei jōsuiki* 37.1 (5: 55). The contemporary names for this device are given in *Wamyō ruijūshō*, p. 252; *Nihon shoki* 618 8/1; *Engi shiki*, p. 990; and elsewhere.

34 Miyoshi Kiyoyuki's tenth-century missive claims that "in China there is a weapon of this name, but it is not as powerful or trenchant as ours." *Honchō monzui*, p. 51 (914 4/28 Miyoshi Kiyoyuki *iken fuji*).

35 *Shoku Nihon kōki* 835 9/13. For discussions concerning the form of the *ōyumi*, see Friday, *Hired Swords*, 41–3; Friday, "Pushing Beyond the Pale: The Yamato Conquest of the *Emishi* and Northern Japan," 14–15; Toda Yoshimi, "Kokuga gunsei no keisei katei," 12–32; Nakamura Akizō, "Fujiwara Hirobumi no ran," 215–18; Kawai, *Gempei kassen*, 27; Kondō, *Yumiya to tōken*, 15, 107–8. Discussions and illustrations of *oxybeles*, *lithobolos*, *ballista*, and similar devices appear in Peter Connolly, *Greece and Rome at War*, 281–3; John Warry, *Warfare in the Classical World: An Illustrated Encyclopedia of Weapons, Warriors, and Warfare in the Ancient Civilizations of Greece and Rome*, 78–9, 187; and Ralph Payne-Gallwey, *The Crossbow: Its Construction, History and Management*, 259–64, 300–8.

36 *Honchō monzui*, p. 51 (914 4/28 Miyoshi Kiyoyuki *iken fuji*); *Shoku Nihon kōki*, 837 2/8; *Ruijū sandaikyaku*, pp. 219–20 (837 2/8 *Mutsu no kuni ge*).

37 *Ruijū sandaikyaku*, pp. 209–17, 219–20 (*daijōkanpu* dated 814 5/21, 837 2/8, 838 7/25, 869 3/7, 11/29, 870 5/19, 871 8/16, 875 1/13, 879 2/5, 880 8/7, 8/12, 894 8/21, 9/13, 895 7/20, 11/2, 12/9, 901 4/5).

38 *Honchō monzui*, p. 51 (914 4/28 Miyoshi Kiyoyuki *iken fuji*).

39 *Ryō no gige*, p. 185.

40 *Sandai jitsuroku* 881 4/25; *Heian ibun* doc. 4609.

41 *Shoku Nihon kōki*, 837 2/8; *Ruijū sandaikyaku*, pp. 209–17, 219–20, 553 (*daijōkanpu* dated 753 10/21, 814 5/21, 837 2/8, 838 7/25, 869 3/7, 11/29, 870 5/19, 871 8/16, 875 1/13, 879 2/5, 880 8/7, 8/12, 894 8/21, 9/13, 895 7/20, 11/2, 12/9, 901 4/5); *Honchō monzui*, p. 51 (914 4/28 Miyoshi Kiyoyuki *iken fuji*). Wm. Wayne Farris, "Japan to 1300," 54; Farris, *Heavenly Warriors*, 116–17.

42 The first crossbow trigger mechanism was discovered in Tsukidate-chō, Miyagi prefecture, in June of 1999; a month earlier what is believed to be the stock of a Yayoi-era crossbow was unearthed in Izumo-shi, Shimane prefecture. See "Yahari 'do' wa sonzai ka"; "Jitsuyōhin no 'do' shutsudo: Miyagi · Chikudate no Ōkyo-seki Nara-Heian jidai seidōsei no hikigane"; "Chūgoku-shiki 'do' ga shutsudo: Yayoi makki kokunai de hajimete"; Iwashiro Masao, "Kodai ōyumi fukugen no kokoromi: ōyumi fukugen katei de miete kita watakushi no kenkyūhō."

43 Farris, *Heavenly Warriors*, 113–16, 118–19, "Japan to 1300," 53–4. Other historians have remarked on the presence of hand-crossbows in early Japan, but none concludes, as Farris does, that these were ever widely used by Japanese armies. The current consensus is that the *ōyumi* mentioned in the sources was something other than a

NOTES

hand-held crossbow. See, for example, Toda, "Kokuga gunsei," 12–32; Nakamura, "Fujiwara Hirobumi no ran," 215–18; Kawai, *Gempei kassen*, 40–3; Kondō, *Yumiya to tōken*, 15, 107–8; Kondō, *Chūsei-teki bugu*, 146, 148–9, 204–5; or Sasama, *Nihon kassen bugu jiten*, 35–7.

44 "Yahari 'do' wa sonzai ka"; Naitō Akira, "Kodai no yumi 'do' fukugen"; Iwashiro, "Kodai 'do' fukugen." For illustrations and explanations of various crossbow trigger mechanisms, see George M. Stephens, *Crossbows: From Thirty-Five Years with the Weapon*, 70–1; William Reid, *The Lore of Arms*, 29; David Harding, ed., *Weapons: An International Encyclopedia from 5000 BC to 2000 AD*, 102; Payne-Gallwey, *The Crossbow*, 96–9; and Joseph Needham, "Part VI, Military Technology: Missiles and Sieges," 126–35.

45 Needham, "Military Technology," 126.

46 *Heian ibun* doc. 4609; *Sandai jitsuroku* 881 4/25.

47 "Mutsuwaki," p. 30; *Gempei jōsuiki*, 37.1 (5: 55); *Nihon shoki* 685 11/4; *Sandai jitsuroku* 866 8/15.

48 *Lan chēn tzu*, quoted in Needham, "Military Technology," 123.

49 *Wu ching tsung yao*, quoted in Needham, "Military Technology," 122.

50 The lack of discipline among the ranks of state troops was dramatized by the battle of Koromo River in 789, in which a government army of more than 4,000 was routed by 1,200 or so *emishi* cavalrymen. Only 275 officers and men were killed or wounded in the actual fighting, but 1,036 were drowned while trying to run away, and another 1,250 made it across the river, but only after abandoning their weapons and armor. For details, see Friday, "Pushing Beyond the Pale," 13–20; or Farris, *Heavenly Warriors*, 47–120.

51 Suzuki Masaya, *Katana to kubi-tori: Sengoku kassen isetsu*, 14–26; Kondō, *Yumiya to tōken*, 4–9.

52 Richard F. Burton, *The Book of the Sword*, xv–xvi.

53 See, for example, *Kojiki* v. 19 or 35; *Azuma kagami* 1203 10/10. Suzuki, *Katana to kubi-tori*, 35–6.

54 Kondō, *Chūsei-teki bugu*, 57–9; Seki, "'Bu' no kōgen," 14.

55 Kondō (*Chūsei-teki bugu*, 57–9) cites *Azuma kagami* 1244 4/21 as an early example of "*sayamaki*" and *Heihanki* 1169 3/13 as the first appearance of "*koshi-gatana*."

56 See, for example, *Sandai jitsuroku* 878 6/7; *Shōyūki* 1011 9/29; *Konjaku monogatarishū* 23.15, 25.13; *Kokon chomonjū* 9:12:335 (1: 409–13); *Kojidan* 317 (2: 41); *Azuma kagami* 1200 2/2, 1200 4/8. The principal exception to this usage rule seems to have been in cases in which *katana* were used to cut off the heads of fallen enemies; the verb in such instances was usually "*kaku*." Kondō observes that the difference in function between *tachi* and *katana* is particularly clear in the *Shōyūki*. His *Chūsei-teki bugu*, 64–70, features a near-comprehensive list of *Shōyūki* passages in which either term appears. See also Kondō, *Yumiya to tōken*, 121–30; Seki, "'Bu' no kōgen," 10–14.

57 Kondō, *Chūsei-teki bugu*, 59–62. The earliest appearance of "*uchi-gatana*" in the sources seems to be 1107 (*Heian ibun* doc. 1679). Other early references include *Sankeiki* 1179 5/19 and *Azuma kagami* 1192 1/21.

58 Ogasawara Nobuo, "Tōken gaisetsu," 8–9. Photographs of Kofun-era swords appear in Murano Takao, ed., "Nihon no katana: Tetsu no waza to bu no kokoro," 38–59.

59 Sasaki, "Tetsu to Nihon-tō," 35–8, 44–6, 54–7; Shimomukai Tatsuhiko, "Kokuga to bushi"; Farris, *Heavenly Warriors*, 102–3. Most of the known examples have been found in the northeast, mainly in Iwate and Aomori prefectures, leading some scholars to postulate that the *warabite katana* was developed by the *emishi* inhabitants of the region. But the oldest *warabite katana* yet discovered have been found in seventh-century tombs in Ibaraki prefecture, suggesting that this type of sword originated in eastern Japan and was carried into *emishi* lands by Yamato settlers, soldiers and traders.

NOTES

60 Sasaki Minoru, "Nihon-tō to ōyoroi no seiritsu katei: kinzoku kōkogakuteki tachiba kara no kōsatsu"; Ishii Masakuni, *Warabite katana: Nihontō no shigen ni kansuru ikkōsatsu*; Suzuki Keizō, "Kuge no ken no nasho to kōzō"; Ogasawara Nobuo, *Nihontō no rekishi to kanshō*; Kondō, *Chūsei-teki bugu*, 215–17. Photographs of *warabite katana*, *kenuki-gata tachi* and *chokutō* appear in Murano, "Nihon no katana," 59–63, 78, 90, 95, 144. A photograph of a thirteenth-century *tachi* mounting (with a wrapped wooden hilt) designed to look like a *kenuki-gata tachi* is given on p. 146, and photographs of Heian and Kamakura period *tachi* blades and mountings are on pp. 90–154.

61 This thesis has sometimes been expanded upon to argue that the connection between curved blades and cavalry originated with the *emishi* rather than with the Yamato Japanese. The fact that the first curved sword, the *warabite-tō*, has been found mostly in the northeast, and may, therefore, have been developed by the *emishi*, and the fact that the *emishi* were known as horsemen, suggests to some that it may have been designed for cavalry use. From thence, it is argued, it was probably adopted by the Yamato Japanese, who became acquainted with its efficiency during the "pacification" wars of the late eighth century, and evolved into the *kenuki-gata tachi* and/or the medieval *tachi*. Ogasawara Nobuo, "Tōken gaisetsu," 12–14; Sasama Yoshihiko, *Nihon katchū · bugu jiten*, 450–2; Sasaki "Nihon-tō to ōyoroi," 35–8; Sasaki, "Tetsu to Nihon-tō," 54–7; Shimomukai, "Kokuga to bushi."

62 Sasama, *Nihon katchū · bugu jiten*, 451; Sasaki, "Tetsu to Nihon-tō," 40; Kondō Yoshikazu, "Buki kara mita nairanki no sentō," 70–3. Kondō argues that the use of the single-edged *katana* primarily as a thrusting weapon was dictated by its length.

63 Kondō, "Buki kara mita nairanki," 70–3.

64 The following discussion is condensed from H. Russell Robinson, *Japanese Arms and Armor*, 13–17; Bottomly and Hopson, *Arms and Armour*, 15–18; and Sasaki, "Tetsu to Nihon-tō," 52–3.

65 Fujio Shin'ichirō, "Yayoi jidai no tatakai," 16–19; Sasama, *Nihon katchū · bugu jiten*, 370–1. References to the use of *hoko* in battle appear as late as the thirteenth century; see, for example, *Azuma kagami* 1201 5/14.

66 *Hoko* were also used for displaying the heads of slain enemies, which were impaled on the end of the weapon and paraded through the capital. From the late twelfth century onward, *naginata* were used for the same purpose, although the heads were tied to the latter, rather than impaled on them (*Shōyūki* 996 6/14, 1020 12/26 intercalary; *Heian ibun* doc. 797; *Chūyūki* 1097 3/8, 1110 1/29; *Azuma kagami* 1184 2/13). Numerous illustrations of heads displayed on *naginata* appear in *Heiji monogatari ekotoba* (pp. 15, 16, 34, 35, 39, 43). The fourteenth-century picture scroll *Go-sannen kassen ekotoba* features a particularly interesting depiction of enemy heads impaled on the ends of what appear to be *naginata* (p. 87), but the accompanying text (p. 80) describes them as *hoko*. Presumably the fourteenth-century illustrator did not know the difference between the two weapons.

67 Kondō, *Chūsei-teki bugu*, 99–102. For examples of warriors twirling *naginata*, see *Heike monogatari* (*Engyōbon*) 4. 18, p. 376, which depicts a warrior dubbed "Yagiri Tajima Myōzen" ("Arrow-cutting Myōzen of Tajima") "spinning his naginata like a water wheel, striking arrows and scattering them to the four directions"; or *Taiheiki* (*Keichōbon*) 2.8 ("Morokata tōsan no koto, tsuketari Karasaki-hama no kassen"), which tells of a monk named Kaijitsu "whirling his short naginata like a water wheel" as he attacks an enemy swordsman. An illustration of a warrior twirling a *naginata* appears in *Ishiyama-dera engi*, p. 16.

68 *Honchō seiki* 1146 3/9; *Heian ibun* doc. 2583; Kondō, *Chūsei-teki bugu*, 85.

69 *Shunki* 1040 4/11; *Chūyūki* 1097 3/08, 1110 1/29; *Heian ibun* doc. 2023; *Azuma kagami* 1201 5/14. Kondō, *Chūsei-teki bugu*, 80–8. Kondō speculates that the now-standard orthography, a compound meaning "reaping sword" (薙刀), was adopted,

based on the usage of the weapon, in order to avoid confusion with regular swords of unusual length, which, by the fifteenth century, were known as "*nagakatana*" (written 長刀). One of the earliest appearances of the modern orthography is the *Heike monogatari (Engyōbon)*; see, for example 4.18 (p. 374). But the same text uses the "long sword" orthography interchangeably with the "reaping sword" one; see 4.18 (p. 376).

70 *Kamakura ibun* doc. 32830. Kondō, *Chūsei-teki bugu*, 89–92; Conlan, "Innovation or Application?," 11–12, 18. Conlan's analysis of casualty reports indicates that, while only 2 percent of the wounds reported during the fourteenth century were ascribed to *yari*, the fifteenth century witnessed a marked increase in the use of these weapons. The *Taiheiki emaki* depicts warriors armed with *naginata* in nearly every battle scene, but contains no illustrations of warriors fighting with *yari*. The character most often used today for "*yari*" (槍) appears in sources at least as far back as the ninth century (see, for example, *Sandai jitsuroku* 881 4/25), but the reading "*yari*" is a modern usage, probably adopted out of confusion resulting from its use in the compound "*sōjutsu*" (槍術) for the late medieval and early modern art of spearmanship. In medieval and earlier texts, this character referred to a *hoko*, not a *yari* of the sort that were deployed in later medieval warfare.

71 Kondō, *Chūsei-teki bugu*, 90–1. Kondō argues that the pool cue-like thrusting method employed for the *yari* was probably the inspiration for the character (鑓), used to write "*yari*" in medieval texts. This character, he notes, is a *kokuji*, invented in Japan, and combines the character for metal with one meaning "to slide" (*suberu*). The *yari*, he concludes, was a purely Japanese invention, while the *hoko*, which was a direct adaptation of Chinese weapons, evolved into the *naginata* and/or became relegated to ceremonial functions after the twelfth century.

72 *Mōko shūrai ekotoba* shows a *kumade* being employed in naval warfare (p. 96) and in defense of fortifications (p. 73). *Zenkunen kassen ekotoba*, p. 38, depicts a warrior on foot using a *kumade* to pull another from his mount. Use of the *kumade* from horseback is portrayed in *Ishiyama-dera engi*, p. 73; and *Kasuga gongen kenki e*, 13.13.

73 Kondō, *Chūsei-teki bugu*, 113–29. Kondō notes that corresponding passages in variant texts of works such as *Heike monogatari* transpose "*teboko*" and "*konaginata*" according to a regular pattern: the *Engyōbon*, *Nakadobon*, *Genpei jōsuiki* and *Yashirobon* versions of the text refer to "*teboko*" where the *Kakuichi-bon*, *Shibusenjōbon*, *Minabebon* and others speak of "*konaginata*." He argues that the name "*teboko*" probably derives from the shape of the blade itself, which appears to have been straight, like the *hoko*, and from the fact that it was used mainly for thrusting and stabbing, like the *hoko*; while the term "*konaginata*" comes from the structure of the blade, which was tanged, like a *naginata*.

74 Suzuki, *Katana to kubi-tori*, 69–74; Sasama, *Nihon katchū · bugu jiten*, 163, 224, 400, 453, 499.

75 "Wei chih"; Fujimoto Masayuki, "Bugu to rekishi I: tate," 41–4; Morita Tei, "Kodai sentō ni tsuite," 178.

76 Morita, "Kodai sentō," 177–9; Fujimoto, "Bugu to rekishi I," 45–7; Sasama, *Nihon katchū · bugu jiten*, 425–6.

77 *Go-sannen kassen ekotoba*, pp. 16–17, 45, 50–2; *Mōko shūrai ekotoba*, pp. 80–1; *Konjaku monogatarishū* 25.3, 25.5; *Shōmonki*, pp. 65, 77; *Kokon chomonjū* 6.255 (1: 306); *Heike monogatari (Kakuichi-bon)* vol. 5, Nara enshō (1: 381); *Gempei jōsuiki* 37.1; *Heike monogatari (Engyōbon)* 9.20 (2: 249); *Azuma kagami* 1221 6/06; *Taiheiki (Keichōbon)* 26.3 "Shijōnawate kassen no koto" (4: 158); 34.9 "Ryūsen hiraishi-jō otsuru koto" (4: 176).

78 *Hōnen jōnin eden*, 1: 9. The *Wamyō ruijūshō* (p. 250) includes an entry for a "hand shield" (*tedate*, written with characters meaning "walking shield" [歩楯]), which it explains as "something held by foot soldiers," but it is uncertain whether this is

meant to identify hand-held shields or simply portable ones. Similarly, *Fusō ryakki* 940 2/8 lists among the goods captured following the defeat of Taira Masakado "300 flat shields" (*heidate*), while a head note states that one version of the text substitutes "hand" (*te* 手) for "flat" (*hei* 平). A gloss to the *Wamyō ruijushō* cites this passage as an example of "*tedate*."

79 Fujimoto Masayuki, *Yoroi o matō hitobito*, 12–14; Takahashi Masaaki, *Bushi no seiritsu*, 275–7; Kondō, *Chūsei-teki bugu*, 12–15; Bottomly and Hopson, *Arms and Armour*, 29–33.

80 In 780, and again in 781, the Council of State issued word-for-word identical edicts ordering a changeover from the production of iron to leather armor for its armies. Scholars have made much of these orders, which cite the light weight, ease of manufacture, ruggedness, durability, and "difficulty of penetration by arrows" of leather armor as reasons for the change. Inoue Mitsuo, for example, sees the change as a reflection of the diminishing quality of the *ritsuryō* armies, while Toda Yoshimi and others view it as a fundamental technological improvement adopted as part of a tactical shift to greater reliance on cavalry over infantry, and an important step toward the emergence of the *bushi*. But, while there is little doubt that leather armor was a technological improvement, some caution is in order when assessing the significance – and the magnitude – of the 780 and 781 orders.

First, the changeover was not as comprehensive as the foregoing interpretations would imply it to have been. Both the 780 and the 781 edicts instructed that existing iron armors were not to be retired, but were to continue to be used and repaired; the new policy applied only to armors manufactured thenceforth. Iron armors, particularly ceremonial armors, produced in the capital continued to be made from iron lamellae, even after the 781 edict. And most medieval armors were, as I have noted, composed of a mixture of iron and leather lamellae. Second, there are no particular grounds for any direct association of the changeover to leather armor with a tactical shift to dependence on cavalry. The 780 and 781 orders make no distinctions between armor intended for cavalry or infantry use; they simply cite new specifications for "armors produced in the provinces" in fulfillment of tax obligations. In fact, Miyazaki Takamune argues convincingly that the style of armor referred to by the 780 and 781 orders was not the *ryōtō-kei keikō* out of which the *ōyoroi* worn by mounted *bushi* developed, but the *tankō* thought to be ancestral to the *haramaki* developed for medieval foot soldiers (see below). When, moreover, one considers the composition of the government's armies at this time, it seems certain that the court would have expected the vast majority of the new armors to be worn by infantrymen. Intriguingly, the leather used for these government-issued armors was not the cowhide preferred by medieval armorers, but horsehide, which regulations specified was to be obtained from the skins of dead horses found in government pastures.

Shoku Nihongi 780 8/18; *Ruijū sandaikyaku* p. 561 (781 4/10 *daijō kanpu*); *Engi shiki*, p. 990; Inoue Mitsuo, *Heian jidai no gunji seido*, 88–9; Toda Yoshimi, "Kokuga gunsei"; Toda Yoshimi, "Shoki chūsei bushi no shokunō to shoyaku"; Farris, *Heavenly Warriors*, 101; Miyazaki Takamune, "Bunken kara mita kodai katchū oboegaki: 'tankō' o chūshin ni shite"; Kondō, *Chūsei-teki bugu*, 204–7; Takahashi Masaaki, *Bushi no seiritsu*, 271. For information on the composition of government armies in 780, see Friday, "Pushing."

81 Kondō, "Ōyoroi no seiritsu," 144–6; Fujimoto, *Yoroi o matō hitobito*, 12–17; Bottomly and Hopson, *Arms and Armour*, 29.

82 Bottomly and Hopson, *Arms and Armour*, 12; Fujimoto, *Yoroi o matō hitobito*, 15–17.

83 Matthew Strickland, *War & Chivalry: The Conduct and Perception of War in England and Normandy, 1066–1217*, 169–76. Strickland observes that, while narrative accounts tend to vaunt the effectiveness of mail, manuscript illuminations, medieval chansons

NOTES

and romances frequently depict swords and other bladed weapons cleaving through armor and helmets. There have, he says, never been controlled or scientific tests done on the resistance of mail to edged weapons to help resolve these apparent contradictions, nor is the archeological evidence of much help here. At the same time, he notes that medieval European armor was absolutely not proof against the thrust of the couched lance, which formed the principal attack in the opening stages of a battle.

84 There are no extant examples of designs intermediate between *keikō* and *ōyoroi*, so historians can only guess at the early evolution of this armor. The *Omodaka-odoshi* armor, in the collection of the Ōmishima shrine in Ehime prefecture, is believed by some to be the oldest surviving example of *ōyoroi*, but its precise origins are uncertain. Documentary evidence for dating the origins or surmising the development of early *ōyoroi* is also scarce. The term "*ōyoroi*" itself was not popularized until the early modern period. Early medieval texts most often denote this style of armor simply as "*yoroi*," while later medieval warriors appear to have called it "*shikishō no yoroi*" ("proper/regular/formal armor"). A few documents and entries in chronicles and diaries from the mid-eleventh to the mid-twelfth centuries refer to "*tojikawa*" ("trussed cowhide") armors worn by horsemen, and contrast these with *haramaki*, leading some scholars to conclude that this was an earlier, alternative name for *ōyoroi*. If so, the first appearance of *ōyoroi* in the written record was in 1066. Tsuno Jin's analysis of the evolution of *sane* also points to the origins of *ōyoroi* as having been sometime during the early eleventh century.

"Daijingū shozō jiki"; *Heian ibun* doc. 1679; *Sochiki* 1081 10/18; Suzuki Keizō, "Shikishō no yoroi no keisei ni tsuite"; Sasama, *Nihon katchū · bugu jiten*, 34–42; Seki, "'Bu' no kōgen," 22–3; Takahashi Masaaki, *Bushi no seiritsu*, 25–31, 269–74; Kondō, "Ōyoroi no seiritsu"; Kondō, *Chūsei-teki bugu*, 44–9.

85 Takahashi Masaaki, *Bushi no seiritsu*, 269; Kondō, *Chūsei-teki bugu*, 16; Sasama, *Nihon katchū · bugu jiten*, 97–8; Fujimoto, "Bugu to rekishi I," 46; Fujimoto, *Yoroi o matō hitobito*, 38–53; Robinson, *Japanese Arms*, 17.

86 Examples of this design include the *hōryō-kei keikō* of the Kofun period and the *tankō* of the *ritsuryō* era. The latter should not be confused with the plate armors of the Kofun era, which archeologists also call "*tankō*." This usage is a modern (post-Meiji) convention. The *tankō* worn by the *ritsuryō* armies were of lamellar construction. Kondō, *Chūsei-teki bugu*, 21–7, offers a thoroughgoing discussion of *ritsuryō* period armors.

87 Fujimoto, "Bugu to rekishi I," 46; *Yoroi o matō hitobito*, 38–53; Sasama, *Nihon katchū · bugu jiten*, 43, 95–6.

88 Sasama, *Nihon katchū · bugu jiten*, 34–44, 95–8; Robinson, *Japanese Arms*, 13–17; Bottomly and Hopson, *Arms and Armour*, 12–37. Sasama notes that medieval texts use a number of different character combinations for "*sendan no ita*." He speculates that both plates may have originally been called *sen* (or *zen*) *dan no ita* (literally "plates one layer (*dan*) in front (*zen*) of the main armor") and the other orthographies were adopted later, as homophones. The *kyūbi no ita* (literally, "dove tail plate") he suggests, was probably named for its shape.

89 Sasama Yoshihiko, *Katchū no subete*, 36–64, 75–8; Sasama, *Nihon katchū · bugu jiten*, 296–310; Bottomly and Hopson, *Arms and Armour*, 33–5; Fujimoto, *Yoroi o matō hitobito*, 47.

90 The existence of a family-determined color scheme is asserted in "Hyōshō jinkun yōryaku shō," p. 94. *Azuma kagami* 1189 9/7 depicts a warrior being asked the color of another warrior's armor, in order to identify the other man. Sasama, *Katchū no subete*, 16–22, offers illustrations of thirty-two patterns used in armor lacings and fifteen designs used for armor coverings. The use of armor decoration and other devices as a means of distinguishing allies from enemies during the Nambokuchō wars

NOTES

of the fourteenth century is discussed in Thomas Conlan, "The Nature of Warfare in Fourteenth-Century Japan: The Record of Nomoto Tomoyuki," 317–19. For additional information on family crests, see Nuta Raiyū, *Nihon monshōgaku*.

91 *Engi shiki*, pp. 989–90; *Heian ibun* doc. 1679; Takahashi Masaaki, *Bushi no seiritsu*, 275. While it is difficult to ascertain the precise value of a *hiki* during the early twelfth century, it appears to have been equivalent to about one day's wages for an unskilled laborer. Such workers were paid 15 or 16 *mon* per day during the early tenth century (Takinami Sadako, "Heian-kyō no kōzō," 86–7), when the labor pool was smaller – and demand for an individual worker's services therefore proportionally greater – than it was by the early 1100s. One *mon* was worth one-tenth of a *hiki* from the late Kamakura era onward, but some sources give the exchange rate as 1:25 for earlier periods (*Nihon-shi yōgo jiten*, ed. Nihon-shi yōgo jiten henshū iinkai. Tokyo: Kashiwa shobō, 1979, 704). These figures indicate that a laborer would have needed to work for at least 50, and as many as 133, days to earn the price of one *ōyoroi*. My thanks to William Wayne Farris and Ethan Segal for helping me sort this out.

92 Fujimoto, *Yoroi o matō hitobito*, 43–52; Sasama, *Nihon katchū · bugu jiten*, 101; Kondō, *Chūsei-teki bugu*, 207.

93 Kondō, *Chūsei-teki bugu*, 19–21, 44–9; Sasama, *Nihon katchū · bugu jiten*, 109–14; Fujimoto Masayuki, "Bugu to rekishi III: katchū," 46–7.

94 See, for example, *Heian ibun* doc. 1679; *Azuma kagami* 1201 5/14, 1203 10/10, 1235 9/10; *Mōko shūrai ekotoba*, pp. 21–2, 71–4; *Obusuma Saburō ekotoba*, pp. 32–3.

95 *Gempei jōsuiki* 22.1 (3: 112); *Hōnen jōnin eden*; Sasama, *Nihon katchū · bugu jiten*, 173–80; Kondō, *Chūsei-teki bugu*, 19.

96 Sasama, *Nihon katchū · bugu jiten*, 147–72; Kondō, *Chūsei-teki bugu*, 19–21.

97 Shakadō Mitsuhiro (in "Nambokuchō ki kassen ni okeru senshō") cautions that casualty reports may give a somewhat distorted picture of the wounds sustained on medieval battlefields, inasmuch as details are recorded only in the case of non-lethal injuries; fatalities are not listed by type. Thus, he reminds us, it is possible that the preponderance of wounds to the limbs over injuries to the head and torso cited in the reports reflects the higher fatality rate of the latter, as well as the greater frequency of the former.

98 See, for example, *Shōmonki*, p. 65; *Heian ibun* doc. 797; or *Chōya gunsai*, p. 284 (1058 3/29 *daijōkanpu*). This conclusion is reinforced by the relative numbers given for infantrymen in other references. *Konjaku monogatarishū* 25.5, for example, describes a force of 70 mounted warriors and 30 foot soldiers, while *Heian ibun* doc. 72 and *Midō kampakki* 1017 3/11 refer respectively to troops of 15 or 16 horsemen and 20 or more foot soldiers, and 7 or 8 horsemen and "ten or more foot soldiers."

99 The history of the horse in Japan dates back to at least the early Jōmon period, by which time the animals had found their way into the archipelago from southern China through Kyushu, and from the north, through Korea. Although horses were used as pack animals by the Yayoi period, true equestrian culture arrived in Japan during the early fifth century, becoming widely diffused throughout Kyushu and most of Honshu by the sixth. Kobayashi Yukio, "Jōdai Nihon ni okeru jōba no fūshū"; Mori Kōichi, ed., *Nihon kodai bunka no tankyu 9: uma*; Walter Edwards, "Event and Process in the Founding of Japan"; Sasama Yoshihiko, *Nihon kassen bugu jiten*, 265–9; Takahashi Masaaki, "Bushi to ōken," 18–20; Toyoda Aritsune and Nomura Shin'ichi, "Uma ga daikatsuyaku shita Gempei no tatakai."

100 Toyoda and Nomura, "Uma ga daikatsuyaku," 17–21; Kawai, *Gempei kassen*, 43–7. Hayashida's findings appear in Hayashida Shigeyuki, "Chūsei Nihon no uma ni tsuite" and *Nihon zairai uma ni kansuru kenkyū*. His conclusions concerning the size of medieval horses are corroborated by analyses of horse skeletons unearthed in other archeological sites, the size of medieval saddles, and descriptions of horses in written texts. See Nishimoto Toyohiro, "Kamakura-shi Yuhigahama-Minami kiseki no

shutsudo uma ni tsuite"; Saiki Hideo, "Hakkutsu chōsa kara miru umaya to uma"; and Matsuzaki Masumi, "Bagu kara miru uma," in *Kamakura no bushi to uma*, ed. Uma no hakubutsukan (Tokyo: Meicho shuppan, 1999) 33–8.
101 Toyoda and Nomura, "Uma ga daikatsuyaku," 27–8.
102 Sasama, *Nihon kassen bugu jiten*, 312–29; Takahashi Masaaki, *Bushi no seiritsu*, 197–9.
103 Kondō, *Yumiya to tōken*, 70–1; Sasama, *Nihon kassen bugu jiten*, 347–51.
104 Sasama, *Nihon kassen bugu jiten*, 330–46; Kondō, *Yumiya to tōken*, 71.
105 Kondō, *Yumiya to tōken*, 67–72; Sasama, *Nihon kassen bugu jiten*, 300–11.
106 Kawai Yasushi, "Chūsei bushi no bugei to sensō," 77–8; Kondō Yoshikazu, "Ōyoroi no seiritsu," 154.
107 Harry Holbert Turney-High, *Primitive War: Its Practice and Concepts*, 5–7; van Crevald, *Technology and War*, 1–6, 73–7.
108 van Crevald, *Technology and War*, 319–20.
109 van Crevald, *Technology and War*, 313–16.

4 THE SCIENCE OF WAR

1 See, for example, *Sandai jitsuroku* 887 8/7; "Mutsuwaki," p. 23; *Ruijū fusenshō*, p. 175 (992 10/18 *daijōkanpu*); *Chōya gunsai*, p. 525; *Konjaku monogatarishū* 19.7; *Azuma kagami* 1184 3/28; *Nambokuchō ibun Kyūshū-hen* docs. 3304, 3305.
2 Martin van Crevald, *Technology and War*, 9–23; John Keegan, *A History of Warfare*, 156–234.
3 Kobayashi Yukio, "Jōdai Nihon ni okeru jōba no fūshū"; Suzuki Takeo, "Heian jidai ni okeru nōmin no uma." Reinier H. Hesselink, "The Introduction of the Art of Mounted Archery into Japan," presents an intriguing reconstruction of the relationship between Chinese and Japanese mounted archery.
4 I have confined my attention, in this chapter and elsewhere in the volume, to warfare on land. This decision was motivated principally by editorially imposed constraints on space, but secondarily by the consideration that naval operations played only a very minor role in early medieval campaigns. Satō Kazuo's two-volume *Umi to suigun no Nihonshi* offers an excellent overview of Japanese naval history.
5 Takahashi Masaaki, "Bushi to ōken," 18–20. See also Takahashi, *Bushi no seiritsu: bushizō no sōshutsu*, especially pp. 189–207 and 223–64. The latter presents an idiosyncratic and somewhat problematic perspective on Heian warriors and warfare. For details, see my review ("Review of Takahashi Masaaki, *Bushi no seiritsu/bushizō no sōshutsu*").
6 Kondō Yoshikazu's careful analysis of seventh- to tenth-century legal codes and edicts demonstrates that it was the rank-and-file soldiers of the various court military units who were equipped with bow and arrow, while senior officers carried only swords. This, he argues, suggests that swords were the main symbolic weapons, and that archery was a utilitarian military technology. Moreover, he notes that the *bushi* did not just *retain* an earlier military tradition, they embellished it considerably, introducing better bows, numerous special purpose arrowheads, and new styles of saddles and armor designed specifically to meet the demands of archery from horseback. See Kondō Yoshikazu, "Chūsei bushiron no ichi zentei: ritsuryōseika ni okeru yumiya no ichi."
7 Karl Friday, *Hired Swords: The Rise of Private Warrior Power in Early Japan*, 35–40; Friday, "Pushing Beyond the Pale: The Yamato Conquest of the *Emishi* and Northern Japan," 14–15n. For accounts of the Jinshin War in English, see G. Cameron Hurst III, "An Emperor Who Reigned as Well as Ruled: Temmu Tennō"; or Wm. Wayne Farris, *Heavenly Warriors: The Evolution of Japan's Military, 500–1300*, 41–7. Excellent English-language discussions of the Hidetsugu and Nakamaro rebellions can be

189

NOTES

found in *Heavenly Warriors*, pp. 60–5 and 69–77; Bruce L. Batten, "State and Frontier in Early Japan: The Imperial Court and Northern Kyushu, 645–1185," 172–9; and Joan R. Piggott, *The Emergence of Japanese Kingship*, 128–31.

8   Stephen Morillo, "The 'Age of Cavalry' Revisited," 49–53.
9   While textual sources tend to make only terse references to the presence of foot soldiers in battles, or to ignore them altogether, battle scenes in pictorial sources, such as *Hōnen jōnin eden*, *Obusama Saburō ekotoba*, *Zenkunen kassen ekotoba*, *Go-sannen kassen ekotoba*, *Heiji monogatari ekotoba*, *Heiji monogatari emaki*, *Mōko shūrai ekotoba* and *Taiheiki emaki* feature them prominently. There are, moreover, exceptions to the generally low profile of foot soldiers in written texts. *Shōmonki*, for example, makes frequent mention of foot troops, such as in its account of a battle fought near the Shimozuke *kokuga* in the sixth month of 936, when Masakado used them to disrupt Taira Yoshikane's battle preparations and throw his forces into confusion (pp. 65–7). *Heike monogatari (Engyōbon)* 8.20 (2: 152) describes an attack on Minamoto Yoshinaka in Bizen, for which Senō Kaneyasu conscripts local residents with hunting bows and arrows. Kawai Yasushi, "Jishō · Jūei no nairan to chiiki shakai," 8–10, analyzes this passage in some depth.
10 Takahashi Masaaki is perhaps the most recent proponent of the belief that early *bushi* were attended on the battlefield by grooms, who otherwise took no direct part in the fighting. Arguing that such attendants were necessary because Japanese ponies were wild, mean and very difficult to control, he maintains that two grooms, called "*kuchi-tori*," were normally assigned to each rider, jogging along beside him and holding the reins of his mount while he shot his bow (see Takahashi Masaaki, *Bushi no seiritsu*, 234–8). No such grooms appear, however, in any illustrations of early medieval battles.
11 Morillo, "Age of Cavalry," 51–2; Bernard S. Bachrach, *Early Carolingian Warfare: Prelude to Empire*, 174.
12 Keegan, *History of Warfare*, 160–3, 177–217; Erik Hildinger, *Warriors of the Steppe: A Military History of Central Asia, 500 BC to 1700 AD*; John Masson Smith, jr., "Ayn Jâlūt: Mamlūk Success or Failure?"
13 Hildinger, *Warriors of the Steppe*, 20–3; Keegan, *A History of War*, 162–3; van Crevald, *Technology and War*, 12–13.
14 Modern scholars estimate the maximum effective range for Heian-period mounted archers as somewhere between 10 and 20 meters, and the typical distance at which bowmen of the era fought as around ten to 14 meters. See Kondō Yoshikazu, *Yumiya to tōken: chūsei kassen no jitsuzō*, 119–21; Fujimoto Masayuki, "Bugu to rekishi II: Yumiya," 70; or Kawai Yasushi, *Gempei kassen no kyozō o hagu*, 41–3. Fujimoto (p. 69) also notes that it was difficult for archers to get a full draw in the haste of battle, and when encumbered by the horse, the armor and the need to shoot and dodge the opponent's arrow at the same time. This made the shots even weaker than they would already have been.
15 *Konjaku monogatarishū* 25.3.
16 Karl Friday, "Valorous Butchers: The Art of War during the Golden Age of the Samurai," 13; Fujimoto Masayuki, "Bugu to rekishi II," 69.
17 *Heike monogatari (Engyōbon)* 9.20 (2: 246).
18 *Heike monogatari (Engyōbon)* 5.14 (1: 517).
19 Friday, "Valorous Butchers," 12–13. In an informative discussion of *inuoumono*, a mounted archery game in which bowmen shot blunted arrows at dogs, Saitō Naoyoshi explains that the easiest angle from which to shoot a target while on horseback is directly to one's left side. The next best shooting angle, he says, is diagonally to the rear, while shooting diagonally forward to one's course of travel requires a very tricky feat of balance and timing. See Murakami Sakae and Saitō Naoyoshi, *Kyūdō oyobi kyūdō shi*, 145–6. Saitō's remarks are also discussed and

summarized in Kawai Yasushi, "Jishō · Jūei no sensō to *Heike monogatari*," 19–20. For a description, in English, of *inuoumono* and other forms of mounted archery competition, see G. Cameron Hurst III, *Armed Martial Arts of Japan: Swordsmanship & Archery*, 115–20.
20 *Konjaku monogatarishū* 27.34.
21 *Azuma kagami* 1191 8/1.
22 In recent years a lively debate has developed, principally between Kondō Yoshikazu and Kawai Yasushi, concerning the basic shooting angle for mounted archery and the most likely pattern of maneuver. Kondō maintains, largely on the basis of pictorial evidence, that the basic angle of attack was straight on, with the warriors shooting forward, almost parallel to their direction of travel. Kawai, citing Saitō Naoyoshi's analysis of *inuoumono* (cited above), argues that the preferred shooting angle was directly to the left, as in modern *yabusame* and other mounted archery games, and that the norm was to avoid head-on charges whenever possible – that the ideal was to slip in behind and to the right of an opponent (on his "horse hand" side) where he could not return fire. As I suggested in the main text, however, neither position appears to be entirely correct. See Kondō Yoshikazu, *Chūsei-teki bugu no seiritsu to bushi*, 218–25; Kawai Yasushi, "Jishō · Jūei no sensō," 19–20, or "Chūsei bushi no bugei to sensō: Gempei kassen o chūshin ni," 78–82.
23 Scholars of Western military history have observed that a similar situation seems to have held in Europe during this same (tenth- to fourteenth-century) period. Contrary to the stereotype of knights as uncooperative solo fighters, obsessed with the ideal of single combat, the normal practice seems to have been for groups of ten to forty horsemen to coordinate closely with each other. See, for example Malcolm Vale, *War and Chivalry: Warfare and Aristocratic Culture in England, France and Burgundy at the End of the Middle Ages*, 103–5.
24 *Konjaku monogatarishū* 23.14.
25 *Konjaku monogatarishū* 25.12.
26 *Mōko shūrai ekotoba*, pp. 25–6. An alternative translation appears in Conlan, *Divine Intervention*, 64.
27 *Azuma kagami* 1189 8/10.
28 Friday, "Valorous Butchers," 8. Hayashi Rokurō, *Kodai makki no hanran*, 173, makes a similar observation concerning the objective of early *bushi* warfare. He attributes this, however, to the relative abundance of cultivatable lands relative to the availability of labor to work them. Thus, he argues, to destroy an adversary or his home was of more value than attempting to capture his lands intact, since the elimination of a rival freed valuable workers to be employed on the victor's own lands. Okada Seiichi, "Kassen to girei," 163–5, also characterizes the objectives of Heian-period warfare as centering on the destruction of opponents, but argues that this changed with the confiscations and redistributions of land titles carried out by Yoritomo and his successors. Henceforth, he maintains, the capture of territory became a fundamental premise of Japanese warfare. I disagree with this assessment, for the reasons cited in the main text. Okada's interpretation ignores the fundamental distinction that must be drawn between the capture and occupation of territory as a direct military objective, and the *political* seizure (and redistribution) of assets (including land rights) belonging to subjugated criminals and "enemies of the state."
29 Archer Jones, *The Art of War in the Western World*, 83.
30 Friday, "Valorous Butchers," 18, n. 21.
31 Jones, *Art of War*, 83.
32 Examples of raids appear in numerous Heian-period literary and documentary sources, in addition to *Shōmonki* and other sources for the Masakado rebellion. See, for example, "Mutsuwaki," p. 27; *Konjaku monogatarishū* #23.13, #25.5; *Heian ibun* docs. 797, ho 007, 2090, 2583; *Fusō ryakki* 902/09/26, 919/05/23; *Nihon kiryaku*

NOTES

947/02/14; *Chōya gunsai*, pp. 179–80 (986/10/20 *Sesshō ke ōsesho*); *Chōshūki* 1094/03/08.
33 *Shōmonki*, p. 55.
34 *Shōmonki*, pp. 71–7.
35 *Shōyūki* 1031 3/1; *Sakeiki* 1031 6/27. The Tadatsune affair is discussed in detail in Karl Friday, "Lordship Interdicted: Taira Tadatsune and the Limited Horizons of Warrior Ambition."
36 *Sakeiki* 1034 10/24.
37 *Heian ibun* doc. 1351.
38 Fukuda Toyohiko, *Tōgoku heiran*, 64–6.
39 Theresa Vann's work on twelfth-century Castile ("Twelfth-Century Castile and Its Frontier Strategies") suggests that analogous considerations shaped strategic thinking in medieval Europe. The circumstances of medieval war, she argues, derived from the circumstances surrounding it. Feudal kingdoms lacked the organization and resources available to later states, and could not support large standing armies for extended periods of time. Similarly, no medieval polity could support total war without destroying itself, and could rarely muster the resources to mount large, set-piece battles such as characterized later eras. Ambushes and skirmishes were useful tactics, but not suitable ones around which to build a strategy, inasmuch as no baron could count on long-term, continued success in such tactics. Sieges of castles or towns, on the other hand, involved predictable sequences of events, and usually led to incremental loses or gains, without large loss of life on either side. Fortified positions could also be held with comparatively few troops. For these reasons, concludes Vann, medieval commanders preferred sieges, and most medieval fighting consisted of skirmishes rather than large-scale campaigns.
40 For more on stockades in the northeast, and their role in the government's efforts to establish domain over the *emishi* inhabitants thereof, see Kudō Masaki, *Jōsaku to emishi*; Sekiguchi Akira, *Emishi to kodai kokka*, 122–55; Takahashi Tomio, *Emishi*, 87–103; or Takemitsu Makoto, *Kodai tōhoku: Matsurowanu mono no keifu*, 14–41. In English, see Friday, "Pushing Beyond the Pale," 5–7.
41 "Mutsuwaki," p. 28.
42 "Mutsuwaki," pp. 30–1.
43 While historians long assumed that Heian and Kamakura warriors lived in heavily fortified compounds, called *tachi* or *hōkeikan*, which served dual purposes as residences and fortresses, recent scholarship has cast doubt on this conjecture. Hashiguchi Teishi, "Hōkeikan wa ika ni seiritsu suru no ka," 114–17, offers an excellent overview and summary of the received wisdom on the fortified *bushi* residences of the Heian and Kamakura periods. Takahashi Masaaki, "Kihei to suigun," was among the earliest challenges to the prevailing view. More recent treatments include the Hashiguchi article cited above, his earlier "Chūsei hōkeikan o meguru shomondai," and Nakazawa Katsuaki, *Chūsei no buryoku to jōkaku*.
44 Takahashi Masaaki, "Kihei to suigun," 79–80; Hashiguchi, "Hōkeikan," 119–30. Hashiguchi observes that there are numerous methodological problems involved in researching early medieval warrior dwellings, particularly in identifying what sorts of features became common when. Surviving documentary references, for example, can rarely be linked to archeological sites with complete certainty. Many warrior home sites, moreover, were used continuously for long periods – even centuries – during which they were repeatedly redone and updated. Thus the remains today are unreliable indicators of what the site looked like in its earliest manifestations.
45 Kawai Yasushi, "Jishō · juei no 'sensō' to Kamakura bakufu" Nakazawa, *Chūsei no buryoku*, 161–2.
46 *Heike monogatari* (*Engyōbon*) 9.15 (2: 227).
47 *Gempei jōsuiki* 37.1 (5: 54).

NOTES

48 *Azuma kagami* 1180 11/5, 11/6, 1184 2/5, 2/7, 1188 11/5, 1189 8/10, 1201 5/14. Nakazawa, *Chūsei no buryoku*, 169–75.
49 See, for example, *Kamakura ibun* docs. 29617, 29755; *Sankeiki*, 1179 10/3, 1180 5/26; *Azuma kagami* 1180 5/23, 5/26, 5/27, 8/4, 8/17, 8/25, 10/14, 11/4, 1203 9/17, 10/26, 1213 5/2, 5/3.
50 Nakazawa Katsuaki has tabulated the features of late twelfth-century fortifications, as described in *Azuma kagami*, *Heike monogatari* (*Engyōbon*) and *Heike monogatari* (*Kakuichi-bon*). See the tables he presents in *Chūsei no buryoku*, p. 170.
51 Harry Holbert Turney-High, *Primitive War: Its Practice and Concepts*, 17; Martin H. Brice, *Stronghold: A History of Military Architecture*, 17.
52 Kawai, *Gempei kassen*, 83–4.
53 For ditches and earthworks used in pastures used to enclose pastures, see *Heian ibun* docs. 1509, 1950, 1962, 3223, 3224; or *Kamakura ibun* doc. 3913. Early examples of trenches and moats constructed for military purposes include *Azuma kagami* 1180 5/23, 1187 4/23 and 1189 8/8.
54 *Azuma kagami* 1189 8/7. Kawai, *Gempei kassen*, 84–92. A photograph of the Azukashiyama ditch appears on p. 91 of this volume. While *Azuma kagami* asserts that Yasuhira dammed up the Abukuma River to flood his moat, Kawai points out that this is impossible, inasmuch as the ditch is more than 2 meters higher in elevation than the river.
55 The definitive study of the Mongol defense walls is Yanagita Yoshitaka, "Genkō bōruui to chūsei kaigan sen." Conlan, *Divine Intervention*, 235, cites *Kamakura ibun* doc. 12260 as the earliest documentary reference to the walls.
56 Kawai, "Jishō · Jūei no 'sensō' to Kamakura bakufu," 68. Kawai builds here on the calculations of Kobayashi Seiji.
57 *Heian ibun* docs. 4080, 4131; *Azuma kagami* 1181 3/13, 1187 4/23, 1189 8/7.
58 See, for example, *Azuma kagami* 1180 8/26, 1184 2/7, 1189 8/7, 8/8, 8/9, 8/10, 9/17, 9/20; *Heike monogatari* (*Engyōbon*) 5.15 (1: 519–23), 7.9 (2: 26–8), 9.20 (233–55).
59 *Yagura* appear in late thirteenth- and fourteenth-century picture scrolls depicting late twelfth-century fortifications, and in battle accounts in the various versions of *Heike monogatari*. There are, however, no references to or illustrations of Gempei War-era *yagura* in contemporaneous sources, which raises the possibility that they were a later invention, anachronistically ascribed to twelfth-century *jōkaku* by authors and artists of a later age. The only reference to *yagura* in *Azuma kagami* is the entry for 1201 5/14, which describes the famous warrior woman Hangaku Gozen sitting atop a *yagura* and shooting down attackers, until she was at length felled by an arrow shot from a position in the mountains above and behind the fort she defended.
60 *Azuma kagami* 1189 8/7.
61 See, for example, *Azuma kagami* 1180 11/5, 1184 2/7, or 1213 5/2. Nakazawa Katsuaki, "Chūsei jōkaku-shi shikiron," 37.
62 Conlan, "State of War," 112–18, offers an excellent overview of fourteenth-century castle warfare.
63 *Taiheiki* (*Tenshōbon*) 3.1 (1: 123–7), 3.2 (1: 127–34). Goble (*Kenmu*, 122) speculates that Go-Daigo may have chosen Mount Kasagi because it was the site of an enormous cliff-face sculpture of the Maitreya Buddha, as well as for its fierce garrison of temple warriors. Nakazawa Katsuaki offers an intriguing discussion of the practice of selecting holy or spiritual places as sites for castles during the early medieval period, in "Chūsei jōkaku-shi shikiron," 38–51.
64 *Taiheiki* (*Tenshōbon*) 3.2 (1: 133).
65 *Taiheiki* (*Tenshōbon*) 3.2 (1: 133–4).
66 Nakazawa Katsuaki, "Kūkan to shite no 'jōkaku' to sono tenkai," 207–14.
67 See, for example, *Taiheiki* (*Tenshōbon*) 3.2, 3.3 (1: 136–43).

NOTES

68 *Taiheiki (Tenshōbon)* 3.6 (1: 152); *Taiheiki (Rufubon)* 7.2 (1: 308). *Taiheiki (Tenshōbon)* 7.2 (1: 348) gives the initial numbers for the besieging force as an even more astounding (and even less credible) 1,800,000 horsemen!

69 Ishii Susumu, *Kamakura bakufu*, 117–25. Ishii's conclusions rapidly became the received wisdom on this issue, and remained so until very recently. See, for example, Nishimata Fusō, "Kassen no rūru to manaa"; or Abe Takeshi, *Kamakura bushi no seikai*, 190–6.

70 Satō Shin'ichi, *Nambokuchō no dōran*, 194–5; Amino Yoshihiko, *Mōko shūrai*, 372–3. Satō's and Amino's positions have been restated repeatedly by subsequent scholars; see, for example, Seki Yukihiko, "'Bu' no kōgen: kōchū to yumiya."

71 Kawai, "Jishō · Jūei no 'sensō' to Kamakura bakufu"; Abe Takeshi, *Kamakura bushi no seikai*, 204–11; Okada Seiichi, "Kassen to girei"; Futaki Ken'ichi, *Chūsei buke no sakuhō*, 40–66; Kondō Yoshikazu, "Buki kara mita nairanki no sentō"; Imai Seinosuke, "Kassen no kikō."

72 Hans Delbrück, *Warfare in Antiquity*, 34–5; Delbrück, *The Barbarian Invasions*, 227.

73 For a dissenting view, arguing that the warfare of the 1180s did *not* involve significantly greater numbers of troops than had earlier battles, see Farris, *Heavenly Warriors*, 269–70, 272–3, 291–2, 300–2, 392–3.

74 See, for example, *Teishin kōki* 940 1/13; *Midō kanpakki* 1017, 3/11; *Nihon kiryaku* 1028 8/05; *Chōya gunsai*, p. 284 (1058 3/29 daijōkanpu); *Konjaku monogatarishū* 25.5; *Heian ibun* docs. 372, 797.

75 *Shōmonki*, p. 121; *Fusō ryakki* 939 11/21, 940 2/8; *Honchō seiki* 941.

76 *Gokuyō* 1180 9/9, 12/5, 12/27, 1181 2/1, 2/17, 1183 6/5, 7/21, 1184 3/6. Farris, *Heavenly Warriors*, 392–3, offers a table showing the numbers of troops involved in twenty major battles of the Gempei War, as described in the six major sources for the conflict.

77 Kawai, *Gempei kassen*, 60–7; "Jishō · Jūei no 'sensō,' to Kamakura bakufu," 64–5.

78 *Azuma kagami* 1180 8/26, 1180 12/1, 1184 2/5, 1184 2/7, 1189 8/8, 1189 8/10, 1189 9/9, 1213 5/2, 1213 5/3, 1221 6/12, 1221 6/14; *Mōko shūrai ekotoba*. See also Conlan, *Divine Intervention*, which features English translations of many of the main sources for information of the Mongol invasions.

79 See, for example, *Azuma kagami* 1208 10/21, 1221 6/19. Kawai, *Gempei kassen*, 21.

80 *Gempei jōsuiki* 22.1 (3: 115); *Hōgen monogatari (Nakaraibon)*, quoted in Takahashi Masaaki, *Bushi no seiritsu*, 246.

81 Kondō Yoshikazu appears to have been the first scholar to make this observation; see *Yumiya to tōken*, 187–97. It is also worth recalling that the anecdotes in the various wartales concerning the behavior of individual warriors, during the closing stages of battles, are the portions of the texts most heavily shaped by later raconteurs – and therefore the least reliable sections of the tales.

82 *Azuma kagami* 1180 8/25.

83 Conlan, "State of War," 65; Suzuki Masaya, *Katana to kubi-tori*, 78–80; Shakadō Mitsuhiro, "Nambokuchō ki kassen ni okeru senshō," 37–8.

84 Conlan, "State of War," 77–80; Imai Seinosuke, "Kassen no kikō." Conlan further demonstrates that the term *"nobushi,"* which some historians have associated with peasant infantrymen fighting in massed formation, in fact designated a style of combat rather than a class of combatant. *Nobushi*, he argues, were simply warriors who fought "crouching in fields," as the literal meaning of the word implies – that is, troops who fought on foot, from behind cover. Contemporaneous records clearly show that such men came from diverse social backgrounds, and included high-ranking *bushi* as well as peasants. See "State of War," 76–7.

NOTES

5 THE CULTURE OF WAR

1 Wm. Wayne Farris, *Heavenly Warriors: The Evolution of Japan's Military, 500–1300,* 8–9; Robert L. O'Connell, *Of Arms and Men: A History of War, Weapons, and Aggression,* 13–29.
2 Ishii Shirō, *Nihonjin no kokka seikatsu,* 14–24.
3 Eiko Ikegami, *The Taming of the Samurai: Honorific Individualism and the Making of Modern Japan,* 97–8; her portrait of early medieval warfare (pp. 97–103) appears to have been drawn primarily from Ishii Shirō's work, cited above. Other examples of recent scholarship that have portrayed early medieval warfare as ritualized include: Nishimata Fusō, "Kassen no rūru to manaa"; Okada Seiichi, "Kassen to girei"; Seki Yukihiko, "'Bu' no kōgen: kōchū to yumiya"; H. Paul Varley, *Warriors of Japan as Portrayed in the War Tales*; Takahashi Masaaki, *Bushi no seiritsu: bushizō no sōshutsu*; Farris, *Heavenly Warriors,* 8–9, 132–3, 231–3, 237–8, 269–70, 298–300; and Farris, "Japan to 1300," 60–2, 66–7. The image of ritual and formalism in early medieval warfare has been virtually reified in popular and textbook accounts. See, for example, Mikiso Hane, *Premodern Japan: A Historical Survey,* 73–4; Stephen R. Turnbull, *The Book of the Samurai: The Warrior Class of Japan,* 19, 22–36; Turnbull, *The Lone Samurai and the Martial Arts,* 14–28; John Newman, *Bushido: the Way of the Warrior,* 13–14, 16–17.
4 *Konjaku monogatarishū* 25.6, 29.5; *Kokon chomonjū* 9.13.347, 9.12.333.
5 See, for example, "Mutsuwaki," pp. 23, 25–6; *Azuma kagami* 1180 8/26, 1184 4/21, 1205 6/22, 1221 6/6, 1241 11/29.
6 Matthew Strickland observes that, "despite drawing on established concepts, honor [is] ultimately a personal issue . . . governed by the conscience and self-esteem of the individual." Matthew Strickland, *War & Chivalry: The Conduct and Perception of War in England and Normandy, 1066–1217,* 125–31.
7 *Heian ibun* doc. 640.
8 "Mutsuwaki," p. 23.
9 "Mutsuwaki," p. 28.
10 "Mutsuwaki," p. 23.
11 Thomas Conlan, "State of War: The Violent Order of Fourteenth Century Japan," 172.
12 Karl Friday and with Seki Humitake, *Legacies of the Sword: The Kashima-Shinryū and Samurai Martial Culture,* 61.
13 *Konjaku monogatarishū* 25.1, 25.4, 25.6, 27.34; *Shōmonki,* pp. 105–7, 127–9; "Mutsuwaki," pp. 27, 30–1; *Azuma kagami* 1190 1/6, 1213 5/3; *Kojidan* #312; *Shōyūki* 1028 7/10; *Heike monogatari (Engyōbon)* 9.20 (2: 233); *Chūyūki* 1108 1/29. For fuller information on early *bushi* religious attitudes, see: Conlan, "State of War," 170–202; Gomi Fumihiko, *Sassei to shinkō: bushi o saguru*; Takahashi Masaaki, *Bushi no seiritsu,* 189–99; or Irumada Nobuo, *Musha no yō ni,* 257–94. Futaki Ken'ichi, *Chūsei buke no sakuhō,* 63–6, discusses of the idea of taboos on the battlefield, and their relationship to practical concerns.
14 *Konjaku monogatarishū* 19.7.
15 *Hōgen monogatari (Nakaraibon)* 26–7.
16 Karl Friday, "Mononofu: The Warrior of Heian Japan," 82–5; Friday, "Valorous Butchers: The Art of War during the Golden Age of the Samurai," 8–9. The *Nakaraibon Hōgen monogatari,* from which this passage is drawn, is thought to have been compiled shortly before 1318 (Yamagishi and Takahashi, *Hōgen monogatari [Nakaraibon] to kenkyū,* 146).
17 "Shin sarugakki," p. 138.
18 *Konjaku monogatarishū* 25.3.

NOTES

19 Recounted in *Konjaku monogatarishū* 25.5.
20 *Konjaku monogatarishū* describes Morotō's brother-in-law only as "a son of the [former] governor of Nōtō ____ Koremichi," known by the sobriquet of Ōkimi ("the great prince"). Noguchi Minoru, however, has identified him as Tachibana Yoshinori, on the basis of entries in a Tachibana family genealogy, which describe Tachibana Koremichi as having been governor of Nōtō, and Yoshinori as "a resident of Mutsu and holder of the Junior Fifth Lower court rank called Ōkimi." See "Gempeitōkitsu no gunji kizoku," 12.
21 William R. Wilson, "The Way of the Bow and Arrow: The Japanese Warrior in the Kojaku Monogatari," 188; Ishii Susumu, *Chūsei bushidan*, 117.
22 *Konjaku monogatarishū* 25.10; 25.4; *Azuma kagami* 1185 6/16.
23 Sasayama Haruo, "Bunken ni mirareru senjutsu to buki," 130–8, discusses of the use of deception and treachery in warfare of the *Kojiki* and *Nihon shoki*.
24 Strickland, *War & Chivalry*, 128–31.
25 *Azuma kagami* 1180 11/4.
26 James Murdoch, *A History of Japan* 1: 580.
27 *Gempei jōsuiki* 27.2 (5: 69).
28 *Shōmonki*, p. 67; *Azuma kagami* 1184 2/7, 1189 8/9, 1189 8/10, 1189 8/12, 1200 1/23, 1213 5/23, 1219 1/27. A mid-thirteenth-century tale collection also features a charming, but obviously fanciful, account of a poetry exchange between Minamoto Yoshiie and Abe Sadatō during Yoshiie's attack on Akita stockade in 1062. The story relates that Sadatō, seeing he has lost, escapes the fort through a back exit, only to be spotted and pursued by Yoshiie, who catches up with him near the Koromo River. As he pursues Sadatō, Yoshiie calls to him to quit running and return to fight, and then recites *"koromo no tate wa hokorobi-nikeri"* ("the woof [*tate*] of your robe [*koromo*] is in tatters," or "your citadel [*tate*] at Koromo is destroyed"). Sadatō pauses, shakes his head, and responds *"toshi o heshi ito no midare no kurushisa ni"* ("having endured the disarray of old threads [*ito*] that have seen many years," or "amid the suffering brought about by the muddling of [battle] plans [*ito*] of many years"). Yoshiie is so impressed that he removes the arrow already fitted to his bow and turns away. *Kokon chomonjū* 9.12.336.
29 See, for example, Judith N. Rabinovitch, *Shōmonki: The Story of Masakado's Rebellion*, 82–3.
30 *Heike monogatari (Kakuichi-bon)* 9.1–16 (2: 164–222).
31 Takahashi Masaaki, *Bushi no seiritsu*, 252–3, discusses the use of decorations on armor, horses and the like as tools for identifying appropriate adversaries.
32 "Hachiman gudōkun," p. 406.
33 *Mōko shūrai ekotoba*; Thomas Conlan, *In Little Need of Divine Intervention: Scrolls of the Mongol Invasions of Japan*, 258. Katō Tomoyasu and Yūi Masatomo, eds., *Nihon shi bunken kaidai jiten*, 891, places the compilation of Hachiman gudōkun between 1299 and 1218. Wm. Wayne Farris offers an alternative translation of the passage as: "Whereas we [Japanese] thought about reciting our pedigrees to each other and battling man-to-man in glory or defeat as was the custom of Japanese armies, in this battle the Mongols assembled at one point in a great force" (*Heavenly Warriors*, 331). The original passage reads 日本軍ノ如ク相互ニ名乗合高名不覚ハ一人宛ノ勝負ト思フ処。此合戦ハ大勢一度寄合テ。
34 *Hōgen monogatari (Nakaraibon)*, p. 15; *Gempei jōsuiki* 37.2 (5: 55), 38.2 (5: 98–9); *Heike monogatari (Engyōbon)* 9.20 (2: 243), 9.21 (2: 256), 9.22 (2: 259); *Heike monogatari (Kakuichi-bon)* 9.6 (2: 188). Of the nineteen examples of *nanori* in the *Kakuichi-bon Heike monogatari*, twelve occur amid charges, while warriors stand before the gates of enemy fortifications, or while warriors wait for the enemy to attack. Two occur after a warrior has defeated another and is about to dispatch him. Three occur while

NOTES

in pursuit of a routed enemy. And only two are addressed to individual opponents squaring off to attack – one of whom then responds by running away.
35 *Gempei jōsuiki* 23.1 (4: 87), 21.4 (3: 103), 38.2 (5: 99).
36 Sasamatsu Hiroshi, "Omae no kasan . . .," offers an interesting look at the custom of insults in medieval Japan.
37 Friday, "Valorous Butchers," 15–16.
38 Kenneth D. Butler, "The *Heike Monogatari* and the Japanese Warrior Ethic"; Butler, "The Heike Monogatari and Theories of Oral Epic Literature"; Butler, "The Textual Evolution of the Heike Monogatari." For more on the fundamental features of oral composition, see Albert Lord, *The Singer of Tales*.
39 Sonam Kachru, "Dogs of War: Examining Warrior Duels in the *Heike monogatari*"; Kachru suggests that this is because the winners are concerned about rewards later, while the apparent losers are in no position to worry about such things. Similar observations can also be made of *nanori* in *Hōgen monogatari* and *Heiji monogatari*. (Taira) Akushichibyōe Kagekiyo's defiant speech to Yoshitsune's men, in *Heike monogatari (Kakuichi-bon)* 11.5 (2: 320–1) appears to be the only exception to the pattern Kachru identifies. In this account, Kagekiyo, ensconced behind a shield, shoots the horse from under the charging Mionoya no Jūrō, and then attempts to chase him down on foot. Jūrō, however, escapes, prompting a frustrated – and winded – Kagekiyo to bellow, "You may have heard tell of me in days of yore, now see me with your own eyes; I am he whom the punks of the capital call Akushichibyōe Kagekiyo, of Kazusa," and then retire from the field.
40 *Heike monogatari (Engyōbon)* 9.20 (2: 251).
41 *Heike monogatari (Engyōbon)* 9.20 (2: 245); *Gempei jōsuiki* 27.2 (5: 55–6).
42 Strickland, *War & Chivalry*, 133–8; Joseph Ober, "Classical Greek Times," 13–17; James Turner Johnson, *Just War Tradition and the Restraint of War*, 126; Robert C. Stacey, "The Age of Chivalry," 36–8.
43 "Mutsuwaki," p. 25
44 "Mutsuwaki," p. 26.
45 Strickland, *War & Chivalry*, 176–82, raises similar considerations with regard to infantrymen in medieval Europe.
46 See Karl Friday, "*Bushidō* or Bull? A Medieval Historian's Perspective on the Imperial Army and the Japanese Warrior Tradition," for a comparison of modern and medieval Japanese ideas on military ethics.
47 *Gempei jōsuiki* 38.2 (5: 98–9).
48 *Azuma kagami* 1189 9/7, 9/13. *Azuma kagami* 1184 3/28 offers another example of a warrior (Taira Shigehira) arguing that there is no disgrace to capture.
49 Kawai Yasushi, "Jishō · Jūei no nairan to chiiki shakai," 11–12.
50 Thomas Conlan, "The Nature of Warfare in Fourteenth-Century Japan: the Record of Nomoto Tomoyuki," 320–1.
51 *Ryō no gige*, p. 191.
52 *Nihon kiryaku* 794 10/28, 992 11/30; *Chōshūki* 1094 3/8.
53 *Shoku Nihongi* 764 9/18; *Fusō ryakki* 940 2/8; *Nihon kiryaku* 941 8/7; *Heian ibun* docs. 520, 795, 797; *Chōya gunsai*, pp. 286–7 (1117 5/5 Kebiishi-chō kudashi-bumi).
54 *Nihon kiryaku* 992 12/2; *Chūyūki* 1097 3/8, 1108 1/19, 1/29, 1110 1/29; *Suisaki* 1063 2/16; *Azuma kagami* 1189 8/11.
55 *Azuma kagami* 1189 8/8; *Obusuma Saburō ekotoba*, p. 15.
56 Kuroda Hideyo, "Kubi o kakeru," 18–20. The incident involving Yoritomo appears in *Utsunomiya daijin kizuiki* 1189 10/19 (in *Dainihon shiryō*, series 4 vol. 2). Yoshitsune's sacrifice of prisoners is described in *Heike monogatari (Kakuichi-bon)* 11.2 (2: 308). Kuroda also cites *Heike monogatari (Kakuichi-bon)* 12.5 (2: 391), in which Yoshitsune orders that heads taken in battle be "made offerings to the war gods."

NOTES

57 For more on *buke kojitsu*, see G. Cameron Hurst III, "The Warrior as Ideal for a New Age," 226–31.
58 My summary of Muromachi-era procedures for inspecting heads is from Futaki Ken'ichi, *Chūsei buke no sakuhō*, 59–63.
59 Conlan, "Nature of Warfare," 311–13; Suzuki Masaya, *Katana to kubi-tori: Sengoku kassen isetsu*, 86–105. The earliest example of an order against head-hunting dates from 1138; see *Nanbokuchō ibun Chūgoku · Shikoku hen* doc. 773.
60 Conlan, "Nature of Warfare," 311–13; Suzuki, *Katana to kubi-tori*, 86–105.
61 For a fuller description of the role of temples in the socio-political and economic structure of early medieval Japan, see Mikael Adolphson, "Enryakuji: An Old Power in a New Era"; Martin Collcutt, *Five Mountains: The Rinzai Zen Monastic Institution in Medieval Japan*; or Joan R. Piggott, "Hierarchy and Economics in Early Medieval Todaiji."
62 *Kokon chomonjū* 9:12:333.
63 *Konjaku monogatarishū* 25.11.
64 *Konjaku monogatarishū* 25.7; the same tale appears in *Ujishūi monogatari* 2.10. For an account of just how formidable an opponent this bandit, Hakamadare, could otherwise be, see *Konjaku monogatarishū* 29.19.
65 See, for example, *Shōmonki*, 99, 117–19, 125–7; "Mutsuwaki," pp. 27, 31–4; *Chōya gunsai* 986 10/20 *Sesshō ke ōsesho*, pp. 179–80; *Konjaku monogatarishū* 23.13, 25.1, 25.5; *Heian ibun* docs. 797, ho 7, 2090, 2583; *Fusō ryakki* 902 9/26, 919 5/23; *Nihon kiryaku* 947 2/14; *Chūyūki* 1094 3/8.
66 *Shōmonki*, 117–19; *Konjaku monogatarishū* 25.1.
67 *Konjaku monogatarishū* 29.25.
68 *Obusuma Saburō ekotoba*, p. 15; this kidnapping is illustrated on pp. 18–19.
69 *Heian ibun* doc. 339.
70 *Obusuma Saburō ekotoba*, pp. 3, 15, 24–6.
71 *Konjaku monogatarishū* 25.11.
72 Thomas Nagel, "War and Massacre," 8–13.
73 Archer Jones, *The Art of War in the Western World*, 121.

EPILOG

1 Thomas Conlan, "State of War: The Violent Order of Fourteenth Century Japan," 87–124.
2 May Elizabeth Berry, *The Culture of Civil War in Kyoto*, xxvi–xxxii.
3 On this point see Thomas Conlan, "Largesse and the Limits of Loyalty in the Fourteenth Century."

REFERENCES AND BIBLIOGRAPHY

Primary sources

Azuma kagami. In *Shintei zōho kokushi taikei.* Tokyo: Yoshikawa kōbunkan, 1968.
Ban dainagon ekotoba. Nihon no emaki, vol. 2. Komatsu Shigemi, gen. ed. Tokyo: Chūō kōronsha, 1987.
Buki kōshō. Shintei zōho kojitsu sōsho, vols. 19–20. Tokyo: Yoshikawa kōbunkan, 1977.
Chōshūki. In *Zōho shiryō taisei.* Kyoto: Rinsen shoten, 1965.
Chōya gunsai. In *Kokushi taikei.* Tokyo: Yoshikawa kōbunkan, 1964.
Chūyūki. In *Zōho shiryō taisei.* Kyoto: Rinsen shoten, 1965.
"Daijingū shozō jiki." In *Jingibu* 1.3, vol. 2 of *Gunsho ruijū,* ed. Hanawa Hōkinoichi. Tokyo: Zoku gunsho ruijū kanseikai, 1932.
Dainihon shiryō. Series 1–4. Tokyo: Tōkyō daigaku shuppankai, 1901–.
Denryaku. 5 vols. In *Dainihon kokiroku.* Tokyo: Iwanami shoten, 1960–70.
Engi shiki. In *Shintei zōho kokushi taikei.* Tokyo: Yoshikawa kōbunkan, 1937.
Fusō ryakki. In *Kokushi taikei.* Tokyo: Yoshikawa kōbunkan, 1965.
Gempei jōsuiki. 6 vols, ed. Nagahara Hajime. Tokyo: Shinjinbutsu ōraisha, 1989.
Gokuyō. 3 vols. Tokyo: Kokusho kankō kai, 1906–7.
Gonijō Moromichi ki. In *Dainihon kokiroku,* vol. 5. Tokyo: Iwanami shoten, 1956.
Gonki. In *Zōho shiryō taisei.* Kyoto: Rinsen shoten, 1965.
Go-sannen kassen ekotoba. Nihon no emaki, vol. 20. Komatsu Shigemi, gen. ed. Tokyo: Chūō kōronsha, 1988.
"Goseibai shikimoku." In *Buke bu* 1, vol. 17 of *Shinkō gunsho ruijū,* ed. Hanawa Hōkinoichi. Tokyo: Meicho fukyūkai, 1930, 357–65.
"Goseibai shikimoku tsuikahō." In *Chūsei hōsei shiryōshū,* ed. Ikeuchi Yoshisuke and Satō Shin'ichi, vol. 1. Tokyo: Iwanami shoten, 1955–78.
"Hachiman gudōkun." In *Jingibu,* vol. 1 of *Gunsho ruijū,* ed. Hanawa Hōkinoichi. Tokyo: Zoku gunsho ruijū kanseikai, 1932, 386–416.
Heian ibun. 15 vols. Tokyo: Tōkyōdō, 1965–.
Heihanki. In *Zōho shiryō taisei.* Kyoto: Rinsen shoten, 1965.
Heiji monogatari, ed. Tochigi Yoshitada *et al. Shin Nihon koten bungaku taikei,* vol. 43. Tokyo: Iwanami shoten, 1992.
Heike monogatari ekotoba. Nihon no emaki, vol. 12. Komatsu Shigemi, gen. ed. Tokyo: Chūō kōronsha, 1988.
Heike monogatari (Engyōbon). 4 vols, ed. Kitahara Yasuo and Ogawa Eiichi. Tokyo: Bensei shuppan, 1990.

Heike monogatari (Kakuichi-bon). 2 vols, ed. Takagi Ichinosuke *et al*. *Nihon koten bungaku taikei*, vols. 32–3. Tokyo: Iwanami shoten, 1960.
Hōgen monogatari, ed. Tochigi Yoshitada *et al*. *Shin Nihon koten bungaku taikei*, vol. 43. Tokyo: Iwanami shoten, 1992.
Hōgen monogatari (Nakaraibon) to kenkyū, ed. Yamagishi Tokuhei and Takahashi Teiichi. Toyohashi: Mikan kokubun shiryō kankokai, 1959.
Honchō monzui. In *Kokushi taikei*. Tokyo: Yoshikawa kōbunkan, 1965.
Honchō seiki. In *Kokushi taikei*. Tokyo: Yoshikawa kōbunkan, 1964.
Hōnen jōnin eden. *Zoku Nihon no emaki*, vols. 1–3. Komatsu Shigemi, gen. ed. Tokyo: Chūō kōronsha, 1990.
Hyakurenshō. In *Kokushi taikei*. Tokyo: Yoshikawa kōbunkan, 1965.
"Hyōshō jinkun yōryaku shō." In *Buke bu*, vol. 25.1 of *Zoku gunsho ruijū*, ed. Haniwa Hōkinoichi. Tokyo: Zoku gunshoruijū kanseikai, 1931, 77–102.
Ishiyama-dera engi. *Nihon no emaki*, vol. 16. Komatsu Shigemi, gen. ed. Tokyo: Chūō kōronsha, 1988.
Jōkyūki, ed. Tochigi Yoshitada *et al*. *Shin Nihon koten bungaku taikei*, vol. 43. Tokyo: Iwanami shoten, 1992.
Kamakura ibun. 15 vols (to date). Tokyo: Tōkyōdō, 1971–.
Kanjin. In *Nihon shisō taikei 8, kodai seiji shakai shisō*. Tokyo: Iwanami shoten, 1986, 167–84.
Kasuga gongen kenki e. *Zoku Nihon no emaki*, vols. 13–14. Komatsu Shigemi, gen. ed. Tokyo: Chūō kōronsha, 1991.
"Kemmu shikimoku." In *Buke bu* 1, vol. 17 of *Shinkō gunsho ruijū*, ed. Hanawa Hōkinoichi. Tokyo: Meisho fukyūkai, 1930, 380–2.
"Kemmu shikimoku tsuika-hō." In *Buke bu* 1, vol. 17 of *Shinkō gunsho ruijū*, ed. Hanawa Hōkinoichi. Tokyo: Meisho fukyūkai, 1930, 366–406.
Koji ruien. 51 vols, Tokyo: Yoshikawa kōbunkan, 1999.
Kojidan, ed. Kobayashi Yasuharu. *Koten bunko*, vols. 60–2. Tokyo: Gendai shichōsha, 1981.
Kojiki. *Kojiki taisei*, vol. 7. Hisamatsu Sen'ichi *et al*., gen. eds. Tokyo: Heibonsha, 1958.
Kokon chomonjū. In *Shintei zōho kokushi taikei*. Tokyo: Yoshikawa kōbunkan, 1985.
Konjaku monogatarishū. In *Nihon koten bungaku zenshū*. Tokyo: Shōgakkan, 1971.
Kugyō bunin. In *Shintei zōhō kokushi taikei*. Tokyo: Yoshikawa kōbunkan, 1928.
Midō kampakki. In *Dainihon kokiroku*. Tokyo: Iwanami shoten, 1952.
Mōko shūrai ekotoba. *Nihon no emaki*, vol. 13. Komatsu Shigemi, gen. ed. Tokyo: Chūō kōronsha, 1988.
"Mutsuwaki." In *Kassen bu*. *Gunsho ruijū*. Tokyo: Shoku gunsho ruijū kanseikai, 1941.
Nambokuchō ibun Chūgoku · Shikoku hen. 6 vols., ed. Matsuoka Hisatō. Tokyo: Tōkyōdō, 1987–95.
Nambokuchō ibun Kyūshū-hen. 7 vols., ed. Seno Seiichirō. Tokyo: Tōkyōdō, 1985–92.
Nihon kiryaku. In *Shintei zōho kokushi taikei*. Tokyo: Yoshikawa kōbunkan, 1985.
Nihon shoki. In *Shintei zōho kokushi taikei*. Tokyo: Yoshikawa kōbunkan, 1985.
Nihonkoku genzaisho mokuroku, ed. Abe Ryūichi and Nagasawa Kikuya. *Nihon shomoku taisei*, vol. 1. Tokyo: Kyukoshoin, 1979.
Obusuma Saburō ekotoba – Ise shimmeisho utaawase. *Zoku Nihon no emaki*, vol. 18. Komatsu Shigemi, gen. ed. Tokyo: Chūō kōronsha, 1992.
"Ōtoku gannen nōdaiki." In *Zoku zoku gunsho ruijū*, ed. Haniwa Hōkinoichi. Tokyo: Takeiki insatsusho, 1909–.

Ruijū fusenshō. In *Kokushi taikei.* Tokyo: Yoshikawa kōbunkan, 1964.
Ruijū sandaikyaku. In *Shintei zōho kokushi taikei.* Tokyo: Yoshikawa kōbunkan, 1983.
Ryō no gige. In *Shintei zōho kokushi taikei.* Tokyo: Yoshikawa kōbunkan, 1985.
Ryō no shūge. In *Shintei zōho kokushi taikei.* Tokyo: Yoshikawa kōbunkan, 1985.
Sakeiki. In *Zōho shiryō taisei.* Kyoto: Rinsen shoten, 1965.
Sandai jitsuroku. 2 vols. In *Shintei zōho kokushi taikei.* Tokyo: Yoshikawa kōbunkan, 1986.
Sankeiki. In *Zōho shiryō taisei.* Kyoto: Rinsen shoten, 1965.
Sata mirensho. Zoku gunsho ruijū, vol. 25. Haniwa Hōkinoichi and Ōda Tōjirō, gen. eds. Tokyo: Heibun sha, 1924.
Seiji yōryaku. In *Shintei zōho kokushi taikei.* Tokyo: Yoshikawa kōbunkan, 1984.
"Shin sarugakki." In *Nihon shisō taikei,* vol. 8 *Kodai seiji shakai shisō.* Tokyo: Iwanami shoten, 1986.
Shōki mokuroku. In *Dainihon kokiroku.* Tokyo: Iwanami shoten, 1959–.
Shoku Nihon kōki. In *Shintei zōho kokushi taikei.* Tokyo: Yoshikawa kōbunkan, 1987.
Shoku Nihongi. In *Shintei zōho kokushi taikei.* Tokyo: Yoshikawa kōbunkan, 1986.
Shōmonki, ed. Hayashi Rokurō. Tokyo: Imaizumi seibunsha, 1975.
Shōyūki. In *Dainihon kokiroku.* Tokyo: Iwanami shoten, 1959.
Shunki. In *Zōho shiryō taisei.* Kyoto: Rinsen shoten, 1965.
Sochiki. Zōho shiryō taisei, vol. 5. Kyoto: Rinsen shoten, 1965.
Suisaki. Zōhō shiryō taisei, vol. 12. Kyoto: Rinsen shoten, 1965.
Taiheiki (Keichōbon). 5 vols, ed. Yamashita Hiroaki. *Shinko Nihon koten shūsei.* Tokyo: Shinkosha, 1977.
Taiheiki (Rufubon). 5 vols, ed. Yamashita Hiroaki. *Shinchō Nihon koten shūsei.* Tokyo: Shinchōsha, 1998.
Taiheiki (Tenshōbon). 4 vols, ed. Hasegawa Tadashi. *Shinpen Nihon koten bungaku zenshū,* vols. 54–7. Tokyo: Shōgakkan, 1998.
Taiheiki emaki, ed. Miya Tsugio and Satō Kazuhiko. Tokyo: Kawade shobō shinsha, 1992.
Teishin kōki. In *Dainihon kiroku.* Tokyo: Iwanami shoten, 1956.
Tōken zukō. Shintei zōho kojitsu sōsho, vol. 19. Tokyo: Yoshikawa kōbunkan, 1977.
Ujishūi monogatari, ed. Kobayashi Chishō. *Nihon koten bungaku zenshū.* Tokyo: Shōgakkan, 1973.
Utsubo monogatari, ed. Kōno Tama. *Nihon koten bungaku taikei,* vol. 10. Tokyo: Iwanami shoten, 1959.
Wamyō ruijūshō (Shobon shūsei wamyō ruijūshō). Tokyo: Rinsen shoten, 1968.
"Wei chih." (Sanguo chih, "Weishu tungi chuan," Weiren hsiang). In *Shinwa kara rekishi e,* vol. 1, ed. Inoue Mitsusada. Tokyo: Chūō kōronsha, 1965, 214–20.
Zenkunen kassen ekotoba – Heiji monogatari emaki – Yūki kassen ekotoba. Zoku Nihon no emaki, vol. 17. Komatsu Shigemi, gen. ed. Tokyo: Chūō kōronsha, 1992.

Secondary sources

Abe Takeshi. *Kamakura bushi no seikai.* Tokyo: Tōkyōdō shuppan, 1994.
Abe Yukio. "Heiji monogatari Hachiman Tarō Yoshiie no kenkyū rombunshū." *Miyashrio gakuin jo dai* 57 (1982): 25–44.
Adolphson, Mikael. "Enryakuji: An Old Power in a New Era." In *The Origins of Japan Medieval World: Courtiers, Clerics, Warriors, and Peasants in the Fourteenth Century,* ed. Jeffrey P. Mass. Stanford, CA: Stanford University Press, 1997, 237–60.

———. *The Gates of Power: Monks, Courtiers and Warriors in Premodern Japan*. Honolulu: University of Hawaii Press, 2000.
Aida Jirō. *Mōko shūrai no kenkyū*. Tokyo: Yoshikawa kōbunkan, 1958.
Akagi Shizuko. "Gutei no Heishi." *Kodai bunka shiron 3* (1982): 1–7.
Akashi Kazunori. "Kodai-chūsei kazokuron no mondaiten." *Kaihō* 23 (1985): 1–7.
Akita Shō. "Chihō kanga to sono shūhen: kokushisei no keisei o megutte." *Shōnai kokōgaku* 19 (1985): 1–11.
Akutō kenkyūkai, ed. *Akutō no chūsei*. Tokyo: Iwata shoin, 1998.
Allmand, Christopher. "War and the Non-Combatant in the Middle Ages. In *Medieval Warfare: A History*," ed. Maurice Keen. New York: Oxford University Press, 1999, 253–72.
Altham, E. A. *The Principles of War*. London: Macmillan, 1914.
Amdur, Ellis. "The History and Development of the Naginata." *Journal of Asian Martial Arts* 4, no. 1 (1995): 32–49.
Amino Yoshihiko. *Akutō to kaizoku: Nihon chūsei no shakai to seiji*. Tokyo: Hōsei daigaku shuppankyoku, 1995.
———. "Commerce and Finance in the Middle Ages: the Beginnings of 'Capitalism'." *Acta Asiatica* 81 (Sept 2001): 1–19.
———. *Mōko shūrai*. *Nihon no rekishi*, vol. 10. Tokyo: Shogakukan, 1974.
———. "Shōen koryōsei no keisei to kōzō." In *Tōchiseidoshi*, ed. Takeuchi Rizō. Tokyo: Yamakawa shoten, 1973, 173–274.
———. "Umino ryōshu · umi no bushidan." In *Bushi to wa nan darō ka*, ed. Takahashi Masaaki and Yamamoto Kōji. Tokyo: Asahi shimbunsha, 1994, 44–57.
Amino Yoshihiko, Sasamatsu Hiroshi and Ishii Susumu. *Chūsei no tsumi to batsu*. Tokyo: Tōkyō daigaku shuppankai, 1983.
Anderson, L. J. *Japanese Armour*. New York: Lionel Leventhal, 1968.
Aoki Kazuo. "Ritsuryō zaisei." In *Nihon rekishi 3, kodai 3*, ed. Ienaga Saburō *et al*. Tokyo: Iwanami shoten, 1962, 115–46.
Aoyama Mikiya. "Chūsei bushi ni okeru kanshoku no juyō: bushi no tekiō to kanshoku no henshitsu." *Nihon rekishi* 577 (June 1996): 24–41.
Arai Takashige. *Chūsei akutō no kenkyū*. Tokyo: Yoshikawa kōbunkan, 1990.
———. "Nambokuchō nairan no hyōka o megutte." In *Sōten Nihon no rekishi vol. 4 chūsei hen*, ed. Minegishi Sumio. Tokyo: Shinjimbutsu ōraisha, 1991.
Arnesen, Peter J. *The Medieval Japanese Daimyo: The Ouchi Family's Rule of Suo and Nagato*. New Haven, CT: Yale University Press, 1979.
———. "The Provincial Vassals of the Muromachi Shoguns." In *The Bakufu in Japanese History*, ed. Jeffrey P. Mass and William Hauser. Stanford, CA: Stanford University Press, 1985, 99–129.
———. "The Struggle for Lordship in Late Heian Japan: The Case of Aki." *Journal of Japanese Studies* 10, no. 1 (1984): 101–41.
———. "Suo Province in the Age of Kamakura." In *Court and Bakufu in Japan: Essays in Kamakura History*, ed. Jeffrey Mass. New Haven, CT: Yale University Press, 1982, 92–120.
Asakawa Kan'chi. Documents of Iriki. Westport, CT: Greenwood Press, 1974.
———. *Land and Society in Medieval Japan*, ed. Committee for the Publication of Dr. K. Asakawa's Works. Tokyo: Japan Society for the Promotion of Science, 1965.
Ashida Tōichi. "Nihon ritsuryō jidai no tōchi shōyū ken ni tsuite." *Hōgaku jaanaru* 33 (1982): 31–74.

REFERENCES AND BIBLIOGRAPHY

Ayton, Andrew. "Arms, Armor and Horses." In *Medieval Warfare: A History*, ed. Maurice Keen. New York: Oxford University Press, 1999, 186–208.

Bachrach, Bernard S. *Early Carolingian Warfare: Prelude to Empire*. Philadelphia: University of Pennsylvania Press, 2001.

———. "Early Medieval Demography: Some Observations on the Methods of Hans Delbrück." In *The Circle of War in the Middle Ages: Essays on Medieval Military and Naval History*, ed. Donald J. Kagay and L. J. Andrew Villalon. Woodbridge, Suffolk: Boydell Press, 1999, 3–20.

Bainton, Roland H. *Christian Attitudes Toward War and Peace: A Historical Survey and Critical Re-evaluation*. New York: Abingdon Press, 1960.

Bartlett, Robert, and Angus MacKay, eds. *Medieval Frontier Societies*. Oxford: Oxford University Press, 1989.

Batten, Bruce L. "Provincial Administration in Early Japan: From Ritsuryo kokka to Ocho kokka." *Harvard Journal of Asiatic Studies* 53, no. 1 (June 1993): 103–34.

———. "State and Frontier in Early Japan: the Imperial Court and Northern Kyushu, 645–1185." PhD. dissertation, Stanford University, 1989.

Bay, Alexander R. "Bugei and Heihō: Military Skills and Strategy in Japan from the Eighth to Eleventh Centuries." MA thesis, University of Oregon, 1998.

Berry, Mary Elizabeth. *The Culture of Civil War in Kyoto*. Berkeley: University of California Press, 1994.

Blacker, Carmen. *The Catalpa Bow: A Study of Shamanistic Practices in Japan*. London and Winchester, MA: Allen & Unwin, 1975.

Bloomberg, Catherine. *Samurai Religion: Some Aspects of Warrior Manners and Customs in Feudal Japan*. New York: Uppsale, 1977.

Bock, Felicia, trans. *Engi-shiki: Procedures of the Engi Era Books I–IV*. Tokyo: Monumenta Nipponica Monograph, 1970.

Borgen, Robert. *Sugawara no Michizane and the Early Heian Court*. Cambridge, MA: Harvard University Press, 1985.

Bottomly, I., and A. P. Hopson. *Arms and Armour of the Samurai: The History of Weaponry in Ancient Japan*. New York: Crescent Books, 1988.

Brandt, R. B. "Utilitiarianism and the Rules of War." In *War and Moral Responsibility*, ed. Marshall Cohen, Thomas Nagel and Thomas Scanlon. Princeton, NJ: Princeton University Press, 1974, 25–45.

Brewster, Jennifer, trans. *Fujiwara no Nageko, The Emperor Horikawa Diary (Sanuki no Suke Nikki)*. Honolulu: University of Hawaii Press, 1978.

Brice, Martin H. *Stronghold: A History of Military Architecture*. New York: Schocken Books, 1985.

Brower, Robert H. "The Reizei Documents." *Monumenta Nipponica* 36, no. 4 (1981): 445–62.

Brown, Delmer, and Ishida Ichirō, trans. and eds. *The Future and the Past: A Translation and Study of the Gukansho, An Interpretive History of Japan Written in 1219*. Berkeley: University of California Press, 1979.

Brown, R. Allen. *Origins of English Feudalism*. London: Allen & Unwin, 1973.

Brownlee, John S. "Crisis as Reinforcement of the Imperial Institution – The Case of the Jōkyū Incident of 1221." *Monumenta Nipponica* 30, no. 2 (1975): 193–201.

———. "Shōkyū War and the Political Rise of Warriors." *Monumenta Nipponica* 1, no. 2 (1969): 59–77.

Brunner, Otto. *Land and Lordship: Structures of Governance in Medieval Austria*, trans.

Howard Kaminsky and James Van Horn Melton. Rev. edn, Philadelphia: University of Pennsylvania Press, 1992.

"Buki · bugu no shōsan: Nishotani iseki no hatten." In *Tsuwamono no jidai: kodai makki no tōgoku shakai*, ed. Maizō bunkazai Sentaa. Tokyo: Yokohama-shi rekishi hakubutsukan, 1998, 17–32.

Burton, Richard F. *The Book of the Sword*. New York: Dover, 1987 (orig. pubn 1884).

Butler, Kenneth D. "The *Heike Monogatari* and the Japanese Warrior Ethic." *Harvard Journal of Asian Studies* 29 (1969): 93–108.

———. "The *Heike Monogatari* and Theories of Oral Epic Literature." *Bulletin of the Faculty of Letters, the Seikei University* 2 (1966): 37–54.

———. "The Textual Evolution of the *Heike Monogatari*." *Harvard Journal of Asiatic Studies* 26 (1966): 5–51.

"Chūgoku-shiki 'do' ga shutsudo: Yayoi makki kokunai de hajimete." *Asahi shinbun*, 12 (May 1999): 3.

Clausewitz, Carl von. *On War*, trans. Michael Howard and Peter Paret. Princeton, NJ: Princeton University Press, 1976 (orig. pubn 1832).

Clayburn, P. M. "Japanese Castles." *History Today* 15 (1965): 20–8.

Cogan, Thomas J., trans. *The Tale of the Soga Brothers*. Tokyo: University of Tokyo Press, 1987.

Collcutt, Martin. *Five Mountains: The Rinzai Zen Monastic Institution in Medieval Japan*. Cambridge, MA: Harvard University Press, 1981.

The Columbia Dictionary of Quotations. Microsoft Bookshelf 98 edition, 1998.

Conlan, Thomas. *In Little Need of Divine Intervention: Scrolls of the Mongol Invasions of Japan*. Ithaca, NY: East Asia Program, Cornell University, 2001.

———. "Innovation or Application? The Role of Technology in War." Paper presented at the Association for Asian Studies annual meeting, Boston, MA, 13 March 1999.

———. "Largesse and the Limits of Loyalty in the Fourteenth Century." In *The Origins of Japan's Medieval World: Courtiers, Clerics, Warriors, and Peasants in the Fourteenth Century*, ed. Jeffrey P. Mass. Stanford, CA: Stanford University Press, 1997, 39–64.

———. "The Nature of Warfare in Fourteenth-Century Japan: The Record of Nomoto Tomoyuki." *Journal of Japanese Studies* 25, no. 2 (1999): 299–330.

———. "State of War: the Violent Order of Fourteenth Century Japan." Ph.D. dissertation, Stanford University, 1998.

Connolly, Peter. *Greece and Rome at War*. Englewood Cliffs, NJ: Prentice-Hall, 1981.

Coulborn, Rushton, ed. *Feudalism in History*. Princeton, NJ: Princeton University Press, 1956.

Davis, David L. "Ikki in Late Medieval Japan." In *Medieval Japan: Essays in Institutional History*, ed. John W. Hall and Jeffrey P. Mass. New Haven, CT: Yale University Press, 1974, 221–47.

Deguchi Hisanori. "Monogatari to shite no byōbue: Ichinotani kassen-zu byōbu o megutte." *Gunki to katarimono* 36 (March 2000): 63–73.

Delbrück, Hans. *The Barbarian Invasions*, trans. Walter J. Renfroe, Jr. Lincoln: University of Nebraska Press, 1990 (orig. pubn 1921).

———. *Warfare in Antiquity*, trans. Walter J. Renfroe, Jr. Lincoln: University of Nebraska Press, 1990 (orig. pubn 1920).

DeVries, Kelly. "God and Defeat in Medieval Warfare: Some Preliminary Thoughts." In *The Circle of War in the Middle Ages: Essays on Medieval Military and Naval History*, ed. Donald J. Kagay and L. J. Andrew Villalon. Woodbridge, Suffolk: Boydell Press, 1999, 87–97.

———. *Infantry Warfare in the Early Fourteenth Century*. Woodbridge, Suffolk: Boydell Press, 1996.

d'Entreves, A. P., ed. *Aquinas: Selected Political Writings*. trans. J. G. Dawson. Oxford: Blackwell, 1965.

Edwards, Walter. "Event and Process in the Founding of Japan." *Journal of Japanese Studies* 9, no. 2 (1983): 265–95.

Endō Motō. "Shuba no tō no kōdō to seikaku." In *Nihon kodai shi ron'en*, ed. Endō Motō sensei shōju kinen kai. Tokyo: Kokusho kangyōkai, 1983, 3–17.

———. "Masakado no ran zengo no kantō chiiki no shingyō girei." *Nihon kodaishi ronsō*, 1983, 389–410.

Farris, Wm. Wayne. *Heavenly Warriors: The Evolution of Japan's Military, 500–1300*. Cambridge, MA: Harvard University Press, 1992.

———. "Japan to 1300." In *War and Society in the Ancient and Medieval Worlds: Asia, the Mediterranean, Europe, and Mesoamerica*, ed. Kurt Raaflaub and Nathan Rosenstein. Cambridge, MA: Center for Hellenic Studies, Harvard University, 1999, 47–70.

———. *Population, Disease, and Land in Early Japan, 645–900*. Cambridge, MA: Harvard University Press, 1985.

Fernandez-Armesto, Filipe. "Naval Warfare after the Viking Age, c.1100–1500." In *Medieval Warfare: A History*, ed. Maurice Keen. New York: Oxford University Press, 1999, 230–52.

Fissel, Mark Charles. *English Warfare 1511–1642*. Warfare and History. Jeremy Black, gen. ed. London and New York: Routledge, 2001.

Friday, Karl. "Bushidō or Bull? A Medieval Historian's Perspective on the Imperial Army and the Japanese Warrior Tradition." *History Teacher* 27, no. 3 (May 1994): 339–49.

———. "Futile Warlords: Provincial Rebellion in the Mid-Heian Age." Paper prepared for Conference "Centers and Peripheries in Heian Japan," Harvard University, June 11–13, 2002.

———. *Hired Swords: The Rise of Private Warrior Power in Early Japan*. Stanford, CA: Stanford University Press, 1992.

———. "Kisha no ayumi no ikkōsatsu: chūsei Nihon ni okeru kokka to bunka to gijutsu." *Tōkyō daigaku shiryō hensanjō kenkyū kiyō* 11 (March 2000): 21–35.

———. "Lordship Interdicted: Taira Tadatsune and the Limited Horizons of Warrior Ambition." In *Centers and Peripheries in Heian Japan*, ed. Edward Kamens and Mikael Adolphson. Cambridge, MA: Harvard University Press, forthcoming.

———. "Mononofu: The Warrior of Heian Japan." MA thesis, University of Kansas, 1983.

———. "Pushing Beyond the Pale: The Yamato Conquest of the *Emishi* and Northern Japan." *Journal of Japanese Studies* 23, no. 1 (1997): 1–24.

———. "Review of Takahashi Masaaki, *Bushi no seiritsu/bushizō no sōshutsu*." *Shigaku zasshi* 109, no. 11 (Nov 2000): 112–20.

———. "Teeth and Claws: Provincial Warriors and the Heian Court." *Monumenta Nipponica* 43, no. 2 (1988): 153–85.

———. "Valorous Butchers: The Art of War during the Golden Age of the Samurai." *Japan Forum* 5, no. 1 (April 1993): 1–19.

Friday, Karl, with Seki Humitake. *Legacies of the Sword: The Kashima-Shinryū & Samurai Martial Culture*. Honolulu: University of Hawaii Press, 1997.

Frois, Luis. *Nichiō bunka hikaku*. vol. 11 of *Taikōkai jidai sōsho*, trans. Okada Akio. Tokyo: Iwanami shoten, 1965.
Fujimoto Masayuki. "Bugu to kassen no hembō." In *Shūkan asahi hyakka Nihon no rekishi* vol. 12. Tokyo: Asahi shimbunsha, 1986.
———. "Bugu to rekishi I: tate." *Rekishi to chiri* 418 (1990): 40–52.
———. "Bugu to rekishi II: yumiya." *Rekishi to chiri* 421 (1990): 58–72.
———. "Bugu to rekishi III: katchū." *Rekishi to chiri* 424 (1990): 41–59.
———. "Chūsei no eiga ni mieru chūsei jōkaku." *Chūsei jōkaku kenkyū* 8 (July 1994): 4–43.
———. *Yoroi o matō hitobito*. Tokyo: Yoshikawa kōbunkan, 2000.
Fujio Shin'ichirō. "Yayoi jidai no tatakai ni kansuru shomondai: tetsu · tetsusōzai no jittai t tatakai." In *Jinrui ni totte tatakai to wa 2, tatakai no shisutemu to taigai senryaku*, ed. Matsugi Takehiko and Udagawa Takehisa. Tokyo: Tōyō shorin, 1999, 12–55.
Fujioka Kenjiro. "Historical Development of Japanese Cities: Ancient and Feudal Ages." In *Japanese Cities: A Geographical Approach*. Tokyo: Association of Japanese Geographers, 1970, 13–16.
Fukuda Ikuō. *Musha no yo*. Tokyo: Yoshikawa kōbunkan, 1995.
Fukuda Keikichi. "Zenkyūnen kassen to Sadatō densetsu." *Kawauchi kodaishi ronshū* 5 (1989): 47–67.
Fukuda Toyohiko. "Bushi = zaichiryōshu-ron to bushi = geinōjin-ron no kankei." *Nihon rekishi* 601 (June 1998): 98–104.
———. *Chūsei seiritsuki no gunsei to nairan*. Tokyo: Yoshikawa kōbunkan, 1995.
———. "Fujiwara Sumitomo no ran." In *Heian ōchō no bushi*, ed. Yasuda Motohisa. Senran Nihonshi. Tokyo: Daiichi hōgen, 1988, 76–83.
———. ed. *Ikusa. Chūsei o kangaeru*. Tokyo: Yoshikawa kōbunkan, 1993.
———. "Kodai makki no yōhei to yōhei taichō." In *Chūsei Nihon no shosō*, ed. Yasuda Motohisa sensei tainin kinen ronshū kangyō iinkai. Tokyo: Yoshikawa kōbunkan, 1989, vol. 5, 459–89.
———. "Ōchō gunsei kikō to nairan." In *Iwanami kōza Nihon rekishi 4 (kodai)*. Tokyo: Iwanami shoten, 1976, 81–120.
———. "Rekishigaku kara mita Nishinotani kiseki no igi." In *Tsuwamono no jidai: kodai makki no tōgoku shakai*, ed. Maizō bunkazai Sentaa. Tokyo: Yokohama-shi rekishi hakubutsukan, 1998, 116.
———. "Senshi to sono shūdan." In *Ikusa*, ed. Fukuda Toyohiko. Tokyo: Yoshikawa kōbunkan, 1993, 76–129.
———. *Taira Masakado no ran*. Tokyo: Iwanami shoten, 1981.
———. "Taira Masakado no ran." In *Heian ōchō no bushi*, ed. Yasuda Motohisa. Senran Nihonshi. Tokyo: Daiichi hōgen, 1988, 65–74.
———. "Taira Masakado o meguru eio densetsu no keisei." *Gekkan hyakka* 238 (1982): 38–43.
———. "Tetsu to uma to Taira Masakado." *Gekkan hyakka* 196 (1974): 6–11.
———. *Tōgoku heiran to mononofu-tachi*. Tokyo: Yoshikawa kōbunkan, 1995.
———. "Tōgoku no uma to tetsu." *Rekishi chiri kyōiku* 518 (May 1994): 14–19.
Futaki Ken'ichi. *Chūsei buke no sakuhō*. Tokyo: Yoshikawa kōbunkan, 1999.
Futomaru Nobuaki. *Senryaku senjutsu heiki jiten Chūgoku chūsei/kindai hen*. *Gurafikku senshi shiriizu*, vol. 7. Tokyo: Gakushū kenkyūsha, 1999.
———. *Senryaku senjutsu heiki jiten Chūgoku kodai hen*. *Gurafikku senshi shiriizu*, vol. 1. Tokyo: Gakushū kenkyūsha, 1996.

Gay, Suzanne Marie. "Muromachi Bakufu in Medieval Kyoto." Ph.D. dissertation, Yale University, 1982.
——. "Muromachi Rule in Kyoto: Administrative and Judicial Aspects." In *The Bakufu in Japanese History*, ed. Jeffrey P. Mass and William Hauser. Stanford, CA: Stanford University Press, 1985, 49–66.
Gillmor, Carroll. "Cavalry, Ancient and Medieval." In *The Reader's Companion to Military History*, ed. Robert Cowley and Geoffrey Parker. New York: Houghton Mifflin, 1996, 74–5.
Goble, Andrew E. "Hojo and Consultative Government." In *Court and Bakufu in Japan: Essays in Kamakura History*, ed. Jeffrey P. Mass. New Haven, CT: Yale University Press, 1982, 168–90.
——. "The Kamakura Bakufu and Its Officials." In *The Bakufu in Japanese History*, ed. Jeffrey P. Mass and William Hauser. Stanford, CA: Stanford University Press, 1985, 31–49.
——. *Kenmu: Go-Daigo's Revolution*. Cambridge, MA: Council on East Asian Studies, Harvard University, 1996.
Gomi Fumihiko. *Azuma kagami no hōhō: jijitsu to shinwa ni miru chūsei*. Tokyo: Yoshikawa kōbunkan, 1990.
——. *Bushi to bunshi no chūseishi*. Tokyo: Tōkyō daigaku shuppankai, 1992.
——. *Fukugen no Nihon shi: Kassen emaki*. Tokyo: Mainichi shimbunsha, 1990.
——. "Kubi no fechishizumu." In *Fukugen no Nihon shi: Kassen emaki*, ed. Gomi Fumihiko. Tokyo: Mainichi shimbunsha, 1990, 74–5.
——. *Sassei to shinkō: bushi o saguru*. Tokyo: Kadokawa sensho, 1997.
——. "Shi-kassen no seikai." In *Fukugen no Nihon shi: Kassen emaki*, ed. Gomi Fumihisa. Tokyo: Mainichi shimbunsha, 1990, 58–9.
——. "Tachi no shakai to sono hensen." In *Shiro to tachi o horu yomu*, ed. Satō Makoto and Gomi Fumihiko. Tokyo: Yamakawa shuppan kai, 1994, 225–42.
Gomi Katsuo. "Kamakura gokenin no ban'yaku kinshi ni tsuite (1)." *Shigaku zasshi* 63, no. 9 (1954).
——. "Kamakura gokenin no ban'yaku kinshi ni tsuite (2)." *Shigaku zasshi* 63, no. 10 (1954).
Gomi Yoshio. "Kamakura bakufu no gokenin taisei: Kyōtō ōbanyaku no tōsei o chūshin ni." *Rekishi kyōiku* 11, no. 7 (1963): 12–19.
Graff, David A. *Medieval Chinese Warfare, 300–900. Warfare and History*. Jeremy Black, gen. ed. London and New York: Routledge, 2002.
Grapard, Allan. *The Protocol of the Gods: A Study of the Kasuga Cult in Japanese History*. Berkeley: University of California Press, 1992.
Grossberg, Kenneth A. *Japan's Renaissance: Politics of the Muromachi Bakufu*. Cambridge, MA: Harvard University Press, 1981.
——. *The Laws of the Muromachi Bakufu*. Tokyo: Monumenta Nipponica Monograph, 1981.
Haga Noboru. "Emishi to henkyō." *Hikaku bunka* 2 (1986): 1–38.
Haldon, John. *Warfare, State and Society in the Byzantine World, 565–1204. Warfare and History*. Jeremy Black, gen. ed. London: UCL Press, 1999.
Hall, Bert S. "The Changing Face of Siege Warfare: Technology and Tactics in Transition." In *The Medieval City under Siege*, ed. Ivy A. Corfis and Michael Wolfe. Woodbridge, Suffolk: The Boydell Press, 1995, 257–76.
Hall, John Cary. "Japanese Feudal Law: The Institutes of Judicature: Being a Translation

of 'Go Seibai Shikimoku'; the Magisterial Code of the Hojo Power-Holders (AD 1932)." *Transactions of the Asiatic Society of Japan* 34 (1906): 1–44.
Hall, John W. *Government and Local Power in Japan 500–1700: A Study Based on Bizen Province*. Princton, NJ: Princeton University Press, 1966.
———. "Kyoto as Historical Background." In *Medieval Japan: Essays in Institutional History*, ed. John W. Hall and Jeffrey P. Mass. New Haven, CT: Yale University Press, 1974, 3–38.
———. "Muromachi Power Structure." In *Japan in the Muromachi Age*, ed. John W. Hall and Toyoda Takeshi. Berkeley: University of California Press, 1977, 39–44.
Hall, John W., and Toyoda Takeshi, eds. *Japan in the Muromachi Age*. Berkeley: University of California Press, 1977.
Hambrick, Charles H. "The Gukansho." *Japanese Journal of Religious Studies* 5, no. 1 (1978): 37–58.
———. "Gukansho: A Religious View of Japanese History." Ph.D. dissertation, University of Chicago, 1971.
Hane, Mikiso. *Premodern Japan: A Historical Survey*. Boulder, CO: Westview Press, 1991.
Harding, David, ed. *Weapons: An International Encyclopedia from 5000 BC to 2000 AD*. New York: St. Martins Press, 1980.
Hare, Kent G. "Apparitions and War in Anglo-Saxon England." In *The Circle of War in the Middle Ages: Essays on Medieval Military and Naval History*, ed. Donald J. Kagay and L. J. Andrew Villalon. Woodbridge, Suffolk: Boydell Press, 1999, 75–86.
Hare, R. M. "Utilitarianism and the Rules of War." In *War and Moral Responsibility*, ed. Marshall Cohen, Thomas Nagel and Thomas Scanlon. Princeton, NJ: Princeton University Press, 1974, 46–61.
Harrington, Loraine F. "Regional Outposts of Muromachi Bakufu Rule: The Kantō and Kyushu." In *The Bakufu in Japanese History*, ed. Jeffrey P. Mass and William Hauser. Stanford, CA: Stanford University Press, 1985, 66–99.
———. "Social Control and the Significance of the Akutō." In *Court and Bakufu in Japan: Essays in Kamakura History*, ed. Jeffrey P. Mass. New Haven, CT: Yale University Press, 1982, 221–50.
Haruda Takayoshi. "Masakado no ran ni okeru buryoku soshiki: toku ni banrui ni tsuite." *Shigen* 2, no. 3 (1967): 44–51.
———. "Taira Masakado no ran no buryoku." In *Kantō no kodai shakai kodaishi ronshū*, ed. Endō Motoo. Tokyo: Meicho shuppan, 1989, 127–62.
Hasegawa Tadashi. "The Early Stages of the *Heike Monogatari*." *Monumenta Nipponica* 22, nos. 1–2 (1967): 65–81.
Hashiguchi Teishi. "Chūsei hōkeikan o meguru shomondai." *Rekishi hyōron* 454 (1988).
———. "Hōkeikan wa ika ni seiritsu suru no ka." In *Sōten Nihon no rekishi 4: Chūsei hen*. Tokyo: Shin jimbutsu ōraisha, 1991.
Hashimoto Yū. *Ritsuryō gundansei no kenkyū*. Ōsaka: Hashimoto shiikōshū kangyōkai, 1982.
Hatada Takashi. *Genkō*. Tokyo: Chūō kōronsha, 1965.
Hattō Sanae. "Kodai ni okeru kazoku to kyōdōtai." *Rekishi hyōron* 424 (1985): 14–23.
———. "Sekkanki ni okeru zuryō no ie to kazoku keitai." *Nihon rekishi* 442 (1985): 1–18.
Hayashi Rokurō. *Kodai makki no hanran*. Tokyo: Kyōikusha, 1977.
———, ed. *Ronshū Taira Masakado kenkyū*. Tokyo: Gendai shisosha, 1975.
Hayashi Tatsusaburo and George Elison. "Kyoto in the Muromachi Age." In *Japan in*

the Muromachi Age, ed. John W. Hall and Toyoda Takeshi. Berkeley: University of California Press, 1977, 15–37.

Hayashida Shigeyuki. "Chūsei Nihon no uma ni tsuite." In *Uma no bunka sōsho 3, chūsei: uma to Nihon.* Tokyo: Baji bunka zaidan, 1995; orig. pubn *Nihon chikusangaku kaihō* 28, no. 5 (1957).

———. *Nihon zairai uma ni kansuru kenkyū.* Tokyo: Nihon chūō keiba kai, 1978.

Hazard, Benjiman H., Jr. "The Formative Years of the Wako, 1223–63." *Monumenta Nipponica* 22, nos. 3–4 (1967): 260–77.

Herail, Francine. Fonctions et fonctionnaires japonais au début du XIème siècle. Paris: Bibliothèque Japonaise, 1971.

———. *Yodo no tsukai: ou le système des quatre envoyés.* Paris: Presses Universitaires de France, 1966.

Hesselink, Reinier H. "The Introduction of the Art of Mounted Archery into Japan." *Transactions of the Asiatic Society of Japan* 4, no. 6 (1991): 27–47.

Hildinger, Erik. *Warriors of the Steppe: A Military History of Central Asia, 500 BC to 1700 AD.* New York: Sarpedon, 1997.

Hirada Kōji, ed. "Nihon kodaishi sōgō bunken mokuroku." *Kenkyū to shiryō* 7 (1990): 1–147.

Hirada Toshiharu. *Sōhei to bushi.* Tokyo: Nihon kyōbunsha, 1965.

Hirakawa Minami. "Tōhoku daisensō jidai." In *Kodai no chihōshi*, ed. Takahashi Takashi, vol. 6. Tokyo: Asakura shoten, 1978, 156–92.

Hirano Tomohiko. "Kondeisei seiritsu no haikei to sono yakuwari." In *Nihon kodaishi ronkō*, ed. Saeki Arikiyo. Tokyo: Yoshikawa kōbunkan, 1980, 271–316.

Hiraoka Sadaumi. "Sōhei ni tsuite." In *Nihon shakai keizaishi kenkyū.* Tokyo, 1967, 547–82.

Hishinuma Kazunori. "Kamakura bakufu jitō gokeninsei no keisei to tsuitōshi." *Kokushigaku* 159 (3 1996): 61–92.

Hiyoshi Shōichi. *Nihon sōhei kenkyū.* Tokyo: Kokushokan gyōkai, 1972.

Hodate Michihisa. *Heian jidai. Nihon no rekishi*, vol. 3. Tokyo: Iwanami juniya shinsho, 1999.

———. "Kodai makki no tōgoku to ryūjū kizoku." In *Chūsei tōgokushi no kenkyū*, ed. Chūsei tōgokushi kenkyūkai. Tokyo: Tōkyō daigaku shuppankai, 1988, 3–22.

Hori Kyotsu. "Economic and Political Effects of the Mongol Wars." In *Medieval Japan: Essays in Institutional History*, ed. John W. Hall and Jeffrey P. Mass. New Haven, CT: Yale University Press, 1974, 184–200.

Horiuchi Kazuaki. "Akutō no keizu (1)." *Ritsumeikan bungaku* 521 (June 1991): 300–23.

———. "Akutō no keizu (2)." *Ritsumeikan bungaku* 523 (March 1991): 84–110.

———. "Heian chūki no kebiishi no buryoku ni tsuite." In *Ronkyū Nihon kodai shi*, ed. Yamaō Yukihisa. Tokyo: Gakuseisha, 1979, 341–62.

Hoshino Hitoshi. "Shugo · jitō kō." *Shigaku zasshi* 25, no. 29 (1918).

Howard, Michael. "Constraints on Warfare." In *The Laws of War: Constraints on Warfare in the Western World*, ed. Michael Howard, George J. Andreopoulos and Mark R. Shulman. New Haven, CT: Yale University Press, 1994, 1–11.

Howard, Michael, George J. Andreopoulos and Mark R. Shulman. *The Laws of War: Constraints on Warfare in the Western World.* New Haven, CT: Yale University Press, 1994.

Hurst, G. Cameron III. *Armed Martial Arts of Japan: Swordsmanship & Archery.* New Haven, CT: Yale University Press, 1998.

———. "An Emperor Who Reigned as Well as Ruled: Temmu Tennō." In *Great Historical Figures of Japan*, ed. Murakami Hyoe and Thomas J. Harper. Tokyo: Japan Culture Institute, 1978, 16–27.

———. *Insei: Abdicated Sovereigns in the Politics of Late Heian Japan 1086–1185*. New York: Columbia University Press, 1976.

———. "The Kōbu Polity: Court–Bakufu Relations in Kamakura Japan." In *Court and Bakufu in Japan*, ed. Jeffrey P. Mass. New Haven, CT: Yale University Press, 1982, 3–28.

———. "Structure of the Heian Court: Some Thoughts on 'Familial'." In *Medieval Japan: Essays in Institutional History*, ed. John W. Hall and Jeffrey P. Mass. New Haven, CT: Yale University Press, 1974, 39–59.

———. "The Warrior as Ideal for a New Age." In *The Origins of Japan's Medieval World: Courtiers, Clerics, Warriors, and Peasants in the Fourteenth Century*, ed. Jeffrey P. Mass. Stanford, CA: Stanford University Press, 1997, 208–33.

Ichimura Takao. "Sengokki jōkaku no keitai to yakuwari o megutte." In *Sōten Nihon no rekishi* 4, ed. Minegishi Sumio. Tokyo: Shinjimbutsu ōraisha, 1991, 282–300.

Ihara Imaasao. "'Ikusa' to minshū: 'yamakoya' o chūshin ni." *Rekishi hyōron* 511 (1992): 33–43.

Ike Takashi. "Buke kan'isei sairon." *Nihon rekishi* 577 (June 1996): 42–63.

Ike Tōru. "Nihon chūsei no sensō to heiwa." *Ikkō ronsō* 101, no. 4 (1989): 50–69.

Ikegami, Eiko. *The Taming of the Samurai: Honorific Individualism and the Making of Modern Japan*. Cambridge, MA: Harvard University Press, 1995.

Imai Seinosuke. "Kassen no kikō." In *Gunki monogatari no seisei to hyōgen*, ed. Yamashita Hiroaki. Tokyo: Wasen shoin, 1995, 31–46.

———. "Kiba musha ga uma yori oriru toki." *Gunki to katarimono* 36 (March 2000): 26–37.

Inoue Mitsuo. *Heian jidai no gunji seido no kenkyū*. Tokyo: Yoshikawa kōbunkan, 1980.

Inoue Mitsusada et al., eds. *Buke seiken no keisei. Nihon rekishi taikei fukyūban*, vol. 4. Tokyo: Yamakawa shuppansha, 1996.

Irie Kōhei. "Kyūjutsu ni okeru waza to kokoro: Nihon no kyūsha bunka no tokusei." In *Bu to chi no atarashii chihei: taikeiteki budōgaku kenkyū o mezashite,* ed. Shintai undō bunka gakkai. Kyoto: Shōwadō, 1998, 60–74.

Irumada Nobuo. *Musha no yō ni. Nihon no rekishi*. Tokyo: Shūeisha, 1991.

Ishibashi Shōzō. "Emishi no seikai to Hachinohe." *Hachinohe chiiki shi* 13 (1988): 2–50.

Ishii Masakuni. *Warabite katana: Nihontō no shigen ni kansuru ikkōsatsu*. Tokyo: Yūsankaku shuppan, 1966.

Ishii Ryōsuke. "Gunji, keisatsu oyobi kotsu seido." In *Nihon hōseishi gaisetsu*. Tokyo: Kōbundō, 1948, 128–34.

Ishii Shirō. *Nihonjin no kokka seikatsu. Nihon kokuseishi kenkyū*, vol. 2. Tokyo: Tōkyō daigaku shuppankai, 1986.

Ishii Susumu. "Bushidan no hatten." In *Kanagawa kenshi, tsushihen*, vol. 1. Yokohama: Kanagawa-ken, 1981, 347–442.

———. *Chūsei bushidan*. Tokyo: Shogakukan, 1974.

———. "Chūsei seiritsuki gunsei kenkyū no isshiten: kokuga o chūshin to suru gunjiryoku soshiki ni tsuite." *Shigaku zasshi* 78, no. 12 (1969): 1–32.

———. "The Decline of the Kamakura Bakufu." In *Cambridge History of Japan*, vol. 3: *Medieval Japan*, ed. Kozo Yamamura. New York: Cambridge University Press, 1990, 128–74.

———. "The Distinctive Characteristics of the Environs of Kamakura as a Medieval City." *Acta Asiatica* 81 (Sept 2001): 53–71.
———. "The Formation of Bushi Bands (Bushidan)." *Acta Asiatica* 49 (1985): 1–14.
———. *Kamakura bakufu*. Tokyo: Chūō kōronsha, 1965.
———. *Kamakura bushi no jitsuzō*. Tokyo: Heibonsha, 1987.
Ishimoda Shō. "Kamakura bakufu ikkoku jitō-shiki no seiritsu." In *Chūsei no hō to kokka*, ed. Ishimoda Shō and Satō Shin'ichi. Tokyo: Tokyo daigaku shuppan kai, 1960, 1–134.
———. "Kodai makki no hanran." In *Ronshū Taira Masakado kenkyū*, ed. Hayashi Rokurō. Tokyo: Gendai shisosha, 1975, 151–9.
———. *Kodai makki seijishi jōsetsu*. Tokyo: Miraisha, 1964.
———. "Masakado no ran ni tsuite." In *Ronshū Taira Masakado kenkyū*, ed. Hayashi Rokurō. Tokyo: Gendai shisosha, 1975, 192–9.
———. "Taira Tadatsune no ran ni tsuite." In *Kodai makki seijishi josetsu*. Tokyo: Miraisha, 1956, 182–96.
Isomura Yukio. "Hokubu Kyūshū no kodai bōei shisetsu." In *Shiro to tachi o horu yomu*, ed. Satō Makoto and Gomi Fumihiko. Tokyo: Yamakawa shuppan kai, 1994, 119–56.
Itō Hitomi. "Kamakura bushi Ōba-shi no jimbutsuzō: shoki bushi shakai no arikata." *Kamakura* 74 (Jan 1994): 12–25.
Itō Kaoru. "Nishinotani iseki shutsudo ibutsu no kinzokugakuteki kaiseki." In *Tsuwamono no jidai: kodai makki no tōgoku shakai*, ed. Maizō bunkazai Sentaa. Tokyo: Yokohama-shi rekishi hakubutsukan, 1998, 134–43.
Iwashiro Masao. "Kodai ōyumi fukugen no kokoromi: ōyumi fukugen katei de miete kita watakushi no kenkyūhō." *Wakōdi ningen kankei kiyō* 5 (March 2001): 105–25.
"Jitsuyōhin no 'do' shutsudo: Miyagi · Chikudate no Ōkyo-seki Nara-Heian jidai seidōsei no hikigane." *Asahi shinbun* (22 June 1999): 30.
Johnson, James Turner. *Just War Tradition and the Restraint of War*. Princeton, NJ: Princeton University Press, 1981.
Jones, Archer. *The Art of War in the Western World*. Chicago: University of Illinois Press, 1987.
Jones, Richard L. C. "Fortifications and Sieges in Western Europe, c.800–1450." In *Medieval Warfare: A History*, ed. Maurice Keen. New York: Oxford University Press, 1999, 163–85.
Kagay, Donald J., and L. J. Andrew Villalon, eds. *The Circle of War in the Middle Ages: Essays on Medieval Military and Naval History*. Woodbridge, Suffolk: Boydell Press, 1999.
Kachru, Sonam. "Dogs of War: Examining Warrior Duels in the *Heike monogatari*." University of Georgia, 2000.
Kaizu Ichirō. "Chūsei kokka kenryoku to akutō." *Rekishigaku kenkyū* 646 (June 1993): 9–18.
———. "Kassen no senryokusū." *Nihonshi kenkyū* 388 (Dec 1994): 88–97.
———. "Kassen teoi chūmon no seiritsu." *Reki haku kenkyū hōkoku* 48 (March 1992): 149–59.
———. *Mōko shūrai: taigai sensō no shakaishi*. Tokyo: Yoshikawa kōbunkan, 1998.
Kamens, Edward, and Mikael Adolphson, eds. *Centers and Peripheries in Heian Japan*. Cambridge, MA: Harvard University Press, forthcoming.
Kameyama Sumio. "Chūsei shōki Tōgoku bushi no seikatsu ishiki to seishin no saikōzō: Kumagai Naozane o chūshin ni." *Tōkyō nōkō daigaku ippan kyōiku kiyō* 27 (1990): 1–51.

Kamiya Satoshi. "Yayoi jidai no yumiya: kinōgawa kara mita yajiri no jūryōka 1." *Kodai bunka* 52, no. 10 (Oct 2000): 20–31.

———. "Yayoi jidai no yumiya: kinōgawa kara mita yajiri no jūryōka 2." *Kodai bunka* 52 (Dec 2000): 20–30.

Kanda James. "Methods of Land Transfer in Medieval Japan." *Monumenta Nipponica* 23, no. 4 (1978): 379–405.

Kanegae Hiroyuki. "Heian jidai no 'kuni' to 'tachi'." In *Shiro to tachi o horu yomu*, ed. Satō Makoto and Gomi Fumihiko. Tokyo: Yamakawa shuppan kai, 1994, 91–118.

Kaneko Arichika. *Nihon no dentō bajutsu: bajō bugei hen*. Tokyo: Nichibō shuppansha, 1995.

Kanezashi Shōzō. "Suigun to senjutsu." In *NHK rekishi e no shōtai 5: Muteki Yoshitsune gundan*, ed. Toyoda Aritsune and Nomura Shin'ichi. Tokyo: Nihon hōsō shuppan kyōkai, 1990, 99–105.

Kasamatsu Hiroshi. "Omae no kasan . . .." In *Chūsei no tsumi to batsu*, ed. Amino Yoshihiko *et al*. Tokyo: Tōkyō daigaku shuppankai, 1983, 1–14.

———. "Undated Statements of Accusation and Rebuttal." *Acta Asiatica* 81 (Sept 2001): 31–52.

———. "Youchi." In *Chūsei no tsumi to batsu*, ed. Amino Yoshihiko *et al*. Tokyo: Tōkyō daigaku shuppankai, 1983, 89–102.

Katō Tomoyasu and Yūi Masatomo, eds. *Nihon shi bunken kaidai jiten*. Tokyo: Yoshikawa kōbunkan, 2000.

Katsumata Shizuo. "The Structure of the Sekkyō 'Sanshō dayū': Time and Space Sacred and Profane." *Acta Asiatica* 81 (Sept 2001): 20–30.

Katsuno Ryūshin. *Sōhei*. Tokyo: Tōbundō, 1955.

Kawai Kazuo, and Kenneth A. Grossberg. "Shogun and Shugo: The Provincial Aspects of Muromachi Politics." In *Japan in the Muromachi Age*, ed. John W. Hall and Toyoda Takeshi. Berkeley: University of California Press, 1977, 65–87.

Kawai Yasushi. "Chūsei bushi no bugei to sensō: Gempei kassen o chūshin ni." In *Kamakura bushi to uma*, ed. Baji bunka zaidan and Uma no hakubutsukan. Tokyo: Meicho shuppan, 1999, 71–86.

———. *Gempei kassen no kyozō o hagu*. Tokyo: Kōdansha, 1996.

———. "Genji shōgun to bushi shakai." In *Bushi to wa nan darō ka*, ed. Takahashi Masaaki and Yamamoto Kōji. Tokyo: Asahi shinbunsha, 1994, 58–72.

———. "Jishō · Jūei no nairan to chiiki shakai." *Rekishi gaku kenkyū* 11, no. 730 (1999): 2–13.

———. "Jishō · Jūei no sensō to *Heike monogatari*." *Gunki to monogatari* 36 (March 2000): 15–25.

———. "Jishō · Juei no 'sensō' to Kamakura bakufu." *Nihonshi kenkyū* 344 (April 1991): 60–90.

———. "Kamakura shoki no sensō to zaichi shakai." *Chūsei nairanshi kenkyū* 12 (May 1992): 2–15.

———. "Kawachi Ishikawa Genji no 'hōki' to *Heike monogatari*." *Jimbun gakuhō* 306 (March 2000): 45–78.

———. "Ōshū kassen nōto." *(Kusukage joshi tanki daigaku) bunka kenkyū* 3 (1989): 1–40.

Kawajiri Akio. "Masakado no ran to Hitachi no kuni." *Nihon rekishi* 527 (April 1992): 1–18.

———. "Shimōsa kokufu o yakiuchi shita Taira Koreyoshi." *Chiba shigaku* 20 (April 1992): 26–35.

———. "Taira Yoshifumi to Masakado no ran." *Chiba kenshi kenkyū* 1 (Feb 1993): 36–52.
Kawane Yoshihira. "Chūsei Nihon ni okeru gunchūjō monjo yōshiki no seiritsu." *Hisutoria* 140 (Sept 1993): 65–84.
Kawashima Shigehiro. "Suruga no kuni ni okeru Taira Masakado no ran." *Chihōshi Shizuoka* 20 (April 1992): 44–70.
Keegan, John. *A History of Warfare*. New York: Knopf, 1993.
Keen, Maurice, ed. *Medieval Warfare: A History*. New York: Oxford University Press, 1999.
Kennedy, Hugh. *The Armies of the Caliphs: Military and Society in the Early Islamic State*. Warfare and History. Jeremy Black, gen. ed. London and New York: Routledge, 2001.
Kierman, Frank A., Jr., and John K. Fairbank, eds. *Chinese Ways in Warfare*. Cambridge, MA: Harvard University Press, 1974.
Kierstad, Thomas E. *The Geography of Power in Medieval Japan*. Princeton, NJ: Princeton University Press, 1992.
Kikuchi Tetsuo. "Emishi (kai) setsu saikō." *Shikan* 120 (1989): 100–14.
Kiley, Cornelius J. "Estate and Property in the Late Heian Period." In *Medieval Japan: Essays in Institutional History*, ed. John W. Hall and Jeffrey P. Mass. New Haven, CT: Yale University Press, 1974, 109–26.
———. "Imperial Court as a Legal Authority in the Kamakura Age." In *Court and Bakufu in Japan: Essays in Kamakura History*, ed. Jeffrey Mass. New Haven, CT: Yale University Press, 1982, 29–44.
———. "Provincial Administration and Land Tenure in Early Heian." In *Cambridge History of Japan*, vol. 2: *Heian Japan*, ed. Donald H. Shively and William McCullough. New York and Cambridge: Cambridge University Press, 1999, 236–340.
———. "State and Dynasty in Archaic Yamato." *Journal of Japanese Studies* 3, no. 1 (1973): 25–49.
Kitagawa, Hiroshi, and Bruce T. Tsuchida, trans. *The Tale of the Heike*. Tokyo: University of Tokyo Press, 1975.
Kitayama Shigeo. "Sekkan seiji." In *Iwanami kōza Nihon rekishi kodai 4*. Tokyo: Iwanami shoten, 1962, 1–40.
Knox, Bernard. "Trojan War." In *The Reader's Companion to Military History*, ed. Robert Cowley and Geoffrey Parker. New York: Houghton Mifflin, 1996, 479–80.
Knutsen, Roald M. *Japanese Polearms*. London: Holland Press, 1963.
Kobayashi Hiroko. *The Human Comedy of Heian Japan: A Study of the Secular Stories in the 12th Century Collection of Tales, Konjaku Monogatarishu*. Tokyo: Centre for East Asian Cultural Studies, 1979.
Kobayashi Kazuoka. "Akutō to nambokuchō no 'sensō'." *Rekishi hyōron* 583 (Nov 1998): 33–46.
Kobayashi Kazutoshi. "Iru: kyūdō ni okeru te no uchi no rikigaku." *Sūri kagaku* 181 (July 1978).
Kobayashi Shōji. "Fujiwara Sumitomo no ran sairon." *Nihon rekishi* 499 (1989): 1–19.
———. "Fune ikusa." In *Ikusa*, ed. Fukuda Toyohiko. Tokyo: Yoshikawa kōbunkan, 1993, 210–39.
Kobayashi Yukio. "Jōdai Nihon ni okeru jōba no fūshū." *Shirin* 34, no. 3 (1951): 173–90.
Komai Yumiko. "Kebiishi no seritsu ni kansuru." *Kansai gakuin shigaku* 10 (1981): 69–92.

Kondō Yoshikazu. "Buki kara mita chūsei bushiron." *Nihonshi kenkyū* 416 (April 1997): 26–47.
———. "Buki kara mita nairanki no sentō." *Nihonshi kenkyū* 373 (Sept 1993): 60–74.
———. "Chūsei bushiron no ichi zentei: ritsuryōsei-ka ni okeru yumiya no ichi." In *Chūsei no kūkan o yomu*, ed. Gomi Fumihiko. Tokyo: Yoshikawa kōbunkan, 1995, 212–46.
———. "Chūsei sentō shiryō to shite no gunki monogatari no ichi: Zenkūnen kassen emaki to Heike monogatari no kankei o chūshin ni." In *Gunki bungaku to sono shūen*, ed. Kajiwara Masaaki. Tokyo: Kyūko shoin, 2000, 135–57.
———. *Chūsei-teki bugu no seiritsu to bushi*. Tokyo: Yoshikawa kōbunkan, 2000.
———. "Gunki monogatari kara mita chūsei no buki no shiyō to sentō." *Gunki to katarimono* 36 (March 2000): 3–14.
———. "Nihon no yumiya: sono katachi to hataraki." In *Bushi to wa nan darō ka*, ed. Takahashi Masaaki and Yamamoto Kōji. Tokyo: Asahi shimbunsha, 1994, 42–3.
———. "Ōyoroi no seiritsu: yūshoku kojitsu no kenchi kara." In *Tsuwamono no jidai: kodai makki no tōgoku shakai*, ed. Maizō bunkazai Sentaa. Tokyo: Yokohama-shi rekishi hakubutsukan, 1998, 144–54.
———. "Umayumi to yabusame: sono shahō ni tsuite." *Nihon rekishi* 630 (Nov 2000): 18–25.
———. *Yumiya to tōken: chūsei kassen no jitsuzō*. Tokyo: Yoshikawa kōbunkan, 1997.
———. "'Utsu' to 'Kiru': Nihon-tō o minaosu." In *Bushi to wa nan darō ka*, ed. Takahashi Masaaki and Yamamoto Kōji. Tokyo: Asahi shimbunsha, 1994, 24–5.
Koromogawa Jin. "Chūsei zenki no kemmon jiin to buryoku." *Nempō chūseishi kenkyū* 25 (May 2000): 1–28.
———. "Sōhei kenkyūshi to sono kadai." *Atarashii rekishigaku no tame ni* 227 (June 1997): 1–9.
Koyanagi Kazuhiro. "Chinzei ni okeru ikan no shutsugen to tenkai." In *Shiro to tachi o horu yomu*, ed. Satō Makoto and Gomi Fumihiko. Tokyo: Yamakawa shuppan kai, 1994, 157–90.
Kubota Tadashi. "Nihon de no yari senjutsu no suii to sono tokuchō: ōshū no rei to no hikaku kara." *Gunji shigaku* 36, no. 1 (June 2000): 74–87.
Kudō Keiichi. "Chakudōjō gunchūjō no seiritsu jōken oboegaki." In *Azuma kagami no sōgōteki kenkyū*. Tokyo: Heisei gan-san nendo Mombushō kagaku kenkyūhi hojokin kenkyū seika hōkokusho, 1991, 74–9.
Kudō Masaki. *Jōsaku to emishi. Kōkogaku raiburari*. Tokyo: Nyū saiensusha, 1989.
———. "Kodai emishi no shakai: kōeki to shakai soshiki." *Rekishi hyōron* 434 (1986): 13–35.
———. "Kodai emishi to sono bunka." *Miyashiro rekishi kagaku kenkyū* 30 (1989): 1–6.
———. "Tōhoku kodaishi to jōsaku." *Nihonshi kenkyū* 136 (1973): 17–33.
Kumagai Kimio. "Emishi no seiyaku." *Nara kodaishi ronshū* 1 (1985): 15–26.
Kume Kunitake. "*Taiheiki* wa shigaku ni eki nashi" (1891). In *Shigaku, shigaku hōhō ron*, vol. 3 of *Kume Kunitake rekishi chosakushū*. Tokyo: Yoshikawa kōbunkan, 1990, 144–80.
Kuroda Hideo. *Sugata to shigusa no chūseishi: ezu to emaki no fukei kara*. Tokyo: Heibonsha, 1986.
———. "Kubi o kakeru." *Gekkan hyakka* 306 (1988): 13–21.
———. *Nazo kaki Nihon shi: ega shiryō o yomu. NHK ningen daigaku*, nos. 1–3 gekki. Tokyo: Nihon hōsō shuppan kyōkai, 1999.
Kuroda Kōichirō. "Jingū kebiishi no kenkyū." *Nihonshi kenkyū* 107 (1969): 1–20.

Kuroda Toshio. "Chūsei kokka to tennō." In *Iwanami kōza Nihon no rekishi 6: chūsei 2*. Tokyo: Iwanami shoten, 1967, 261–301.

———. *Jisha seiryoku*. Tokyo: Iwanami shoten, 1980.

———. *Nihon chūsei no kokka to shūkyō*. Tokyo: Iwanami shoten, 1975.

Kuwabara Shigerō. "Tōgoku no jōkaku." In *Shiro*, ed. Ueda Masaaki. Tokyo: Shakaishisōsha, 1997, 103–28.

Lewis, Archibald. *Knights and Samurai: Feudalism in Northern France and Japan*. London: Temple Smith, 1979.

Lord, Albert. *The Singer of Tales*. New York: Cambridge University Press, 1960.

McCullough, Helen C. *Genji & Heike: Selections from The Tale of Genji and The Tale of the Heike*. Stanford, CA: Stanford University Press, 1994.

———. trans. *Okagami, The Great Mirror: Fujiwara Michinaga and his Times*. Princeton, NJ: Princeton University Press, 1980.

———. trans. *The Taiheiki: A Chronicle of Medieval Japan*. Rutland, VT: Tuttle, 1979.

———. "A Tale of Mutsu." *Harvard Journal of Asiatic Studies* 25 (1964 5): 178–211.

———. trans. *The Tale of the Heike*. Stanford, CA: Stanford University Press, 1988.

———. trans. *Yoshitsune: A 15th Century Japanese Chronicle*. Tokyo: Tokyo University Press, 1966.

McCullough, William. "Azuma Kagami Account of the Shōkyū War." *Monumenta Nipponica* 23 (1968): 102–55.

———. "Japanese Marriage Institutions in the Heian Period." *Harvard Journal of Asian Studies* 27 (1967): 103–67.

———. "Shōkyūki and Azuma Kagami: Sources for the Shōkyū War." Ph. D. dissertation, University of California, Berkeley, 1962.

———. "Shōkyūki: An Account of the Shōkyū War of 1221." *Monumenta Nipponica* 19, nos. 1–4 (1964): 163–215, 186–221.

McCullough, William, and Helen C. McCullough, trans. *A Tale of Flowering Fortunes: Annals of Japanese Aristocratic Life in the Heian Period*. Stanford, CA: Stanford University Press, 1980.

McGuinness, Diane, ed. *Dominance, Aggression and War*. New York: Paragon, 1987.

Maeda Kumiko. "Chūsei Setonai suiun to kaizokushū Murakami-shi." *Tachibana shigaku* 15 (Oct 2000): 30–53.

Maizō bunkazai sentaa, ed. *Tsuwamono no jidai: kodai makki no tōgoku shakai*. Tokyo: Yokohama-shi rekishi hakubutsukan, 1998.

Mallett, Michael. "Mercenaries." In *Medieval Warfare: A History*, ed. Maurice Keen. New York: Oxford University Press, 1999, 209–29.

Mass, Jeffrey P. *Antiquity and Anachronism in Japanese History*. Stanford, CA: Stanford University Press, 1992.

———, ed. *Court and Bakufu in Japan: Essays in Kamakura History*. New Haven, CT: Yale University Press, 1982.

———. *The Development of Kamakura Rule 1180–1250: A History With Documents*. Stanford, CT: Stanford University Press, 1979.

———. "The Early Bakufu and Feudalism." In *Court and Bakufu in Medieval Japan: Essays in Kamakura History*, ed. John W. Hall and Jeffrey P. Mass. New Haven, CT: Yale University Press, 1982, 123–42.

———. "Emergence of the Kamakura Bakufu." In *Medieval Japan: Essays in Institutional History*, ed. John W. Hall and Jeffrey P. Mass. New Haven, CT: Yale University Press, 1974, 127–56.

———. *Family, Law, and Property in Japan, 1200–1350*. Occasional Papers in Japanese Studies no. 2000-3. Boston: Edwin O. Reischauer Institute of Japanese Studies, 2000.

———. "Formative Period of Kamakura Justice." *Transactions of the International Conference of Orientalists in Japan* 21 (1976): 148–50.

———. "Jitō Land Possession in the Thirteenth Century: The Case of Shitaji Chūbun." In *Medieval Japan: Essays in Institutional History*, ed. John W. Hall and Jeffrey P. Mass. New Haven, CT: Yale University Press, 1974, 157–83.

———. "The Kamakura Bakufu." In *Medieval Japan*, ed. Kozo Yamamura. *The Cambridge History of Japan*, vol. 3. New York: Cambridge University Press, 1990, 46–88.

———. *Kamakura Bakufu: A Study in Documents*. Stanford, CA: Stanford University Press, 1976.

———. *Lordship and Inheritance in Early Medieval Japan: A Study of the Kamakura Sōryō System*. Stanford, CA: Stanford University Press, 1989.

———. "Of Hierarchy and Authority at the End of the Kamakura." In *The Origins of Japan's Medieval World: Courtiers, Clerics, Warriors, and Peasants in the Fourteenth Century*, ed. Jeffrey P. Mass. Stanford, CA: Stanford University Press, 1997, 17–38.

———. ed. *The Origins of Japan's Medieval World: Courtiers, Clerics, Warriors, and Peasants in the Fourteenth Century*. Stanford, CA: Stanford University Press, 1997.

———. "Origins of Kamakura Justice." *Journal of Japanese Studies* 3, no. 2 (1977): 299–322.

———. "Patterns of Provincial Inheritance in Late Heian Japan. *Journal of Japanese Studies* 9, no. 1 (1983): 67–96.

———. "Translation and Pre-1600 History." *Journal of Japanese Studies* 6, no. 1 (1980): 61–88.

———. *Warrior Government in Medieval Japan: A Study of the Kamakura Bakufu, Shugo and Jitō*. New Haven, CT: Yale University Press, 1974.

———. "What Can We Not Know About the Kamakura Bakufu?" In *The Bakufu in Japanese History*, ed. Jeffrey P. Mass and William Hauser. Stanford, CA: Stanford University Press, 1985, 13–31.

———. *Yoritomo and the Founding of the First Bakufu*. Stanford, CA: Stanford University Press, 1999.

Masuda Toshinobu. "Masakado no ran no seijishiteki bunseki." In *Kodaishi kenkyū no kadai to hōhō*, ed. Inoue Tatsuo. Tokyo: Kokusho kangyōkai, 1989, 173–92.

Matsugi Takehiko. "Kofun jidai no busō to sensō." In *Jinrui ni totte tatakai to wa 2, tatakai no shisutemu to taigai senryaku*, ed. Matsugi Takehiko and Udagawa Takehisa. Tokyo: Tōyō shorin, 1999, 56–80.

Matsugi Takehiko, and Udagawa Takehisa, eds. *Jinrui ni totte tatakai to wa 2, tatakai no shisutemu to taigai senryaku*. Tokyo: Tōyō shorin, 1999.

Matsuhara Hironobu. *Kodai no chihō gōzoku*. Tokyo: Yoshikawa kōbunkan, 1988.

Matsumoto Kazuo. "Nambokuchō shoki Kamakura-fu gunji taisei ni kansuru ikkōsatsu." *Komonjo kenkyū* 41–2 (Dec 1995): 63–80.

Matsumoto Masaharu. "Seiishi to seitōshi." *Nihon rekishi* 477 (1987): 20–39.

Matsumoto Shimpachirō. "Shōmonki no inshō." In *Ronshū Taira Masakado kenkyū*, ed. Hayashi Rokurō. Tokyo: Gendai shisosha, 1975, 160–77.

———. "Shōmonki no inshō." *Bungaku* 19, no. 10 (1951): 6–21.

Matsumoto Yūsuke. "8 seiki kara 9 seiki shōtō ni kakete no Mutsu-Dewa azetchi." *Shishu* 24 (1989): 44–8.

Matsushima Shūichi. "Heiji no ran ni tsuite." *Nihon rekishi* 469 (1987): 15–32.
Matsuzaki Masumi. "Bagu kara miru uma." In *Kamakura no bushi to uma*, ed. Uma no hakubutsukan. Tokyo: Meicho shuppan, 1999, 33–8.
Mayu Hiromichi, ed. *Chūō shūken kokka e no michi: Senran Nihonshi* vol. 1. Tokyo: Daiichi hōgen shuppan kabushiki kaishi, 1988.
Minamoto Yasushi. *Gekiroku Nihon no kassen: Masakado to Sumitomo no hanran*. Tokyo: Tokyo supotsu shimbunsha, 1979.
Minegishi Sumio. "Kamakura akugenta to Ōkura kassen." *Miura kobunka* 43 (1988).
Minobe Shigekatsu. "The World View of Genpei Seisuiki." *Japanese Journal of Religious Studies* 9, nos. 2–3 (1982): 213–33.
Minobuya Tetsuichi. "Kebiishi to kiyome." *Hisutoria* 87 (1980): 57–78.
Miya Tsugio. *Kassen emaki*. Tokyo: Kadokawa shoten, 1977.
Miyagawa Mitsuru, with Cornelius J. Kiley. "From Shōen to Chigyō: Proprietory Lordship and the Structure of Local Power." In *Japan in the Muromachi Age*, ed. John W. Hall and Toyoda Takeshi. Berkeley: University of California Press, 1977, 89–107.
Miyake Chōhyōe. "Masakado no ran no kenkyū zentei: toku ni shūba no tō o chūshin to shite." In *Ronshū Taira Masakado kenkyū*, ed. Hayashi Rokurō. Tokyo: Gendai shisosha, 1975, 178–91.
Miyata Keizō. "Kamakura bakufu ni yoru Minamoto Yuitsune tsuitō." *Hisutoria* 173 (Jan 2001): 177–202.
———. "Kamakura bakufu seiritsuki no gunji taisei." *Kodai bunka* 50, no. 11 (Nov 1998): 1–19.
Miyazaki Takamune. "Bunken kara mita kodai katchū oboegaki: 'tankō' o chūshin to shite." In *Kansai daigaku kōkogaku kenkyūshitsu 30 shūnen kinen kōkogaku ronsō*, ed. Kansai daigaku kōkogaku kenkyūshitsu 30 shūnen kinen kai. Kyoto: Kansai daigaku, 1983.
Mizuno Yū. "Jinshin no ran." In *Ikusa*, ed. Ōbayashi Taryō. Tokyo: Shakai shisōsha, 1984, 179–204.
———. *Nihon kodai ōchō shiron jōsetsu*. Tokyo: Komiyama shoten, 1954.
Mori Katsumi. "International Relations Between the 10th and the 16th Centuries and the Development of Japanese International Conciousness." *Acta Asiatica* 2 (1961): 69–93.
Mori Kōichi, ed. *Nihon kodai bunka no tankyu 9: uma*. Tokyo: Shakai shisōsha, 1974.
Mori Toshio. "Yumiya no hattatsu." In *Fukugen no Nihon shi: Kassen emaki*, ed. Gomi Fumihisa. Tokyo: Mainichi shimbunsha, 1990, 42–3.
———. "Yumiya no iryoku (1)." In *Fukugen no Nihon shi: Kassen emaki*, ed. Gomi Fumihisa. Tokyo: Mainichi shimbunsha, 1990, 38–9.
———. "Yumiya no iryoku (2)." In *Fukugen no Nihon shi: Kassen emaki*, ed. Gomi Fumihisa. Tokyo: Mainichi shimbunsha, 1990, 40–1.
Morillo, Stephen. "The 'Age of Cavalry' Revisited." In *The Circle of War in the Middle Ages: Essays on Medieval Military and Naval History*, ed. Donald J. Kagay and L. J. Andrew Villalon. Woodbridge, Suffolk: Boydell Press, 1999, 45–58.
Morita Tei. "Heian chūki kebiishi ni tsuite no kakusho." *Nihonshi kenkyū* 12 (1972): 51–63.
———. "Heian zenki o chūshin shita kizoku no shiteki buryoku ni." *Shigen* 15 (1972): 70–84.
———. "Heian zenki tōgoku no gunji mondai ni tsuite." In *Kaitaiki ritsuryō seiji shakaishi no kenkyū*. Tokyo: Kokusho kangyōkai, 1983.

———. "Kebiishi ni tsuite." In *Nihon kodai kanshi seido shi kenkyū jōsetsu*. Tokyo: Gendai sozokusha, 1967.
———. "Kebiishi no kenkyū." *Shigaku zasshi* 78, no. 9 (1969): 1–44.
———. "Kebiishi seiritsu no zentei." *Nihon rekishi* 255 (1969): 62–77.
———. *Kenkyūshi ōchō kokka*. Tokyo: Yoshikawa kōbunkan, 1980.
———. "Kodai sentō ni tsuite." In *Heian shōki kokka no kenkyū*. Tokyo: Gendai sōzōsha, 1970, 170–90.
———. *Ōchō seiji*. Tokyo: Kyōikusha, 1979.
———. "Sumitomo no ran ni tsuite." *Jimbun kagaku shakai kagaku kiyō* 40 (1991): 15–23.
———. *Zuryō*. Tokyo: Kyōikusha, 1978.
Morris, Dana Robert. "Land and Society." In *Cambridge History of Japan*, vol. 2: *Heian Japan*, ed. Donald H. Shively and William McCullough. New York and Cambridge: Cambridge University Press, 1999, 183–235.
———. "Peasant Economy in Early Japan, 650–950." Ph.D. dissertation, University of California, Berkeley, 1980.
Morris, Ivan. "Marriage in the World of Genji." *Asia* 11 (1968): 54–77.
———. *The Nobility of Failure: Tragic Heroes in the History of Japan*. New York: Holt, Rinehart & Winston, 1976.
———. *The World of the Shining Prince: Court Life in Ancient Japan*. New York: Knopf, 1964.
Motogi Yasuo. "Bushiron kenkyū no genjō to kadai." *Nihonshi kenkyū* 421 (Sept 1997): 63–78.
Moyer, K. E. *Violence and Aggression*. New York: Paragon, 1987.
Murai Shōsuke. "The Boundaries of Medieval Japan." *Acta Asiatica* 81 (Sept 2001): 72–91.
Murai Yasuhisa, ed. *Heian ōchō no bushi: Senran Nihonshi* vol. 2. Tokyo: Daiichi hōgen shuppan kabushiki kaishi, 1988.
———. "Meibō o tatematsuru." In *Heian ōchō no bushi*, ed. Yasuda Motohisa. *Senran Nihonshi*. Tokyo: Daiichi hōgen, 1988, 104–5.
———. "Shūba no tō to shūsen no tomogara." In *Heian ōchō no bushi*, ed. Yasuda Motohisa. *Senran Nihonshi*. Tokyo: Daiichi hōgen, 1988, 84–7.
Murakami Sakae, and Saitō Naoyoshi. *Kyūdō oyobi kyūdō shi*. Tokyo: Heibonsha, 1935.
Murano Takao, ed. "Nihon no katana: Tetsu no waza to bu no kokoro." In *Nihon no katana: Tetsu no waza to bu no kokoro*. Tokyo: Tōkyō kokuritsu hakubutsukan, 1997.
Murdoch, James. *A History of Japan*, 3 vols. New York: F. Unger, 1964 (orig. pubn 1910–26).
Nagahara Keiji. "Land Ownership under the Shoen-Kokugaryo System." *Journal of Japanese Studies* 1, no. 2 (1975): 269–96.
———. "The Social Structure of Early Medieval Japan." *Hitotsubashi Journal of Economics* 1, no. 1 (1960): 90–7.
Nagai Hajime. "Gundansei teihaigo no heishi." *Kokugakuin zasshi* 89, no. 9 (1988): 46–59.
———. "Kondeisei ni tsuite no saikentō: Heianki kondei o chūshin to shite." *Shigaku kenkyū shūroku* 8 (1983): 30–9.
Nagaoka Hideo. "'Gunki mono' no zentei · hōga." *Kokugakuin kō kiyō* 20 (1987): 25–66.
Nagauchi Mitsuhiro. "Azuma kagami ni miru Yajima no tatakai ni tsuite." *Gunsho* 20 (April 1993): 20–7.

Nagel, Thomas. "War and Massacre." In *War and Moral Responsibility*, ed. Marshall Cohen, Thomas Nagel and Thomas Scanlon. Princeton, NJ: Princeton University Press, 1974, 3–24.
Naitō Akira. "Kodai no yumi 'do' fukugen." *Mainichi Shimbun Miyagi* (20 April 2000).
Nakahara Toshiaya. "Shishi shinchū no mushi: sōhei." In *Heian ōchō no bushi*, ed. Yasuda Motohisa. *Senran Nihonshi*. Tokyo: Daiichi hōgen, 1988, 94–7.
——. "Zuishin." In *Heian ōchō no bushi*, ed. Yasuda Motohisa. *Senran Nihonshi*. Tokyo: Daiichi hōgen, 1988, 102–3.
Nakamura Akizō. "Fujiwara Hirobumi no ran." In *Ikusa*, ed. Ōbayashi Taryō. Tokyo: Shakai shisōsha, 1984, 205–24.
Nakamura Hirasato. "Senran seppuku no kigen." *Rettō no bunkashi* 11 (Oct 1998): 161–87.
Nakamura Ken. "Chūsei no daiku · tōkō · imonoshi to gijutsu." In *Kodai · chūsei no gijutsu toshakai*, ed. Miura Keiichi. *Gijutsu no shakaishi* vol. 1. Tokyo: Yūhikaku, 1982.
Nakazawa Katsuaki. "Chūsei jōkaku-shi shikiron: sono shinsci o sagaru." *Shigaku zasshi* 102, no. 11 (Nov 1993): 33–58.
——. *Chūsei no buryoku to jōkaku*. Tokyo: Yoshikawa kōbunkan, 1999.
——. "Kūkan to shite no 'jōkaku' to sono tenkai." In *Shiro to tachi o horu yomu*, ed. Satō Makoto and Gomi Fumihiko. Tokyo: Yamakawa shuppan kai, 1994, 191–224.
Nakazawa Shin'ichi. *Akutōteki shikō*. Tokyo: Heibonsha, 1994.
Naoki Kōjirō. *Nihon kodai heiseishi no kenkyū*. Tokyo: Yoshikawa kōbunkan, 1968.
Naruse Kanji. *Jissen tōdan*. Tokyo: Jitsugyō no Nihonsha, 1941.
——. *Rinsen tōjutsu*. Tokyo: Niken shobō, 1944.
——. *Tatakau Nihontō*. Tokyo: Jitsugyō no Nihonsha, 1940.
Needham, Joseph. "Part VI, Military Technology: Missiles and Sieges." In *Chemistry and Chemical Technology*, vol. 5 of *Science and Civilization in China*, ed. Robin D. S. Yates. Cambridge and New York: Cambridge University Press, 1994.
Nelson, Thomas. "Bakufu and Shugo under the Early Ashikaga." In *The Origins of Japan Medieval World: Courtiers, Clerics, Warriors, and Peasants in the Fourteenth Century*, ed. Jeffrey P. Mass. Stanford, CA: Stanford University Press, 1997, 78–90.
Newman, John. *Bushido: The Way of the Warrior*. Leicester: Magna Books, 1989.
Nickerson, Peter. "The Meaning of Matrilocality: Kinship, Property, and Politics in Mid-Heian." *Monumenta Nipponica* 48, no. 4 (1993): 429–68.
Nihon-shi yōgo jiten henshū iinkai, ed. *Nihon-shi yōgo jiten*. Tokyo: Kashiwa shobō, 1979.
Niino Naoyoshi. *Kenkyūshi kuni no miyatsuko*. Tokyo: Yoshikawa kōbunkan, 1974.
Niita Hideharu. "Bakufu seiji no tenkai." In *Buke seiken no keisei*, ed. Inoue Mitsusada et al. *Nihon rekishi taikei fukyūban* vol. 4. Tokyo: Yamakawa shuppansha, 1996, 57–70.
Nishida Tomohiro. "Kamakura bakufu kendan taisei no kōzō to tenkai." *Shigaku zasshi* 111, no. 8 (2002): 1–32.
Nishimata Fusō. "Kassen no rūru to manaa." In *Gempei no sōran*, ed. Yasuda Motohisa. Tokyo: Daiichi hōgen, 1988, 146–7.
Nishimoto Toyohiro. "Kamakura-shi Yuhigahama-Minami kiseki no shutsudo uma ni tsuite." In *Kamakura bushi to uma*, ed. Baji bunka zai dan and Uma hakubutsukan. Tokyo: Meicho shuppan, 1999, 21–6.
Nishioka Toranosuke. "Bushi kaikyū kessei no ichiyoin to shite no 'maku' no hatten." In *Shōenshi no kenkyū*. Tokyo: Iwanami shoten, 1953, 301–407.

Nishiyama Ryōhei. "Kodai no tatakai, bōryoku, arasoi." *Nihonshi kenkyū* 452 (April 2000): 46–53.
Nitta Ichirō. *Sumō no rekishi*. Tokyo: Yamakawa shuppansha, 1994.
Noguchi Minoru. "11–12 seiki, Okuwa no seiji kenryoku o meguru shomondai." In *Kōki sekkan jidaishi no kenkyū*, ed. Kodai gakkyōkai. Tokyo: Yoshikawa kōbunkan, 1990, 397–415.
———. "Bandō bushi to uma." In *Kamakura bushi to uma*, ed. Baji bunka zaidan and Uma no hakubutsukan. Tokyo: Meicho shuppan, 1999, 51–70.
———. *Bandō bushidan no seiritsu to hatten*. Tokyo: Kōseisho rinseishūsha, 1982.
———. *Buke no tōryō no jōken: chūsei bushi o minaosu*. Tokyo: Chūō kōronsha, 1994.
———. "Gempeitōkitsu no gunji kizoku." *Gumma shiryō kenkyū* 15 (Oct 2000): 11–13.
———. "Ikusa to girei." In *Ikusa*, ed. Fukuda Toyohiko. Tokyo: Yoshikawa kōbunkan, 1993, 130–53.
———. "Kindai kokumin dōtoku to shite no bushi ninshiki." *Kyōto jōdai gendai shakai kenkyū* 1 (2001): 93–104.
———. "Kokka to buryoku: chūsei ni okeru bushi · buryoku." *Rekishi hyōron* 564 (April 1997): 60–73.
———. "Musashi bushidan no keisei." In *Tsuwamono no jidai: kodai makki no tōgoku shakai*, ed. Maizō bunkazai Sentaa. Tokyo: Yokohama-shi rekishi hakubutsukan, 1998, 165–72.
———. "Sumōbito to bushi." In *Chūsei tōgokushi no kenkyū*, ed. Chūsei tōgokushi kenkyūkai. Tokyo: Tōkyō daigaku shuppankai, 1988, 51–76.
———. "Taira Koremochi to Taira Koreyoshi." *Shiyū* 10 (1978).
Nomura Shin'ichi. "Nihon no zairai uma to un'yū uma." In *NHK rekishi e no shōtai 5: Muteki Yoshitsune gundan*, ed. Toyoda Aritsune and Nomura Shin'ichi. Tokyo: Nihon hōsō shuppan kyōkai, 1990, 11–36.
Nonaka Akira. "Ōshū gosannen-ki ketsushitsubu no naiyō." *Kagoshima tandai kennkyū kiyō* 58 (June 1996): 1–20.
Nuta Raiyū. *Nihon monshōgaku*. Tokyo: Shin Jimbutsu ōraisha, 1968.
Ōae Akira. *Ritsuryō seika no shihō to keisatsu: kebiishi seido o chūshin to shite*. Tokyo: Daigaku kyōikusha, 1979.
Ōbayashi Taryō, ed. *Ikusa*. Tokyo: Shakai shisōsha, 1984.
Ober, Joseph. "Classical Greek Times." In *The Laws of War: Constraints on Warfare in the Western World*, ed. Michael Howard, George J. Andreopoulos and Mark R. Shulman. New Haven, CT: Yale University Press, 1994, 12–26.
Ōbinata Katsumi. *Kodai kokka to nenjū gyōji*. Tokyo: Yoshikawa kōbunkan, 1993.
Oborotani Hisashi. "Miyako no samurai · hina no musha: sekkanke to musha." In *Heian ōchō no bushi*, ed. Yasuda Motohisa. *Senran Nihonshi*. Tokyo: Daiichi hōgen, 1988, 137–41.
O'Connell, Robert L. *Of Arms and Men: A History of War, Weapons, and Aggression*. New York: Oxford University Press, 1989.
Ogasawara Nobuo. *Nihontō no rekishi to kanshō*. Tokyo: Kōdansha, 1988.
———. "Tōken gaisetsu." In *Nihon no katana: Tetsu no waza to bu no kokoro*, ed. Murano Takao. Tokyo: Tōkyō kokuritsu hakubutsukan, 1997, 8–34.
Ōhira Satoshi. "Hori no keifu." In *Shiro to tachi o horu yomu*, ed. Satō Makoto and Gomi Fumihiko. Tokyo: Yamakawa shuppan kai, 1994, 57–90.
Okada Seiichi. "Bun'ei, kōan no eki." In *Tōgoku bushi no hakken*, ed. Yasuda Motohisa. *Senran Nihonshi*. Tokyo: Daiichi hōgen, 1988, 49–78.

———. "Kassen to girei." In *Ikusa*, ed. Fukuda Toyohiko. Tokyo: Yoshikawa kōbunkan, 1993, 154–81.

Okuda Masahiro. *Chūsei bushidan to shingyō*. Tokyo: Kashiwa shoten, 1980.

Okuno Nakahiko. "Bushidan keiseishijō yori mita Taira Tadatsune no ran: Shisen ron hihan." *Komeizawa shigaku* 6 (1990): 1–10.

———. "Heian ji no guntō ni tsuite." In *Minashū undō to sabetsu-jōsei*, ed. Minshūshi kenkyūkai. Tokyo: Ōyama kaku, 1985, 5–27.

———. "Kodai Tōhoku to Tōgoku." *Minshūshi kenkyū* 37 (1989): 33–48.

———. "Ōshū gosannen no eki no shinshiryō." *Komezawa shigaku* 7 (June 1991): 18–49.

Okutomi Takayuki. "Gaisetsu jōkyū no ran kara Kamakura bakufu no metsubō made." In *Tōgoku bushi no hakken*, ed. Yasuda Motohisa. *Senran Nihonshi*. Tokyo: Daiichi hōgen, 1988, 5–8.

Ōmori Kingorō. "Taira Masakado jiseki kō." In *Ronshū Taira Masakado kenkyū*, ed. Hayashi Rokurō. Tokyo: Gendai shisosha, 1975, 139–50.

Ōta Kōki. *Mōko shūrai: sono gunji shiteki kenkyū*. Tokyo: Kinshōsha, 1997.

Ōtsuka Hatsushige et al. *Michinoku kodai: emishi no seikai*. Tokyo: Yamakawa shuppansha, 1991.

Ōya Kuninori. *Ōshū Fujiwara godai: Michinoku ga hitotsu ni natta jidai*. Tokyo: Kawade shobō shinsha, 2001.

Oyama Yasunori. "Kodai makki no tōgoku to saigoku." In *Iwanami kōza Nihonshi kodai 4*. Tokyo: Iwanami shoten, 1976, 231–69.

———. "Nihon chūsei seiritsuki no mibun to kaikyū." *Rekishigaku kenkyū* 328 (1967): 26–41.

"Ōyoroi no tanjō." In *Tsuwamono no jidai: kodai makki no tōgoku shakai*, ed. Maizō bunkazai Sentaa. Tokyo: Yokohama-shi rekishi hakubutsukan, 1998, 33–84.

Parker, Geoffrey. "Early Modern Europe." In *The Laws of War: Constraints on Warfare in the Western World*, ed. Michael Howard, George J. Andreopoulos and Mark R. Shulman. New Haven, CT: Yale University Press, 1994, 40–58.

Payne-Gallwey, Ralph. *The Crossbow: Its Construction, History and Management*. London: Holland Press, 1903.

Perrin, Noel. *Giving up the Gun: Japan's Reversion to the Sword, 1543–1879*. Boulder, CO: Shambhala, 1979.

Piggott, Joan R. *The Emergence of Japanese Kingship*. Stanford, CA: Stanford University Press, 1997.

———. "Hierarchy and Economics in Early Medieval Todaiji." In *Court and Bakufu in Japan: Essays in Kamakura History*, ed. Jeffrey P. Mass. New Haven, CT: Yale University Press, 1982, 45–91.

Raaflaub, Kurt, and Nathan Rosenstein, eds. *War and Society in the Ancient and Medieval Worlds: Asia, the Mediterranean, Europe, and Mesoamerica*. Cambridge, MA: Center for Hellenic Studies, Harvard University, 1999.

Rabinovitch, Judith N. *Shōmonki: The Story of Masakado's Rebellion*. Tokyo: Monumenta Nipponica Monograph, 1986.

Reid, William. *The Lore of Arms*. New York: Facts on File, 1976.

Reischauer, Edwin O. "Heiji Monogatari." In *Translations from Early Japanese Literature*, ed. Edwin Reischauer and Joseph Yamagiwa. Cambridge, MA: Harvard University Press, 1972, 269–353.

Robinson, H. Russell. *Japanese Arms and Armor*. New York: Crown Publications, 1969.

REFERENCES AND BIBLIOGRAPHY

Rose, Susan. *Medieval Naval Warfare*. Warfare and History. Jeremy Black, gen. ed. London and New York: Routledge, 2002.
Russell, Frederick H. *The Just War in the Middle Ages*. London and New York: Cambridge University Press, 1975.
Sadler, Arthur L., trans. *The Ten Foot Square Hut and the Tales of the Heike*. Rutland, VT: Tuttle, 1972.
Saiki Hideo. "Hakkutsu chōsa kara miru umaya to uma." In *Kamakura bushi to uma*, ed. Baji bunka zai dan and Uma hakubutsukan. Tokyo: Meicho shuppan, 1999, 27–32.
Sakai Hideya. "Chō to tachi, shūraku to yashiki: tōgoku kodai iseki ni miru tachi no keisei." In *Shiro to tachi o horu yomu*, ed. Satō Makoto and Gomi Fumihiko. Tokyo: Yamakawa shuppan kai, 1994, 21–56.
Sakamoto Akira. "Tōgoku bushi no sōbi kōjō o horu: Yokohama-shi Nishinotani iseki no chōsa seika." In *Tsuwamono no jidai: kodai makki no tōgoku shakai*, ed. Maizō bunkazai Sentaa. Tokyo: Yokohama-shi rekishi hakubutsukan, 1998, 117–33.
Sakamoto Tarō Hakase Kanreki Kinenkai, ed. *Nihon kodaishi ronshū*. Tokyo: Yoshikawa kōbunkan, 1962.
Sansom, George B. *A History of Japan, 1334–1615*. Stanford, CA: Stanford University Press, 1961.
Sasaki Minoru. "Nihon-tō to ōyoroi no seiritsu katei: kinzoku kōkogakuteki tachiba kara no kōsatsu," *Rekishi yaku kenkyū* 730 (Nov 1999): 35–48.
———. "Tetsu to Nihon-tō." In *Ikusa*, ed. Fukuda Toyohiko. Tokyo: Yoshikawa kōbunkan, 1993, 39–75.
Sasaki Muneo. "10–11 seiki no zuryō to chūō seifu." *Shigaku zasshi* 96, no. 9 (1987): 1–36.
Sasama Yoshihiko. *Buke senjin shiryō jiten*. Tokyo: Daiichi shobō, 1992.
———. *Katchū no subete*. Tokyo: PHP kenkyūsho, 1997.
———. *Nihon katchū · bugu jiten*. Tokyo: Kashiwa shobō, 1981.
———. *Nihon kassen bugu jiten*. Tokyo: Kashiwa shobō, 1999.
Sasamatsu Hiroshi. "Omae no kasan . . ." In *Chūsei no tsumi to batsu*, ed. Amino Yoshihiko et al. Tokyo: Tōkyō daigaku shuppan kai, 1983, 1–14.
Sasayama Haruo. "Bunken ni mirareru senjutsu to buki." In *Ikusa*, ed. Ōbayashi Taryō. Tokyo: Shakai shisōsha, 1984, 123–55.
———. *Kodai kokka to guntai*. Tokyo: Chūkō shinsho, 1975.
———. *Nihon kodai efu seido no kenkyū*. Tokyo: Tōkyō daigaku shuppankai, 1985.
Sato, Elizabeth. "Early Development of the Shoen." In *Medieval Japan: Essays in Institutional History*, ed. John W. Hall and Jeffrey P. Mass. New Haven, CT: Yale University Press, 1974, 91–108.
———. "Oyama Estate and Insei Land Policies." *Monumenta Nipponica* 34, no. 1 (1979): 73–99.
Satō Kazuhiko. "Nairanki shakai ni okeru gunsei saisoku to jōhō senryaku." In *Chūsei no hakken*, ed. Nagahara Keiji. Tokyo: Yoshikawa kōbunkan, 1993, 88–109.
Satō Kazuo. *Umi to suigun no Nihonshi*. 2 vols. Tokyo: Hara shobō, 1995.
Satō Makoto. "Kodai · chūsei no shiro to tachi." In *Shiro to tachi o horu yomu*, ed. Satō Makoto and Gomi Fumihiko. Tokyo: Yamakawa shuppan kai, 1994, 3–21.
Satō Makoto, and Gomi Fumihiko. *Shiro to kan wo horu · yomu: kodai kara chūsei e*. Tokyo: Yamakawa shuppansha, 1994.
Satō Shin'ichi. *Nambokuchō no dōran*. Tokyo: Chūō kōronsha, 1972.

———. *Nihon chūsei shi ronshū*. Tokyo: Iwanami shoten, 1990.
———. *Nihon no chūsei kokka*. Tokyo: Iwanami shoten, 1983.
———. *Zōtei Kamakura bakufu shugo sido no kenkyū*. Tokyo: Tōkyō daigaku shuppankai, 1971.
Satō Shin'ichi, with John W. Hall. "Ashikaga Shogun and the Muromachi Bakufu Administration." In *Japan in the Muromachi Age*, ed. John W. Hall and Toyoda Takeshi. Berkeley: University of California Press, 1977, 45–52.
Seki Yukihiko. *Bushidan kenkyū no ayumi: gakusetsu shiteki tenkai*. Tokyo: Shin jimbutsu ōraisha, 1988.
———. "Chūsei shoki no bui to buryoku." *Nihon rekishi* 532 (Sept 1992): 18–35.
———. "Kokuga gunsei to bushi no hassei ha dono yō ni kanren suru ka." In *Sōten no Nihon-shi 4*, ed. Minegishi Sumio. Tokyo: Shim jimbutsu ōraisha, 1991, 14–26.
———. "'Bu' no kōgen: kōchū to yumiya." In *Ikusa*, ed. Fukuda Toyohiko. Tokyo: Yoshikawa kōbunkan, 1993, 1–38.
Sekiguchi Akira. *Emishi to kodai kokka*. Tokyo: Yoshikawa kōbunkan, 1992.
———. "Kodai emishi no dokuya shiyō ni kansuru ikkōsatsu." In *Rekishi to kokoro*, ed. Enomoto Moriyoshi hakase taikan o iwau kai. Tokyo, 1988, 35–41.
Sekiguchi Hiroko. "Kodai kazoku to kon'in keitai." In *Kōza Nihonshi 2*, ed. Rekishigaku kenkyūkai · Nihonshi kenkyūkai. Tokyo: Tokyo daigaku shuppankai, 1984, 287–326.
———. "Nihon kodai gokizokusō ni okeru kazoku no tokushitsu ni tsuite." *Genshi kodai shakai kenkyū* 5 (1979): 195–77.
Selby, Stephen. *Chinese Archery*. Hong Kong: Hong Kong University Press, 2000.
Seoh, M. S. "A Brief Documentary Survey of Japanese Pirate Activities in Korea in the 13th to 15th Centuries." *Journal of Korean Studies* 1 (1969): 23–39.
Shakadō Mitsuhiro. "Nambokuchō ki kassen ni okeru senshō." *Nairanshi kenkyū* 13 (1992): 27–39.
Shibatsuji Shunroku. "Kawanakajima kassen no kyozō to jitsuzō." *Shinano* 52, no. 5 (May 2000): 10–21.
Shimomukai Tatsuhiko. "Kokuga to bushi." In *Iwanami kōza Nihon tsūshi 6: kodai 5*. Tokyo: Iwanami shoten, 1995.
———. "Ōchō kokka gunsei kenkyū no kihon shikaku: 'tsuibu kampu' o chūshin ni." In *Ōchō kokka seishi*, ed. Sakamoto Shōzō. Tokyo: Yoshikawa kōbunkan, 1987, 285–345.
———. "Ōchō kokka kokuga gunsei no kōzō to tenkai." *Shigaku zasshi* 51 (1981): 44–67.
———. "Ōchō kokka kokuga gunsei no seiritsu." *Shigaku kenkyū* 144 (1979): 1–27.
———. "Ōryōshi · tsuibushi no shoruikei." *Hisutoria* 94 (1982): 17–33.
———. "Ritsuryō gunsei to kokuga gunsei." In *Jinrui ni totte tatakai to wa 2, tatakai no shisutemu to taigai senryaku*, ed. Matsugi Takehiko and Udagawa Takehisa. Tokyo: Tōyō shorin, 1999, 81–121.
———. "Shokoku ōryōshi · tsuibushi shiryō shūseitai: shokoku ōryōshi · tsuibushi ni tsuite." *Hiroshima daigaku bungakubu kiyō* 45 (1986): 1–41.
———. "Tenkei Fujiwara Sumitomo no ran ni tsuite no seijishiteki kōan." *Nihonshi kenkyū* 348 (Aug 1991): 1–32.
———. "'Fujiwara Sumitomo no ran' saikentō no tame no ichi shiryō." *Nihon rekishi* 495 (1989): 15–32.
Shimomura Itaru. *Bushi*. Tokyo: Tōkyōdō shuppan, 1993.
Shinoda Minoru. *The Founding of the Kamakura Shogunate*. New York: Columbia University Press, 1960.

Shōji Hiroshi. "Heian shōki kebiishi buryoku no ikkōsatsu." *Gunji shigaku* 23, no. 4 (1988): 17–22.
———. *Henkyō no sōran.* Tokyo: Kyōikusha, 1977.
———. "Kebiishi tsuibu katsudō kōdai katei no ikkōsai." *Shūkyō sahkaishi kenkyū* 2 (1985): 99–116.
Smith, Jr., John Masson. "Ayn Jâlūt: Mamlūk Success or Failure?" *Harvard Journal of Asiatic Studies* 44, no. 2 (1984): 314–20.
Souyri, Pierre François. *The World Turned Upside Down: Medieval Japanese Society,* trans. Käthe Roth. New York: Columbia University Press, 2001.
Stacey, Robert C. "The Age of Chivalry." In *The Laws of War: Constraints on Warfare in the Western World,* ed. Michael Howard, George J. Andreopoulos and Mark R. Shulman. New Haven, CT: Yale University Press, 1994, 27–39.
Steenstrup, Carl. "The Gokurakuji Letter: Hojo Shigetoki's Compendium of Political and Religious Ideas of 13th Century Japan." *Monumenta Nipponica* 32, no. 1 (1977): 1–34.
———. *Hojo Shigetoki (1198–1261) and his Role in the History of Political and Ethical Ideas in Japan.* London: Curzon Press, 1979.
———. "Hojo Shigetoki's Letter of Instruction to his Son, Naga-toki: A Guide to Success in 13th Century Japan." *Acta Asiatica* 36 (1974): 417–38.
———. "The Origins of the Houselaws (Kakun) of the Warriors of Medieval Japan." *Proceedings of the International Association of Historians of Asia,* 7th Conference Bankok 2 (1977): 868–909.
———. "Sata Mirensho: A 14th Century Law Primer." *Monumenta Nipponica* 35, no. 4 (1980): 405–36.
Stephens, George M. *Crossbows: From Thirty-Five Years with the Weapon.* Cornville, AZ: Desert Publications, 1980.
Stramigioli, Giuliana. "Preliminary Notes on the Masakadoki and Taira no Masakado Story." *Monumenta Nipponica* 28, no. 3 (1973): 261–93.
Strickland, Matthew. *War & Chivalry: The Conduct and Perception of War in England and Normandy, 1066–1217.* New York and London: Cambridge University Press, 1996.
Suematsu Yasukazu. "Japan's Relations with the Asian Continent and the Korean Peninsula (Before 950 AD)." *Cashiers d'Historique Mondiale* 4, no. 3 (1958): 671–87.
Suezaki Masumi. "Bagu kara miru uma." In *Kamakura bushi to uma,* ed. Baji bunka zai dan and Uma hakubutsukan. Tokyo: Meicho shuppan, 1999, 33–8.
Sugawara Makoto. "Self-Introduction for Honor: the Hōgen Insurrection." *East* 16, nos. 3–4 (1980): 21–8.
Sugimoto Keizaburō. "Konjaku Monogatari no bushi setsuwa: Heike Monogatari to no kanren ni oite." *Hōsei daigaku bungakubu kiyō* 9 (1963): 26–53.
Sugimoto Masayoshi, and David L. Swain. *Science and Culture in Traditional Japan,* AD 600–1854. Cambridge, MA: MIT Press, 1978.
Sun Tzu. *Ping fa.* In *Sonshi,* ed. Murayama Makoto. Tokyo: Asahi geinō shuppan kabushiki kaisha, 1962.
Suzuki Hideo. "Kamakura bushi no seikai." In *Tōgoku bushi no hakken,* ed. Yasuda Motohisa. *Senran Nihonshi.* Tokyo: Daiichi hōgen, 1988, 134–51.
Suzuki Keizō. "Bunken rikai no tame no busō yōgo no kentō." *Kokugakuin daigaku daigakuin kiyō* 15 (1984): 28–75.
———. "Kuge no ken no nasho to kōzō." *Tōken bijutsu* 343 (1985).

———. "Shikishō no yoroi no keisei ni tsuite." *Kokugakuin zasshi* 63, no. 4 (1962): 1–9.
———. "Ya no kōsei: Yūshoku kojitsu no kenkyū." *Kokugakuin kōtō gakkō kiyō* 1 (1959): 3–44.
Suzuki Kunihiro. "Kuge hō to buke hō." In *Tōgoku bushi no hakken*, ed. Yasuda Motohisa. *Senran Nihonshi*. Tokyo: Daiichi hōgen, 1988, 122–47.
Suzuki Masaya. *Katana to kubi-tori: Sengoku kassen isetsu*. Tokyo: Heibonsha shinsho, 2000.
———. *Teppō to Nihonjin: "teppō shinwa" ga kakushite kita koto*. Tokyo: Yōsuisha, 1997.
Suzuki Susumu. *Nihon kassenshi hyakubanashi*. Tokyo: Tatsukaze shobō, 1982.
Suzuki Takeo. "Heian jidai ni okeru nōmin no uma." *Nihon rekishi* 239 (1968): 42–55.
Suzuki Tetsuyū. "Masakado no ran kara Kamakura bushi e." In *Chūsei no fūkyō o yomu 2 toshi Kamakura to bandō no umi ni kurasu*, ed. Amino Yoshihiko and Ishii Susumu. Tokyo: Shinjimbutsu ōraisha, 1994, 123–54.
Tabata Yasuko. "Kodai, chūsei no 'ie' to kazoku: yōshi o chūshin to shite." *Tachibana joshi daigaku kenkyū kiyō* 12 (1985): 41–67.
Tahara, Mildred M. *Tales of Yamato: A 10th Century Poem-Tale*. Honolulu: Hawaii University Press, 1980.
Takahashi Masaaki. *Bushi no seiritsu: bushizō no sōshutsu*. Tokyo: Tōkyō daigaku shuppankai, 1999.
———. "Bushi o minaosu." In *Bushi to wa nan darō ka*, ed. Takahashi Masaaki and Yamamoto Kōji. Tokyo: Asahi shimbunsha, 1994, 2–7.
———. "Bushi to ōken." In *Bushi to wa nan darō ka*, ed. Takahashi Masaaki and Yamamoto Kōji. Tokyo: Asahi shimbunsha, 1994, 8–23.
———. "Chūsei seiritsuki ni okeru kokka · shakai to buryoku." *Nihonshi kenkyū* 427 (1998).
———. "Kihei to suigun." In *Nihonshi 2 chūsei 1*, ed. Toda Yoshimi. Tokyo: Yūhikaku, 1978, 68–98.
———. *Kiyomori izen*. Tokyo: Heibonsha, 1984.
———. "Nihon chūsei no sentō: yasen no kijōsha o chūshin ni." In *Tatakai no shisutemu to taigai senryaku (Jinrui ni totte tatakai to ha #2)*, ed. Matsugi Takehiko and Udakawa Takehisa. Tokyo: Tōyō shorin, 1999, 193–224.
———. "Tsurugaoka Hachimangū yabusame gyōji no seiritsu." *Atarashii rekishigaku no tame ni* 224 (1996).
Takahashi Masaaki, and Yamamoto Kōji. *Bushi to wa nan darō ka. Asahi hyakka Nihon no rekishi bessatsu: rekishi o yominaosu* vol. 8. Tokyo: Asahi shimbunsha, 1994.
Takahashi Noriyuki. "Buke seiken to sensō · gunyaku." *Rekishigaku kenkyū* 755 (2001): 49–58.
———. "Kamakura bakufu gunsei no kōzō to tenkai." *Shigaku zasshi* 105, no. 1 (Jan 1996): 4–34.
Takahashi Osamu. "Bushidan no shihai ronri to sono hyōzō: Meiei hassho iseki no seititsu." *Rekishi hyōron* 611 (March 2001): 17–33.
Takahashi Takashi. "Fushū no ran." In *Heian ōchō no bushi*, ed. Yasuda Motohisa. *Senran Nihonshi*. Tokyo: Daiichi hōgen, 1988, 28–36.
———. "Gosannen no eki." In *Heian ōchō no bushi*, ed. Yasuda Motohisa. *Senran Nihonshi*. Tokyo: Daiichi hōgen, 1988, 122–8.
———. "Zenkūnen no eki." In *Heian ōchō no bushi*, ed. Yasuda Motohisa. *Senran Nihonshi*. Tokyo: Daiichi hōgen, 1988, 113–21.
Takahashi Tomio. *Bushi no kokoro, Nihon no kokoro*. Tokyo: Kondō shuppansha, 1991.

——. *Bushidō no rekishi*. Tokyo: Shin jimbutsu ōraisha, 1986.
——. *Emishi*. Tokyo: Yoshikawa kōbunkan, 1963.
——. *Hiraizumi no seikai: Fujiwara Kiyohira*. Tokyo: Kiyomizu shinsho, 1983.
——. *Kodai emishi o kangaeru*. Tokyo: Yoshikawa kōbunkan, 1991.
——. "Kodai kokka to henkyō." In *Iwanami kōza Nihon rekishi kodai 3*. Tokyo: Iwanami shoten, 1962, 229–60.
Takashima Hideyuki. "Masakado no ōken." *Gumma shiryō kenkyū* 15 (Oct. 2000): 1–19.
Takayama Kahoru. "Shirakawa inseiki ni okeru kebiishi no issokumen: bunin jōetsu kara mite." *Shōnan shigaku* 7–8 (1986): 64–98.
Takayanagi Mitsutoshi, and Suzuki Tōru. *Nihon kassenshi*. Tokyo: Gakugei shorin, 1968.
Takemitsu Makoto. *Kodai tōhoku: Matsurowanu mono no keifu*. Tokyo: Chūō seihan, 1994.
Takeuchi Rizō. "Shōki no bushidan." In *Nihon jimbutsu shi taikei*, vol. 1, ed. Kawasaki Yasuyuki. Tokyo: Asakura shoten, 1961, 194–214.
Takinami Sadako. "Heian-kyō no kōzō." In *Kodai o kangaeru: Heian no miyako*, ed. Sasayama Haruo. Tokyo: Yoshikawa kōbunkan, 1991.
Tanaka Katsuya. *Emishi kenkyū*. Tokyo: Shinsensha, 1992.
Tanaka Minoru. "Kamakura shoki no seiji katei: kenkyū nenkan o chūshin ni shite." *Rekishi kyōiku* 11 (1963): 19–26.
"Tetsu o kagaku suru." In *Tsuwamono no jidai: kodai makki no tōgoku shakai*, ed. Maizō bunkazai Sentaa. Tokyo: Yokohama-shi rekishi hakubutsukan, 1998, 107–15.
Tien Chen-Ya. *Chinese Military Theory*. Oakville, Ontario: Mosaic Press, 1992.
Toda Yoshimi. "Kokuga gunsei no keisei katei." In *Chūsei no kenryoku to minshū*, ed. Nihonshi kenkyūkai shiryō kembukai. Tokyo: Sōgensha, 1970, 5–44.
——. "Shoki chūsei bushi no shokunō to shoyaku." In *Nihon no shakaishi* vol. 4, ed. Asao Naohiro *et al*. Tokyo: Iwanami shoten, 1986, 247–71.
"Tōgoku bushidan no genzō." In *Tsuwamono no jidai: kodai makki no tōgoku shakai*, ed. Maizō bunkazai Sentaa. Tokyo: Yokohama-shi rekishi hakubutsukan, 1998, 93–106.
Tonomura, Hitomi. "Women and Inheritance in Japan's Early Warrior Society." *Comparative Studies in Society and History* 32, no. 3 (1990): 592–623.
Torao Toshiya. "Nara Economic and Social Institutions." In *Medieval Japan*, ed. Delmer M. Brown. *The Cambridge History of Japan* vol. 1. New York: Cambridge University Press, 1993, 415–52.
Toyoda Aritsune, and Nomura Shin'chi, eds. *Muteki Yoshitsune gundan*. *NHK rekishi e no shōtai*, vol. 5. Tokyo: Nihon hōsō shuppan kyōkai, 1990.
——. "Uma ga daikatsuyaku shita Gempei no tatakai." In *NHK rekishi e no shōtai 5: Muteki Yoshitsune gundan*, ed. Toyoda Aritsune and Nomura Shin'ichi. Tokyo: Nihon hōsō shuppan kyōkai, 1990, 11–36.
Toyoda Takeshi. *Bushidan to sonraku*. Tokyo: Yoshikawa kōbunkan, 1963.
Tsukamoto Manabu. "Buryoku to minshū." *Rekishi hyōron* 511 (Nov 1992): 1–11.
Tsuge Hideomi. *Historical Development of Science and Technology in Japan*. Tokyo: Kokusai bunka shinkokai, 1968.
Tsuno Jin. "Kodai kozane yoroi no tokuchō." In *Tsuwamono no jidai: kodai makki no tōgoku shakai*, ed. Maizō bunkazai Sentaa. Tokyo: Yokohama-shi rekishi hakubutsukan, 1998, 155–64.

Tsunoda Ryusaku, and L. Carrington Goodrich, eds. and trans. *Japan in the Chinese Dynastic Histories: Later Han Through Ming Dynasties*. Pasadena, CA: P. D. & Ione Perkins, 1951.

Turnbull, Stephen R. *Battles of the Samurai*. London: Arms and Armour Press, 1987.

———. *The Book of the Samurai: The Warrior Class of Japan*. New York: Gallery Books, 1982.

———. *The Lone Samurai and the Martial Arts*. London: Arms and Armour Press, 1990.

———. *Samurai Warriors*. Poole, Dorset: Blandford Press, 1987.

———. *The Samurai: A Military History*. New York: Macmillan, 1976.

Turney-High, Harry Holbert. *Primitive War: Its Practice and Concepts*. Columbia: University of South Carolina Press, 1949.

Ueda Hironori. "Nihon kodai no buki." In *Ikusa*, ed. Ōbayashi Taryō. Tokyo: Shakai shisōsha, 1984, 43–122.

Urushibara Tetsu. "Nambokuchō shoki ni okeru bakufu gunji seido no kisoteki kōan." In *Nihon chūsei seiji shakai no kenkyū*, ed. Ogawa Shin sensei no koki kinen ronshū o kangyō suru kai. Tokyo: Zoku gunsho ruijū kanseikai, 1991, 311–48.

Urushibara Tōru. "Gunchūjō ni kansuru jakkan no kōsatsu." *Komonjo kenkyū* 21 (June 1983): 33–52.

Uwasugi Kazuhiko. "'Tsuwamono' kara bushi e." *Rekishi chiri kyōiku* 518 (1994): 8–13.

Uwayokote Masataka. "Heian chūki no keisatsu jōtai." In *Ritsuryō kokka to kizoku shakai*, ed. Takeuchi Rizō hakase kanreki kinenkai. Tokyo: Yoshikawa kōbunkan, 1969, 511–40.

———. "Kodai makki nairan kenkyū no mondaiten." *Rekishi hyōron* 88 (1957).

———. *Nihon chūsei kokka shi ronkō*. Tokyo: Haniwa shobō, 1994.

———. "Taira Masakado no ran." In *Ronshū Taira Masakado kenkyū*, ed. Hayashi Rokurō. Tokyo: Gendai shisosha, 1975, 267–87.

Vale, Malcolm. *War and Chivalry: Warfare and Aristocratic Culture in England, France and Burgundy at the End of the Middle Ages*. Athens: University of Georgia Press, 1981.

van Crevald, Martin. *Technology and War*. New York: Free Press, 1989.

Vann, Theresa M. "Twelfth-Century Castile and Its Frontier Strategies." In *The Circle of War in the Middle Ages: Essays on Medieval Military and Naval History*, ed. Donald J. Kagay and L. J. Andrew Villalon. Woodbridge, Suffolk: Boydell Press, 1999, 21–31.

Varley, H. Paul, trans. *A Chronicle of Gods and Sovereigns: Jinnō Shōtōki of Kitabatake Chikafusa*. New York: Columbia University Press, 1980.

———. "The Hōjō Family and Succession to Power." In *Court and Bakufu in Japan: Essays in Kamakura History*, ed. Jeffrey P. Mass. New Haven, CT: Yale University Press, 1982, 143–68.

———. *Imperial Restoration in Medieval Japan*. New York: Columbia University Press, 1971.

———. *The Onin War: History of its Origins and Background, with a Selective Translation of the Chronicles of Onin*. New York: Columbia University Press, 1967.

———. "The Place of Gukansho in Japanese Intellectual History. *Monumenta Nipponica* 34, no. 4 (1979): 479–88.

———. *Warriors of Japan as Portrayed in the War Tales*. Honolulu: University of Hawaii Press, 1994.

Verbruggen, J. F. *The Art of Warfare in Western Europe During the Middle Ages: From the Eighth Century to 1340*, trans. Sumner Willard and R. W. Southern. 2nd edn, rev. and enlarged, Woodbridge, Suffolk: Boydell Press, 1997 (orig. pubn 1954).

Wada Hidematsu. "Tsuibushi kō." *Nyoran shawa* 6 (1888).
Wada Tsuyoshi, ed. *Sumō no rekishi*. Tokyo: Sumōten jitsugyō iinkai, 1998.
Waida Manabu. "Sacred Kingship in Early Japan," *History of Religions* 15, no. 4 (1976): 319–42.
Wakita Haruko. "Marriage and Property in Premodern Japan from the Perspective of Women's History." *Journal of Japanese Studies* 1, no. 2 (1984): 321–45.
Walzer, Michael. *Just and Unjust Wars: a Moral Argument with Historical Illustrations*. New York: Basic Books, 1977.
———. "Political Action: The Problem of Dirty Hands." In *War and Moral Responsibility*, ed. Marshall Cohen, Thomas Nagel and Thomas Scanlon. Princeton, NJ: Princeton University Press, 1974, 62–84.
Warry, John. *Warfare in the Classical World: An Illustrated Encyclopedia of Weapons, Warriors, and Warfare in the Ancient Civilizations of Greece & Rome*. New York: Barnes & Noble, 1993.
Watanabe Naohiko. "Kebiishi no kenkyū." In *Nihon kodai kan'i seido no kisoteki kenkyū*. Tokyo: Yoshikawa kōbunkan, 1972, 295–384.
Wilson, William R., trans. *Hōgen Monogatari: A Tale of the Disorder of Hogen*. Tokyo: Monumenta Nipponica Monograph, 1971.
———. "Sea Battle of Dan no Ura." *American* Neptune 28 (1968): 206–22.
———. "The Way of the Bow and Arrow: The Japanese Warrior in the Kojaku Monogatari." *Monumenta Nipponica* 28, nos. 1–4 (1973): 177–233.
Wintersteen, Prescott B., Jr. "The Early Muromachi Bakufu in Kyoto." In *Medieval Japan: Essays in Institutional History*, ed. John W. Hall and Jeffrey P. Mass. New Haven, CT: Yale University Press, 1974, 201–9.
———. "Muromachi Shugo and Hanzei." In *Medieval Japan: Essays in Institutional History*, ed. John W. Hall and Jeffrey P. Mass. New Haven: Yale University Press, 1974, 210–20.
"Yahari 'do' wa sonzai ka." *Gekkan bunkazai hakkutsu shutsudo jōhō* (Dec 1999): 40.
Yamada Nakaba. *Ghenko: The Mongol Invasion of Japan*. London: Smith, Elder, 1916.
Yamaguchi Hideo. "Heian jidai no kokuga to zaichi seiryoku." *Kokushigaku* 156 (May 1995): 91–102.
Yamamoto Kōji. "Kassen ni okeru bunka tairitsu." In *Bushi to wa nan darō ka*, ed. Takahashi Masaaki and Yamamoto Kōji. Tokyo: Asahi shimbunsha, 1994, 26–43.
———. "Kyūgi nitai." In *Bushi to wa nan darō ka*, ed. Takahashi Masaaki and Yamamoto Kōji. Tokyo: Asahi shimbunsha, 1994, 40–2.
Yamamura, Kozo. "The Growth of Commerce in Medieval Japan." In *Cambridge History of Japan*, vol. 3: *Medieval Japan*, ed. Kozo Yamamura. Cambridge and New York: Cambridge University Press, 1989, 344–95.
———, ed. *Medieval Japan. The Cambridge History of Japan*, vol. 3. Cambridge and New York: Cambridge University Press, 1989.
———. "Tara in Transition: A Study of Kamakura Shoen." *Journal of Japanese Studies* 7, no. 2 (1981): 349–91.
Yamanouchi Kunio. "Kondei o meguru shomondai." In *Nihon kodai shi ronsō*, ed. Endō Motō hakasei kanreki kinen. Tokyo: Endō Motō hakasei kanreki kinen Nihon kodaishi ronsō kangyōkai, 1970, 348–70.
Yanagita Yoshitaka. "Genkō bōruui to chūsei kaigan sen." In *Yomigaeru chūsei I: Higashi Ajia no kukusai toshi Hakata*, ed. Amino Yoshihiko et al. Tokyo: Heibonsha, 1988, 180–94.

Yasuda Motohisa. *Bushi sekai no jōmaku*. Tokyo: Yoshikawa kōbunkan, 1973.
———. "Bushidan no keisei." In *Iwanami kōza Nihon rekishi kodai 4*. Tokyo: Iwanami shoten, 1962, 132–60.
———, ed. *Gempei no sōran. Senran Nihonshi*. Tokyo: Daiichi hōgen, 1988.
———. "Gokeninsei seritsu ni kansuru isshiki ron." *Gakushūin daigaku bungakubu kenkyū nempō* 16 (1969): 81–110.
———, ed. *Heian ōchō no bushi. Senran Nihonshi*. Tokyo: Daiichi hōgen, 1988.
———, ed. *Kassen no Nihonshi*. Tokyo: Shufu to seikatsu sha, 1990.
———, ed. *Nambokuchō no nairan. Senran Nihonshi*. Tokyo: Daiichi hōgen, 1988.
———. *Senran*. Tokyo: Kintō shuppansha, 1984.
———. *Shugo to jitō*. Tokyo: Shibundo, 1964.
———, ed. *Tōgoku bushi no haken. Senran Nihonshi*. Tokyo: Daiichi hōgen, 1988.
Yasuda Takayoshi. "Taira Masakado no ran no buryoku." In *Kantō no kodai shakai*, ed. Endō Motō. Tokyo: Meicho shuppan, 1989, 237–62.
Yates, Robin D. S. "Early China." In *War and Society in the Ancient and Medieval Worlds: Asia, the Mediterranean, Europe, and Mesoamerica*, ed. Kurt Raaflaub and Nathan Rosenstein. Cambridge, MA: Center for Hellenic Studies, Harvard University, 1999, 7–46.
Yiengpruksawan, Mimi Hall. *Hiraizumi: Buddhist Art and Regional Politics in Twelfth-Century Japan*. Boston: Harvard East Asian Monographs, 1998.
Yokota Shigeru. "Shōki Kamakura bushi no gyōdō ronri." *Nihon shisōshi* 58 (April 2001): 70–86.
Yoneda Yūsuke. *Kodai kokka to chihō gōzoku*. Tokyo: Kyōikusha, 1979.
Yoneya Toyonosuke. "In hokumen bushi tsuikō: toku ni sōshiki ni tsuite." *Ōsaka sangyō daigaku jimbun kagaku ronshū* 70 (1990): 29–61.
Yoshida Akira. "Heian chūki no buryoku ni tsuite." *Hisutoria* 47 (1967): 1–16.
———. "Masakado no ran ni kansuru 2 · 3 no mondai." *Nihonshi kenkyū* 50 (1960): 6–26; repr. in *Ronshū Taira Masakado kenkyū*, ed. Hayashi Rokurō. Tokyo: Gendai shisosha, 1975, 200–21.
Yoshii Hiroshi. "Ikusa to minshū." In *Ikusa*, ed. Fukuda Toyohiko. Tokyo: Yoshikawa kōbunkan, 1993, 182–209.
Yoshimura Shigeki. "In hokumen kō." *Hōseishi kenkyū* 2 (1953): 45–71.
———. "Takiguchi no kenkyū." *Rekishi chiri* 53, no. 4 (1929): 1–30.
Yoshizawa Mikio. "Kodai gunsei to kiba heiryoku ni tsuite." In *Ritsuryō kokka to kōzō*, ed. Seki Akira sensei koki kinenkai. Tokyo: Yoshikawa kōbunkan, 1989, 147–77.
Yumino Masatake. "Ritsuryō seika no 'buryō' to 'ōryō'." In *Kodai tennōsei to shakai kōzō*, ed. Takeuchi Rizo. Tokyo: Kōsō shobō, 1980, 215–35.
Zaidan hōjin baji bunka zaidan, and Uma no hakubutsukan, eds. *Kamakura bushi to uma*. Tokyo: Meicho shuppan, 1999.

INDEX

Abe Sadatō 138, 140, 149
Abe Takeshi 128
Abe Yoritoki 119, 138–9
Akasaka Castle, battle of 16, 128
akutō ("evil gangs") 56
alliances: among court aristocrats 40–1; benefices and rewards in 54–6, 59, 61, 115, 168; between central and provincial warriors 41–2; between provincial warriors 40–1; cohesion in 54–5, 57, 59–61; effect of ideological constraints on 60; *see also* kinship; loyalty; warbands
Amano Norikage 151
ambush: ethical considerations 140–5; in medieval Europe 144–5; tactical uses of 115–17
Aminabi Tanematsu 66
Amino Yoshihiko 128, 133
Aquinas, Thomas 24
archery, mounted: medieval Japanese tactics 107–11, 114, 132, 190, 191; as technology of steppe nomads 102, 106–7; under *ritsuryō* military system 103–4; *see also* cavalry
Aristotle 20
armies: size of 129–30, 166; strategic vs. tactical organization of 36, 53, 112; *see also* warbands
armor: advantages of lamellar construction 91; decorations on 94; general construction of 90–1; iron vs. leather 186; principal styles of 90; protective value of 96; *see also hara-ate; haramaki; haramaki yoroi; ōyoroi; Ryōtō-shiki keikō*
arrows 70–1
Asaina Yoshihide 2–3
Ashikaga Takauji 54

Ashikaga Yoshiaki 14
Ashikaga Yoshimitsu 14
Ashikaga Yoshiuji 3
Augustine 20, 23
Azuma kagami 27, 51, 114, 142, 144, 147, 153; reliability of 16–17, 130, 132

bakufu see shogunate
Ban dainagon ekotoba 79
battle cries *see nanori*
battle reports 16, 132, 155
benefices *see* alliances, benefices and rewards in
biwa-hōshi (traveling lute players) 15
bows: of Asian steppe nomads 106–7; composite 68–9, 70; length and shape of 69–70; Mongol 68; simple wood 68–70; strength of 69, 107, 129
Brice, Martin 123
Brunner, Otto 144
buke kojitsu (warrior etiquette) 154
buntori see heads, practice of collecting
Burton, Richard 78
bushi see warriors
bushidan see warbands
bushidō 144
Butler, Kenneth 15

Carlyle, Thomas 63
castles *see* fortifications
casualty figures 132
cavalry: tactical uses of 104–5, 128, 129, 164–5; *see also* archery, mounted
chain of command, military: after Jōkyō War 52–3; during Heian period 42–3; *shugo* role in 49, 51–3, 54, 56; under Minamoto Yoritomo 49–51
chokutō see swords
Cicero 20

231

Conlan, Thomas 132, 139, 162
conscription *see* recruitment
Constantine 20
crossbows: Chinese 74, 75, 76–7; construction of 75–6; Greek and Roman 73; hand-held 74–7; *ōyumi* 72–4, 76; tactical uses and limitations 76–7

daijōkan (Council of State) 23, 24–5, 38, 42, 44, 65
Delbrück, Hans 129
dō (also *michi*; *ritsuryō* administrative circuits) 37
dōmaru 96; *see also* armor

ebira see quivers
emaki (illustrated scrolls) 17
emishi 22, 171–2

Farris, William Wayne 75, 135–6, 188
Former Nine Years' War 119, 149
fortifications: component features of 123–5, 127; descriptions of 119, 120, 121–2; purposes of 119, 120, 121, 122, 126–7, 128, 192; siege tactics 120, 125–6, 127
Fujimoto Hidehira 47
Fujimoto Masayuki 116, 162
Fujimoto Yasuhira 47, 124
Fujiwara Chikataka 157
Fujiwara Hirotsugu 104
Fujiwara Kagesue 149–50
Fujiwara Morotō 142–3, 158
Fujiwara Motohira 29
Fujiwara Nakamaro 104
Fujiwara Yasuhira 151
Fujiwara Yasumasa 139, 157
Fujiwara Yasutake 67
Fujiwara Yorinaga 140–1
Fukuda Toyohiko 118
fusetake yumi see bows, composite
Futaki Ken'ichi 128

Gempei jōsuiki (*Gempei seisuiki*) 17
Gempei War 11, 12, 33
Genji *see* Minamoto
Genji monogatari 33
Go-Daigo, Emperor 13–14, 53, 59, 62, 126
gokenin (shogunal vassals) 13; during the Ōshū campaign 48–9; inconsistencies in system 48; recognition as 47, 57, 179–80; under Yoritomo 46–8, 55; *see also* alliances
gokenin yaku (vassal duties) 48–9, 52, 56
Gomi Fumihiko 162
Go-Saga, Emperor 13
Goseibai shikimoku 25, 28
Go-Shirakawa, Emperor 10
grappling 128, 130, 131–2
guerre couverte 31
Gunchūjō see battle reports
gundan (provincial regiments) 35, 64
Gunkimono *see* wartales

hara-ate 95; *see also* armor
haramaki 94–5, 116; *see also* armor
haramaki yoroi 95; *see also* armor
Hatakeyama Shigetada 114, 125, 151
Hayashida Shigeyuki 97
heads, practice of collecting: attempts to eliminate 155; origins of 152; procedures for viewing 152–3, 153–5; purposes of 152, 153
Heiji Incident 10
Heiji monogatari ekotoba 116
Heike *see* Taira
Heike monogatari: development of 15–16, 17; reliability of 15–16, 60, 122, 123, 128, 129, 130, 137, 145–6, 148, 162
Heishi *see* Taira
helmets 93–4; *see also* armor
higo yumi see bows, composite
Hiraizumi 47
Hōgen Incident 10
Hōgen monogatari 140
Hōjō Masako 1, 2
Hōjō Regency 13, 60
Hōjō Yasutoki 3
Hōjō Yoshitoki 1, 2, 4
hoko (socket-headed spear) 85–6, 87, 184
honor *see* temperament, warrior
horses, Japanese: ancestry of 96–7; size of 97; speed and endurance of 97, 107, 130
horseshoes 97
Hyōbushō (Ministry of Military Affairs) 22, 23, 64
Hyōgoryō (Arsenal Bureaus) 64

Ichinotani, Battle of 50–1, 108, 121–2, 148
Ikegami Eiko 136
Imai Seinosuke 129, 132
infantry: in early medieval armies 105–6;

INDEX

tactical uses of 105–6, 128, 129, 130, 132, 164
inheritance, customs governing 57–8
Ishii Shirō 136–7, 145, 149, 155
Ishii Susumu 128, 131, 143
Izumi Shikibu 157

Jingū, Empress-Regent 91
Jinshin War 103
jitō (Kamakura land stewards) 47, 55–6
jōkaku see fortifications
Jōkyū War 13, 131
Jones, Archer 163
jus ad bellum see Just War
jus in bello see Just Warfare
Just War: Chinese conceptions of 21; early Christian conceptions of 20–1; Greek conceptions of 20; in medieval Europe 23–4, 31–2; *ritsuryō* state conceptions of 21–3; Roman conceptions of 20; in tenth- to fourteenth-century Japan 29–30, 33
Just Warfare 134

kaidate (shield walls) 123
Kajiwara Kagetoki 51, 145, 148, 151
Kammu Heishi *see* Taira
Kasuo Tarō Hidekata 114
katana see swords
Kawai Yasushi 47–8, 128, 130, 162
kebiishi-chō (Office of Imperial Police) 36–7, 39, 43, 152, 175, 177
Keegan, John 106
kemmon ("Gates of Power") 26, 49, 133, 156; *see also kugyō*
Kemmu Restoration 13–14, 54
Kemmu shikimoku 25
kenuki-gata katana see swords
kenuki-gata tachi see swords
kido (*kidoguchi*) 125
Kinomi, Battle of 149
kinship: in alliances and warbands 57–9; *sōryō* system 58–9, 179–80
Kiyowara Iehira 29
Kiyowara Sanehira 29
Kiyowara Takenori 119, 140
Kiyowara Takesada 140
kiyumi see bows, simple wood
Kojiki 144
konaginata (hand spear) 88
kondei system 174
Kondō Yoshikazu 79, 86, 88, 128, 162

Konjaku mongatarishū 17, 27, 107, 109, 141, 161
Kublai Khan 52
Kudō Jirō Yukimasa 114
kugyō (senior court officials) 7; *see also kemmon*
kumade 86, 88
Kumagae Naozane 108, 148
Kume Kunitake 16
Kuroda Hideo 153
Kuroda Toshio 26
Kurodō dokoro (Imperial Secretariat) 32
Kusanoki Masashige 54, 126, 127, 128
kuwagata 94; *see also* armor; helmets
kyūbi no ita 93; *see also* armor

Latter Three Years' War 29
loyalty 59–61, 138, 145

marriage customs 9–10
marugi yumi see bows, simple wood
Mass, Jeffrey 9, 57
meigen ("sighing bowstring") 32
Minamoto 9–10, 12, 57
Minamoto (Kiso) Yoshinaka 1
Minamoto Mitsuru 107–8, 111, 141–2, 143
Minamoto Tametomo 109, 141
Minamoto Yorichika 29
Minamoto Yorifusa 29
Minamoto Yorimasa 68–9
Minamoto Yorinobu 26–7, 113, 138, 157, 161
Minamoto Yoritomo: founder of Kamakura shogunate 1; and the Gempei War 11, 12; initial steps to recruit troops 44–5, 59; sacrifice of enemy prisoner 153; synthesis of legal and personal authority 53, 55, 59, 62; use of surprise and deception 144, 145; and warrior class-consciousness 10
Minamoto Yoriyoshi 40, 113, 119, 120, 138, 140, 149
Minamoto Yoshiie 28, 29, 41, 55
Minamoto Yoshitomo 10, 55, 116
Minamoto Yoshitsune 47, 50, 122, 153
miuchi ("insiders") 60–1; *see also* alliances
Miura Yasumura 27
miyako no musha ("warriors of the capital") 8–9, 10; *see also* Minamoto; Taira
Miyoshi Kiyoyuki 72, 74

233

INDEX

Mochihito, Prince 11, 12, 45, 62, 68
Mōko shūrai ekotoba 17, 154
Mongol invasions 52, 113, 124, 134, 147, 166
mononofu see warriors
Moriyoshi, Prince 13
Murdoch, James 145
musha see warriors
Mutsuwaki 17, 119

nagamaki (medieval polearm) 88
naginata (glaive) 86–7, 184, 185
nanori ("name announcing"): in *Azuma kagami* 146, 147; examples of 145, 148; in Heian period texts 146, 147; in *Heike monogatari* 145–6, 148; as literary device 148; in Mongol wars 147; purposes of 146–9; timing of 147
naval warfare 189
Nihon kiryaku 27
nihontō ("Japanese sword") *see* swords
Niita Yoshisada 13, 54
Nishikido Tarō Kunihira 114
nobushi 194
nodachi ("field sword") 88
non-combatants: as "collateral damage" 158, 161–2; definitions of 155–6; and ecclesiastical authority 156; European ideas concerning 156; mercy and compassion for 157–8; warrior responsibilities toward 156

Oba Kageyoshi 109, 110
ōban'yaku (guard duty in the capital) *see gokenin yaku*
Obusuma Saburō 153, 160–1
Obusuma Saburō ekotoba 68, 69
O'Connell, Robert 135
ōdachi ("great sword") 88
Ōe Hiromoto 2, 3, 4
Office of Imperial Police *see kebiishi-chō*
Okada Seiichi 128
ōryōshi ("Envoy to Subdue the Territory") 37–8, 42–3, 176
Ōshū campaign 46, 47–8, 114, 124, 125, 131, 151
ōsode 3, 93, 95; *see also* armor
ōyoroi: construction of 91–3; cost of 94, 95; limitations of 94, 108, 131; origins of 91–2, 187; *see also* armor
ōyumi see crossbows, *ōyumi*

prisoners of war: disposition of (in Japan) 149–50, 151–2, 153; in medieval Europe 149; status of (in Japan) 150–1
private war: among Heian warriors 26–8; in medieval Europe 23–4, 31; need for government sanction for 31–2; under *ritsuryō* law 24–5, 42; under shogunal law 25–6, 30, 33, 115
privatization: of government 6–7; of military force 8–9; of military recruitment *see* recruitment, privatization of; of weapons manufacture *see* weapons manufacture, commercialization of
purposes of war 19, 32–3, 165

quivers 71–2, 73

raiding: destruction caused by 116–18; tactical uses of 117–18, 119, 165
recruitment: during Heian period 42–3; privatization of 35–6, 38–9, 104; under Minamoto Yoritomo 45; under the *ritsuryō* military 34–5
religion: effect on warrior behavior 139–40
reputation 137–8
residences, warrior 121, 192
rewards *see* alliances
ritsuryō legal system: military apparatus 6, 22–3, 34–5, 64–5, 104; office-holding under 7, 35, 38; state structure 22–3, 32, 64; *see also dō (michi)*
ritual: in medieval warfare 135–7, 141–2, 162–3; war as 32–3
ryōtō-shiki keikō 92; *see also* armor

saddles and tack 97–9
sakamogi (brush walls) 123–4
Sammai uchi yumi see bows, composite
samurai *see* warriors
sane (lamellae) 90
Satake Yoshimasa 145
Satō Shin'ichi 128, 133
Segal, Ethan 188
Seiwa Genji *see* Minamoto
sendan no ita 93; *see also* armor
Shakadō Mitsuhiro 96, 132
shields: ancient 89; construction of 89; hand-held 90; usage of 90
shihōchiku yumi see bows, composite
Shō Shirō Takaie 150

234

INDEX

shōen (private estates) 42–3, 54
shogunate: Kamakura, and Hōjō regency 13; Kamakura, end of 13; Kamakura, military role of 25, 44, 52; Kamakura, origins of 10–13
Shōmonki 17, 39, 116, 147
shugo (military governors) 49; *see also* chain of command
sōryō system *see* kinship, *sōryō* system
sōtsuibushi ("tsuibushi in chief") 51
spear *see hoko*; *yari*
Spring and Autumn Annals 156
stirrups 98
Strickland, Matthew 144
Sun Tzu 21
suneate 93; *see also* armor
Suzuki Masaya 131, 132
swords: as cavalry weapons 83–4, 128, 131–2, 184; *chokutō* 80, 82, 83; cross-sectional shape of 82, 83; curved shape of 80–5; *katana* 79–80, 132, 152; *kenuki-gata katana* 80–2; *kenuki-gata tachi* 80–1; methods of forging 84–5; nomenclature for 78–9, 81; as symbols 77–8; *tachi* 79, 80, 132; *wakizashi* 79; *warabite katana* 80–1

tachi see swords
Tachibana Yorisada 140
Taiheiki 16, 126, 127
Taira 9–10, 12, 57
Taira Hirotsune 145
Taira Kiyomori 10, 11, 45
Taira Koremochi 142–3, 158
Taira Kunitada 150
Taira Masakado 11, 12, 28, 116–17, 118, 158
Taira Munetsune 112–13
Taira Naokata 117
Taira Sadamichi 143
Taira Sadamori 159, 161
Taira Saemon 159
Taira Tadatsune 11, 12, 117–18, 138
Taira Tsunemasa 150
Taira Yoshifumi 107–8, 111, 141–2, 143
Taira Yoshikane 117
Takahahi Masaaki 103
Takahashi Noriyuki 45, 48–9
Takezaki Suenaga 113, 147, 154
Takiguchi (imperial bodyguards) 32–3
tax collection 7–8, 64
teboko (hand spear) 88, 185
Temmu, Emperor 103

temperament, warrior: brutality and callousness 18, 159–61; compassion 138, 139, 157–8; courage 149, 160; familial sentimentality 138, 161; honor 137–8, 143, 144–5, 150; pragmatism 139, 140, 158–9, 161; pride 138, 142–3, 145–6, 161; *see also* loyalty
Terao Yoichi Shigekazu 30
tōzama ("outsiders") 60–1; *see also* alliances
tsubushi ("Envoy to Pursue and Capture") 37–8, 42–3, 176
tsuibu kampu (Warrants of Pursuit and Capture) 5, 42, 46
tsuitōshi ("Envoy to Pursue and Strike Down") 38, 42–3
tsuru-bashiri 92; *see also* armor
tsuru-uchi ("striking the bowstring") 32
tsuwamono see warriors
Tsuwamono-zukuri no tsukasa (Office of Weapons Manufacture) 64

Uda, Emperor 32
Usami Heiji Sanemasa 151
utsubo see quivers
Utsubo monogatari 66

vassals *see* alliances; *gokenin*
van Creveld, Martin 100
von Clausewitz, Carl 17

Wada Rebellion 1–5, 131
Wada Yoshimori 1–4, 2, 4, 108, 114
waidate 91–2; *see also* armor
wakizashi see swords
war: alternative purposes for 19–20, 32–3; rules of *see* Just War; Just Warfare
warabite katana see swords
warbands: origins of 39; size of 39–40; structure of 39–42, 59–61; tactical maneuver and cooperation in 112–15; *see also* alliances
Warrants of Pursuit and Capture *see tsuibu kampu*
warrior government *see* shogunate
warriors: class consciousness 10, 61, 133, 149; emergence of 5–9
wartales: reliability of 15–16, 137, 145
weapons: absence of regional variation 99–100; and technological innovation 63–4, 100–1

235

weapons manufacture: commercialization of 66–7; during Heian and Kamakura periods 66–7, 99–100; specialization in 67; under the *ritsuryō* system 64–5
worldview, medieval Japanese 139

yagura (arrow towers) 125, 193
Yamamoto Kōji 162
Yamato Takeru-no-Mikoto 144
yari (tang-headed spear) 86, 87, 128, 185

Yokoyama Tokikane 3
Yūki Tomomura 27
Yuri Korehira 151

Zōhyōryō (Office of Weapons Manufacture) *see Tsuwamono-zukuri no tsukasa*
zuryō (career provincial officials) 8, 9, 38, 41–2

Lightning Source UK Ltd.
Milton Keynes UK
UKOW06f0337020415

248996UK00004B/62/P